S0-FCA-321

LIVING IN
THE DESERT

LIVING IN THE DESERT

CONTEMPORARY HOUSES IN THE DESERT

[1] BUILT TO EMBRACE THE DESERT

[2] BUILT WITHIN THE DESERT

[3] BUILT TO RESIST THE DESERT

About one-third of the world's land mass is covered by desert. The vastness of this arid terrain embodies a mythical quality that instills a fascination frequently reflected in popular culture—such as Michelangelo Antonioni's 1970 film *Zabriskie Point*, in which a series of surreal events unfold in California's Death Valley, in the Mojave Desert. The enigmatic, somewhat desolate landscape has also inspired idealistic and ambitious architectural projects—some utopian, such as Paolo Soleri's Arcosanti, others a dream turned reality, like Taliesin West by Frank Lloyd Wright. The tremendous sense of emptiness and the never-ending horizon paradoxically prompt feelings of possibility: nature abhors a vacuum. The romantic notion of the sublime creates desirability. The harsh conditions of the desert seem to stimulate human yearnings for discovery, challenge, and freedom.

As deserts were first inhabited by mostly nomadic tribes reliant on what nature had to offer, the history of desert architecture is fairly recent and its development still comparably rare. There are exceptions; the deserts of the American West and Southwest are among the most densely populated arid areas of the world. Settlement in the desert is mainly dependent on the ability to sustain life there—with comfort and extra protection in the harsh conditions—and as such has always been subject to experimentation with technological possibilities. The first large permanent settlements, and later cities, were enabled by the complex and labor-intensive construction of railroads and dams, the infrastructure necessary to sustain growth and prosperity. Though subsequent industrial innovations achieved through the extraction of fossil fuels further made the desert habitable and less remote, much of it is still left undiscovered and unpopulated. To live in the desert requires resourcefulness and, in some ways, strong devotion to the forces and life cycles dictated by nature—on a daily basis. Being able to adjust to such extreme secludedness, silence, and self-reliance is necessary for a way of life that is in many ways the complete opposite of the currently prevalent urban ideal of instant access. The British historian Reyner Banham observed after repeated visits to the Mojave beginning in the 1960s, there are only two types of people: those who love the desert and those who hate it.

What remains fully undisputed, though, is the perfect pairing of architecture with the desert. One enhances the other and vice versa. The desert's scale is magnified when trying to grasp it from the single vantage point of a house, and architecture can flourish when set against this radical backdrop. There is a recognizable topography among deserts across the world, naturally resulting from the shared climatic and geographical limitations imposed upon them. Some structures built on this land utilize traditional vernacular methods and knowledge inherited from earlier generations of settlers, while others display novel techniques to tame the inhospitable conditions and support a sustainable future. Covering different regions and architectural convictions, this book looks at the gestures architects have made and the ways convinced desert dwellers have found to define their respective version of the freedom the desert has to offer.

[1] BUILT TO EMBRACE THE DESERT

10 Andrea Zittel
WAGON STATION ENCAMPMENT

16 Barclay & Crousse Architecture
C3 HOUSE

22 Graeme Williamson Architects
SHINGLE HOUSE

28 Canopea
CASA NAHAS

32 Openstudio Architects
SWARTBERG HOUSE

38 Ibarra Rosano Design Architects
LEVIN RESIDENCE

44 Not Vital
HOUSE TO WATCH THE SUNSET

48 Blank Studio
XEROS RESIDENCE

54 Oller & Pejic Architecture
BLACK DESERT HOUSE

62 Rick Joy Architects
DESERT NOMAD HOUSE

68 Doug Aitken
MIRAGE

72 Edward Ogosta Architecture
FOUR EYES HOUSE

78 Studio Cáceres Lazo
GZ HOUSE

Architecture enthusiasts may be familiar with Arthur Wortmann, the first editor of Dutch architecture periodical *Mark*, who used to say that the smaller the window, the easier it is to frame a pleasing view. In the context of an environment with such overwhelming visual stimuli as the extraterrestrial-seeming arid landscapes of this world, the considerations and strategies for inserting oneself into the desert become increasingly elaborate. The view cannot be simply contained, for it is everywhere and inescapable: a 360-degree panoramic experience that often demands a house's entire orientation and floor plan to be meticulously choreographed to coincide with nature's movements. Those drawn to settle in remote and hard-to-access regions, especially the mystical desert, seem to do so specifically to escape oneself and reconnect with the purity of the elements. In response to this impulse, architects come to embrace the environment in a way that exceeds mere fascination, manifesting in three-dimensional structures that aren't simply on the land, but of the land. The desert's scarcity of resources invites the utilization of locally sourced materials with gentle force and suggests a revival of traditional answers to the prevalent climatic conditions. Some—such as rammed-earth walls made from native desert soil—go back as far as the Neolithic Age, thereby bringing the ancient wisdom of peoples who lived in total harmony with nature to the age of modernity and rendering such practices relevant for today.

  The architecture in this chapter is characterized by the various possible forms of worshipful dedication to nature, be it through enhancing its panoramic vistas, following the trajectory of its light, shaping nutritious native soil into solid walls, or imitating its organic colors and shapes. These are houses built for nature, allowing one to experience it from within as much as from without.

Andrea Zittel
WAGON STATION ENCAMPMENT
2012 | Joshua Tree National Park, CA, USA

Since 2000 the artist Andrea Zittel has constructed a living and working environment in the high desert near Joshua Tree National Park. Covering nearly seventy acres (twenty-eight hectares), *A-Z West* functions as the artist's home as well as "testing ground" for art and daily life. The Wagon Station Encampment sits within *A-Z West* and consists of twelve almost identical compact living units, an open-air kitchen, composting toilets, outdoor showers, and a shared communal Wagon Station "living room." Each of the standardized Wagon Stations comes equipped with little more than a mattress, a small shelf, some hooks, and a windowed hatch that can be opened up to the sky. These sculptures provide the most minimal of requirements for living in a manner meant to challenge our assumptions about the daily needs of life. While occupants are not completely exposed to the elements, their proximity to the stark, rocky landscape of California's high desert enables Zittel to test the bare minimum needs for self-sufficiency.

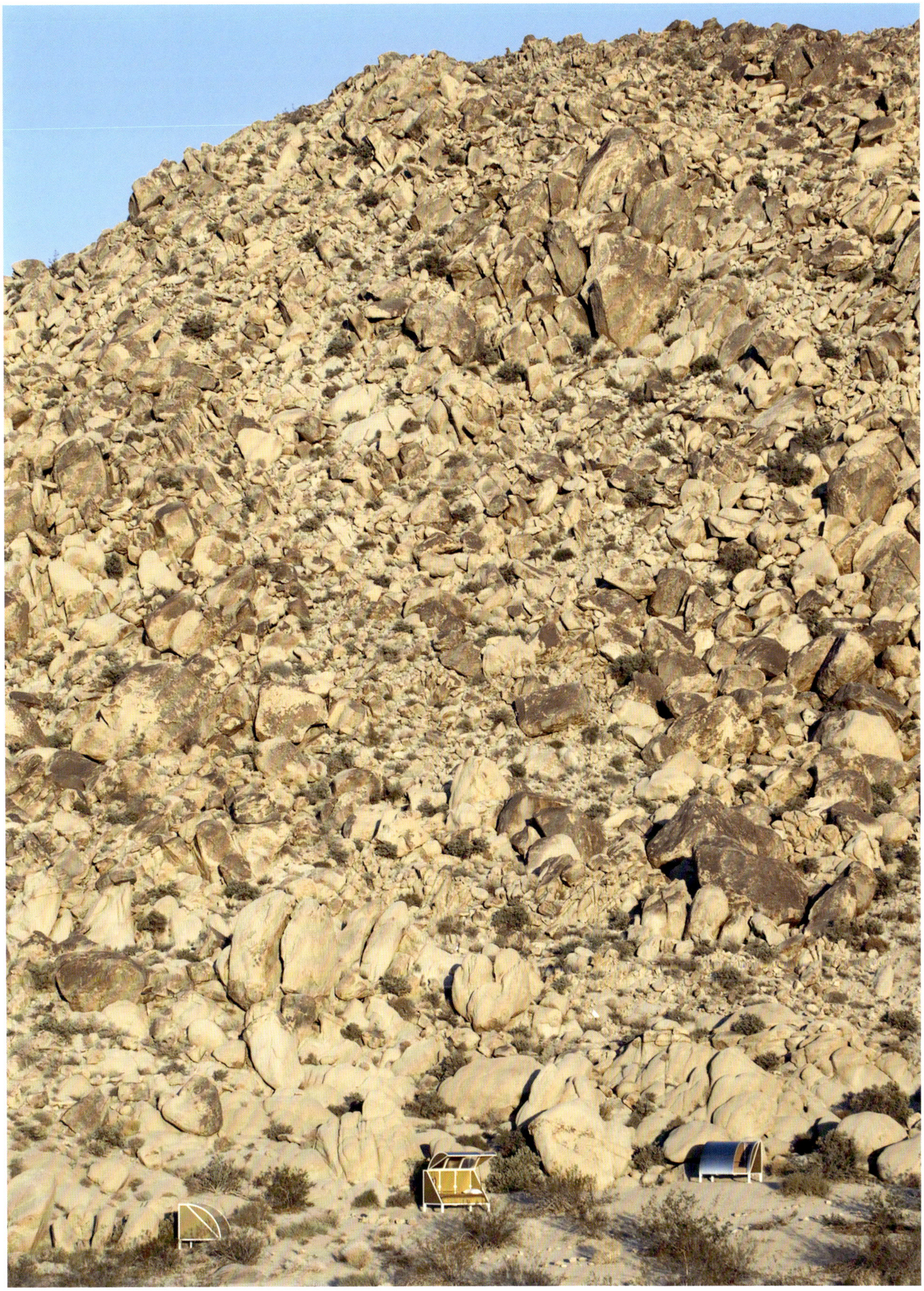

WAGON STATION ENCAMPMENT

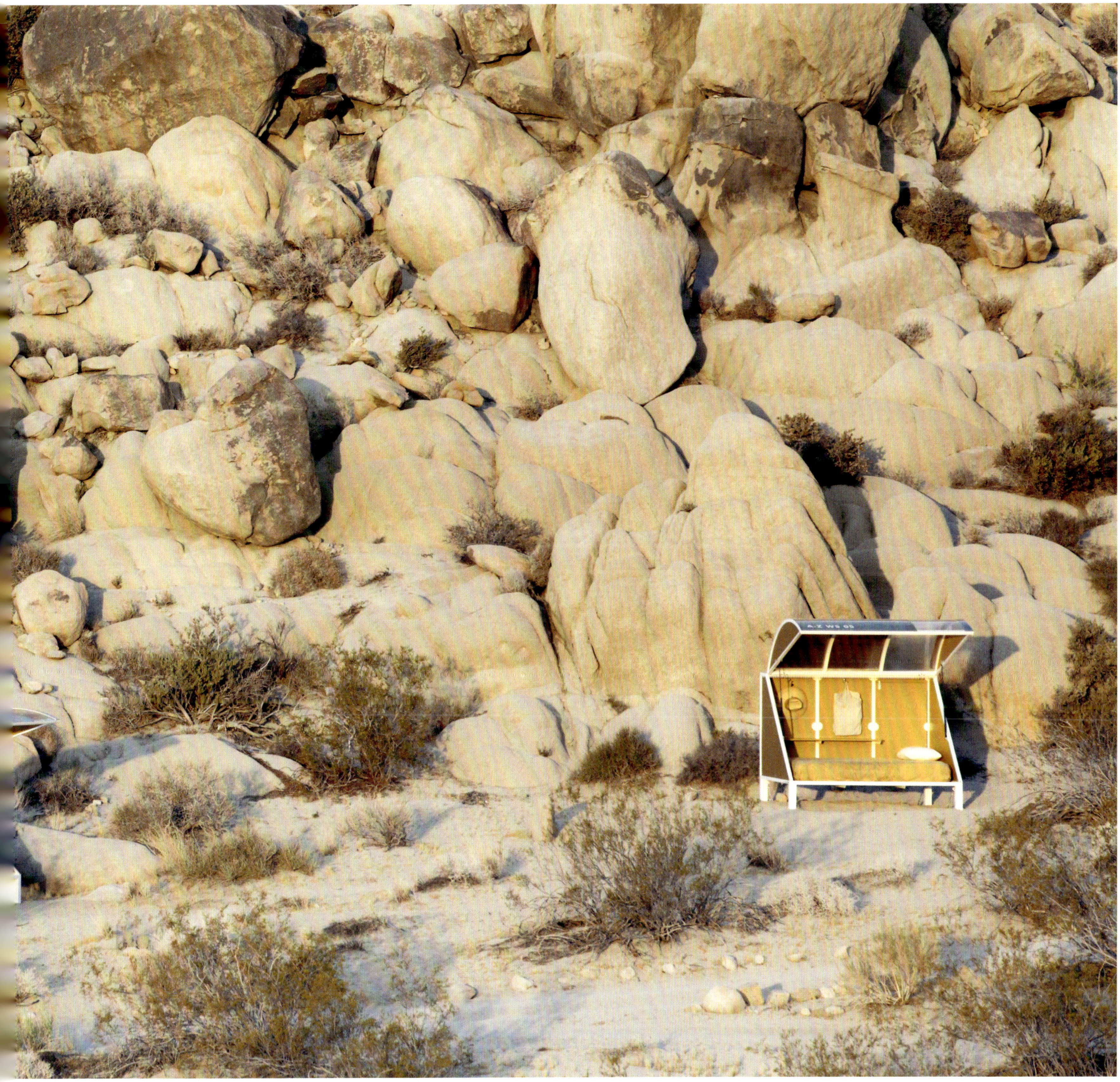

WAGON STATION ENCAMPMENT

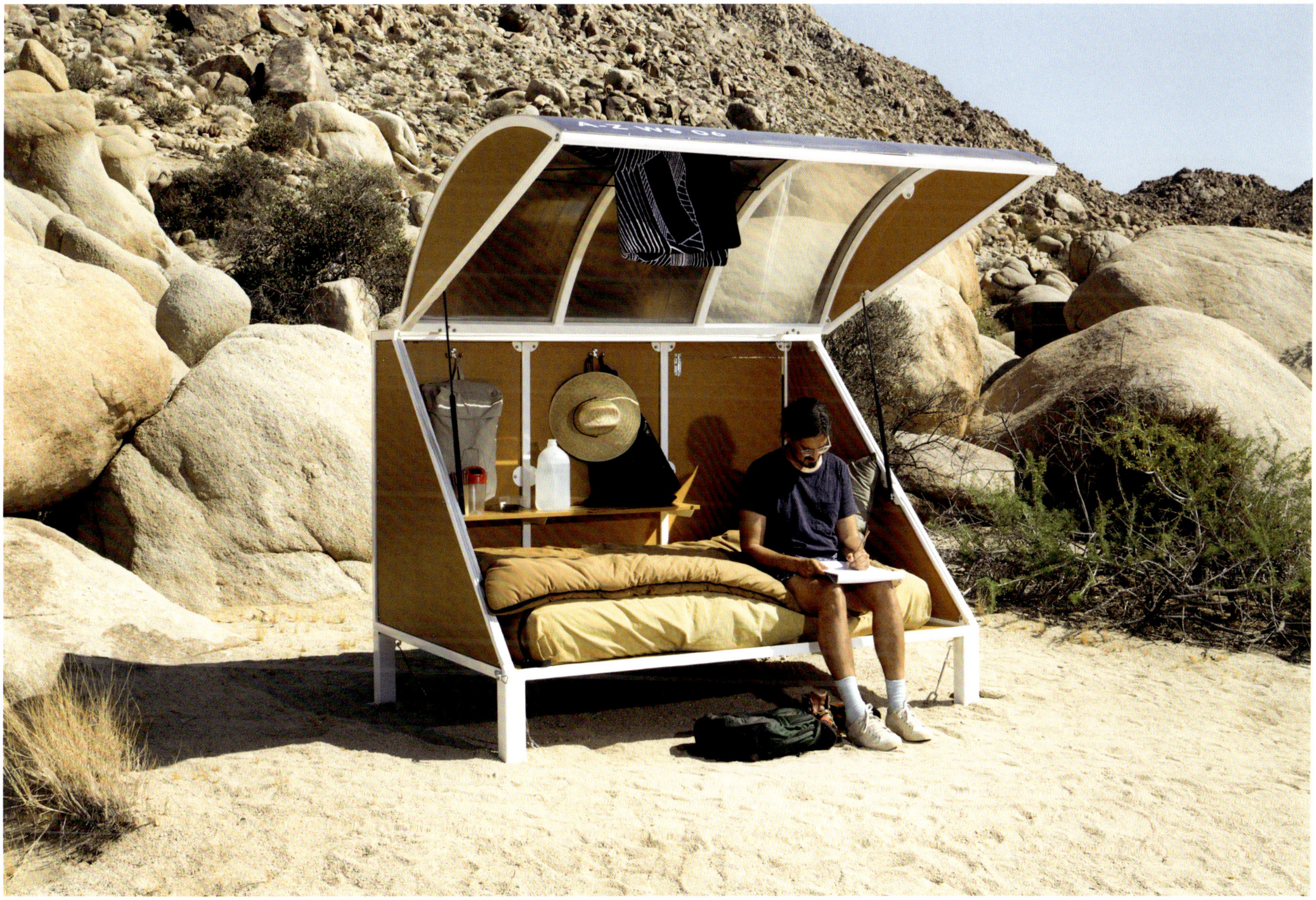

Barclay & Crousse Architecture
C3 HOUSE
2017 | Ancón District, Lima Province, Peru

In Peru where the Andes and the Pacific Ocean meet, the climate is humid yet completely free of rain, and its landscape reveals itself to be otherworldly, even Martian. Although C3 House does not try to imitate the Ancón scenery—as architecture in natural places often attempts to do—it fits in perfectly, as if it had always been part of the topography. Despite the option and good reasons for doing so, it was not the architects' foremost intention to frame the view. Rather than building a dwelling that looks out on the land, they wanted to create a space that would make sense of the land and understand it from the inside.

The layout includes four platforms: one for cars and services, two that shelter the bedrooms, and another dedicated to social activities. The roof is conceived as a series of concrete vaults that evoke a sense of spaciousness, as if there were no roof at all. This feeling of openness is further enhanced as the living room extends seamlessly to the wood-lined terrace, where an infinity pool is situated to face the ocean. While the interior is kept simple and practical, the exterior exposes an extravagance that stems more from an eloquent collage of subtly unusual geometric shapes than from an opulence of materials.

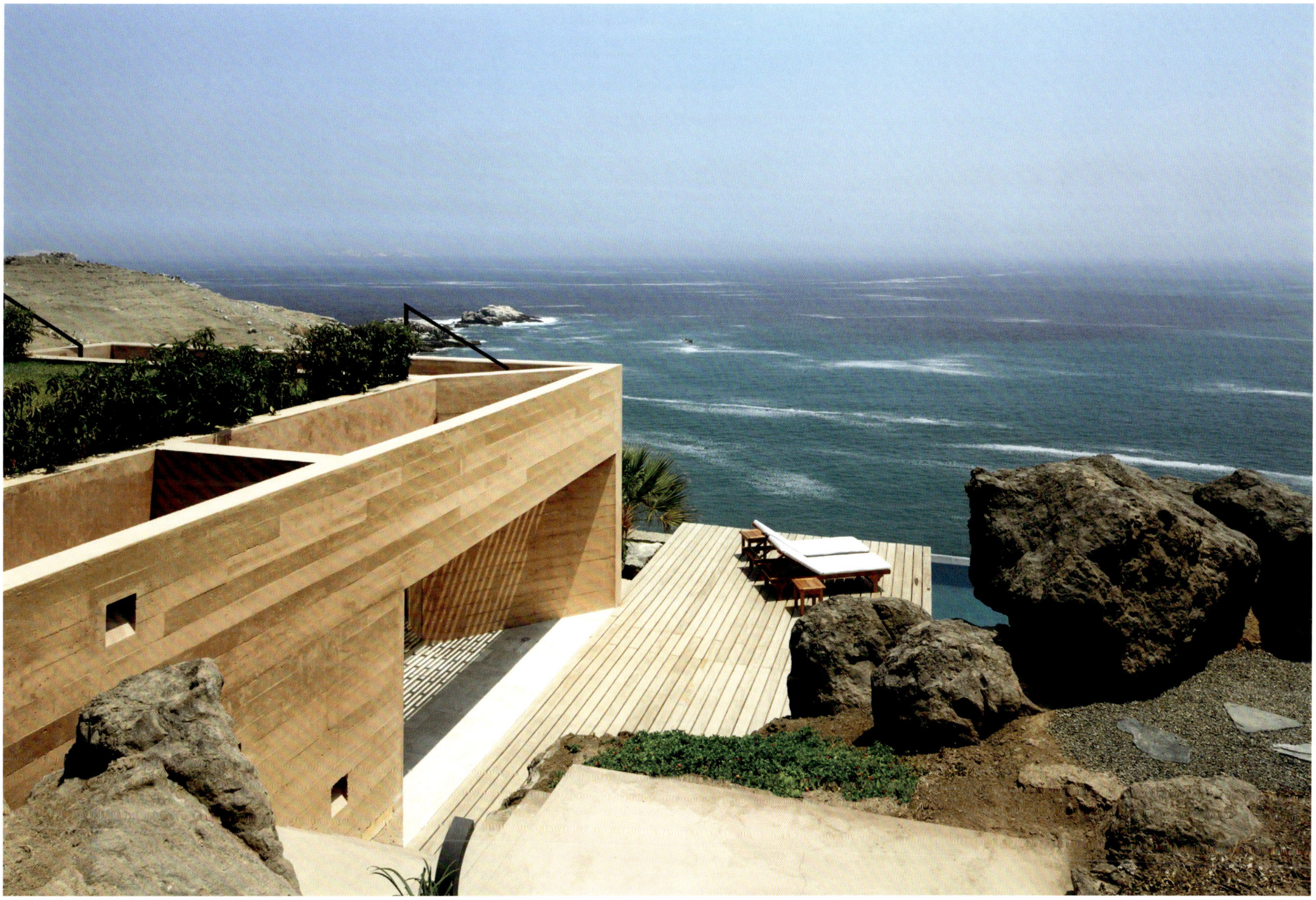

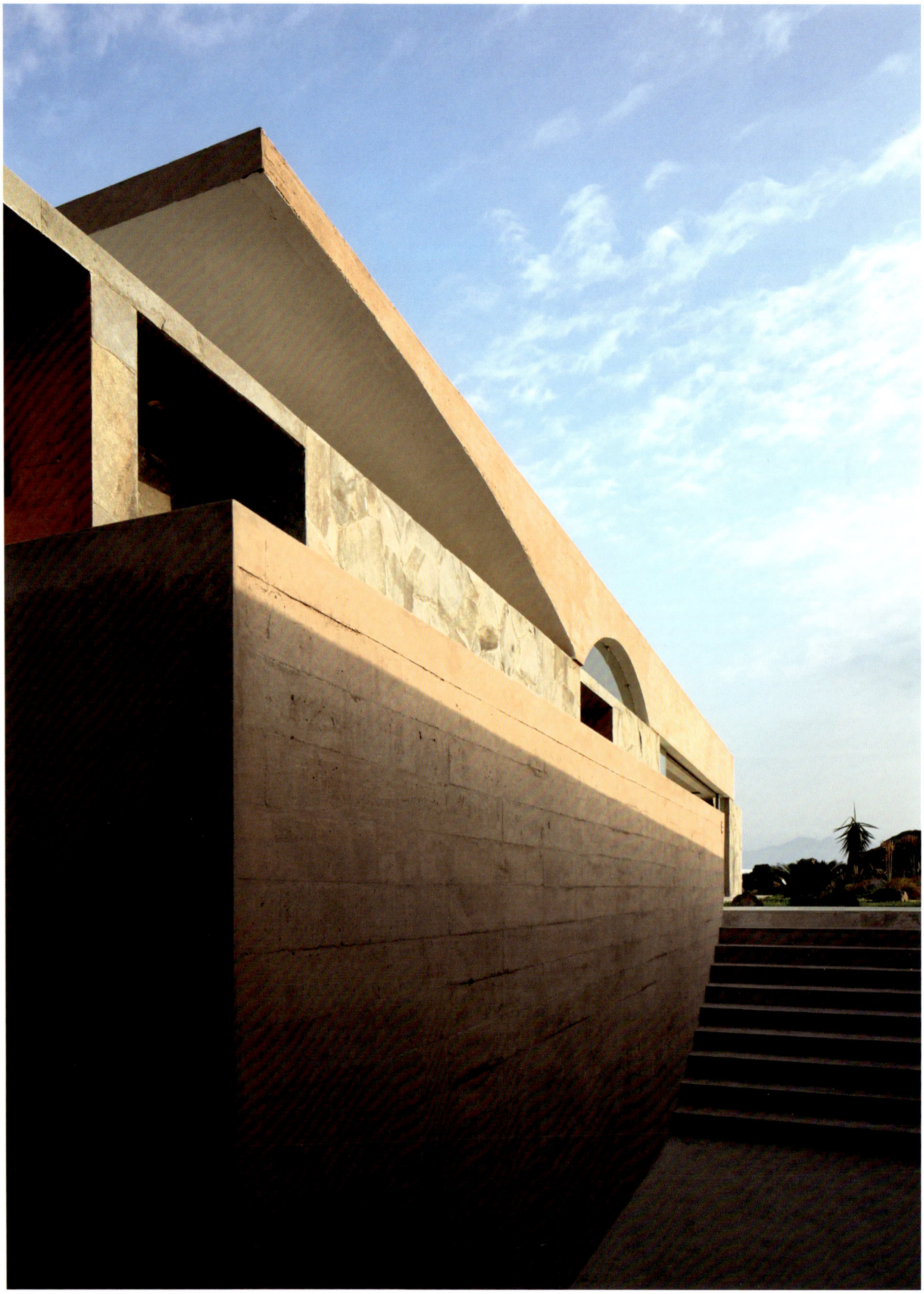

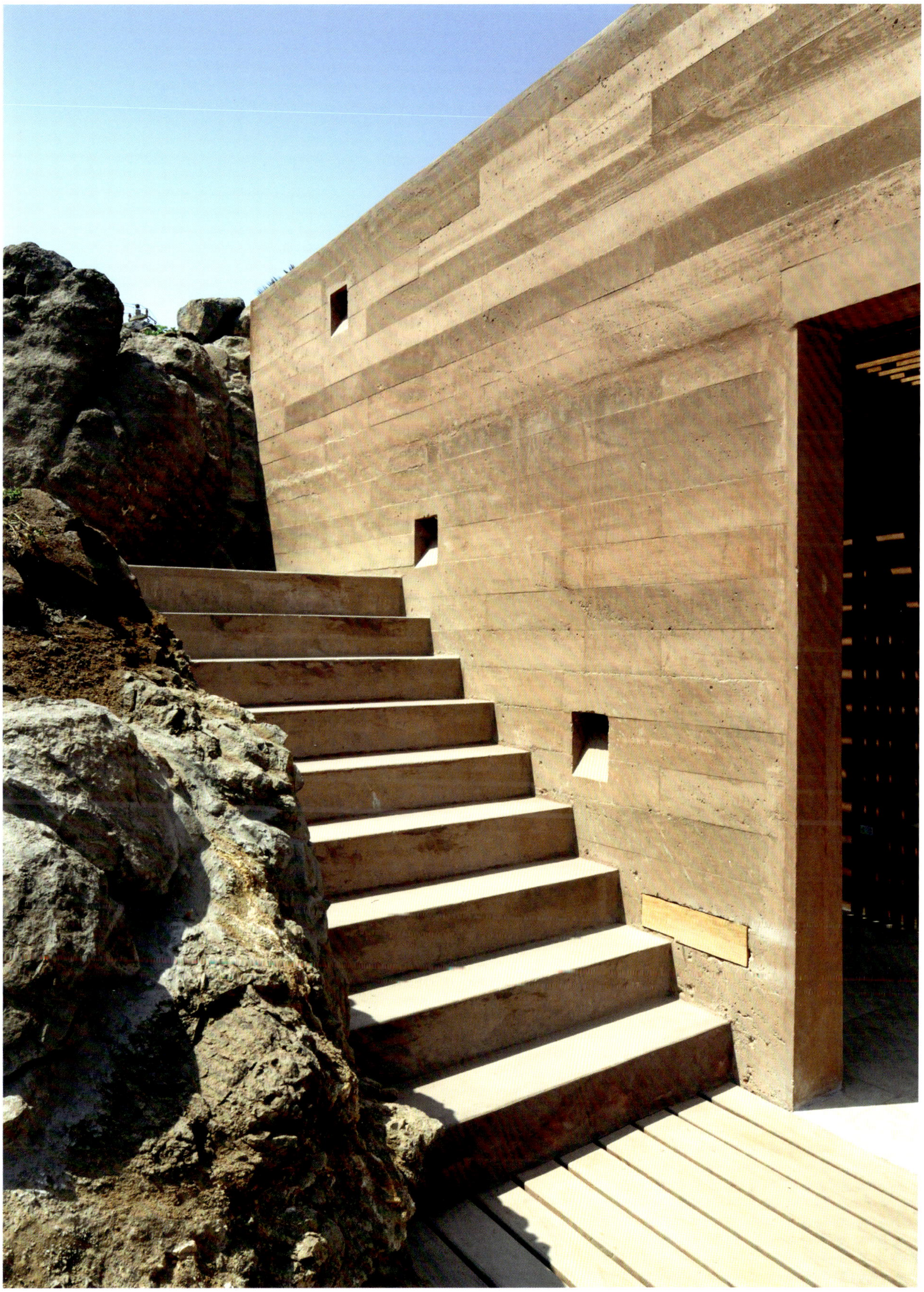

C3 HOUSE

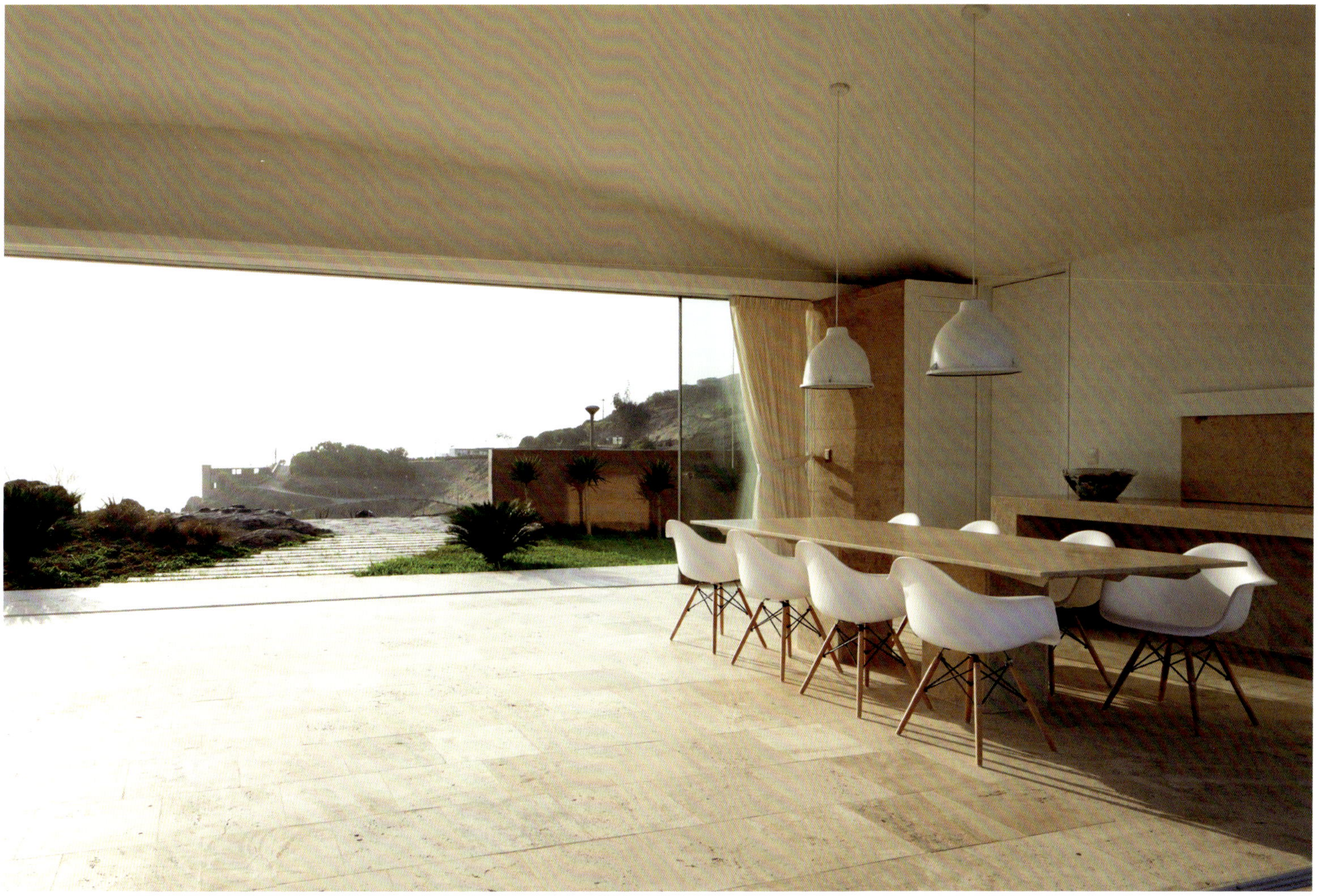

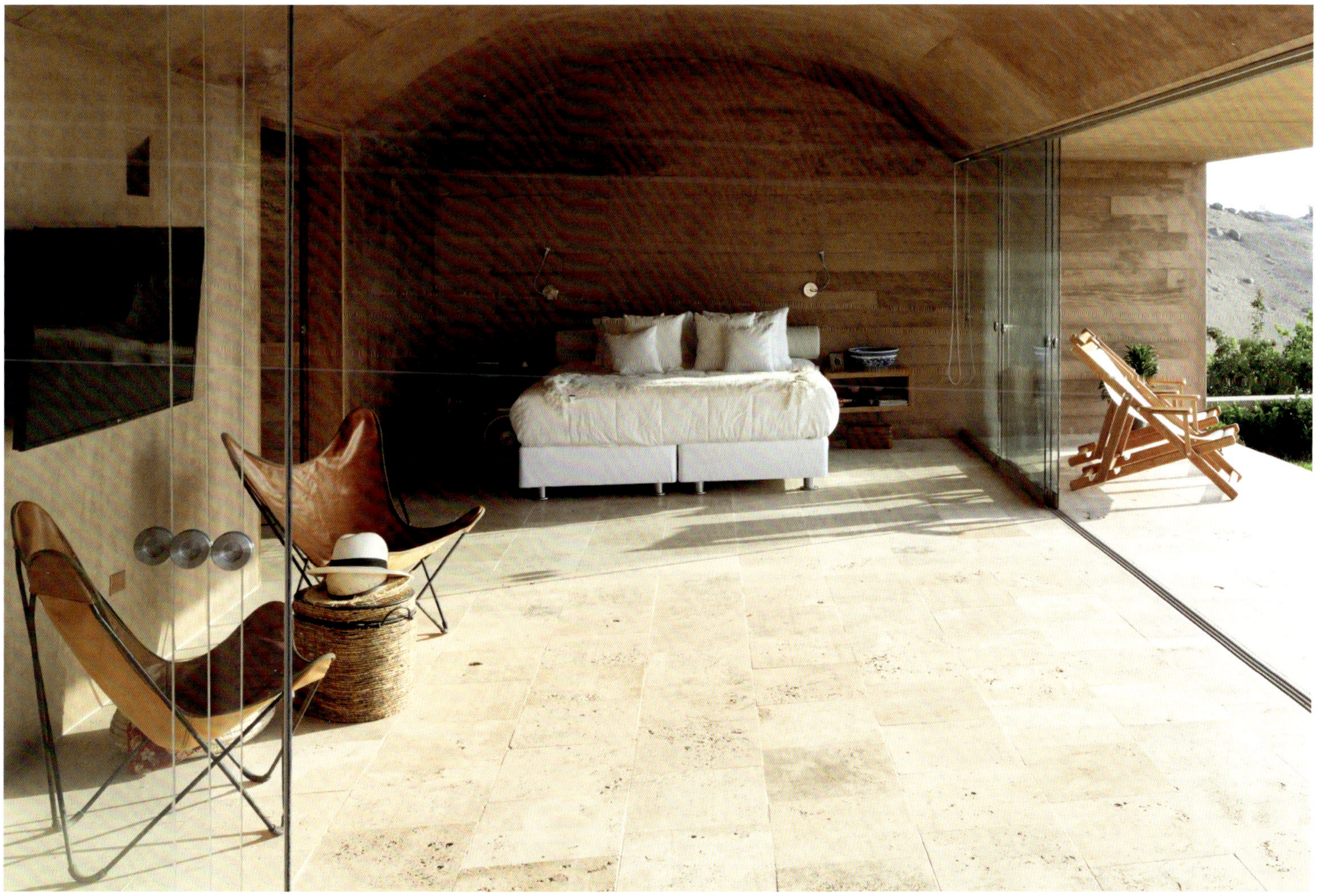

Graeme Williamson Architects
SHINGLE HOUSE
2010 | Dungeness, Kent, UK

As one of eight holiday homes of architectural value designed by formerly Nord Architecture for a British initiative called Living Architecture, Shingle House awaits visitors in Dungeness, on the coast of Kent. The region is attractive for both its postindustrial emptiness as well as its flora and fauna, among the richest in the country. Built in direct proximity to the beach, the home profits from unobstructed views and few neighboring houses.

Thematically, it emulates vernacular architecture of the area by using black-tarred shingles and classic gable roofs—but with a contemporary twist, creating six differently angled roofs through gable walls and compartments of various sizes. This playful geometry is enhanced on the interior, where concrete and white wooden paneling draw attention to slanted ceilings and sharp angles. Fittings are modern without being minimal; instead, a homey feeling is created through a gentle maritime look balanced by dark wooden floors that correspond well with the blurry earth tones of the beach seen through the windows. The dominant light tones of the interior contrast with the dark cladding on the exterior, extravagant and nondescript at the same time.

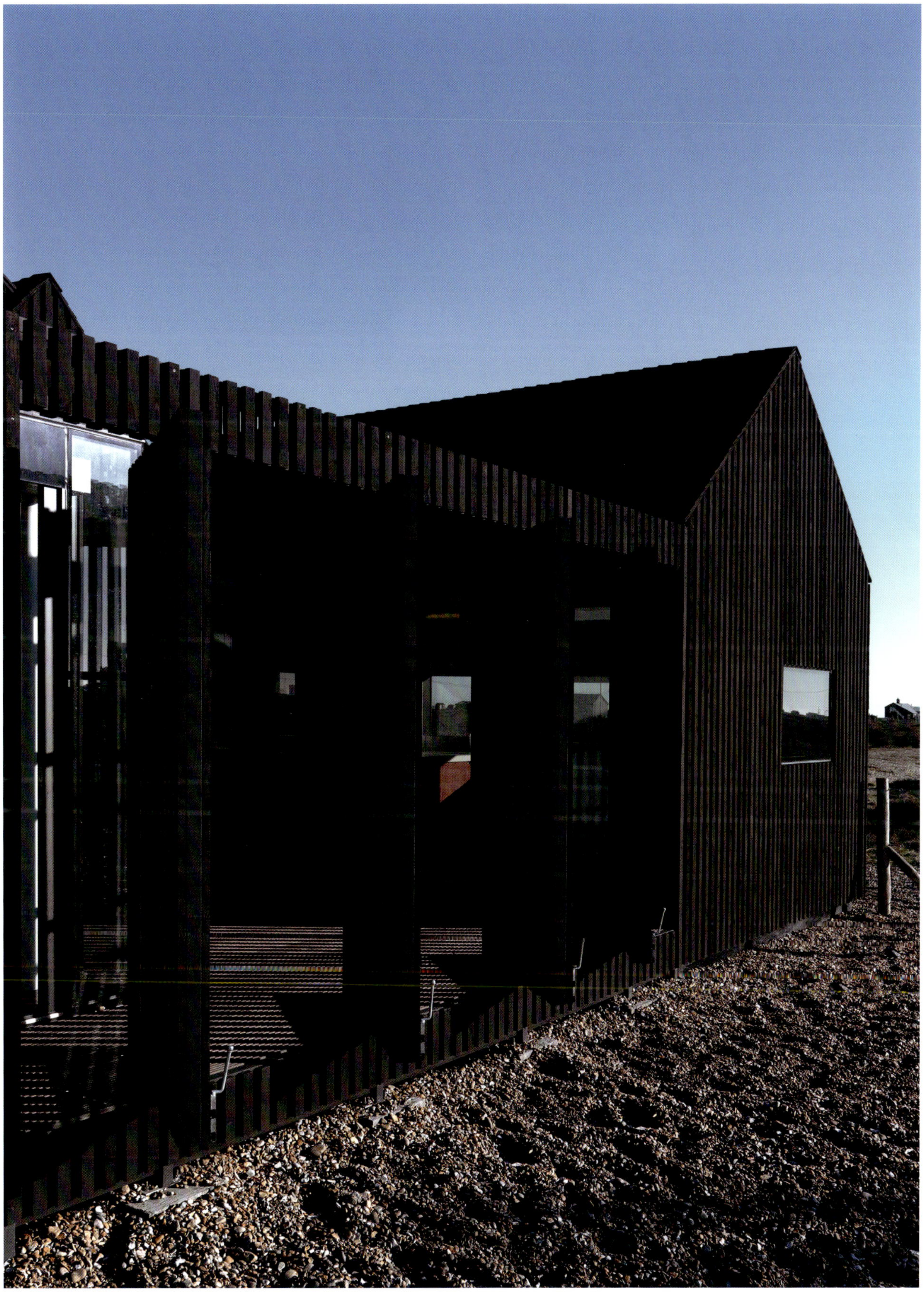

SHINGLE HOUSE

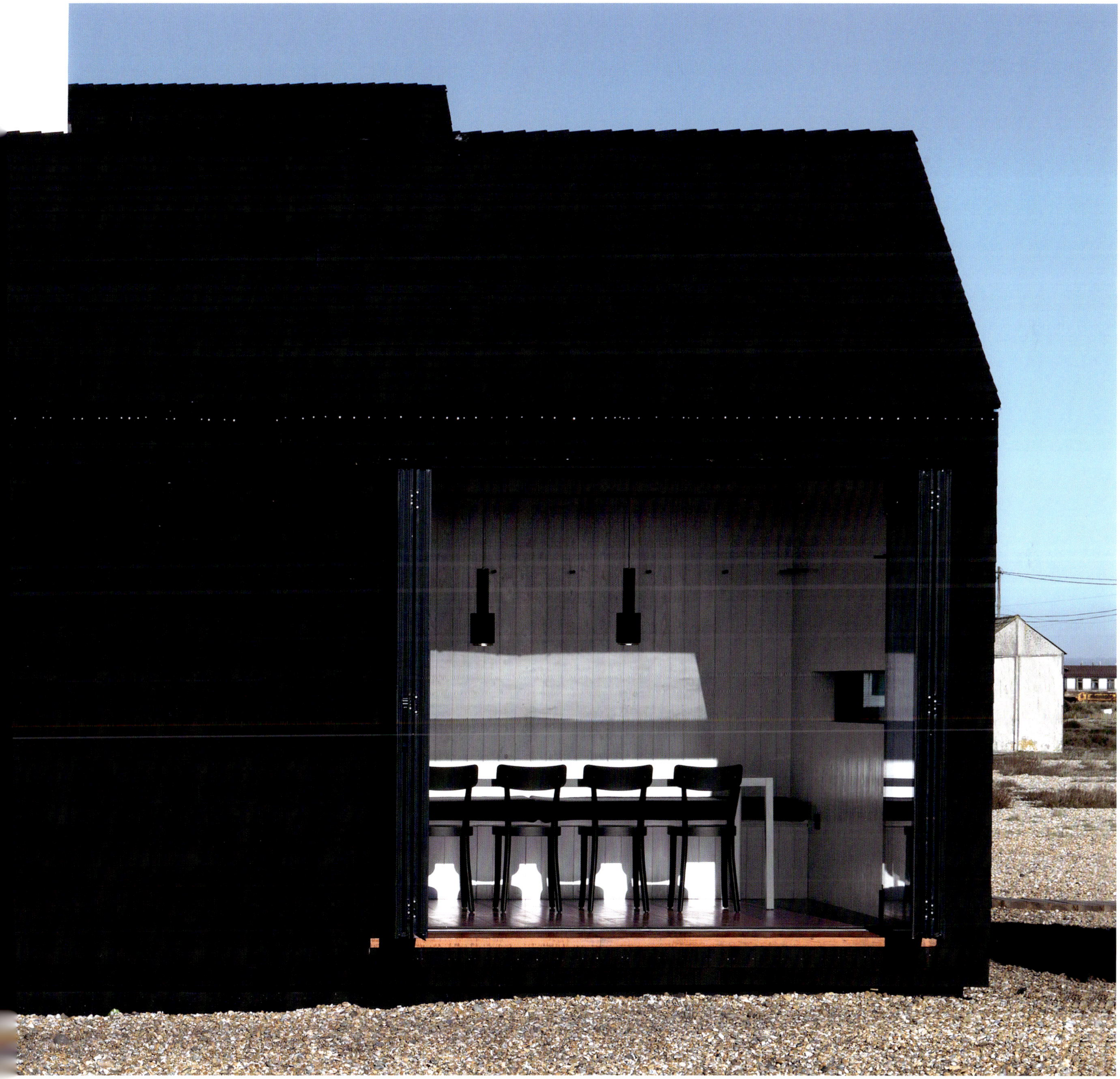

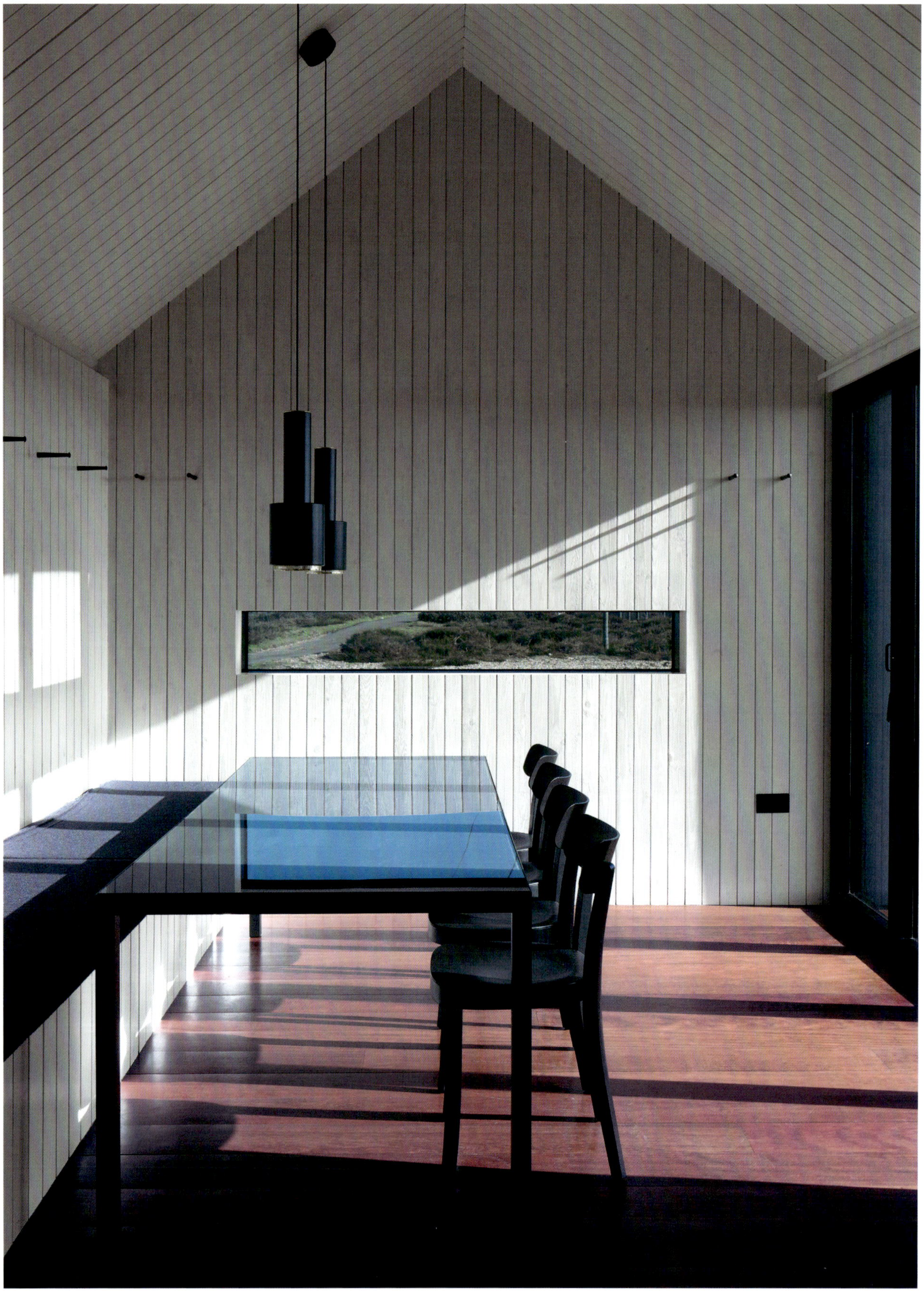

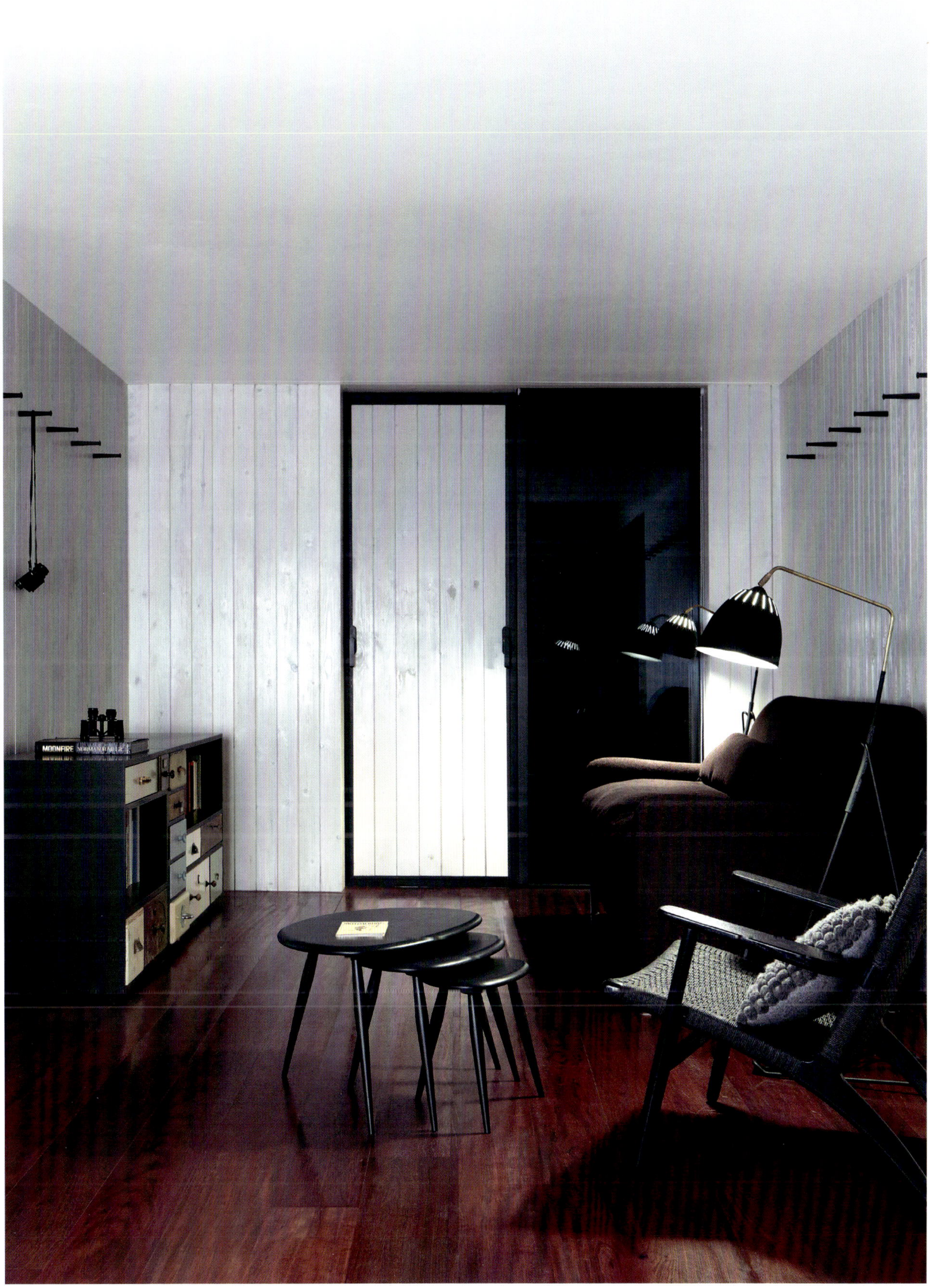

Canopea
CASA NAHAS
2013 | La Ventana, Mexico

The peninsula of Baja California is one of the driest and windiest areas of the vast Sonoran Desert and is especially known for its cactus-rich vegetation. In La Ventana, Casa Nahas sits on a slope shaped by rock formations and native plants. It is a compound of two units—each comprising a living space, kitchen, and bathroom and equipped to house six people—with shared amenities. The structures are designed to take advantage of the spectacular views of the Sierra de la Cacachilas mountain range and the Sea of Cortez while providing thermal efficiency to deflect the at times dizzying heat of the environment. Both units feature barrel-vaulted roofs (one brick, the other concrete), thick walls of rammed earth (visible layers of compacted clay and sand, which slowly absorb and release heat), locally crafted blue floor tiles to keep cool underfoot, and pergolas made with Palo de Arco—Mexico's native trumpet tree—for outdoor shade.

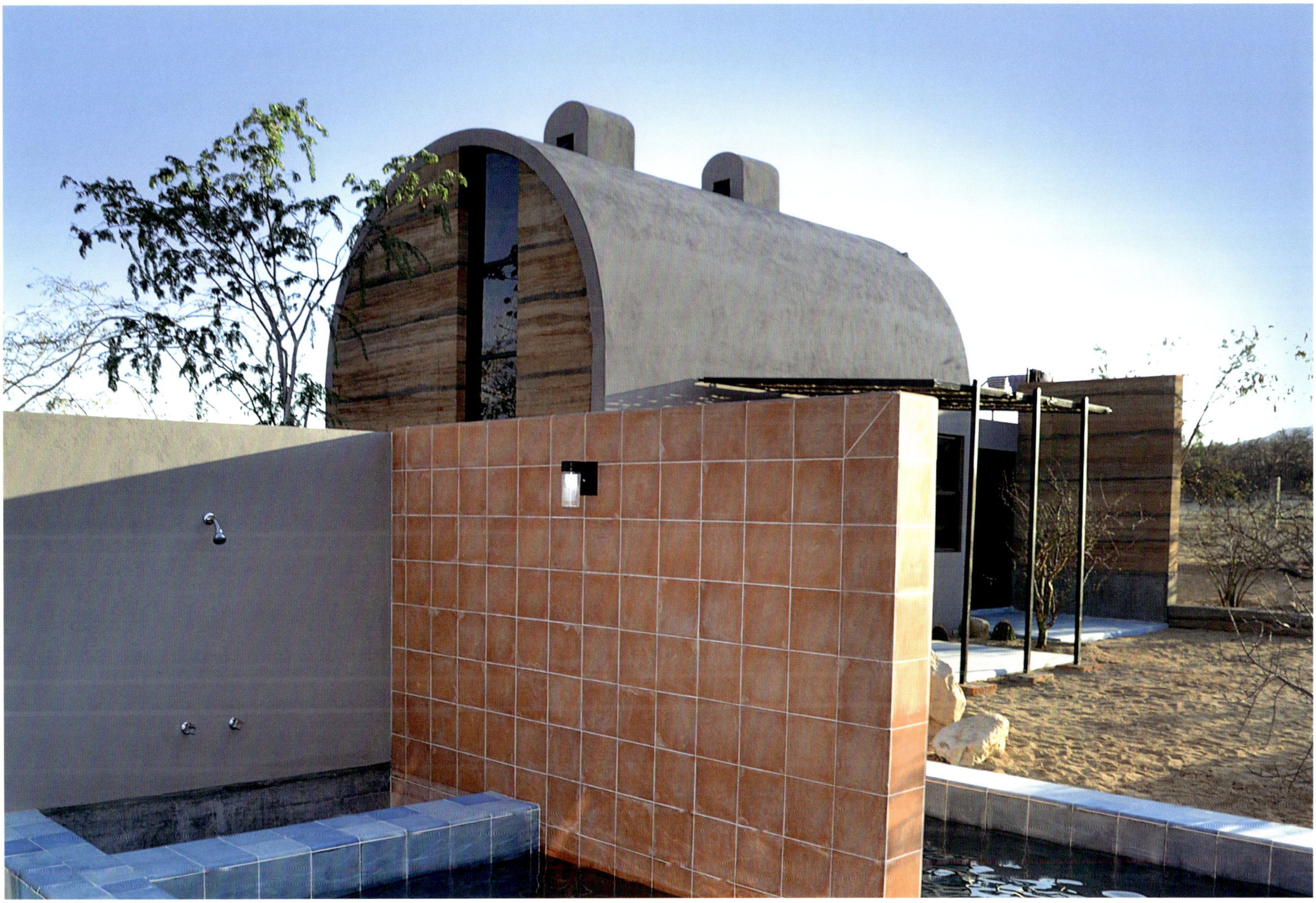

CASA NAHAS

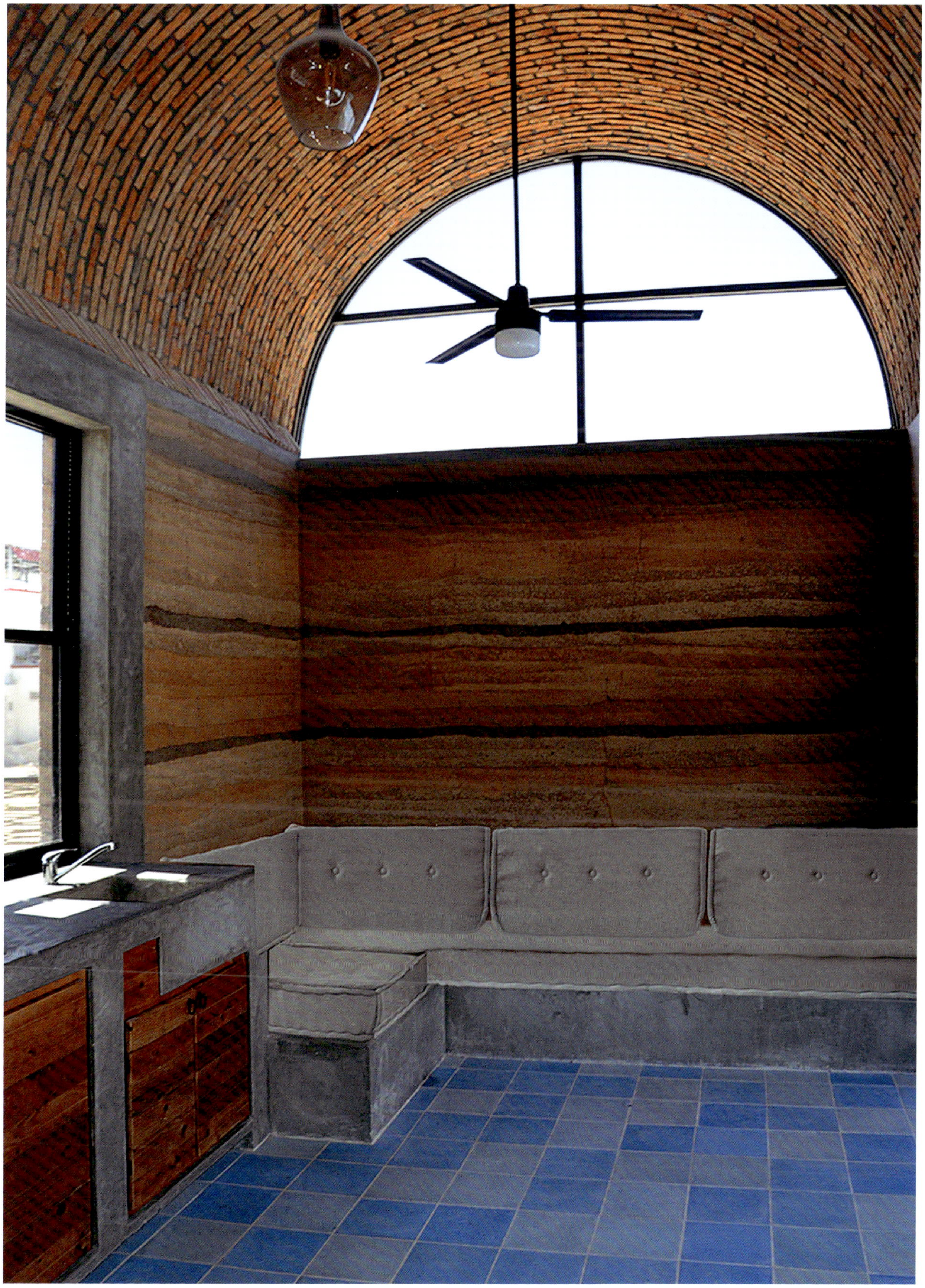

Openstudio Architects
SWARTBERG HOUSE
2013 | Karoo Desert, South Africa

To those who have encountered the alluring Karoo mountains in South Africa's semidesert region, especially by the approach from the long-winding Swartberg Pass over misty mountains starting just outside the town of Prince Albert, Swartberg House will feel unfamiliar, for it doesn't resemble the local colonial architecture. Whether despite or because of its apparent newness, the thick-walled house is perfectly suited to the harsh temperatures of the region, which typically range from 21 to 104 degrees Fahrenheit (-6 to 40 degrees Celsius). Appearing like a poetic fortress from afar, the house is oriented on an east–west axis to take advantage of the sun's path and majestic mountain views. Continuous gray brick-on-edge floors both inside and outside blur the distinction between exterior and interior living spaces while retaining heat in cold temperatures; the rough-cast plaster walls and ceilings throughout serve the same purpose. The light hits the textured walls in various patterns, disciplined by careful placement and caring details like pivoting vents, slatted shutters, and diagonally articulated light shafts. Large openings framed by delicate ash wood—used for fittings throughout—interrupt the graphic array of light to open up completely onto the veld, or grassland. The roof terrace looks out over vineyards and olive groves and, benefiting from almost no light pollution in the area, offers a clear view of the stars at night.

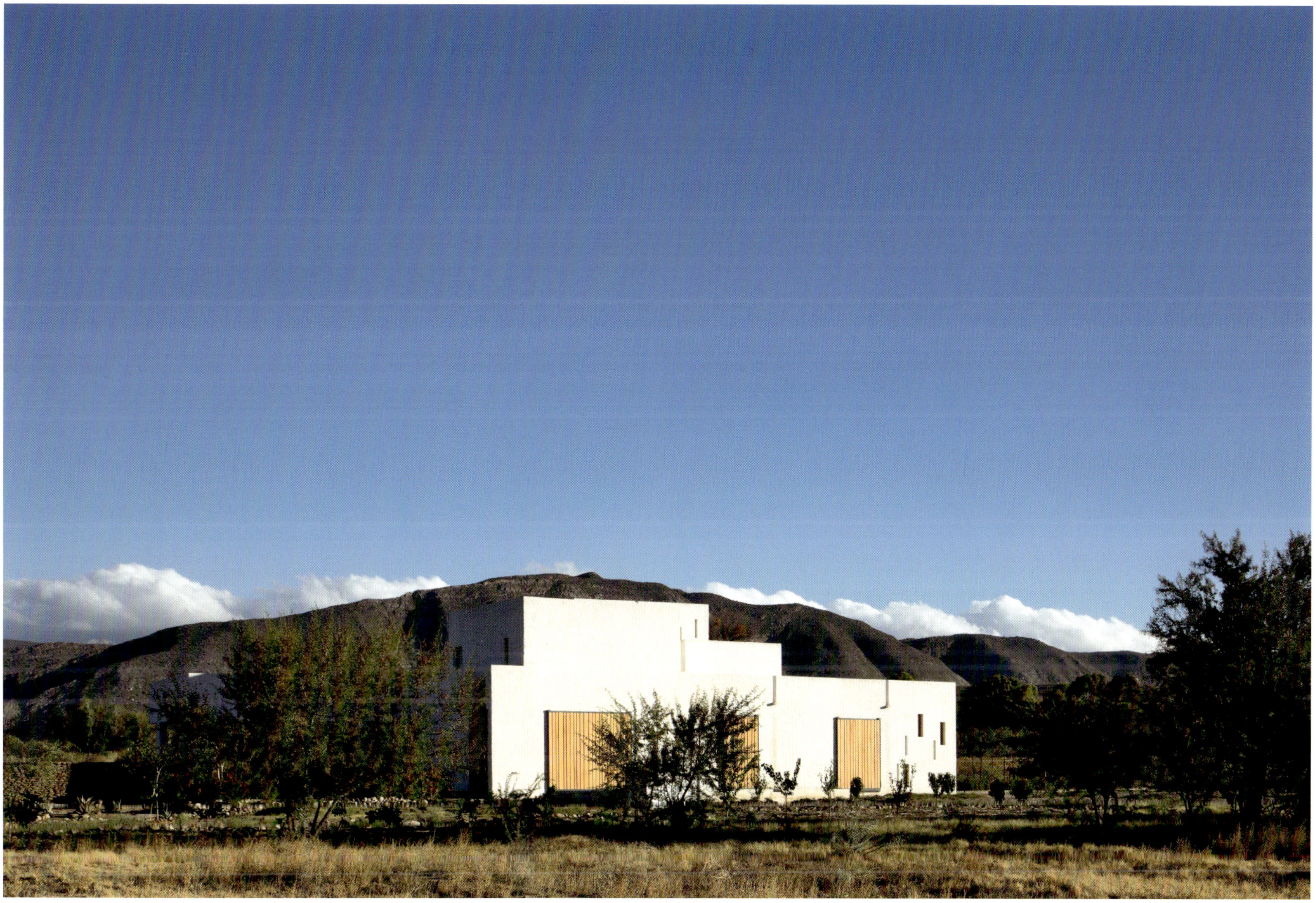

SWARTBERG HOUSE

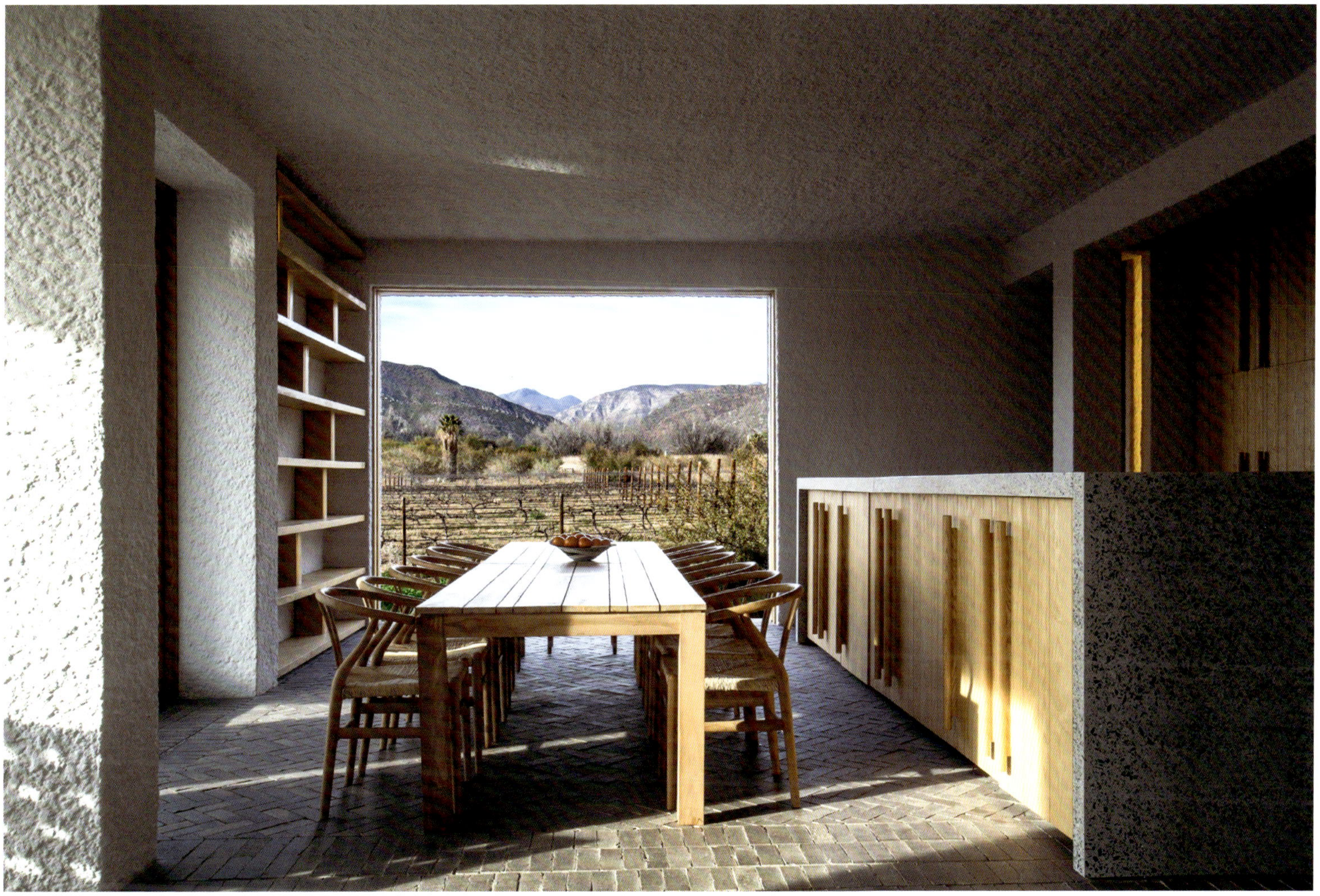

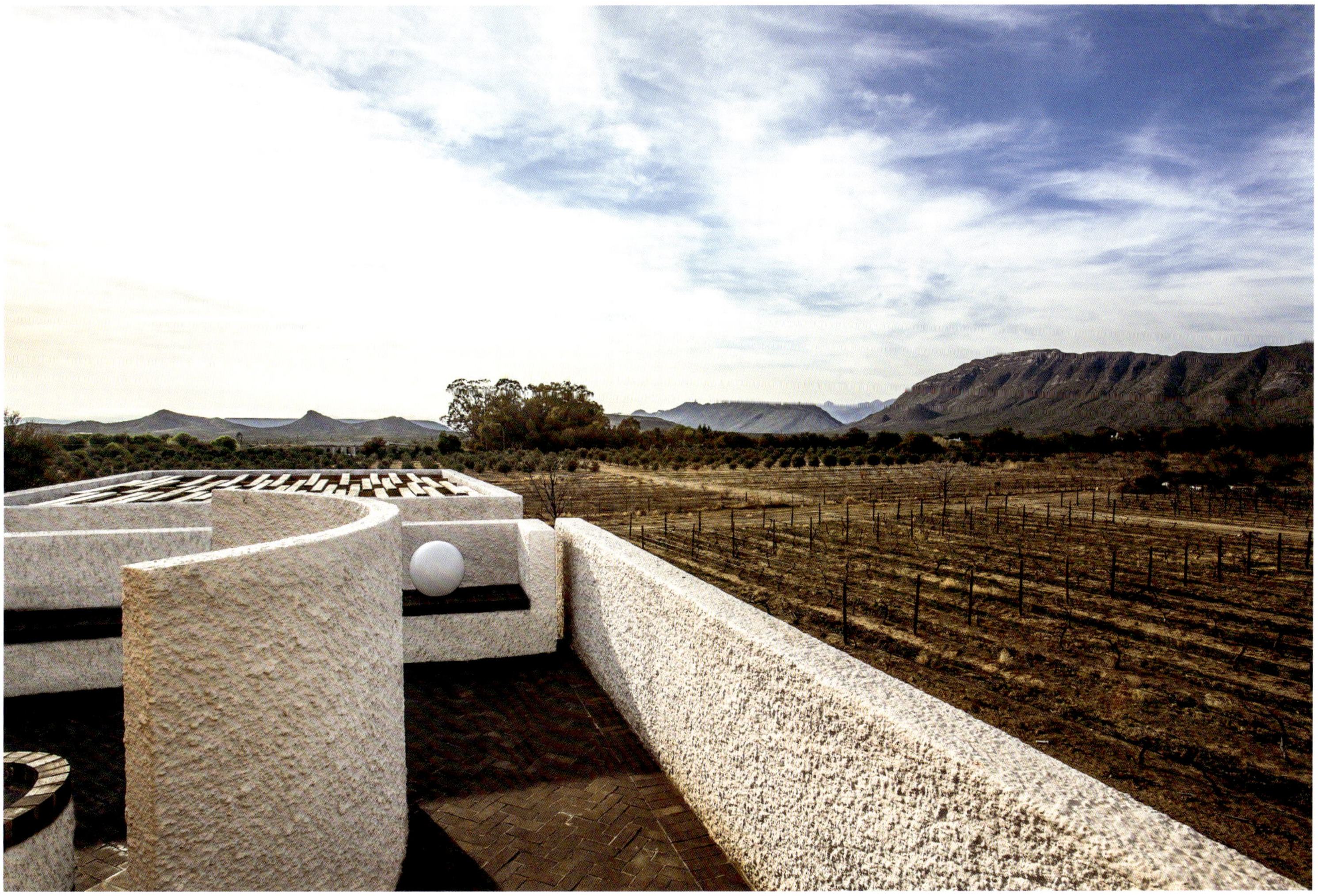

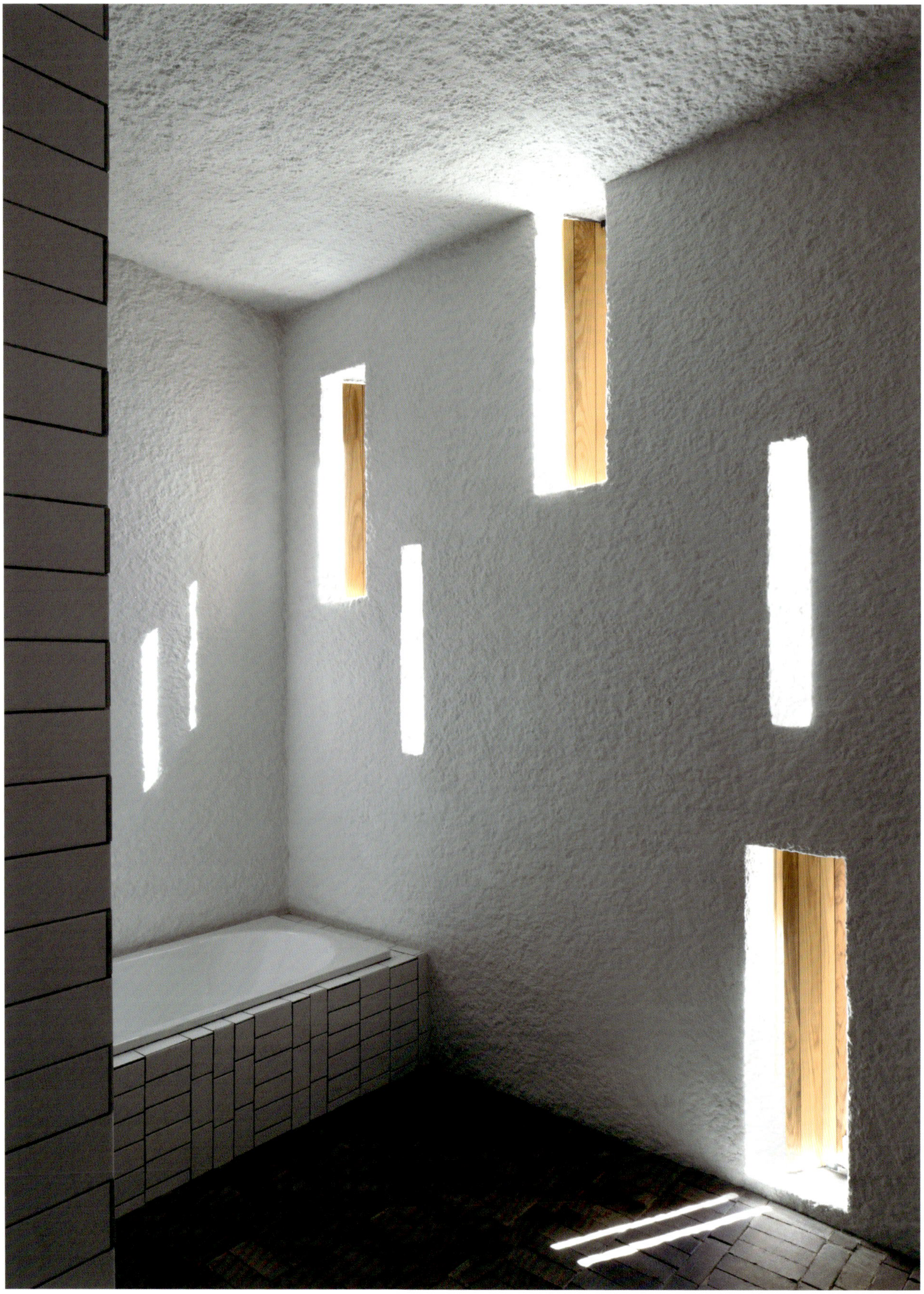

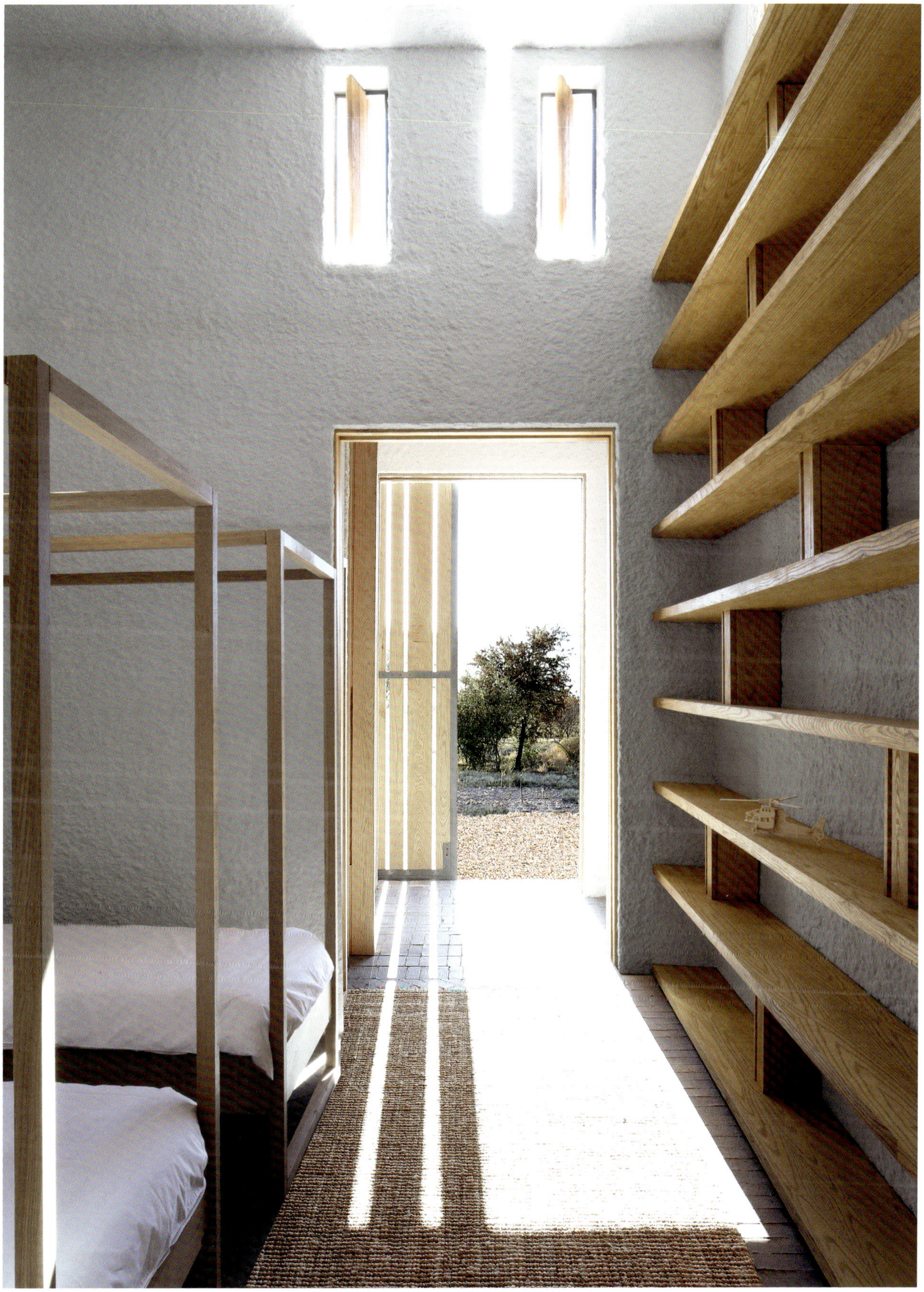

Ibarra Rosano Design Architects
LEVIN RESIDENCE
2012 | Marana, AZ, USA

The odds of imagining that a house situated in the desert would be an all-natural or vernacular-looking structure are high, but to do so would be a fault of logic. Especially in urban zones of Arizona, where architecture is readily connected to the grid, the houses are more often found to be simply in the desert rather than of the desert. The same is true for the Levin Residence in Marana, which sits on Dove Mountain: it is a structure located in the desert, yet it is equipped with all amenities one could have outside the desert too. It doesn't mean that the house is ignorant of the desert, however—quite the opposite, in fact. Every design decision was carefully considered: cantilevered concrete slabs set perpendicular to the topography for optimal solar exposure, cross-ventilation, and framing of views; an exposed slope below the house that provides shady refuge for desert animals; and a bridge to the parking area that allows rainwater to flow beneath. Composed of three simple volumes, the dwelling causes minimal disruption to the terrain and proves that the goal of a high level of comfort can be achieved without disregarding the inhospitable quality of the environment. Visually, the plan is carefully choreographed to expose the void as well as solid vistas, turning the residence into a gallery with the desert as its eternal object.

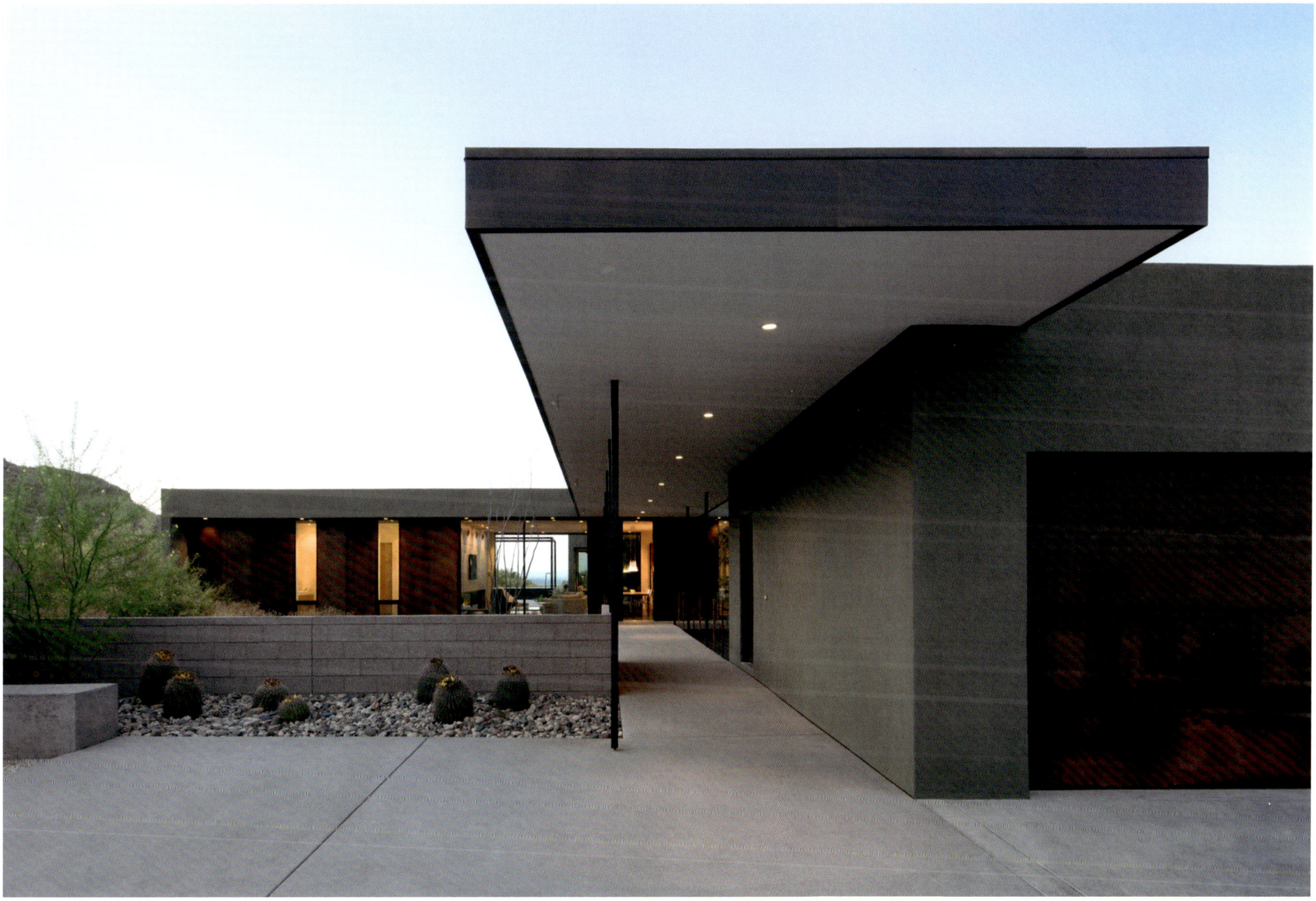

LEVIN RESIDENCE

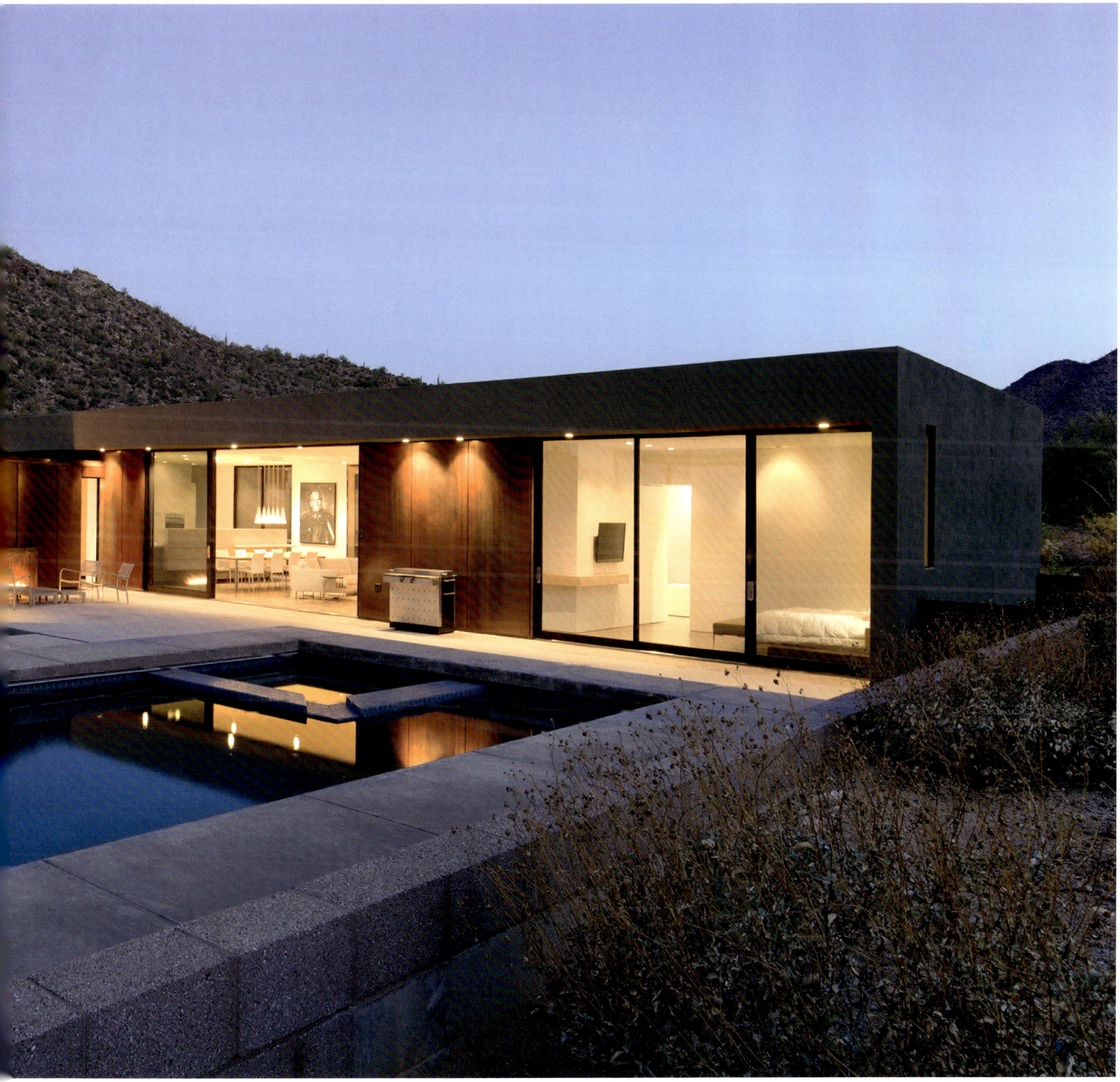

LEVIN RESIDENCE

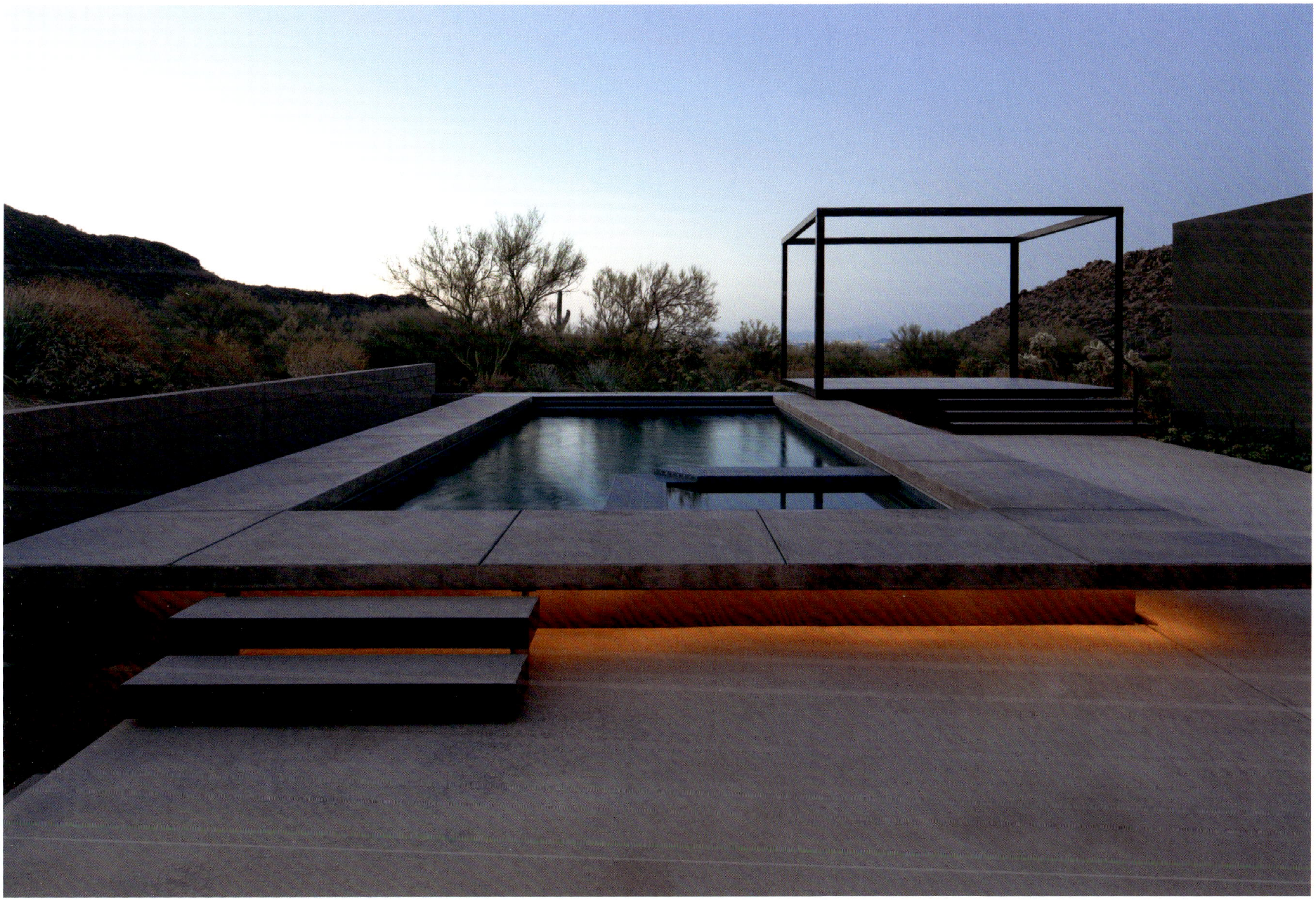

Not Vital
HOUSE TO WATCH THE SUNSET
2005 | Aladab, Niger

Despite its location in Africa's central Sahara, artist Not Vital's House to Watch the Sunset bears an undeniable resemblance to the ancient forms of worship that older civilizations expressed with monuments like the Pyramid of the Sun in Mexico, dating back to about 100 BCE. Part of this impression is conveyed through the geometrical rigorousness—no curves and no unnecessary lines convolute the tower's clear-cut form. To surmount its task, the house of mud and straw builds up with a formalized yet subtle grandeur: the first floor has one door and one window, the second floor features one door and two windows, and the third adds yet another window to the mix. Like a compass, individual staircases to the three floors rise from the ground on the exterior of the building, all facing a different direction. Therefore, each floor must be accessed from the outside rather than from within, imprinting the slight physical strain of the active journey in the mind and thereby closing the circle to ancient worship. Situated in Agadez, Niger, home to nomadic tribes like the Pneu and the Tuareg, the structure points to notions of "home" defined by not only architectural physicality but also the availability of the basic necessities of life. To take the time to closely observe something as mundane and as essential as the sun is a luxury—one that Vital gifts to every visitor.

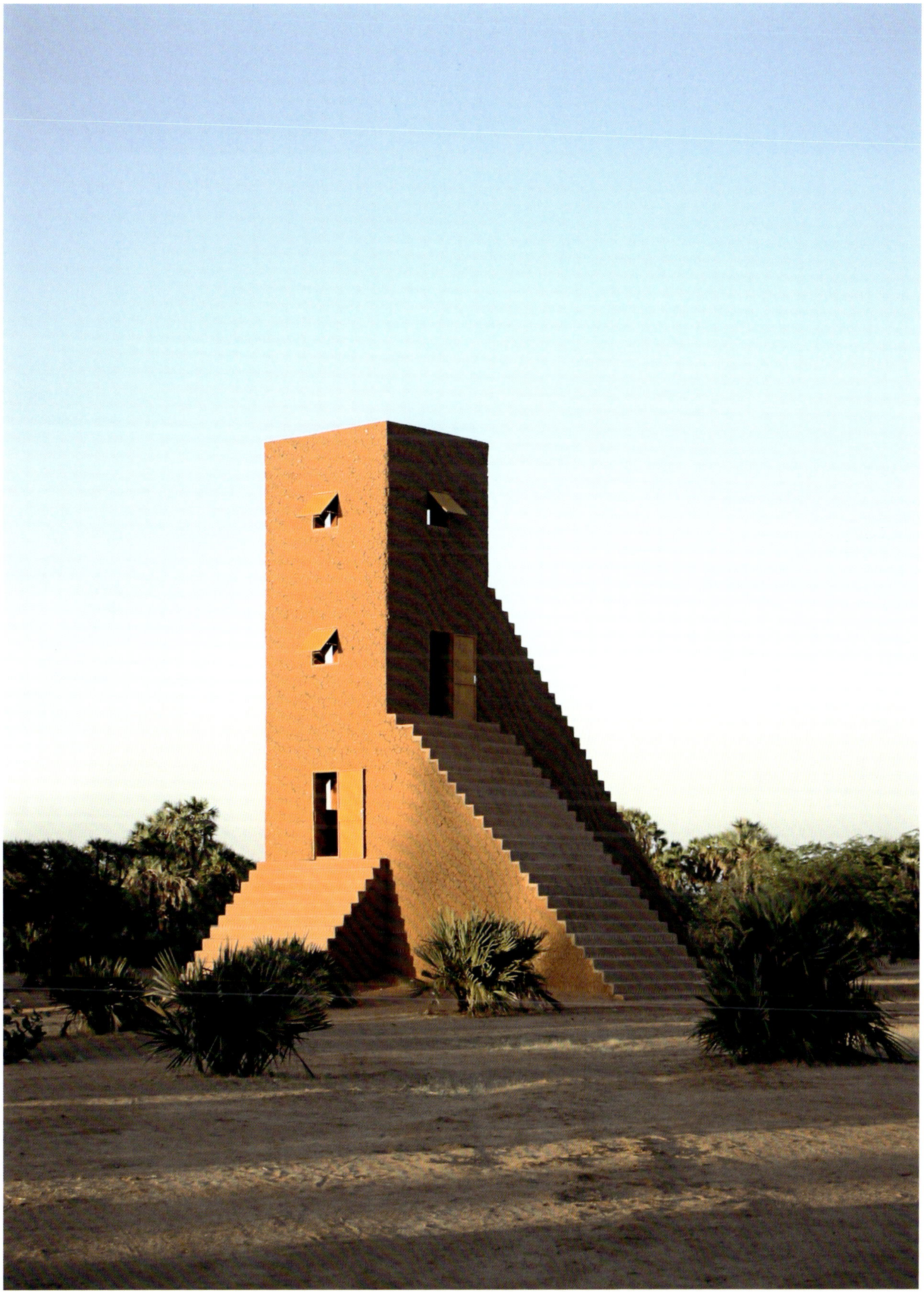

HOUSE TO WATCH THE SUNSET

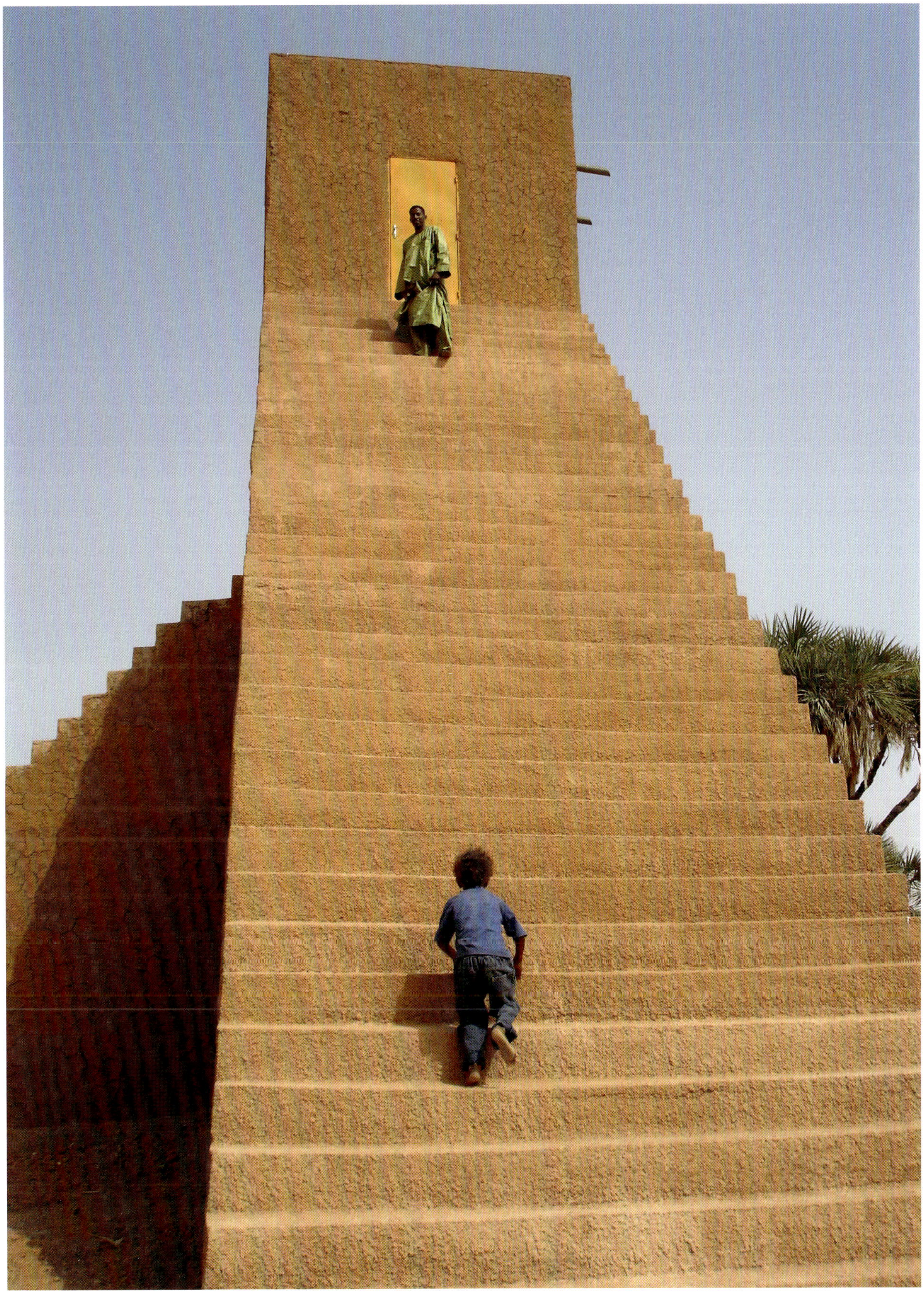

Blank Studio
XEROS RESIDENCE
2006 | Phoenix, AZ, USA

On a narrow plot of land in a Phoenix neighborhood that was originally developed in the 1950s, architect Matthew Trzebiatowski has built a two-story structure to call home and studio. This residence easily fits into the rich architectural culture of Arizona, which has seen vernacular masterpieces and modern experiments built by Frank Lloyd Wright and others. Xeros Residence (*xeros* means "dry" in Greek) has been largely faced with exposed steel—corrugated and mesh—that has weathered over time to deep orange and sandy brown tones that mirror the desert surroundings. The ground floor and the level below grade are dedicated work spaces of Blank Studio, accessed by passing behind a mesh steel panel and water feature that terminates in a small pool. An external flight of stairs leads to the private rooms, further underscoring the separate nature of work and living. The central gallery is followed by a cantilevered master suite and media room, both located on the north facade and completely glazed to allow panoramic mountain views. The form turns an opaque face toward the intense western afternoon sun, while the more exposed sides on the south and east are shielded by an external screen of woven metal mesh. The pop of color from a yellow-glass-framed Juliet balcony appears like a desert bloom.

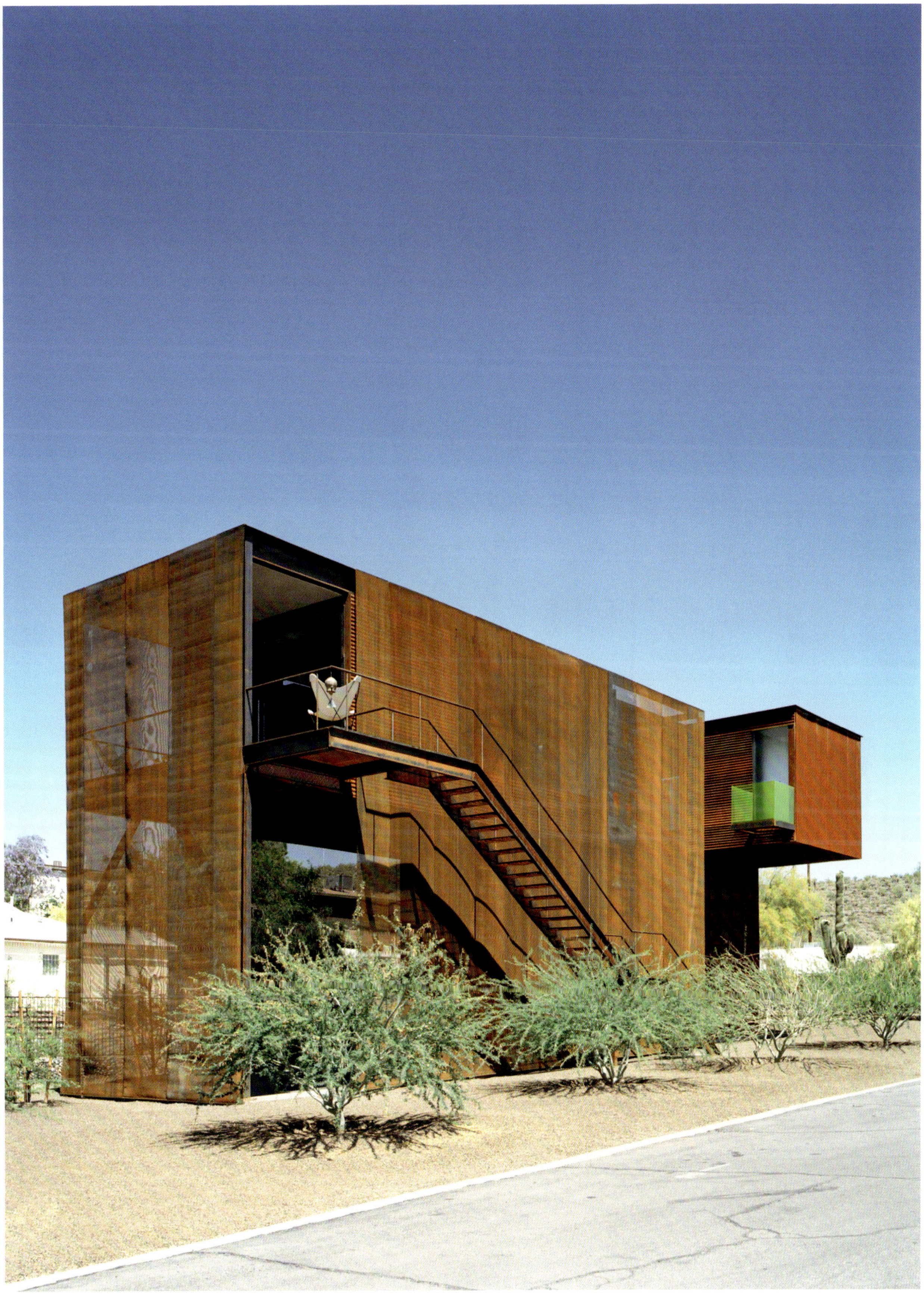

XEROS RESIDENCE

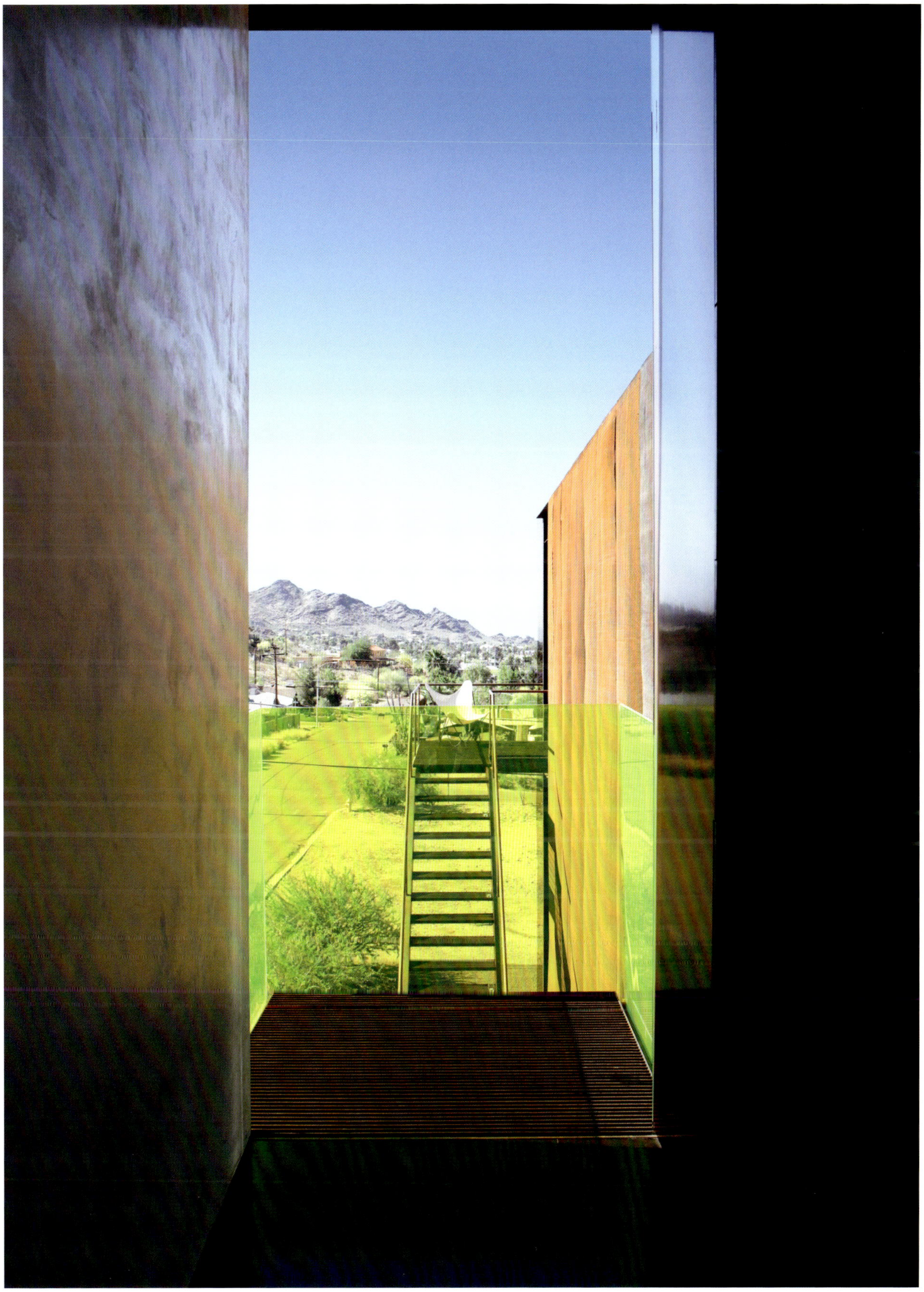

XEROS RESIDENCE

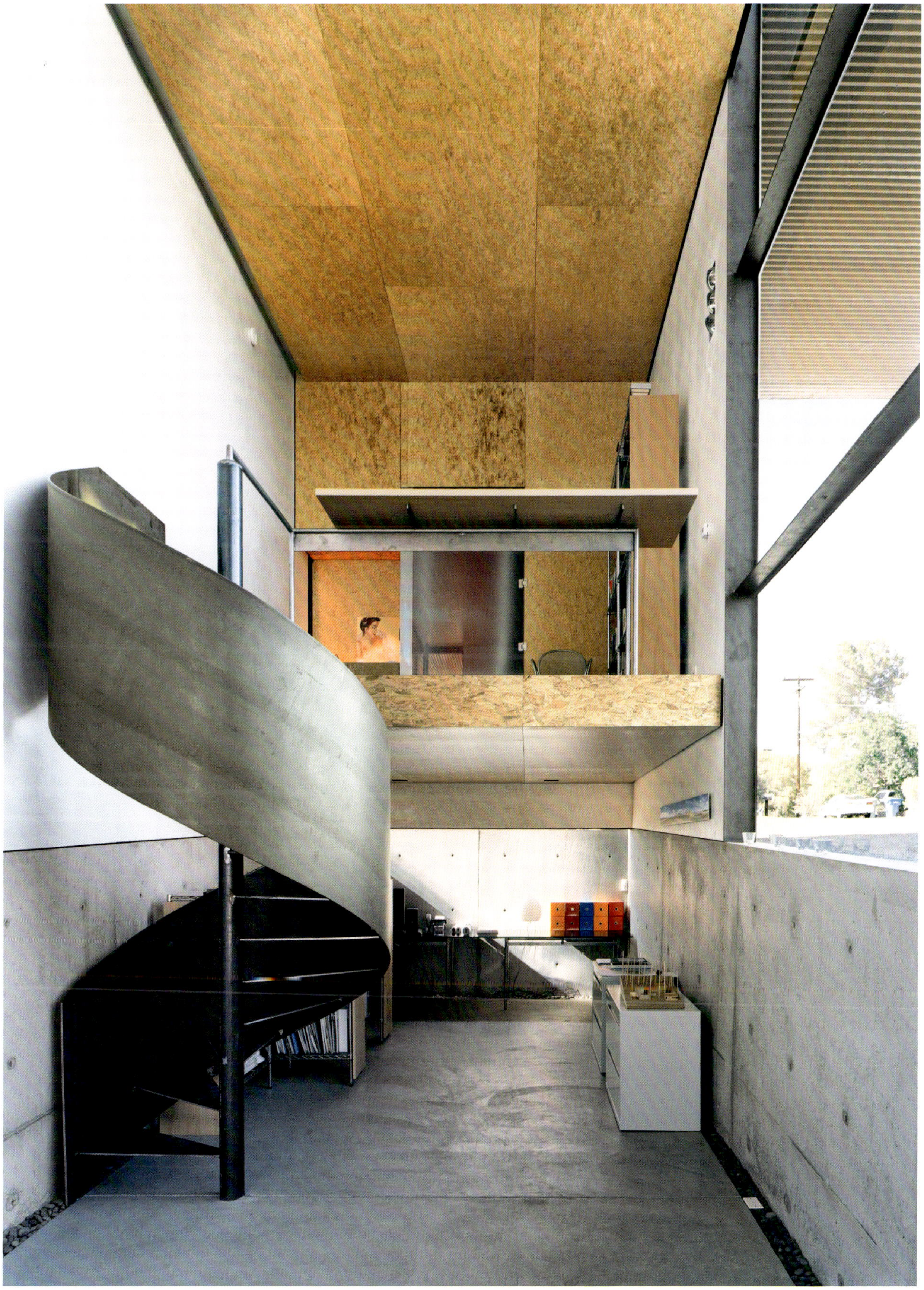

Oller & Pejic Architecture
BLACK DESERT HOUSE
2013 | Yucca Valley, CA, USA

Loosely modeled after the abstract idea of a shadow—an eye-soothing patch of darkness—the black structure sits within the rocky terrain north of Yucca Valley, near Palm Springs and Joshua Tree National Park. Its boldly minimal presence is consciously conceived to offer a stark contrast to the organic softness of the rock formations extending far beyond where the eye can see. Sharp geometric edges stand against nature's backdrop as if to admit that imitation would not have done the natural landscape's grandeur justice. Built with the integrity of modernist ideals, the house features black walls, midnight quartz, high-gloss anthracite, and darkened steel running through both exterior and interior, only interrupted by large floor-to-ceiling window panels, which give undisputed attention to the multi-chromatic brightness of the desert. When the day turns into night, the black house's mood shifts with it. Suddenly, its boldness and color scheme are absorbed by the darkness of the night—thereby giving attention to the star-filled sky and its illumination on the land. This surprising duality is what deeply characterizes the aloof desert dwelling collaboratively designed by client Marc Atlan, a creative director who provided the original concept, and husband-and-wife architecture firm Oller & Pejic from Los Angeles, which brought his vision to fruition.

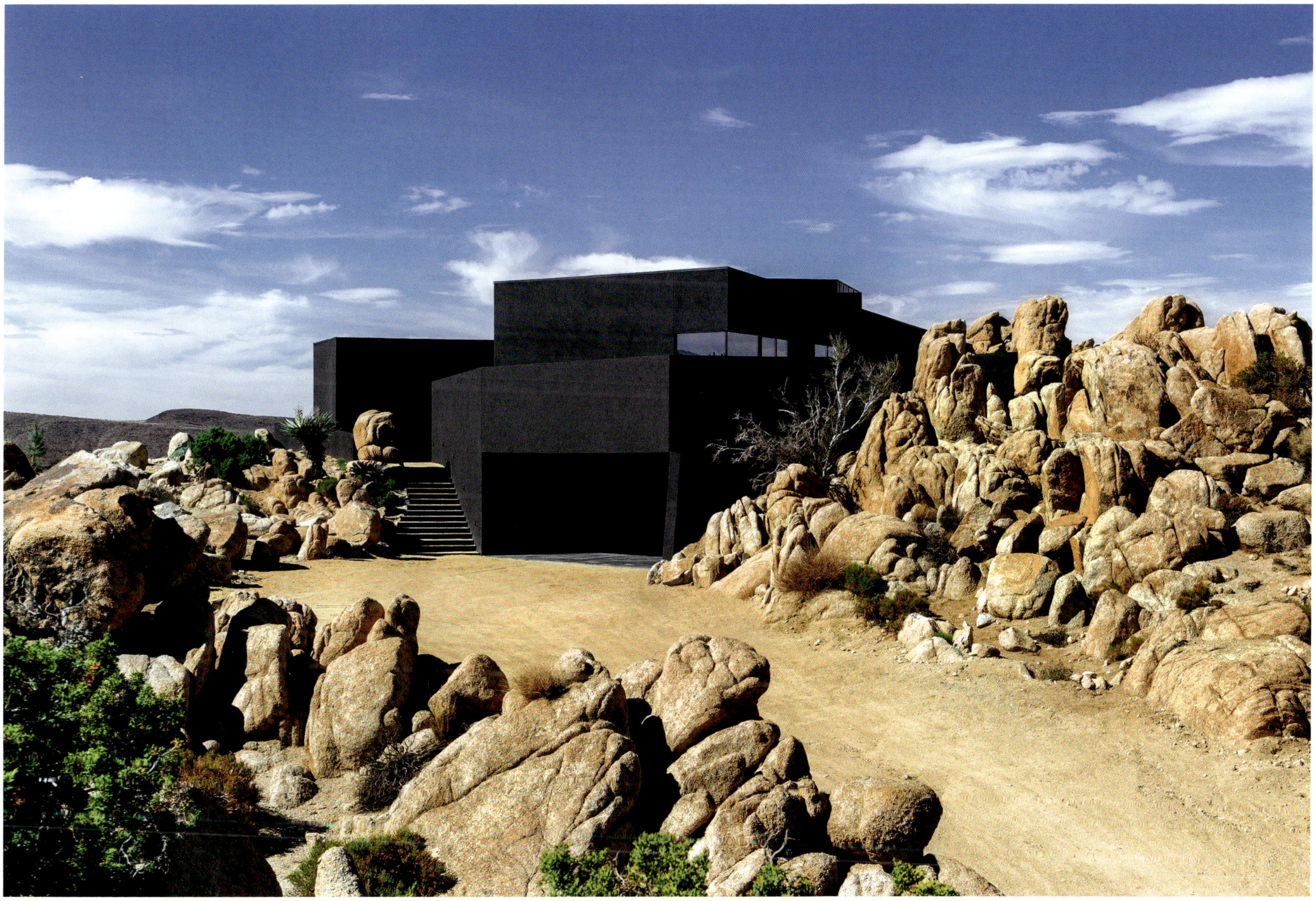

BLACK DESERT HOUSE

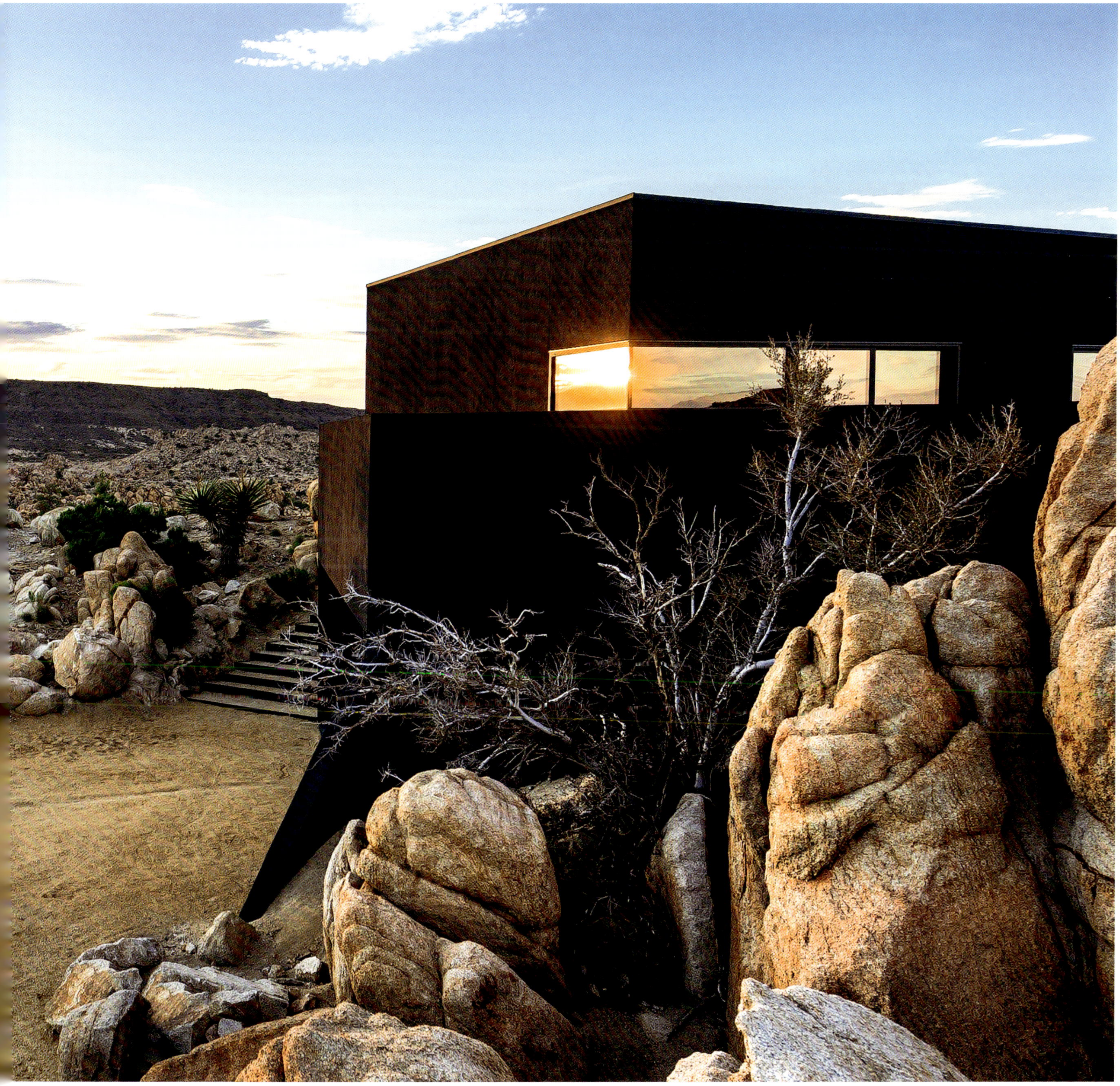

BLACK DESERT HOUSE

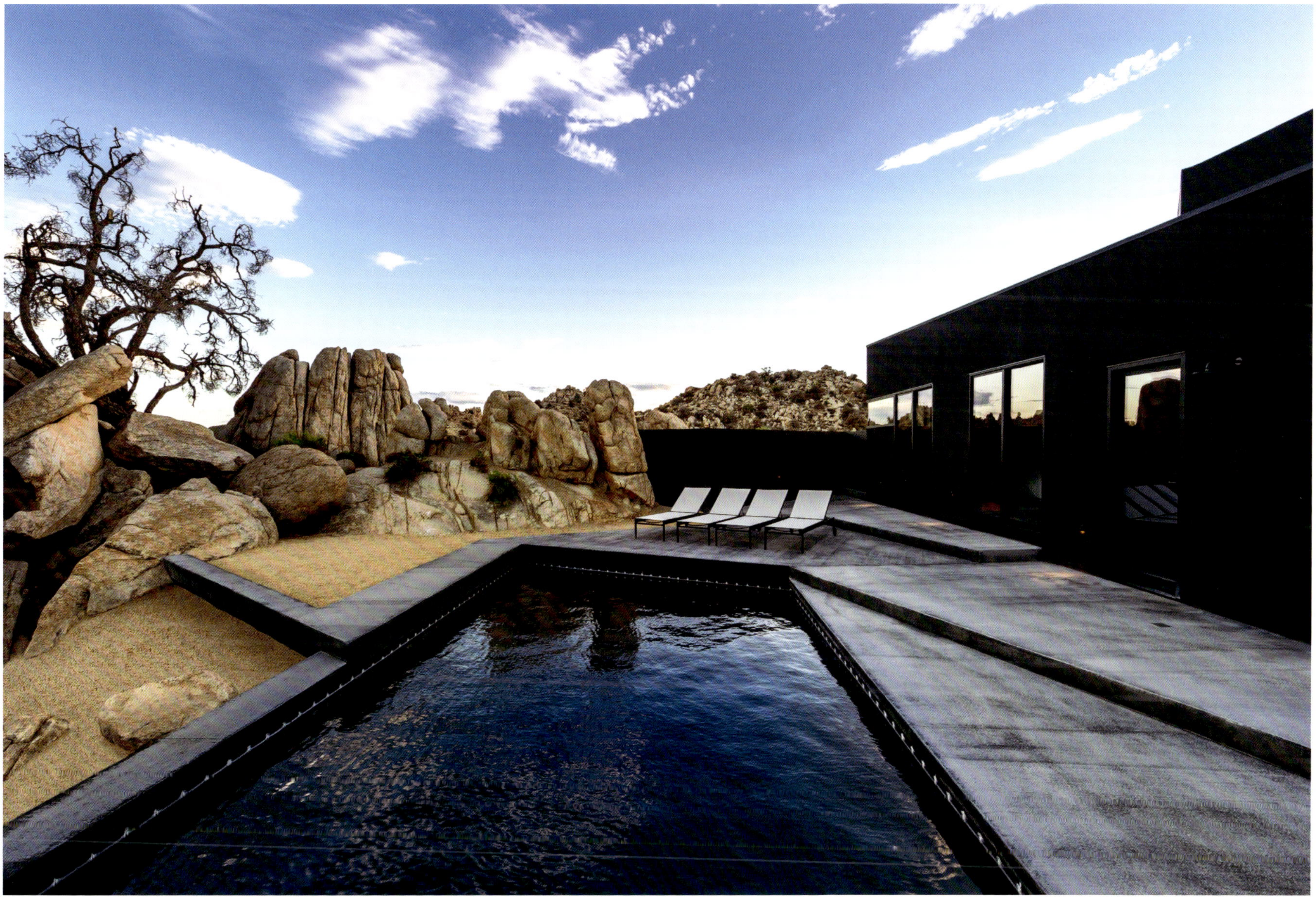

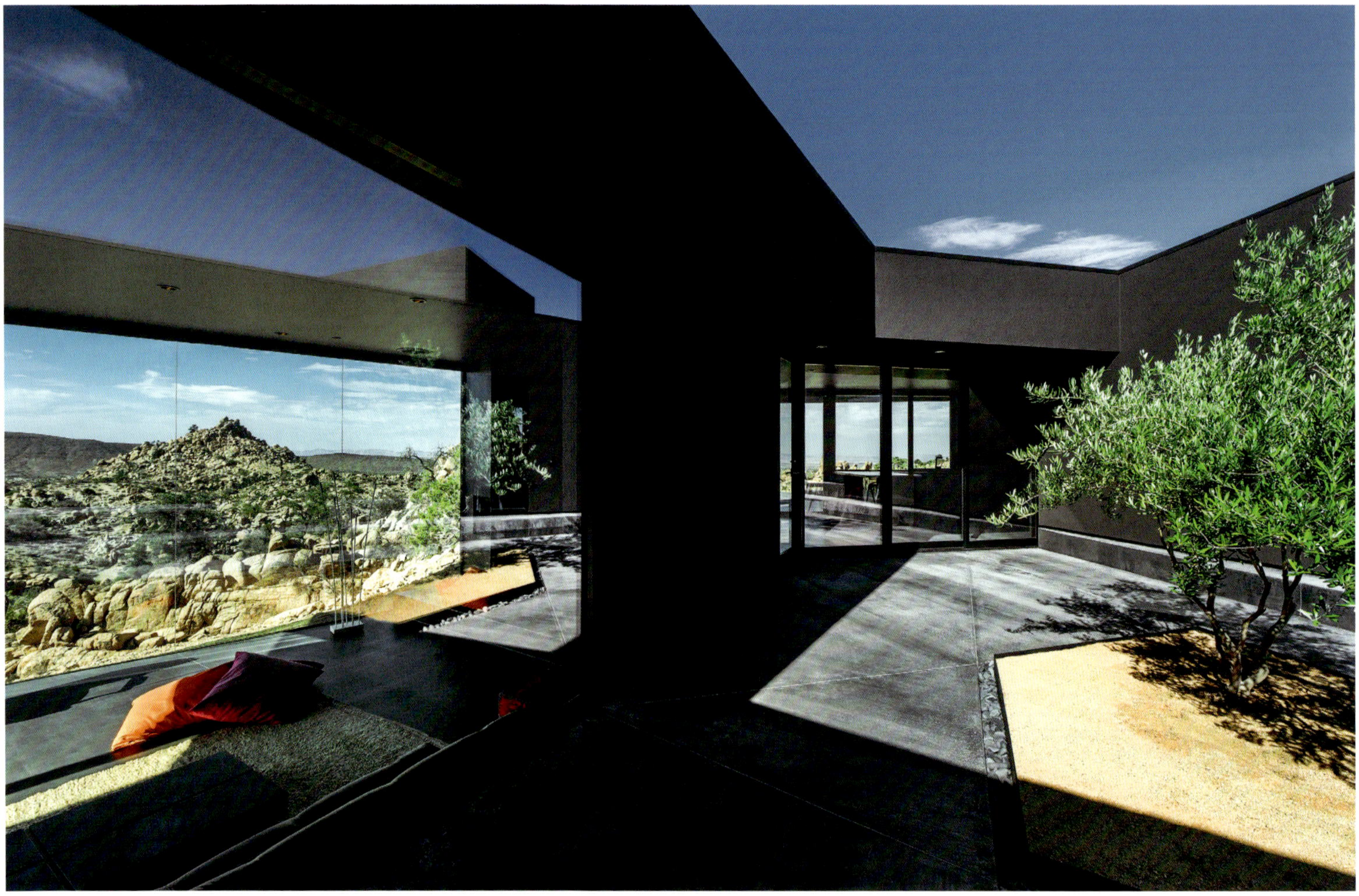

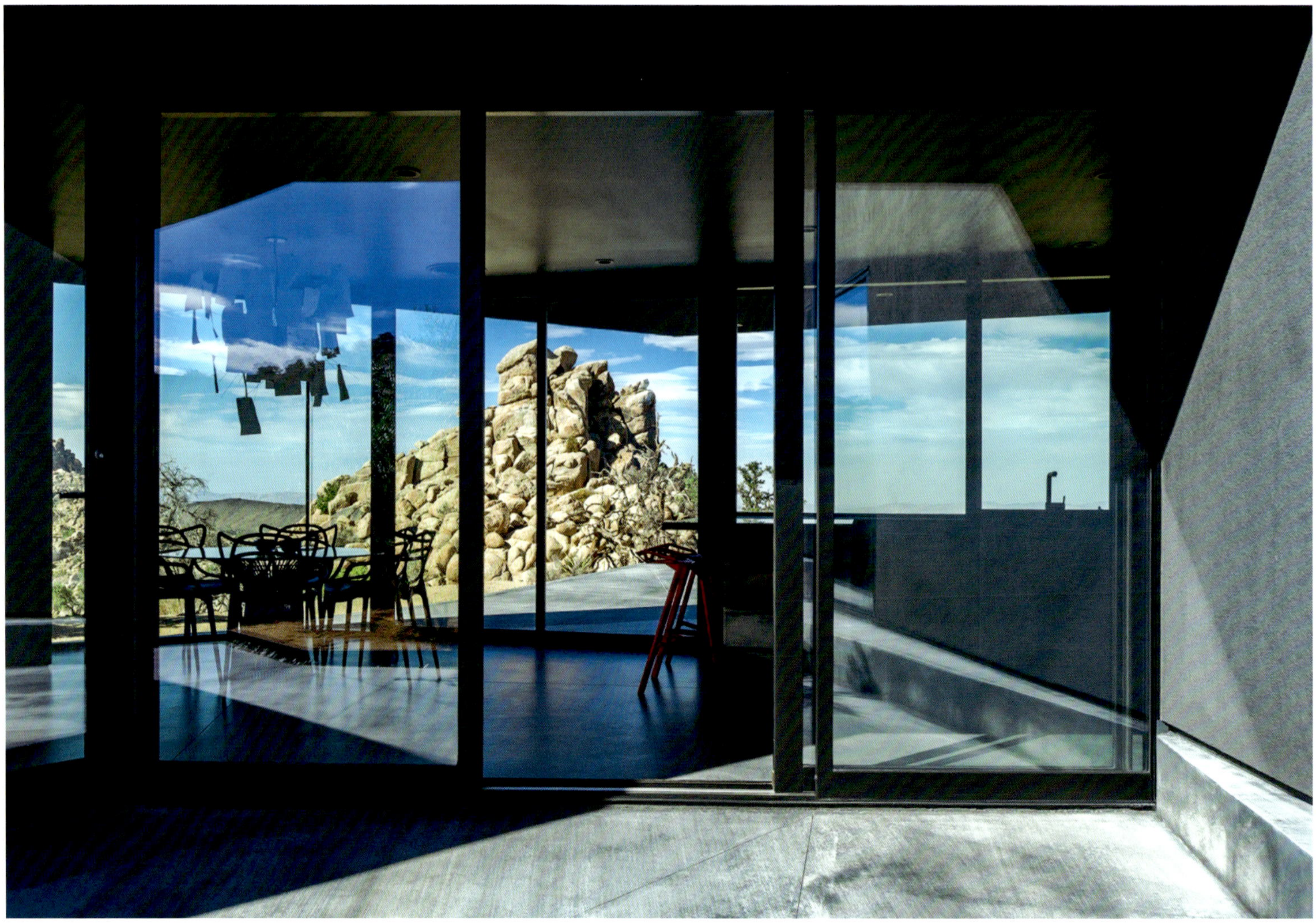

BLACK DESERT HOUSE

Rick Joy Architects
DESERT NOMAD HOUSE
2005 | Tucson, AZ, USA

Tucson is home to the Saguaro National Park, known for its spectacular saguaro cacti, which can grow up to forty feet tall (twelve meters) and—judging from decades of creative travel photography—never fails to astonish generations of tourists. Nestled into this Arizona setting in a secluded bowl-like cradle, three independent volumes look out at the desert vegetation. Each entity consciously frames a different view of the Tucson Mountains through generous glazing: the bedroom affords a view of the sun rising, the living space captures the sun as it sets, and the work studio concentrates on the immediate vista by framing the vegetation like a landscape painting. The main treat is the proximity between bed and land, meaning the first glance of the day is dedicated to nature, which intimately gazes back.

Slightly elevated on stilts, the three cubes emerge as friendly visitors on the land, providing shaded space for small animals and leaving the land mostly untouched. The geometry of the cube—an enduring topic of fascination for artists in the 1960s and 1970s—and the naturally rusted steel-plate cladding lend the dwellings the appearance of minimalist sculpture. This impression is hardly broken by monochrome interiors, uniformly covered in maple veneers. In the sparse landscape, the simplicity of Desert Nomad House adds an achingly beautiful contrast with unexpected subtlety.

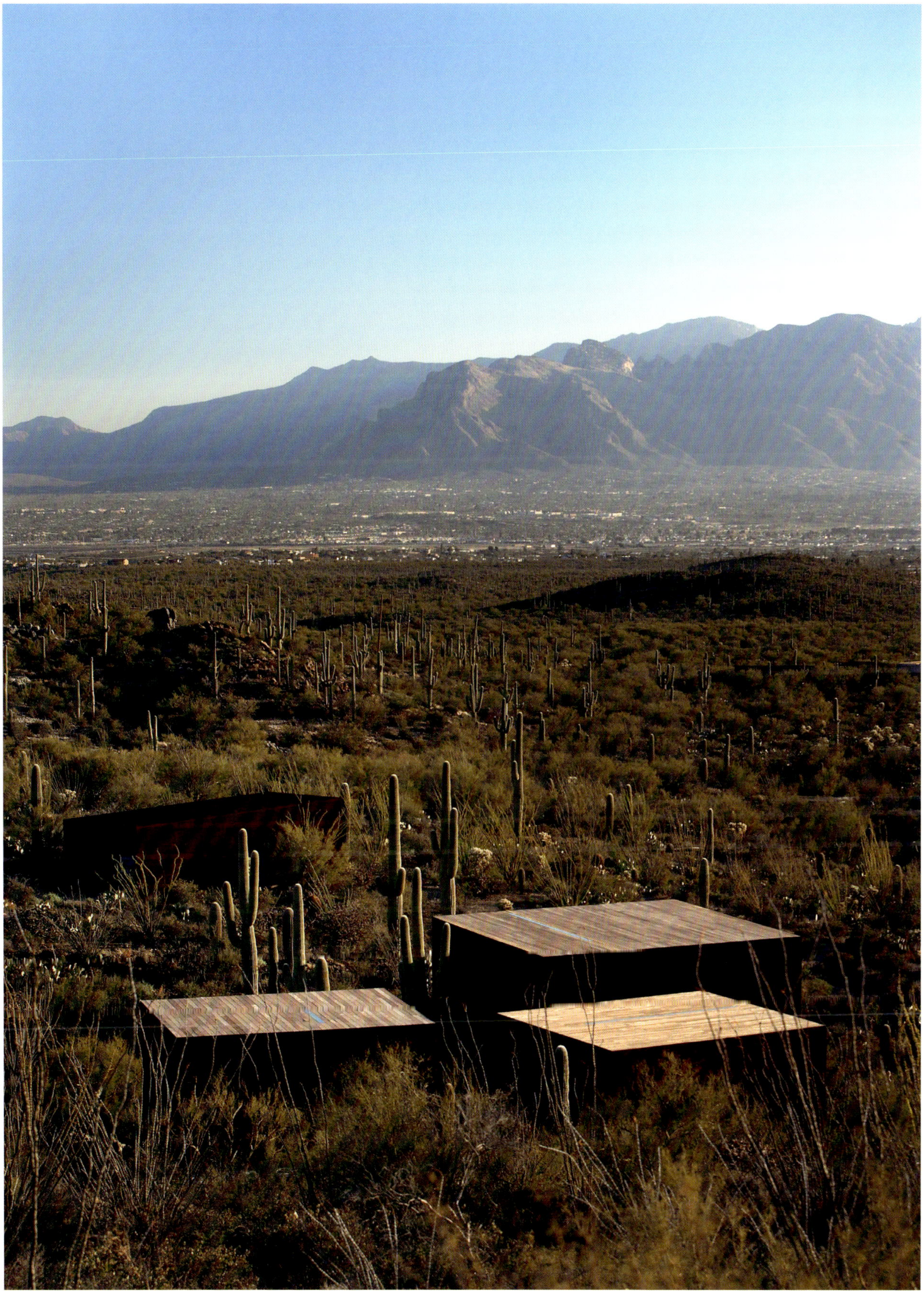

DESERT NOMAD HOUSE 64

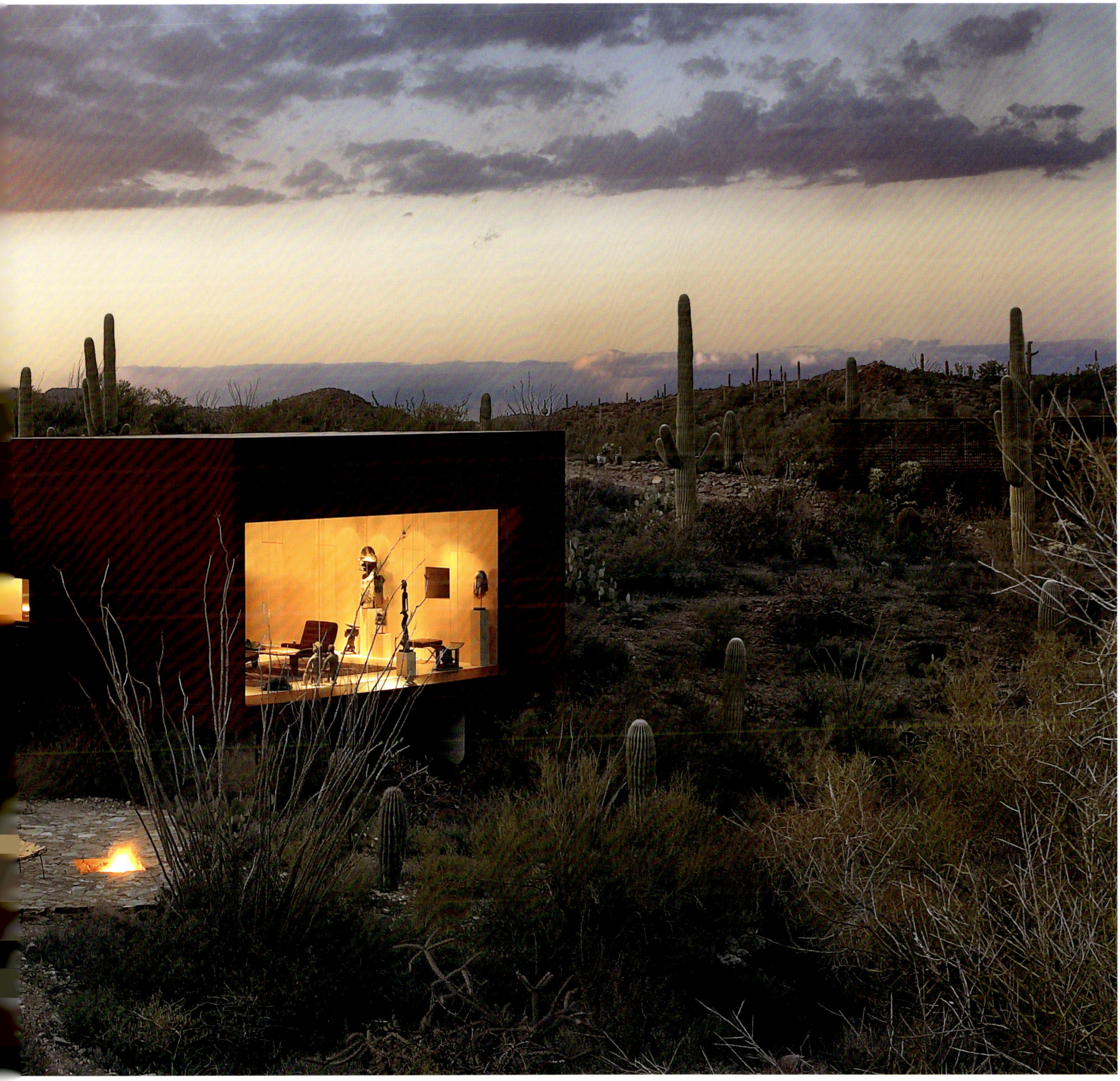

DESERT NOMAD HOUSE

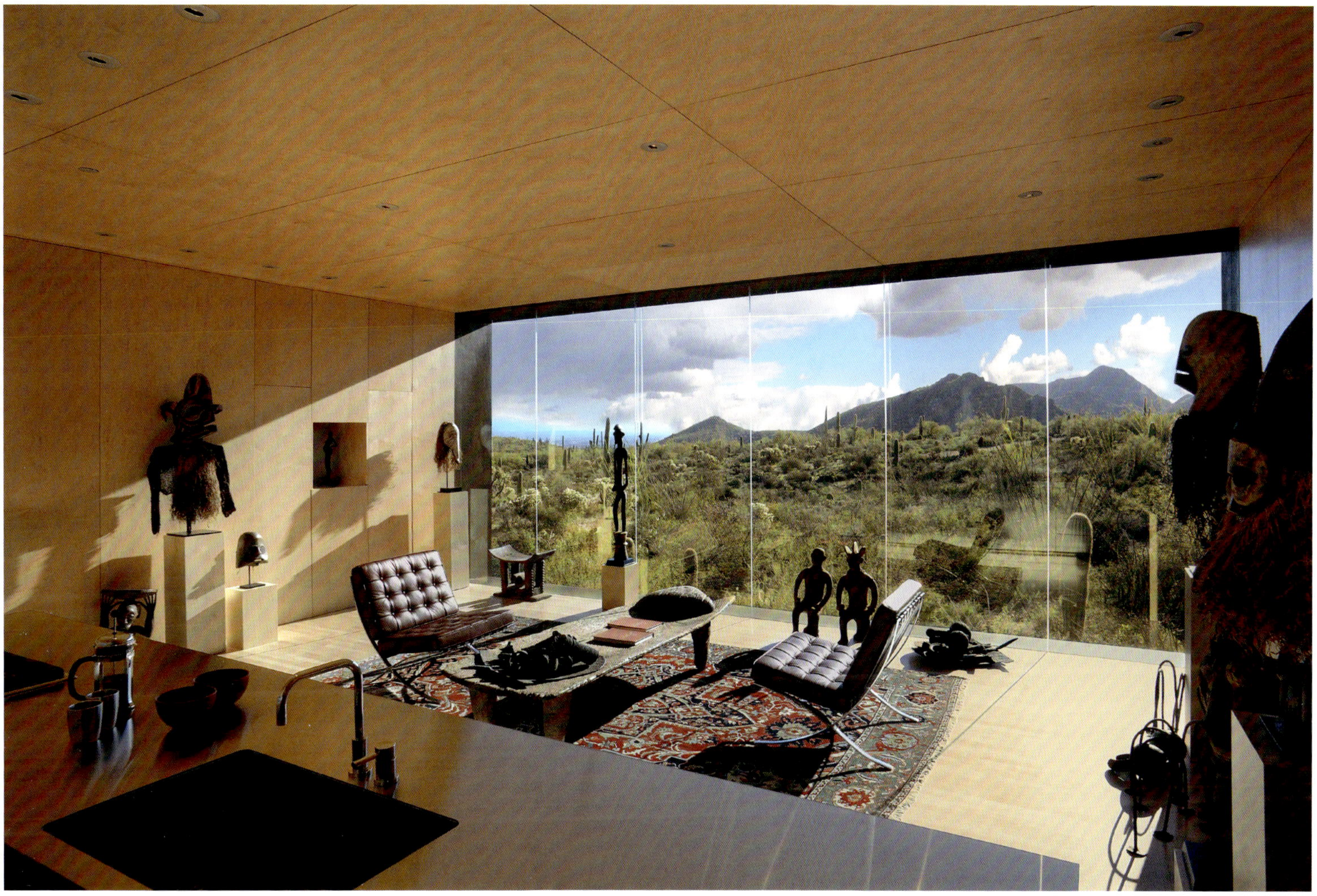

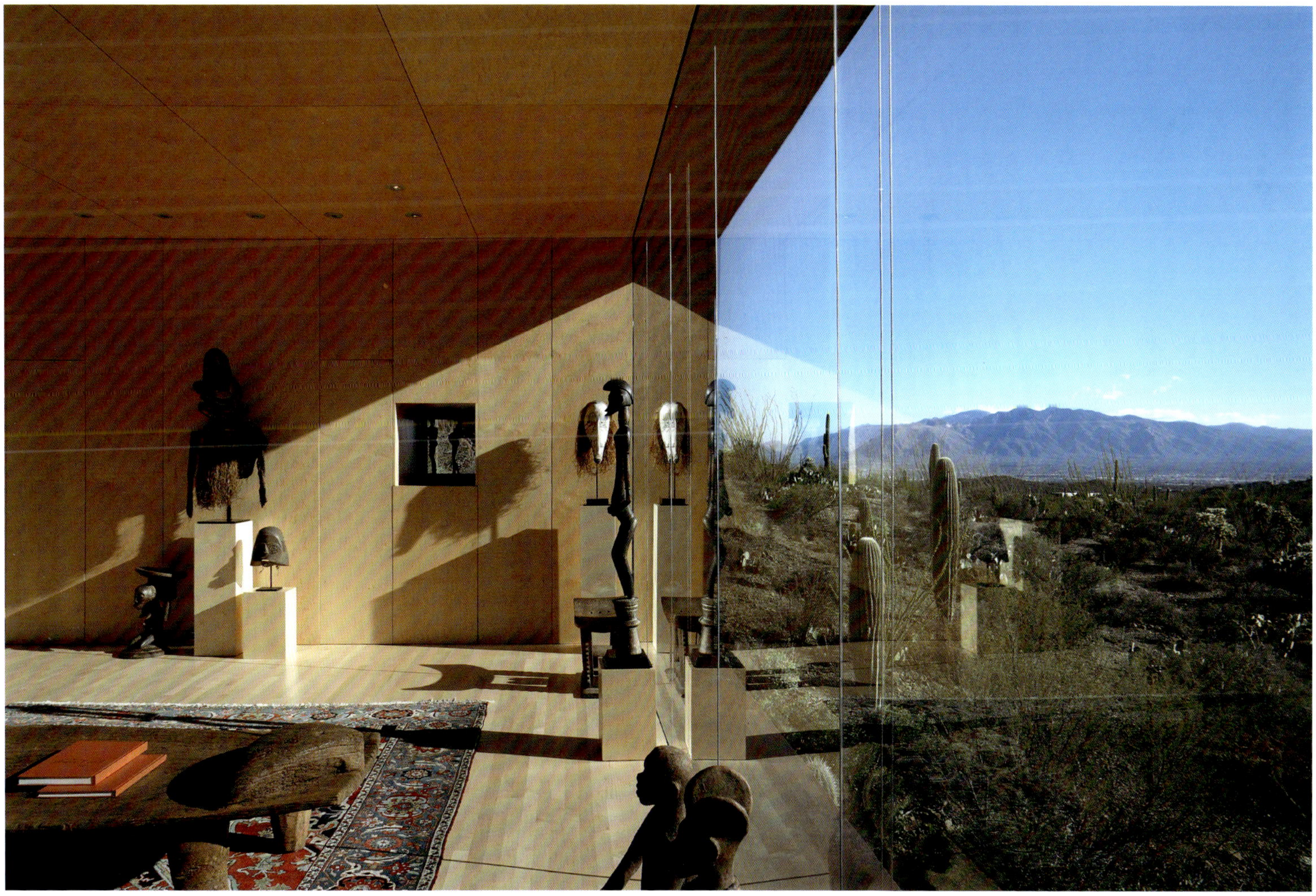

Doug Aitken
MIRAGE
2017 | Palm Springs, CA, USA

Installed in 2017 as part of the inaugural Desert X art biennial, for which artists were asked to respond to the unique conditions of the Coachella Valley, the Mirage house, completely mirrored outside and in, appears as a glowing, otherworldly entity in its rocky desert surroundings. The simplified suburban silhouette is modeled after low-slung ranch-style houses once prevalent in the American West, with the characteristic front porch and gabled roof. Depending on the time of day, light conditions, and angle of the sun, Mirage can either reflect the landscape or disappear into the landscape. Viewing such an intensely reflective mass exposes layers of meaning and sparks questions concerning the future. The region bears a history paved with discovery, expansion, and innovation—of man arriving in the desert and making it available to him. With the urban sprawl of Palm Springs only a few miles away, the success of this mission is indisputable, but the important question is, of course, one about consequences. As modernity increasingly brings overreach into nearly every area of natural habitat, Aitken's functionless installation demands continued personal reflection—both external and internal.

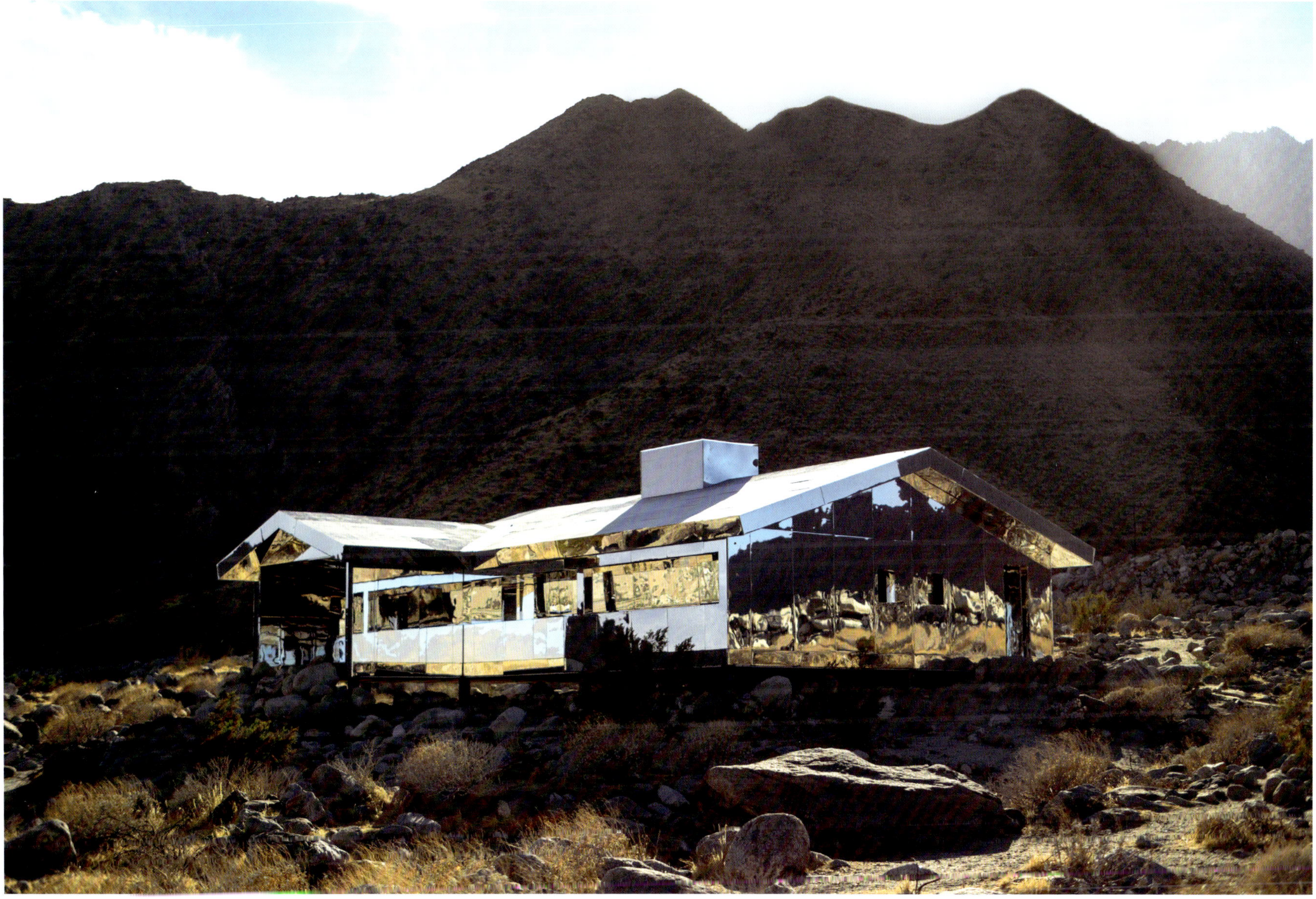

MIRAGE

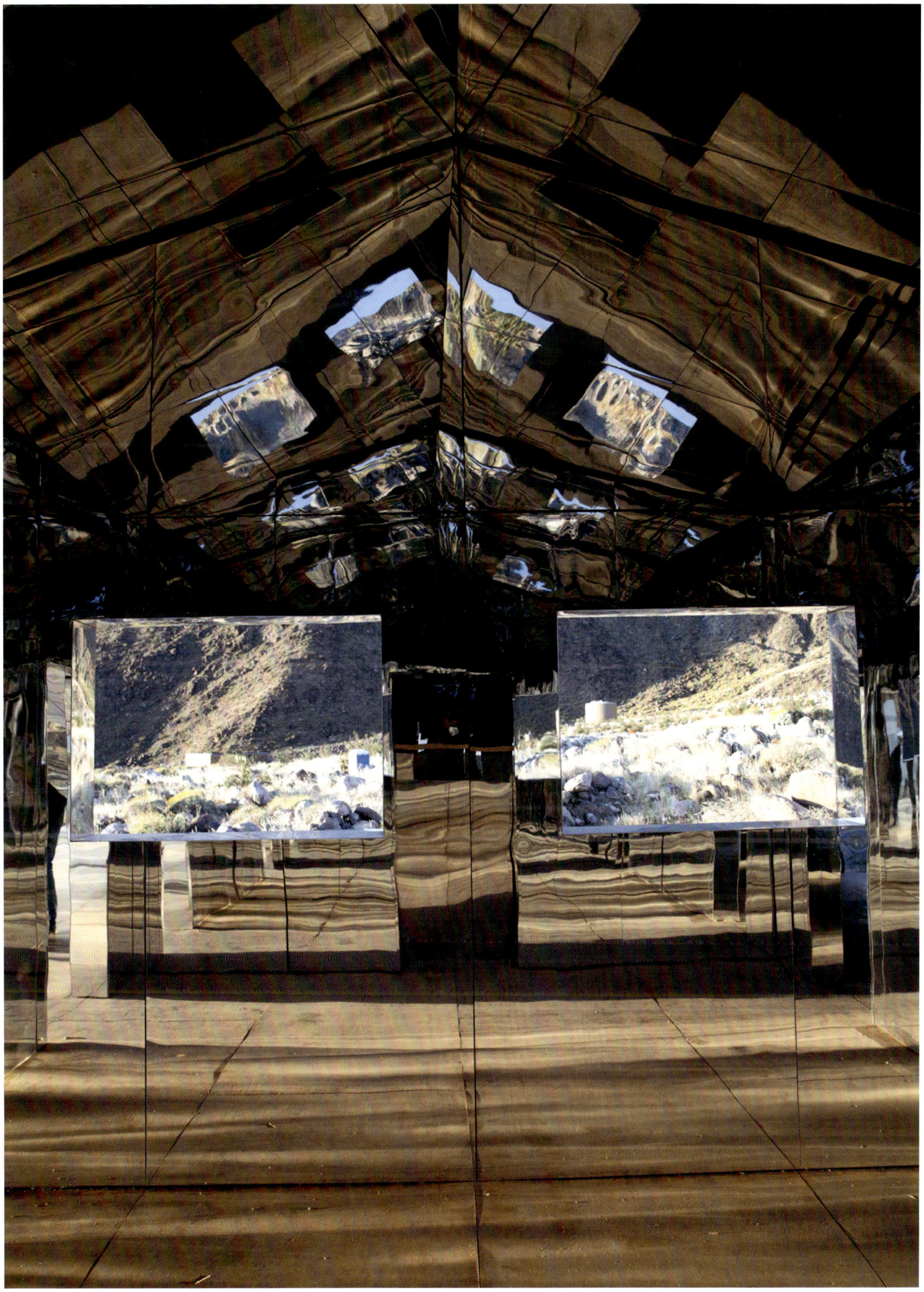

Edward Ogosta Architecture
FOUR EYES HOUSE
2012 | Coachella Valley, CA, USA

There is probably not much that hasn't been seen or done in the Coachella Valley—such is the place. Considering the historic flamboyance of California's desert playground, one could say that the Four Eyes House is an attempt to respond—a house designed for the pleasure of looking. Arranged roughly in the shape of a geometric amoeba, Four Eyes House is one of the most sophisticated objects to be conceived in an arid nature zone. Its monochromatic white surface is nearly a fluorescent white; almost nothing but bright, with minimal interventions of slim metal frames, apertures, and full-frame glazing. Not the slightest attempt has been made to make this house appear like its surroundings. It looks like a smartly dressed—possibly overdressed—guest at a rough-and-tumble affair. Unruly dust, sand, and heat are countered with clinical cleanliness and protruding sharp angles, all elbows. It looks curious, the purposeful cold, blank stare emanating from the ground floor. But this stern mood abruptly gives way to the more lighthearted common spaces within glass-enclosed pavilions. It all finally starts to make sense when the sun goes down and attention is brought to the sleeping towers, four monoliths positioned at the corners of the structure, each one facing a different direction and housing tight quarters with room for only a bed and a commanding solitary view: sunrise or mountains by day, shimmering city lights or star-filled sky by night. In a certain way the home offers freedom, for it is not practical. As a holiday home, it doesn't have to be.

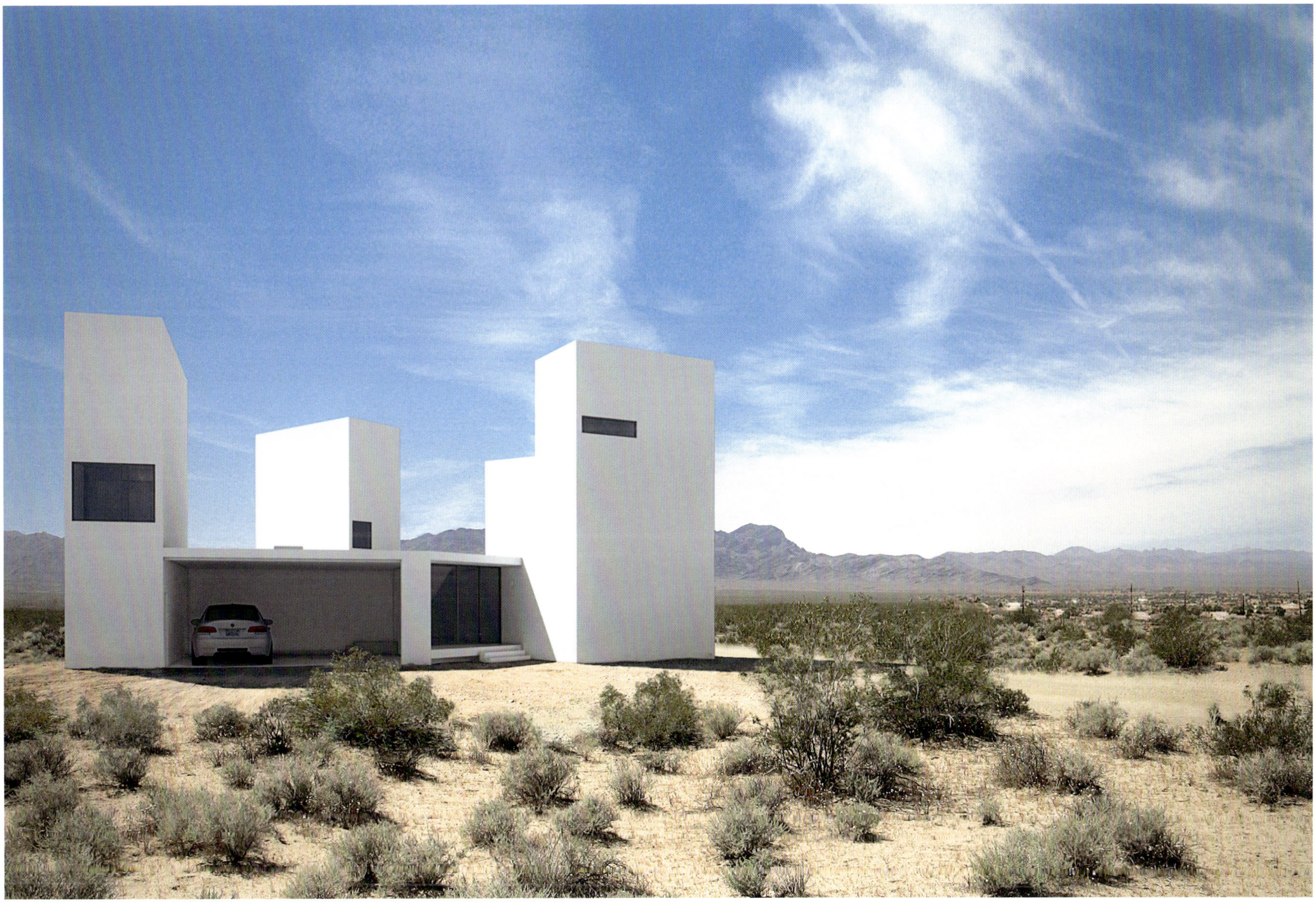

FOUR EYES HOUSE

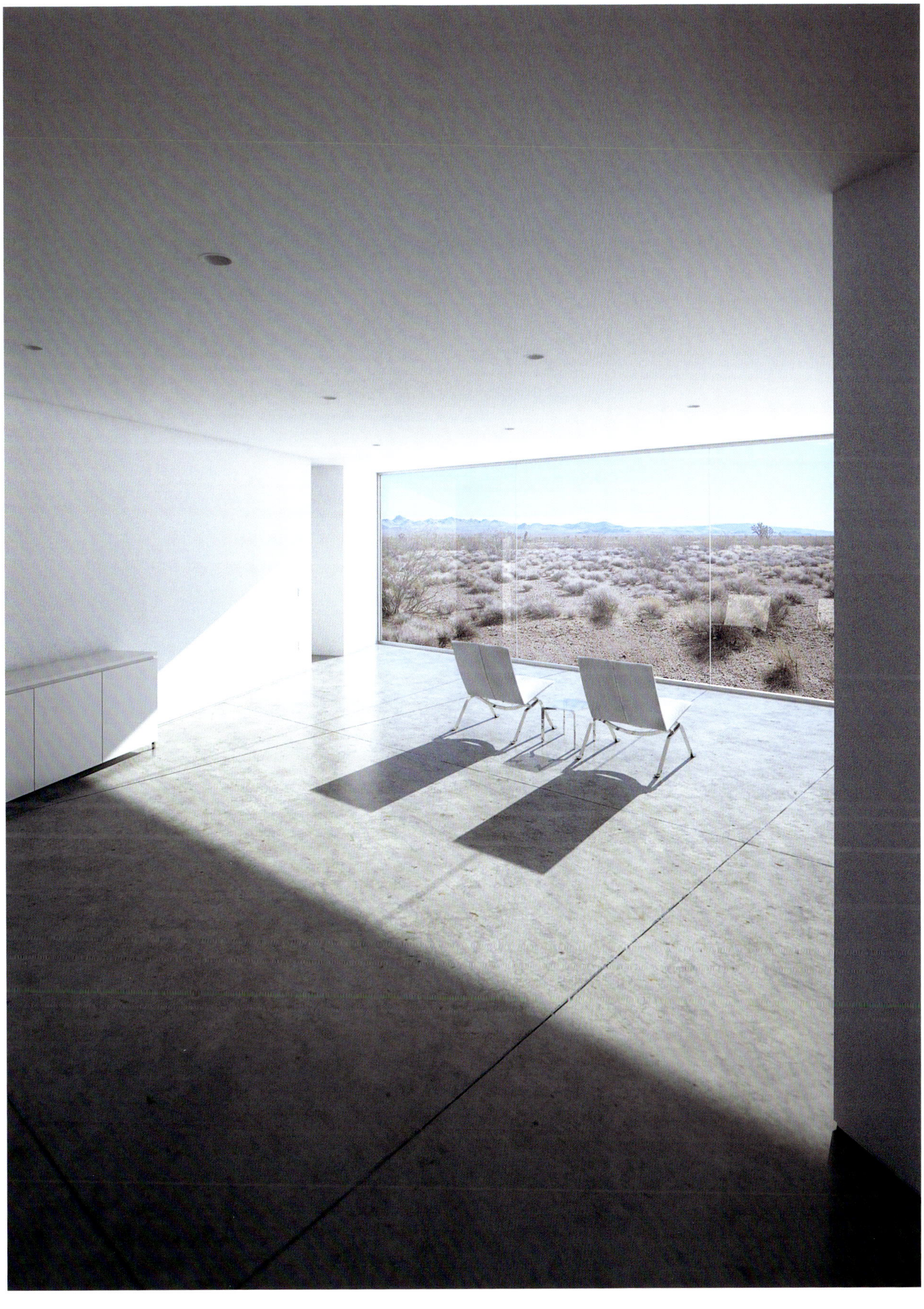

FOUR EYES HOUSE

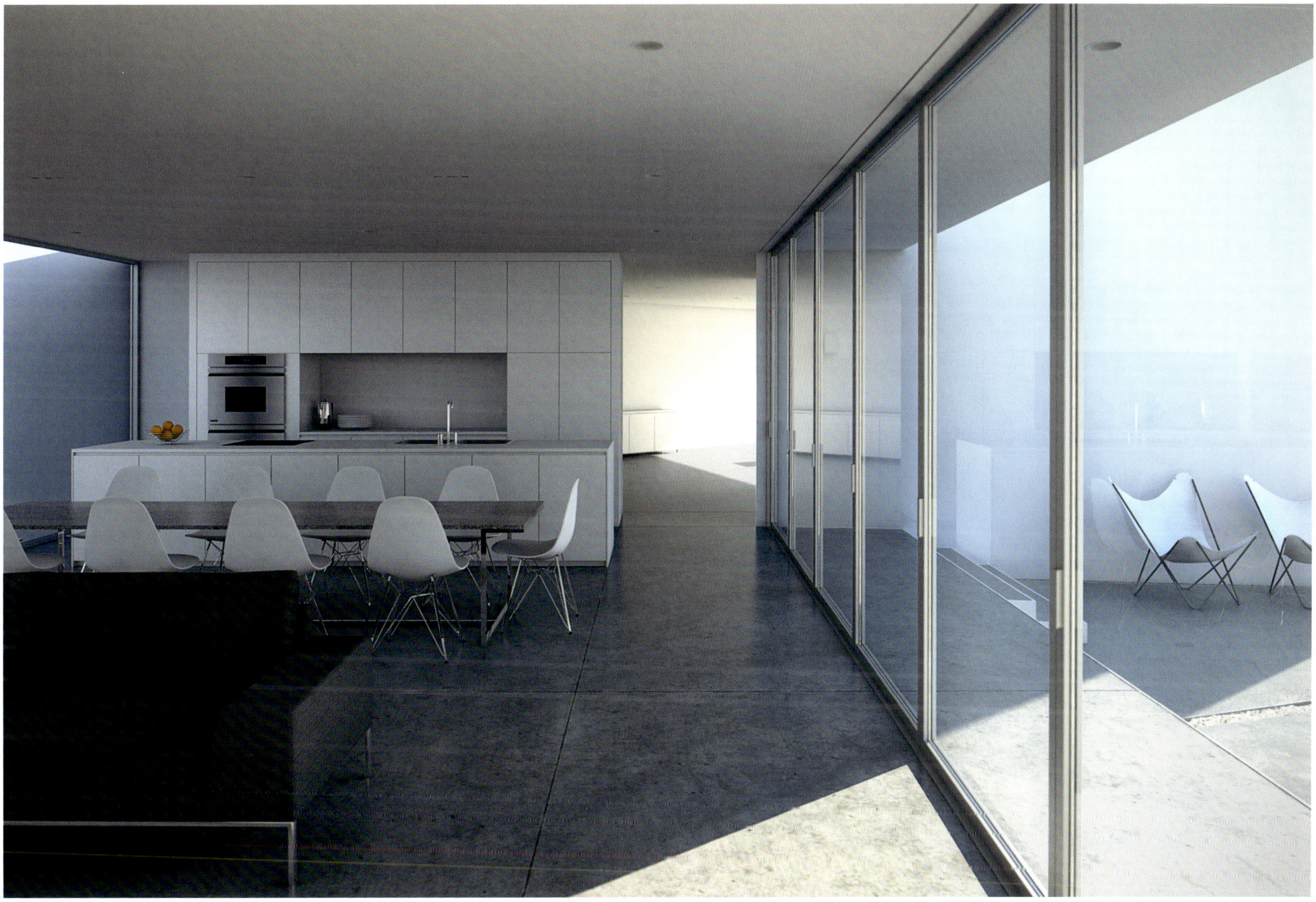

Studio Cáceres Lazo
GZ HOUSE
2016 | Chicureo, Chile

It is easily forgotten that architecture not only provides functional spaces but also is—often mainly—built for pleasure. This project, in Chicureo, Chile, on the outskirts of Santiago, acts as a valid reminder in many ways. First and foremost, it is based on the premise that rooms without a view are unacceptable no matter their purpose. GZ House is shaped accordingly as a long, single-floored progression set high on a mountaintop ascended by a steeply winding road. Like pearls on a necklace, the rooms unfold one after the other, the master bedroom on one side and the children's guest rooms on the other, as if to prepare for a future yet to come. Features that solely fulfill a simple function have been avoided or distorted; the corridor, for example, is not just a corridor but also hall space with sixteen-foot-high (five meters) ceilings and the children's playroom, separated by a small patio. Though it may seem like a minor intervention, it is not. Function often determines the outcome more than anything.

On the exterior, fiber-cement panels clad the entire steel structure, leaving an air vent between the house's skin and envelope for circulation and cooling. The contrast between the rigid utilitarian materials and the free-spirited yet ambitious structure is tangible and nourishing.

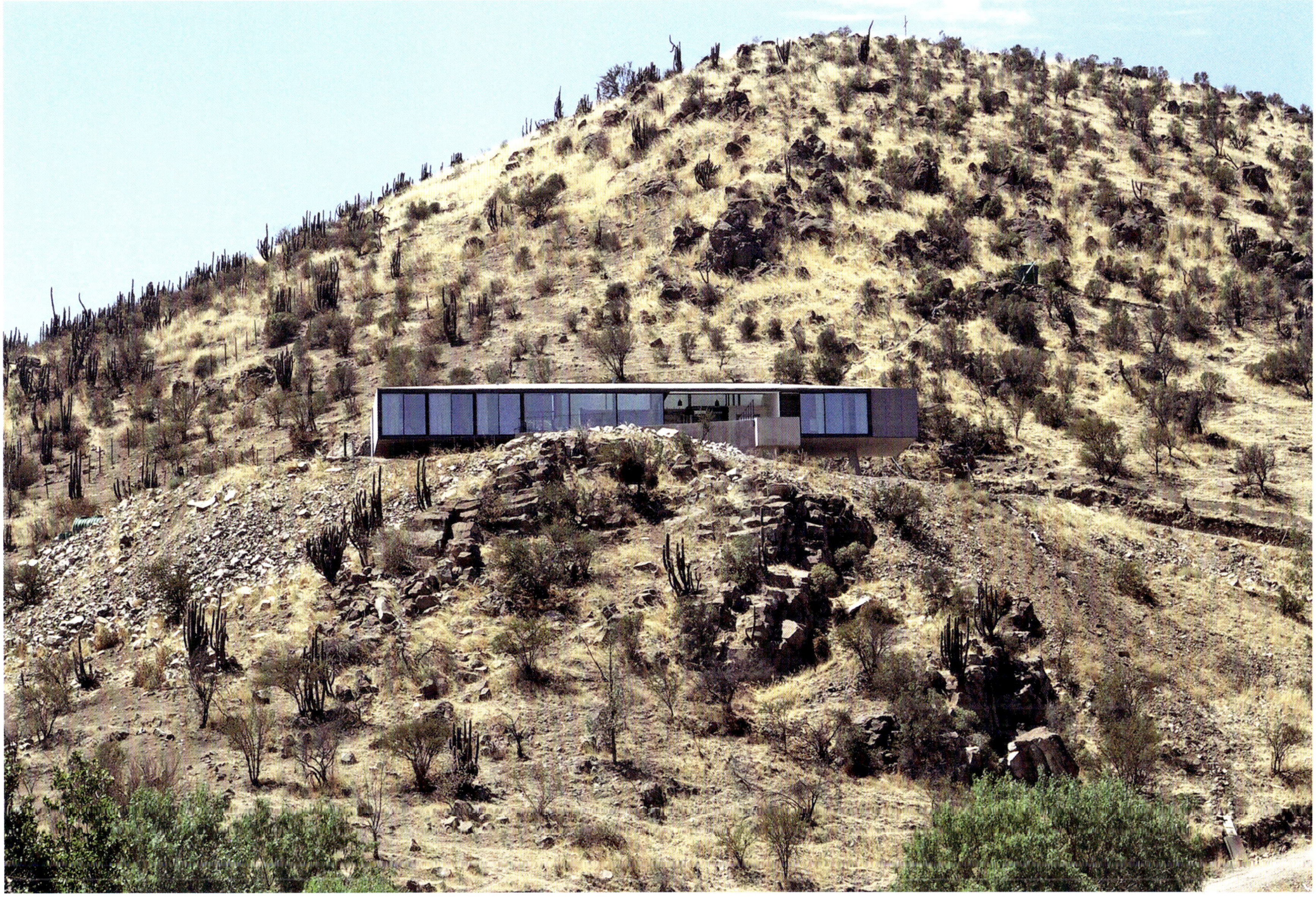

GZ HOUSE

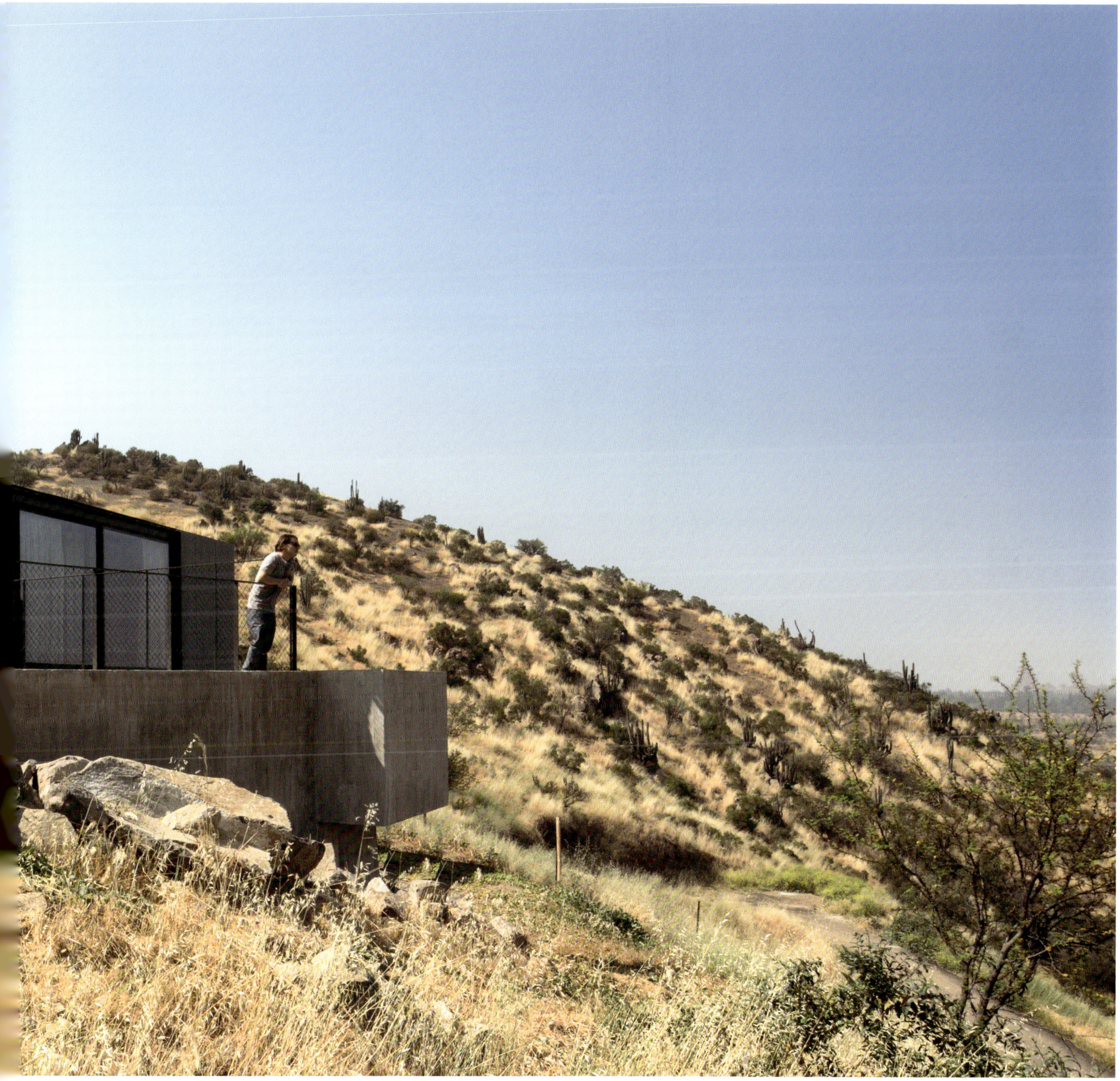

GZ HOUSE

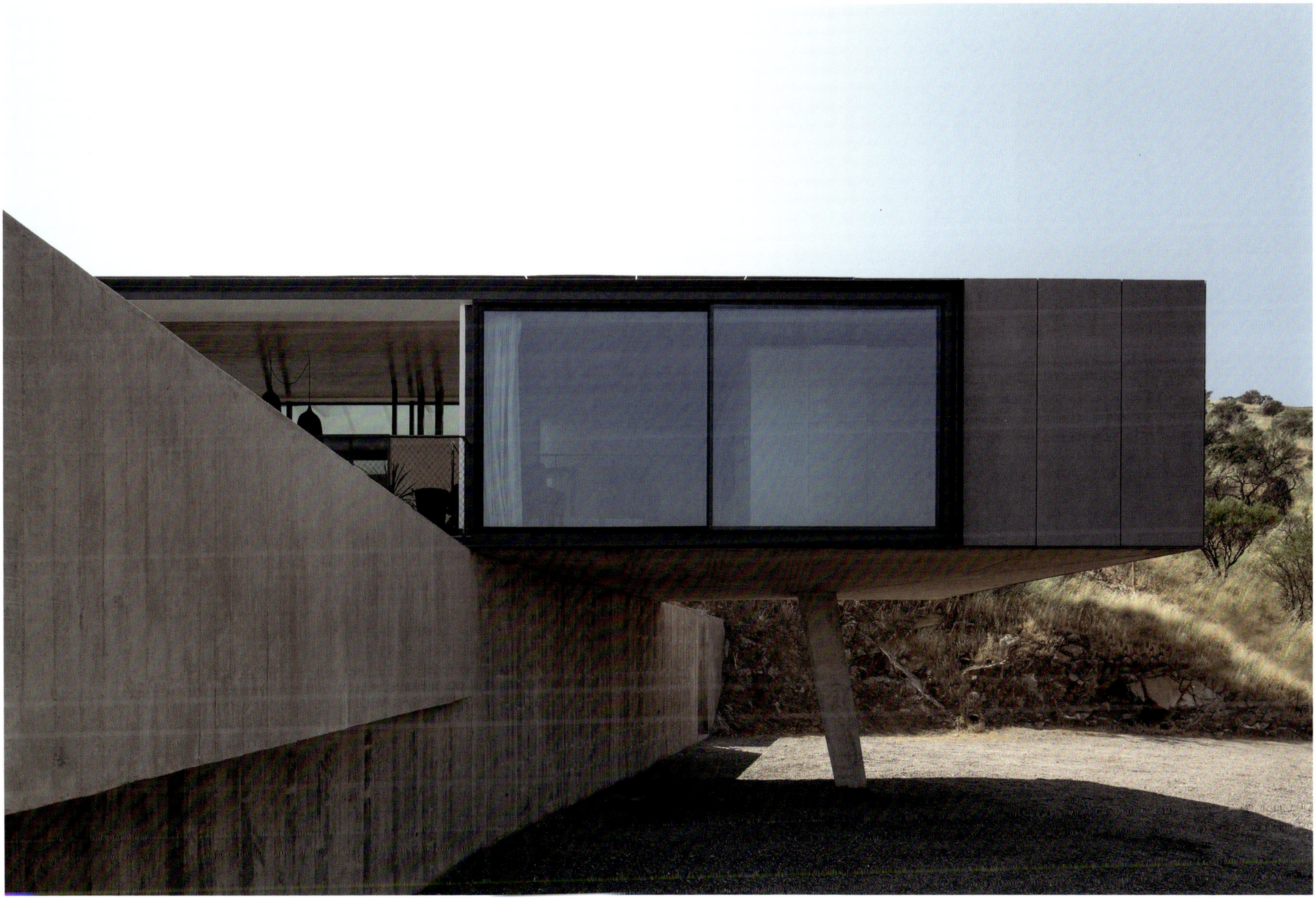

[2] BUILT WITHIN THE DESERT

88 Valerio Olgiati
VILLA ALÉM

92 Selldorf Architects
MESA AT AMANGIRI

98 Imbue Design
HIGH DESERT DWELLING

102 AutonomeForme
DESERTI TASCABILI DJ COMPLEX #2

106 BAM Architects Office
THROUGH GARDENS HOUSE

112 A-I-R, Inc. Darren Petrucci Architect
GHOST WASH HOUSE

116 Carlos Arroyo Arquitectos
CASA ENCUENTRO

122 Marmol Radziner
SCOTTSDALE

128 Olson Kundig
STUDHORSE

136 Studio Ko
VILLA D

140 Gracia Studio
ENCUENTRO GUADALUPE

146 Johnston Marklee
MOUND HOUSE

150 Scott Pask
CASA PASK

158 I-10 Studio
AMANGIRI RESORT

To build in any environment, but especially that of the desert, one must first ask: What is a desert? Words typically used to describe such arid landscapes are *uninhabited, unoccupied, unpeopled, abandoned, evacuated, vacant, vacated, untenanted, tenantless, unfrequented, neglected, secluded, isolated, desolate, lonely, solitary,* and even *godforsaken.* All of these words emphasize the negative space and reference the lack of something, contributing to a sense of nothingness. Yet there is a difference between something that is nothing and something that is lacking. A desert may be simply defined by its lack, by that which it has not, but one could also say that the desert teems with life, if one knows where, or how, to look. There are some life-giving forces that exist in the desert in absolute abundance—light and heat, for example. As architecture has a claim to permanence, it is a virtue of a foresighted construction to include solutions that compensate for prevalent lack, exploit the benefits of available materials, and generate new resources from existing ones, thereby setting up a circular cycle able to sustain itself without—or with only minimal—outside intervention.

The subsequent examples illustrate that there is no one way to suit all desert needs. Every desert topography, every site, and every project has different features and challenges, and must be considered on a unique basis. There is, however, a uniting thread: the projects in this chapter are built together with nature and attempt to kindly give back to it, if only by not depleting it further.

Valerio Olgiati
VILLA ALÉM
2013 | Alentejo, Portugal

Set in the rural cork-forest region of southern Portugal, this dwelling in Alentejo literally unfolds its charm. The main structure of Villa Além is fully contained within a rectangular high-walled concrete courtyard, the top portions of which dramatically fold in or out to alternately provide shade or draw in the strong sunshine. Despite its monumental qualities, from afar the structure seems rather hidden, secluded by the native vegetation rather than powerfully penetrating it.

The dwelling, not visible from the exterior, features walls, floors, and ceilings of reddish-hued concrete constructed from local earth and cast in situ. The structure is broken into multiple programs. The living space opens onto the central courtyard, modeled after the expanse of the Court of the Myrtles at the Alhambra in Granada, thus allowing the garden to expand within the interior. Gateways cut into the courtyard walls provide starkly contrasting vistas of the surrounding landscape. A cave-like curved hallway leads from the public spaces to the bedrooms, enhancing the sense of a private retreat. And, maybe, therein lies the art and appeal of this very special project interspersed in an arid yet rich landscape—its bare radical program unites in harmonious symbiosis with the land.

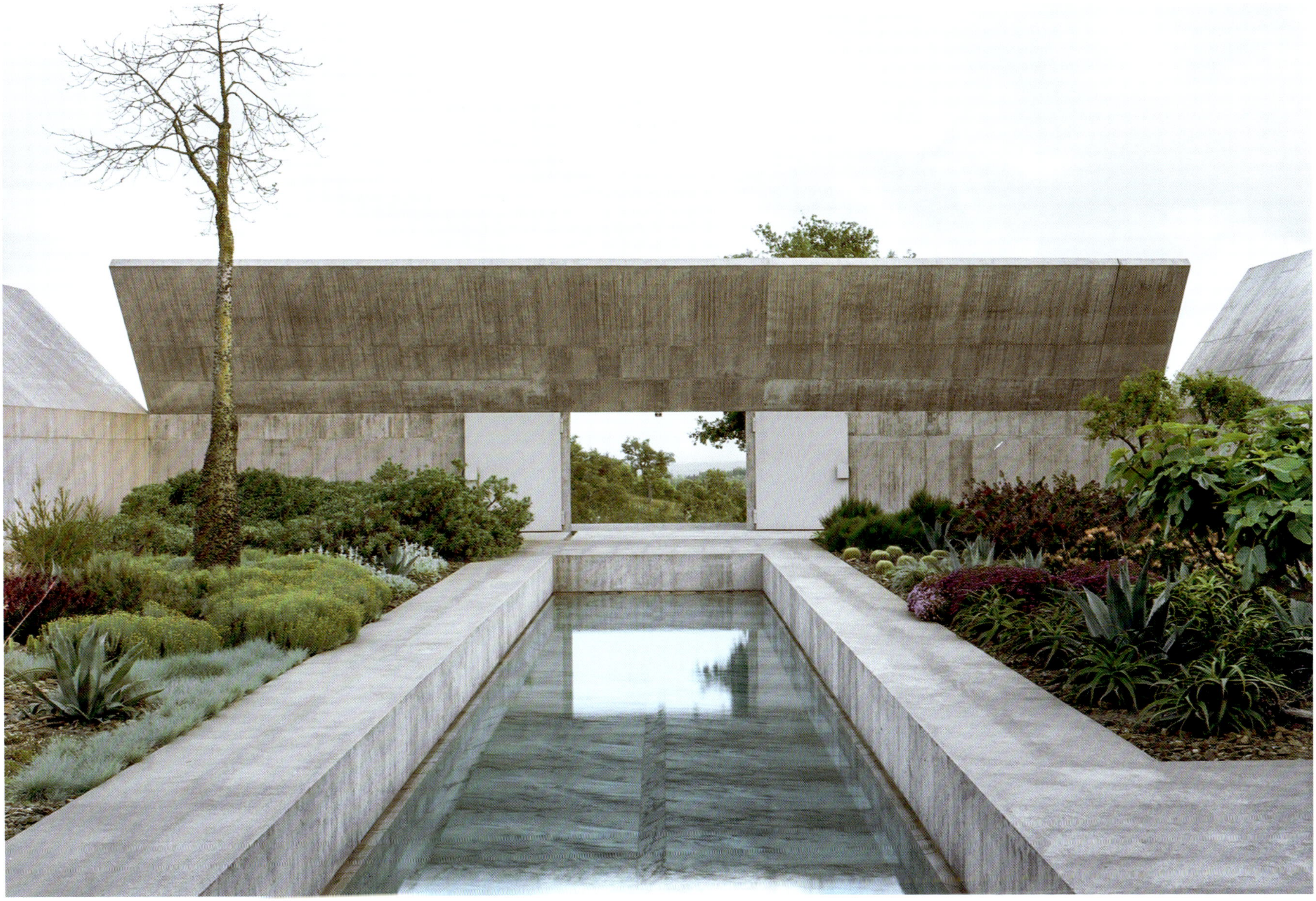

VILLA ALÉM

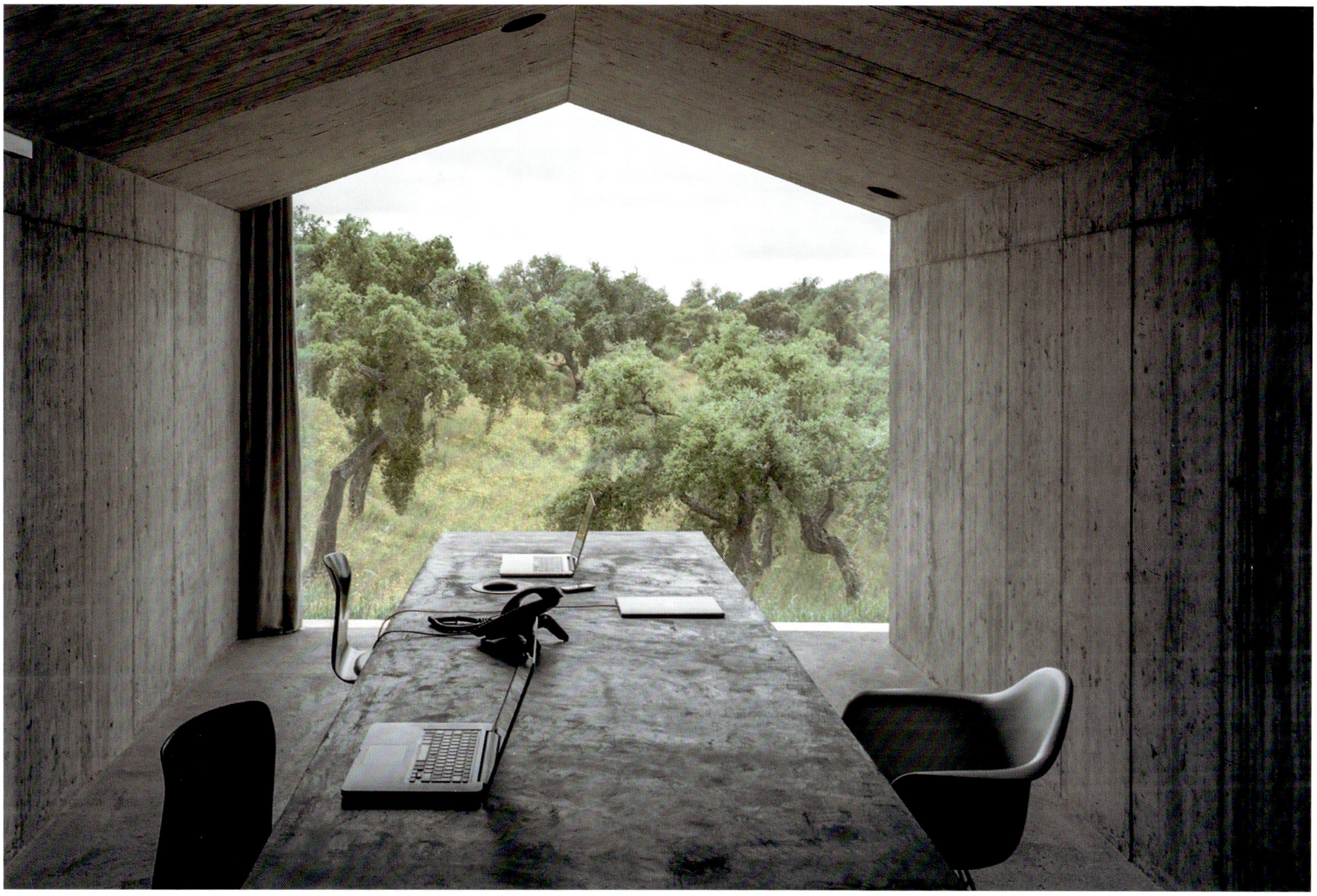

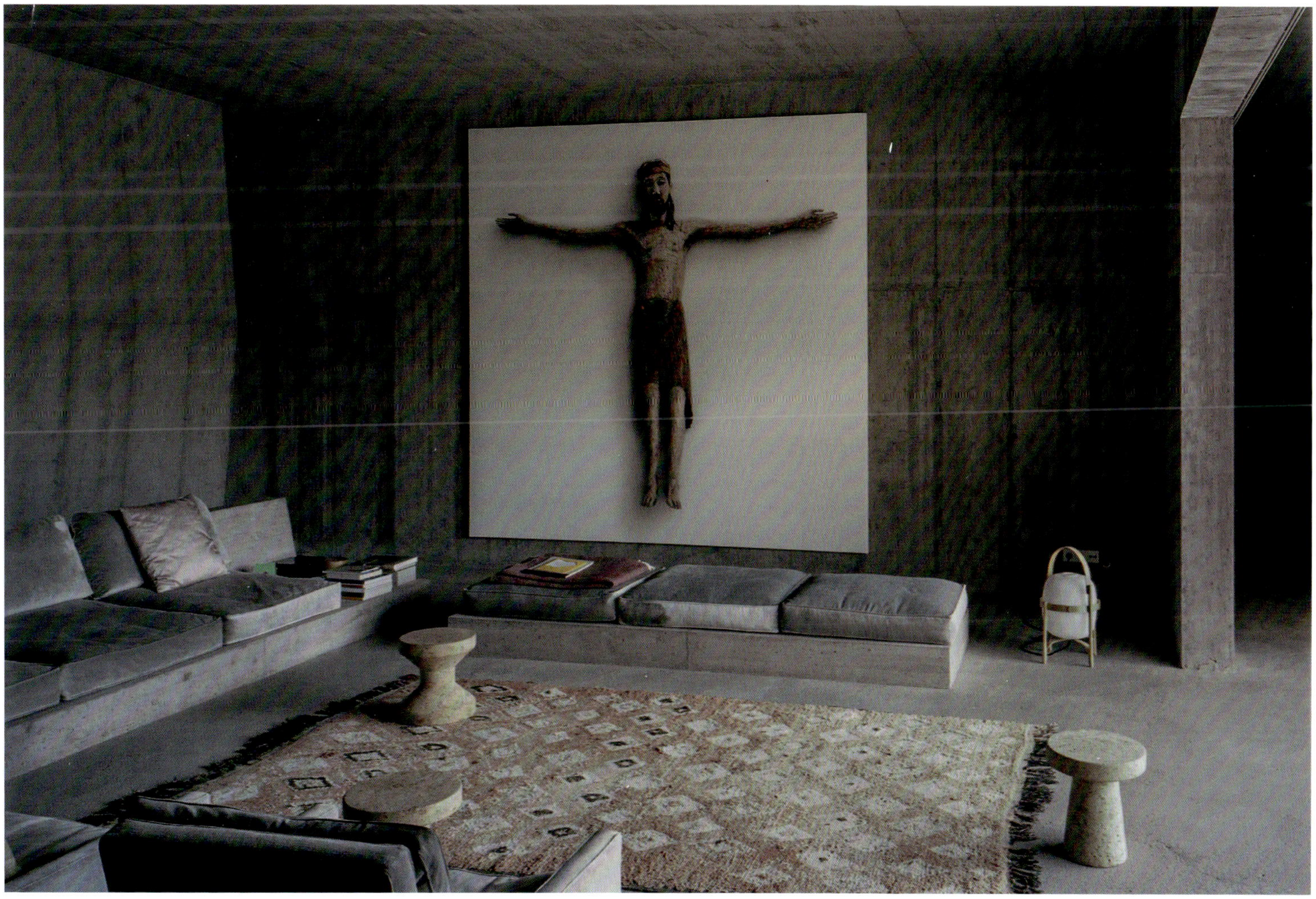

Selldorf Architects
MESA AT AMANGIRI
2011 | Canyon Point, UT, USA

As one of thirty-six planned villas set against the spectacular backdrop of Utah's Canyon Point, the Mesa at Amangiri provides the best of multiple worlds, fusing the comfort and pleasingly appointed interiors of a contemporary luxury hotel with the stark, rugged beauty of the high desert. Residents need only to step outside onto their terrace to fully experience the raw-edged canyon beyond.

Private garden terraces off the bedrooms provide more intimate views. Interestingly, areas of retreat such as the shaded courtyard were designed as a respite from the overwhelming natural vistas. According to the architects, breaks from awe-inspiring landscapes are necessary. In a conscious effort to minimize impact on the land, the buildings and paved roads were sited to reduce effects on the fragile desert flora. Energy usage is moderated through the orientation of buildings to respond to the path of the sun, geothermal heating and cooling, solar water heating, and the implementation of brise-soleils for shade.

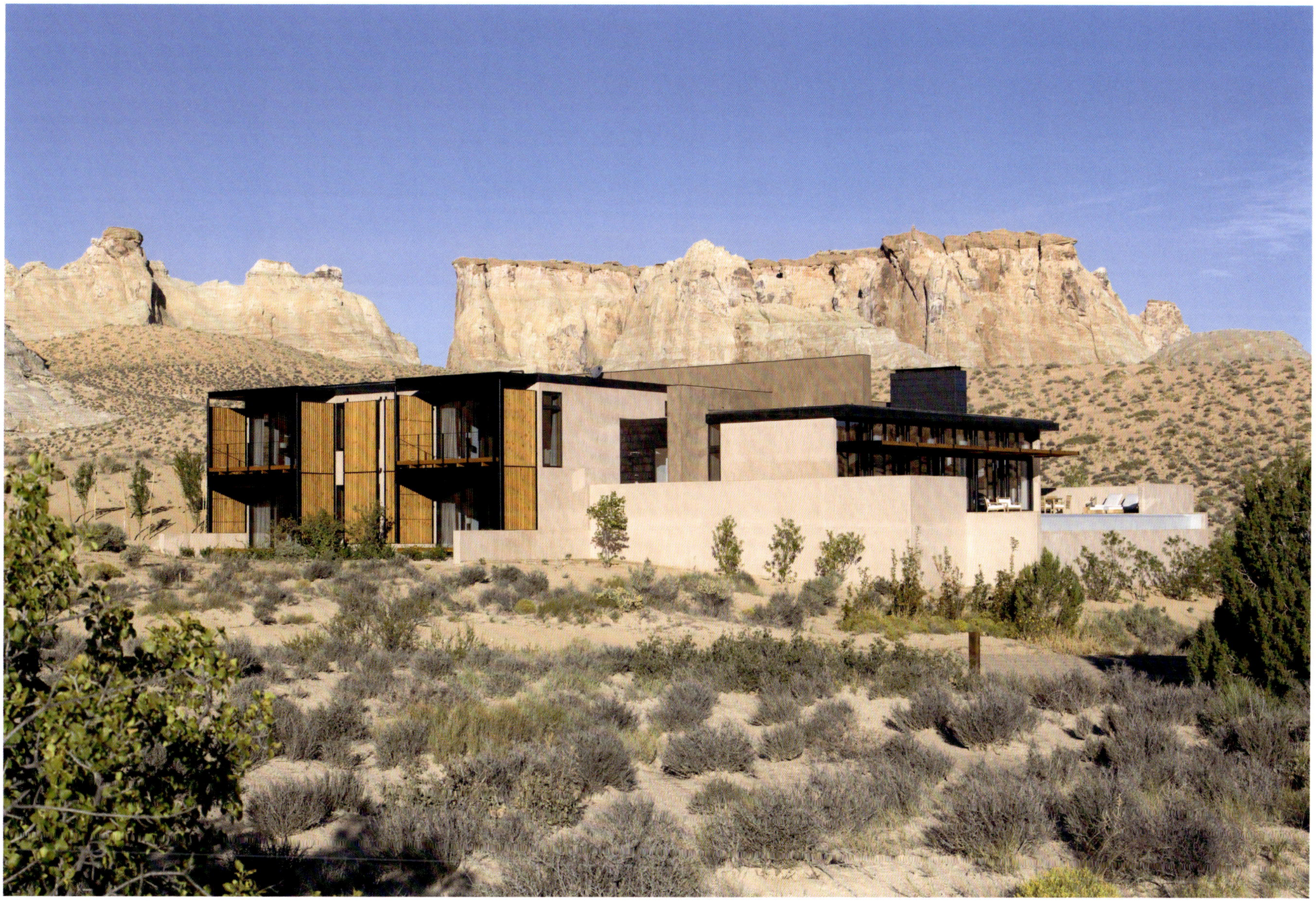

MESA AT AMANGIRI

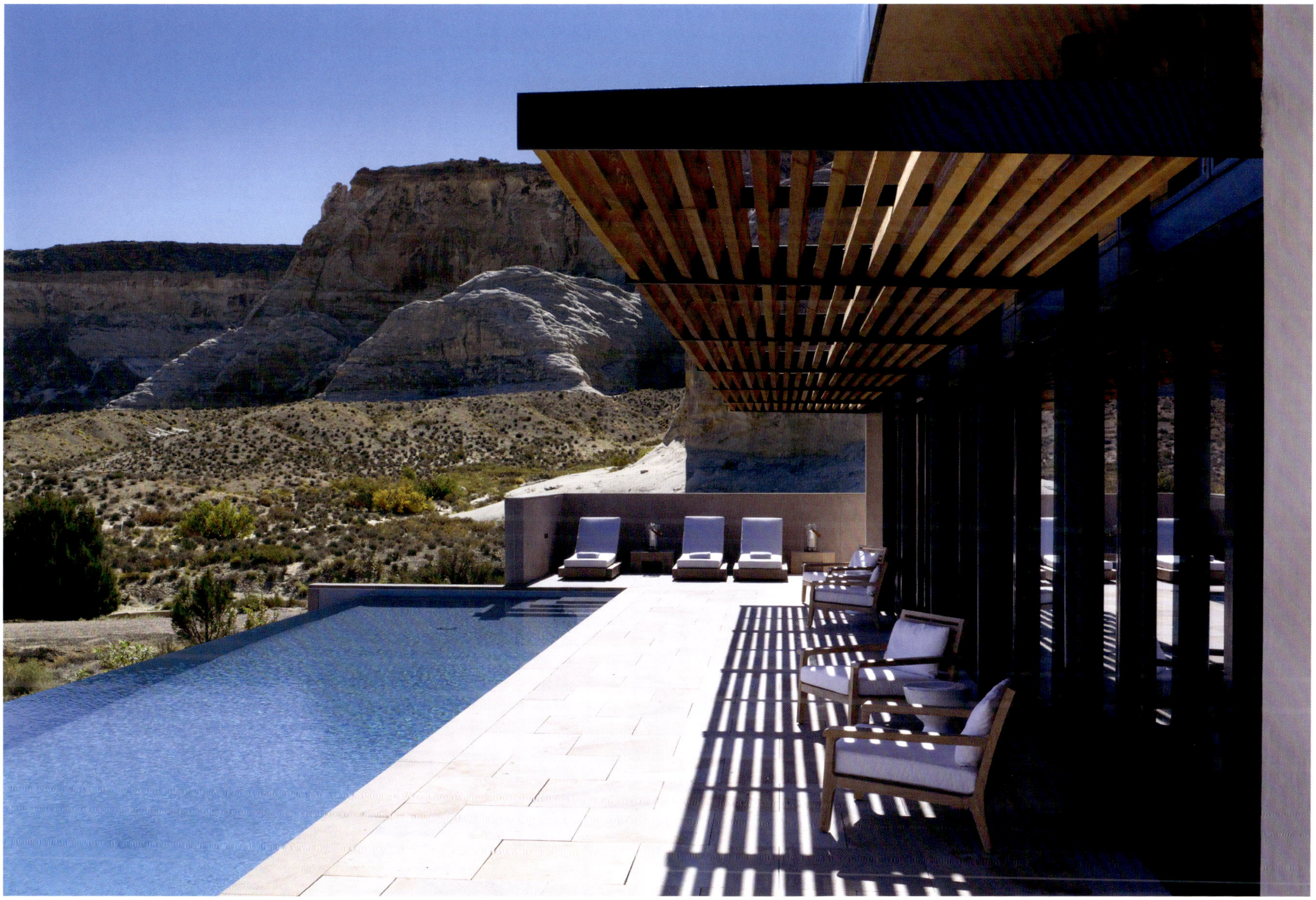

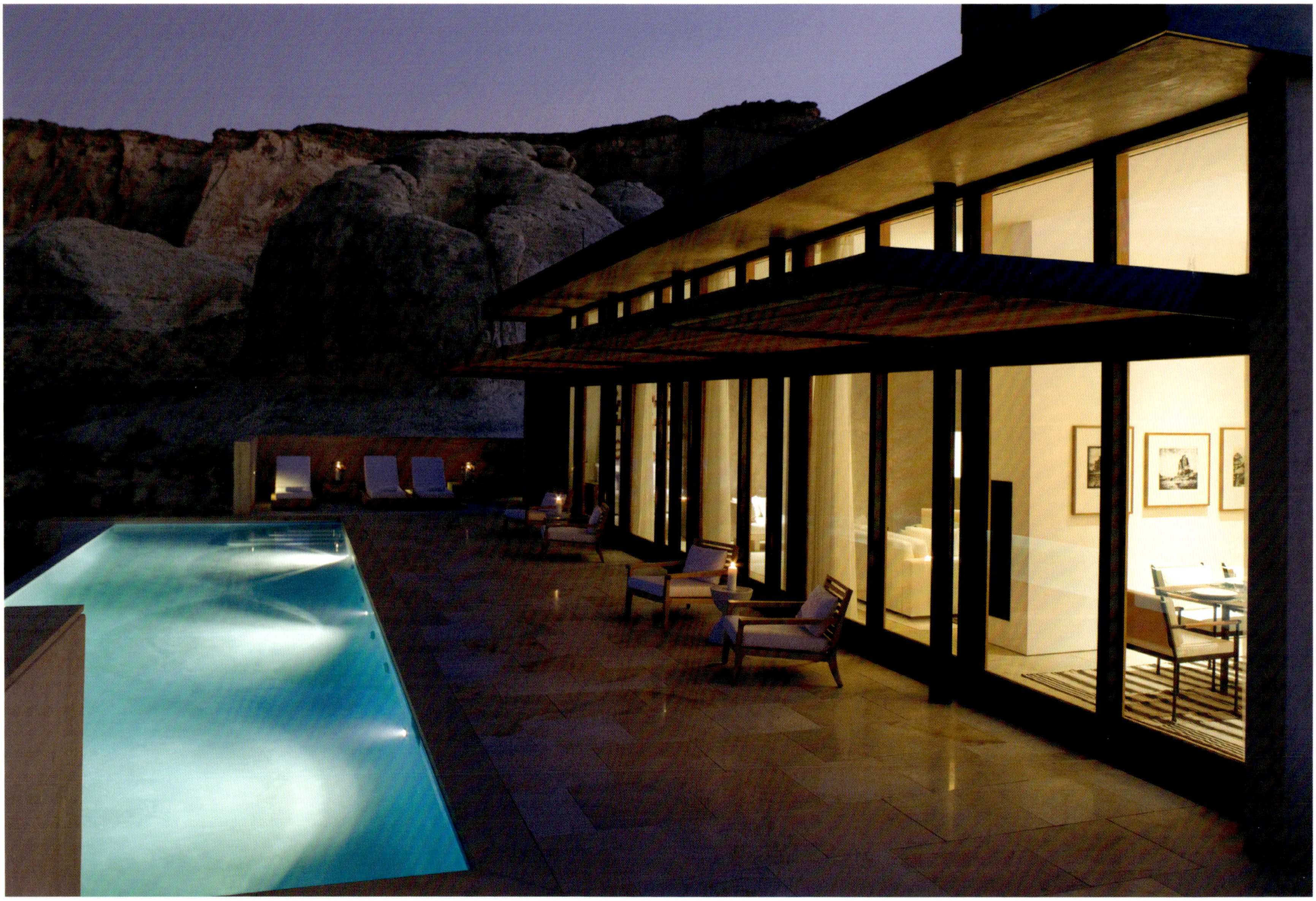

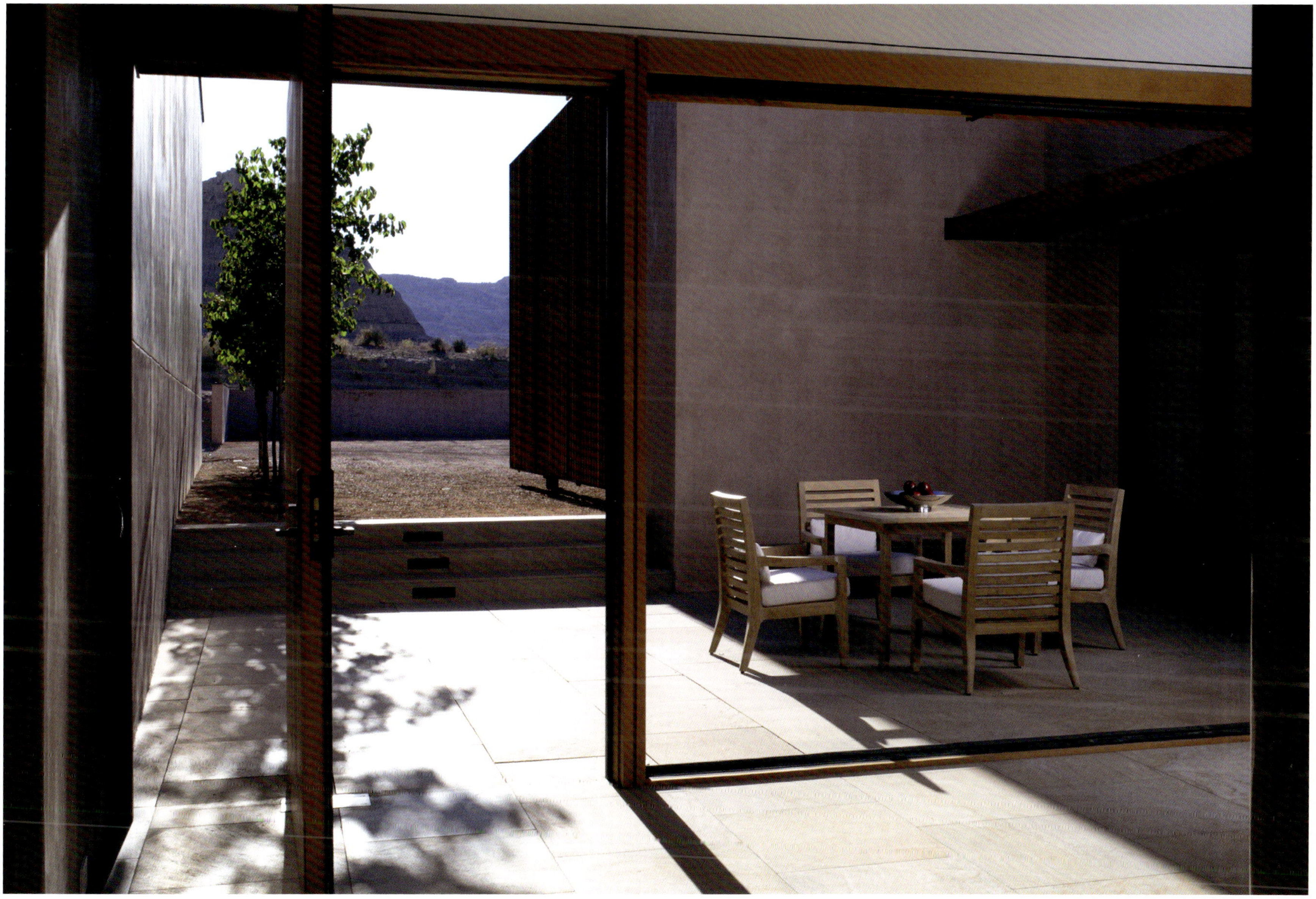

Imbue Design
HIGH DESERT DWELLING
2015 | Capitol Reef National Park, UT, USA

Utah's Capitol Reef National Park is a very impressive landscape of golden canyons, red monoliths, and striking rock formations. Within this rocky setting in Torrey, the three volumes of High Desert Dwelling—main residence, guesthouse, and garage—point their slanted corrugated-steel roofs toward the sky as if they were part of the landscape too. The steel, which also clads part of the facade and is rusted to a deep red through exposure to the elements over time, perfectly displays the fact that nature simply does imperfect best. Two L-shaped modules intersect to form the main living area, with gabled ceilings and fully glazed walls framed by fragrant cedarwood, exposing exceptional vistas. Long sections of the house have horizontal windows to capture everything beyond. No surrounding view is intended to go unnoticed, too big would be the loss. The interior is designed with intimate nooks and gathering spaces, a welcoming feeling that is enhanced by the sight through the windows of nearby juniper trees waving in the breeze. It was a heartfelt desire of the clients to leave as much vegetation untouched as possible, and floor plans were adjusted to grant their wish. Looking at High Desert Dwelling from afar or slightly above supports the notion that this is a house that doesn't want to simply be in nature but wants to become a part of nature itself.

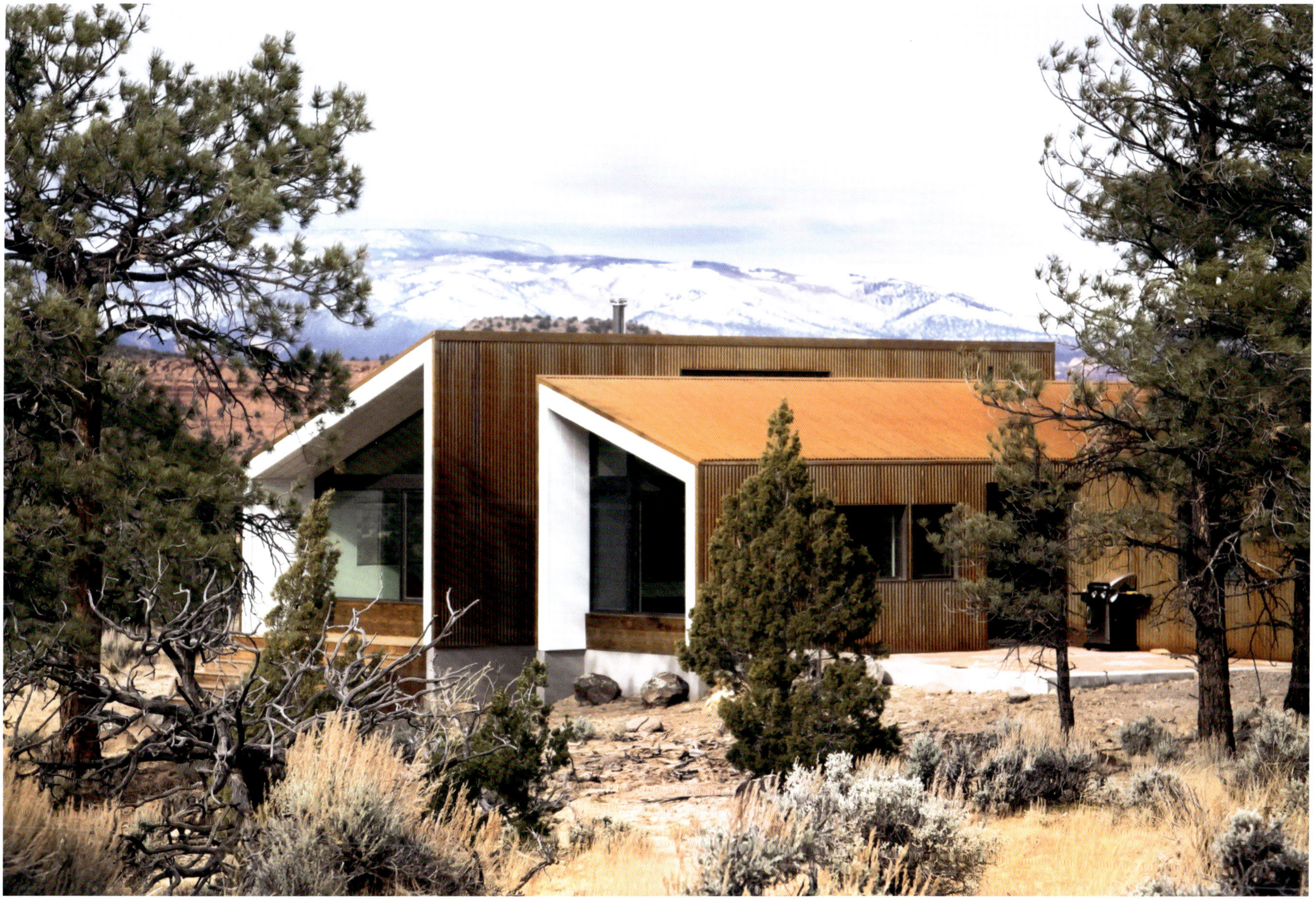

HIGH DESERT DWELLING

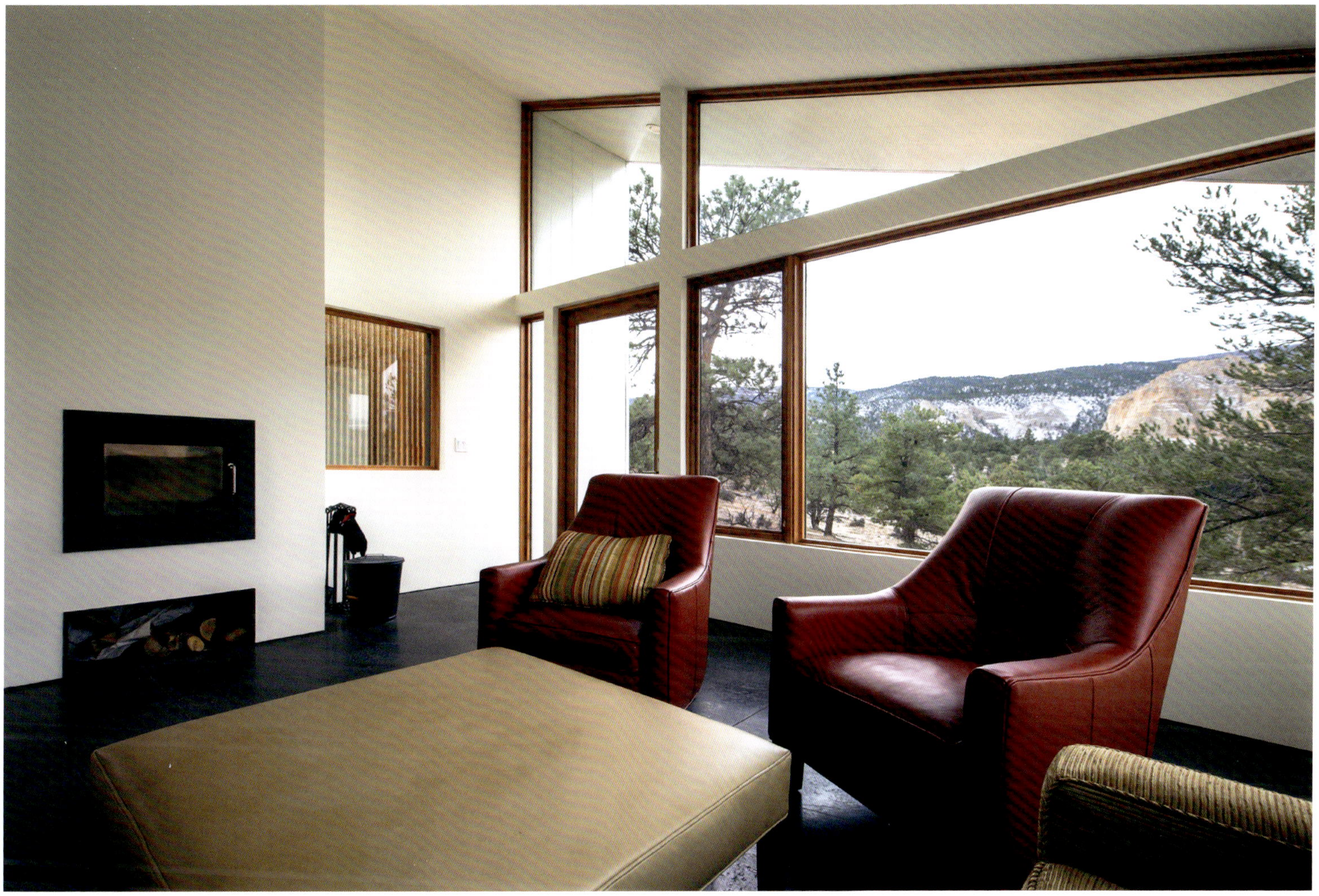
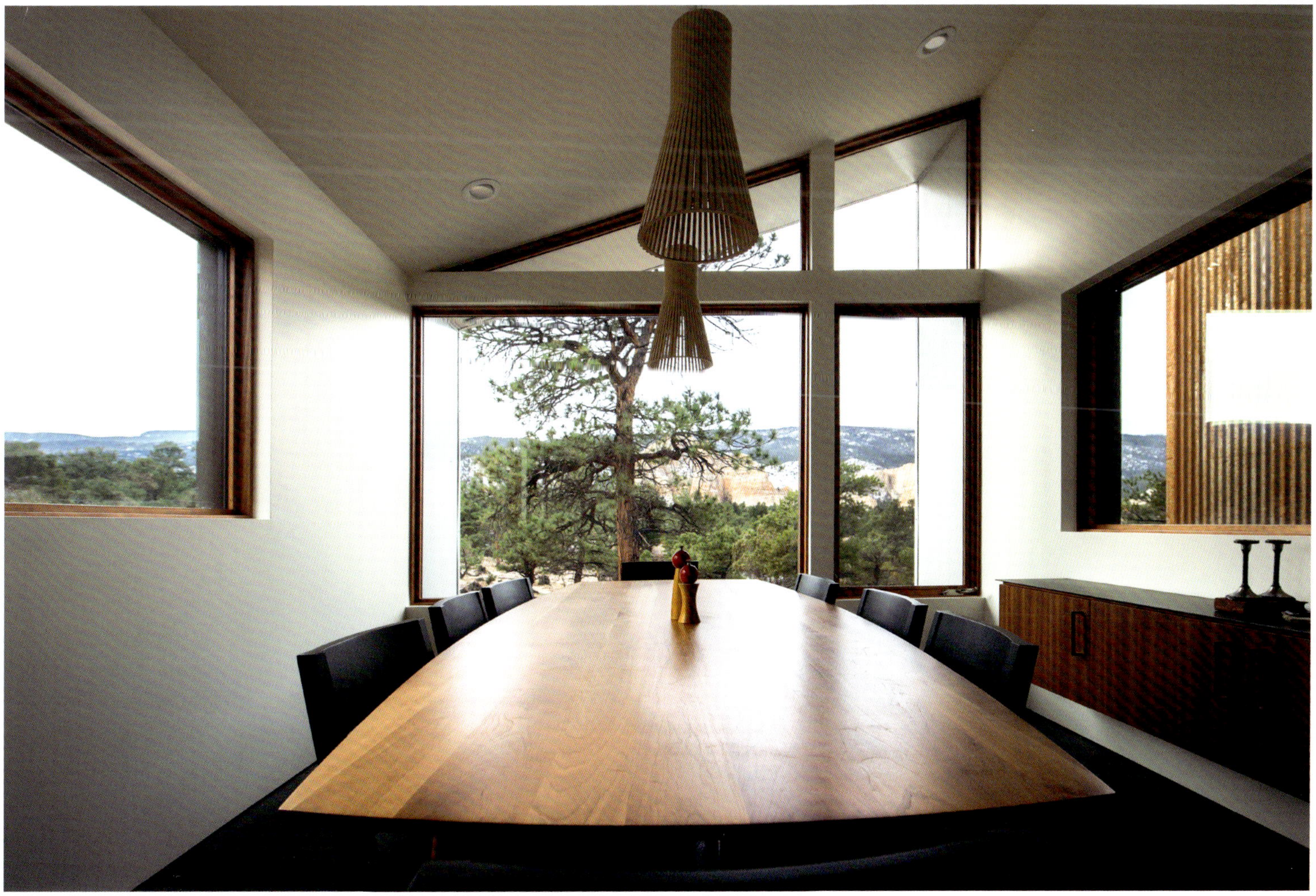

AutonomeForme Architettura
DESERTI TASCABILI DJ COMPLEX #2
2017 | Djerba, Tunisia

It is one of the island of Djerba's majestic features to be overlooking the sea as well as the desert—a view that Deserti Tascabili DJ Complex #2 benefits from too. As one of two buildings on the site made from traditionally Tunisian whitewashed stone, it houses a center for art and poetry in the Mediterranean. The second building provides inspirational private amenities for artist residencies.

Following the historic building practices of the island's Islamic and Jewish residents, Marco Scarpinato and AutonomeForme Architettura have collaborated to create a modern layout while utilizing local techniques of construction and traditional solutions for the natural cooling of rooms, such as extraordinarily thick walls. Doing so not only reduced the environmental impact but also enabled the house to offer a calm respite from the technologically accelerated pace of modern life outside its protective walls—an aspirational atmosphere adopted from Peter Sloterdijk's influential 2009 book *You Must Change Your Life*.

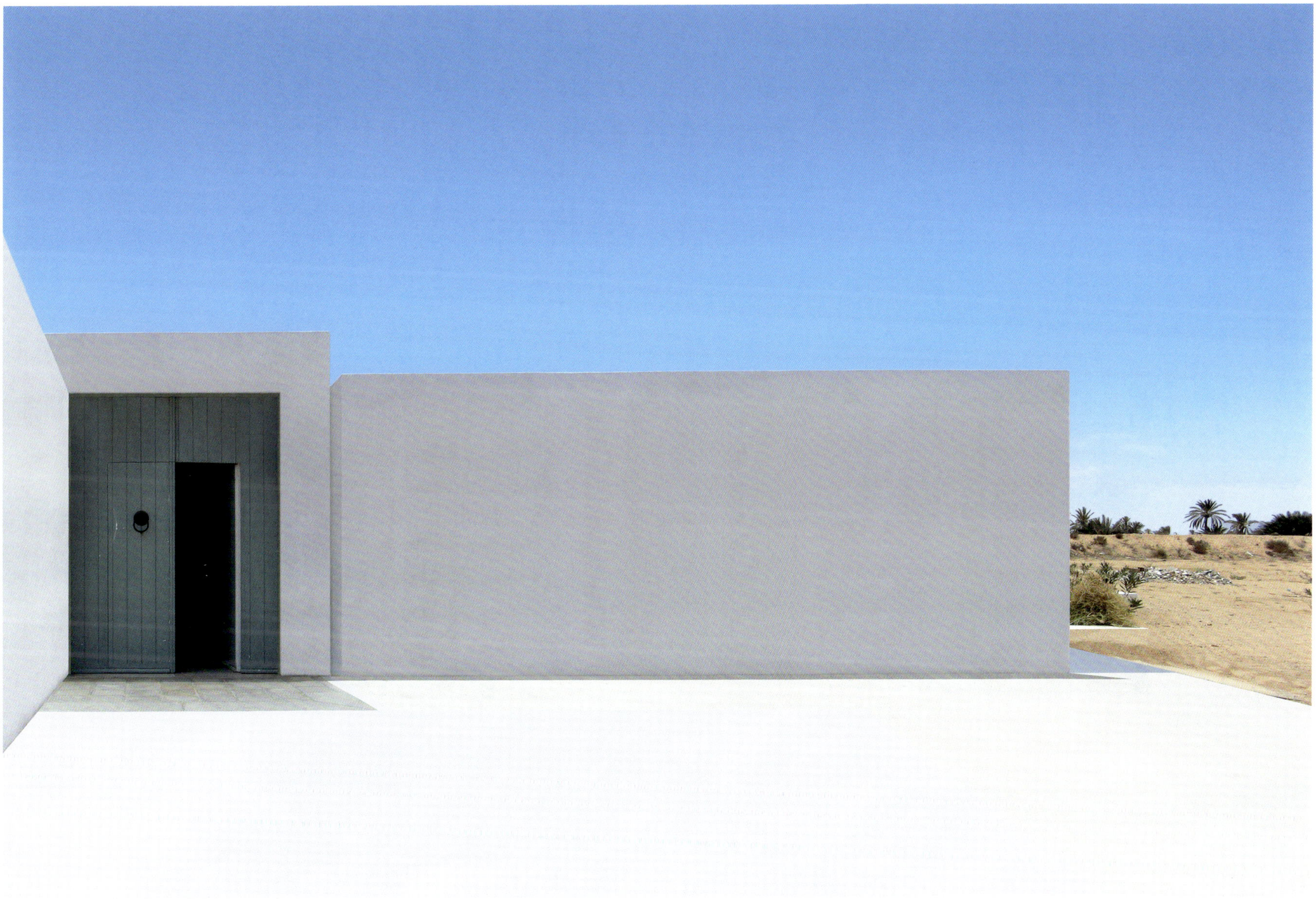

DESERTI TASCABILI DJ COMPLEX #2

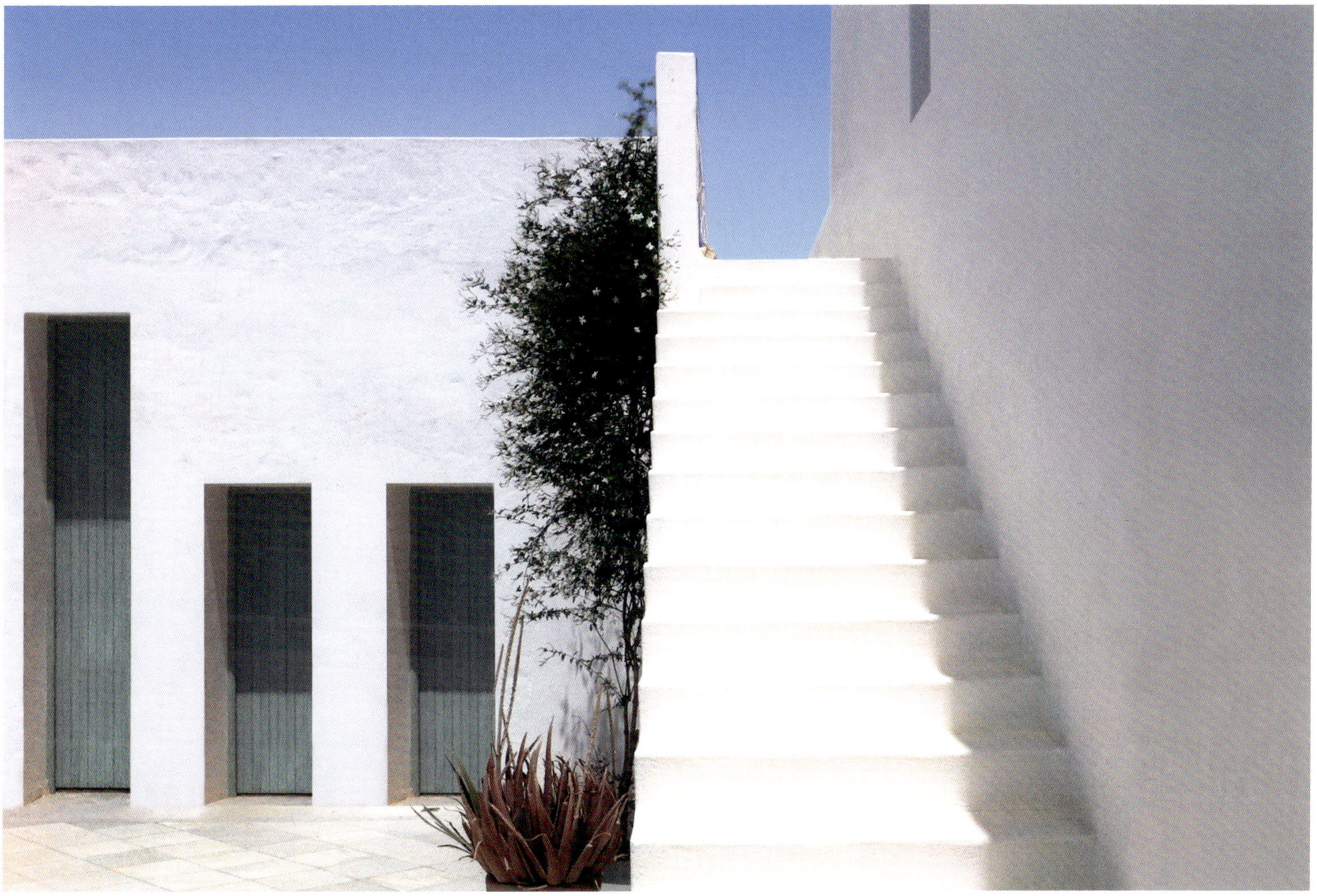

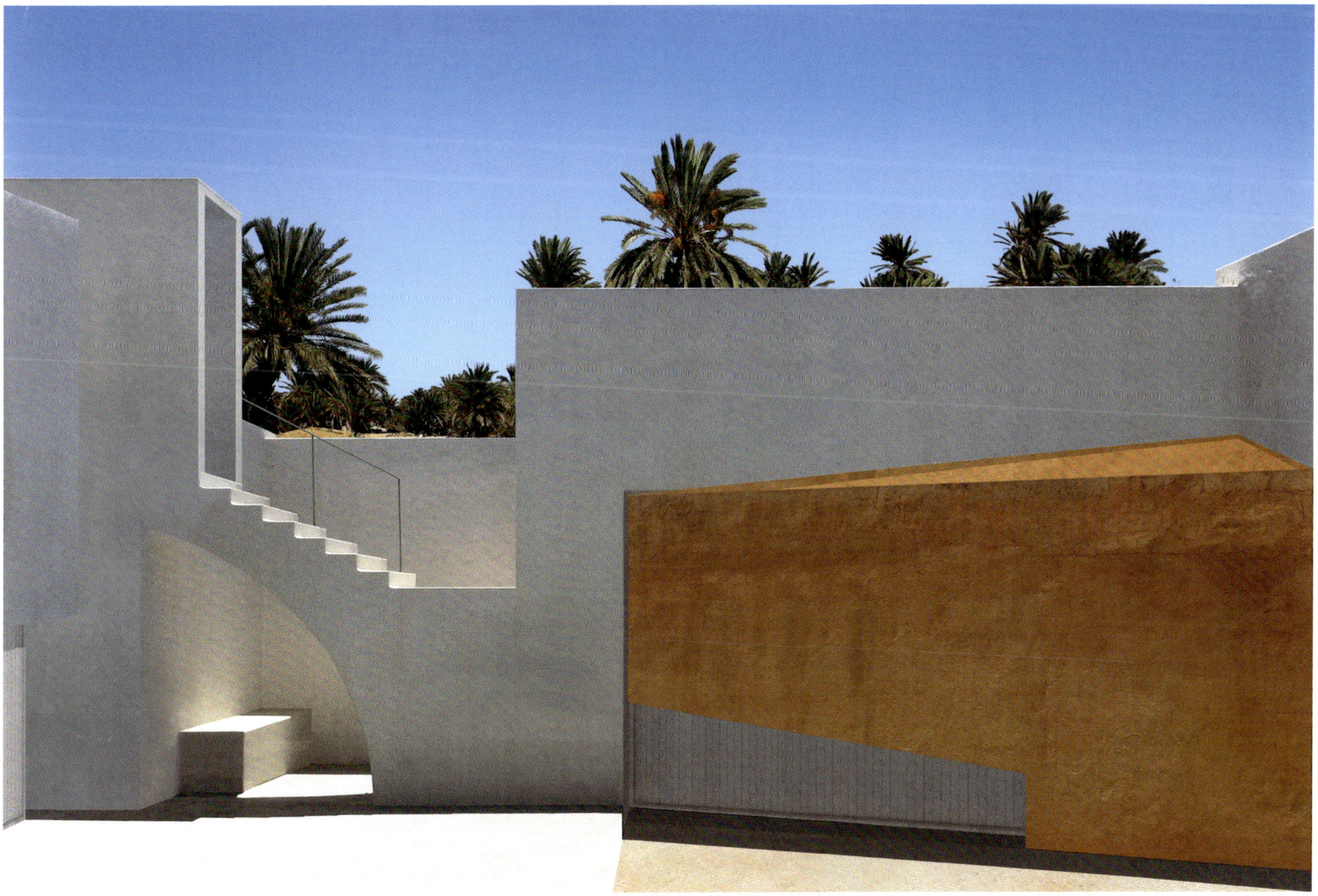

BAM Architects Office
THROUGH GARDENS HOUSE
2017 | Parvaneh Village, Borkhar County,
Isfahan Province, Iran

Through Gardens House is a home in the village of Parvaneh built for a resident who wanted to spend his retirement years in a tranquil setting far from the bustling city life of Isfahan. Though it may well be the most modern house in the rural village, it doesn't stand out from neighboring dwellings or the surrounding nature on purpose; the color of the sanded walls follows Iran's traditional desert palette. To keep costs low and to create something novel without losing touch with the local heritage, the house has been sprayed with an innovative plaster made of sand, dung, and straw. Its exterior shapes are dominated by neoclassical straightness and radical simplicity, providing a poetically bare frame to be filled with life. This characteristic carries over to the interior, which features the same bold bareness, with rectangular rooms arranged in a U-shape around a small central courtyard. The house is designed for silence. The only architectural adornments to break the all-white stucco on the inside are black built-in details or occasional brick. The remote desert of Iran is a place to cherish the simplicity of life—and nature itself.

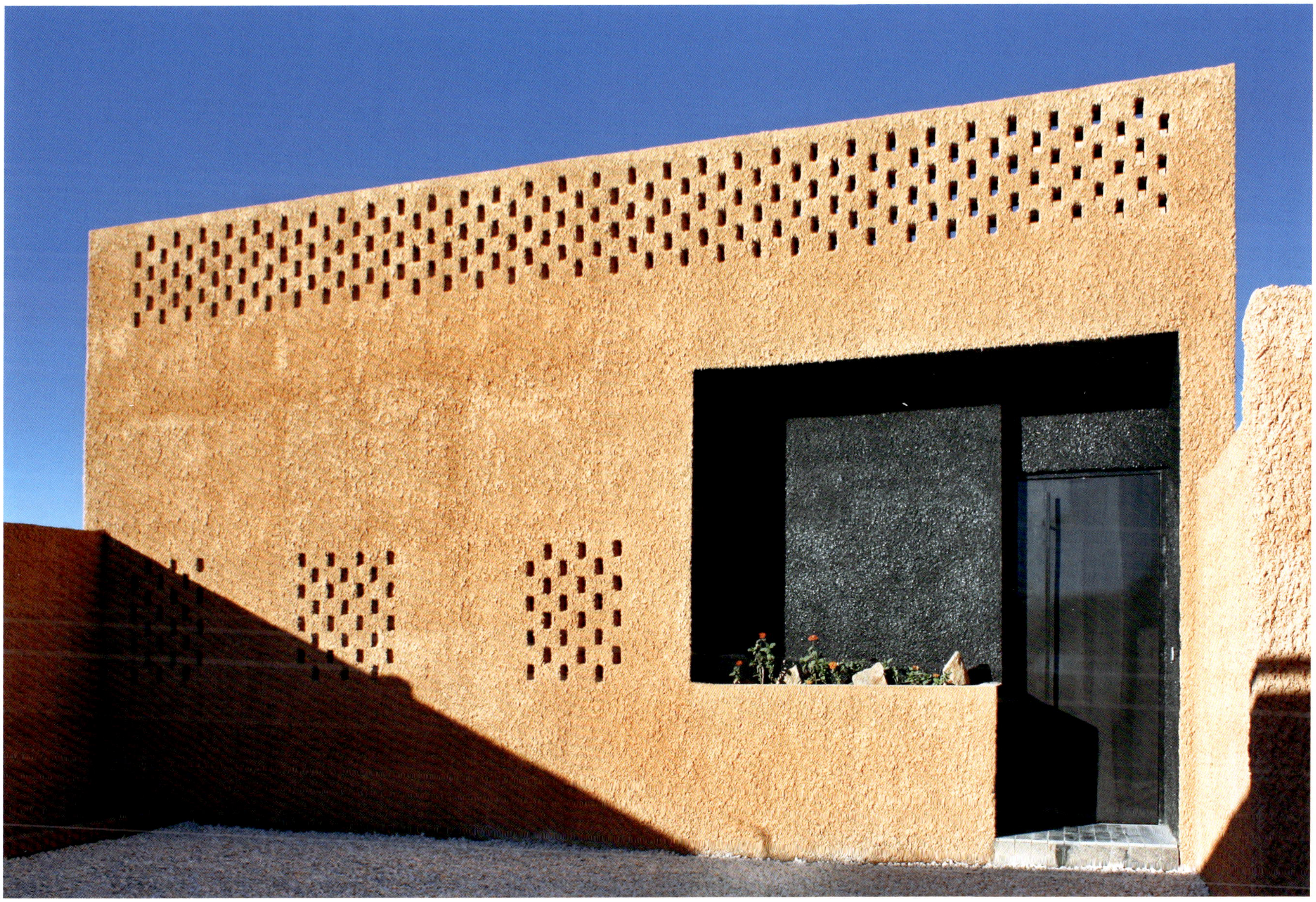

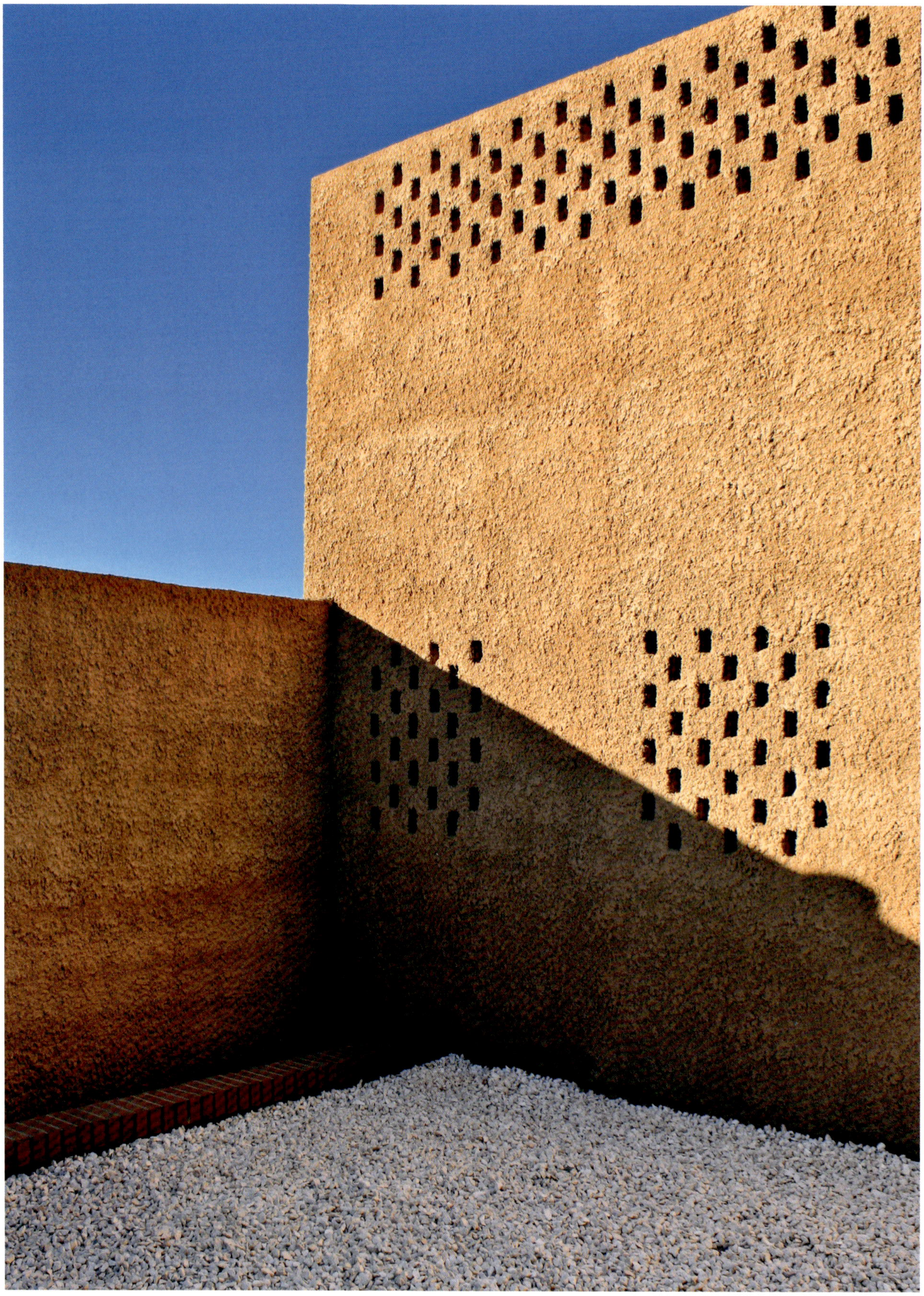

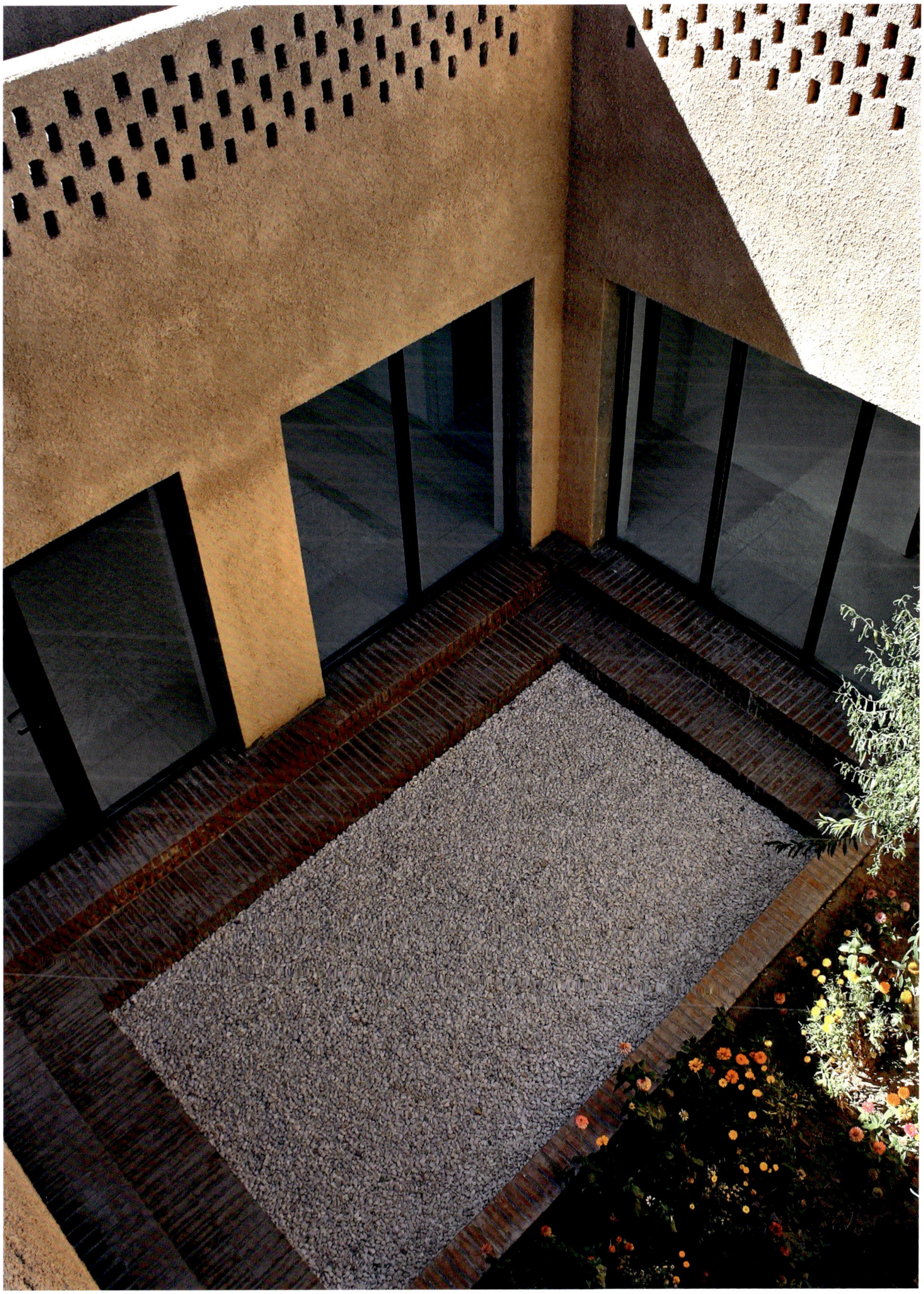

THROUGH GARDENS HOUSE

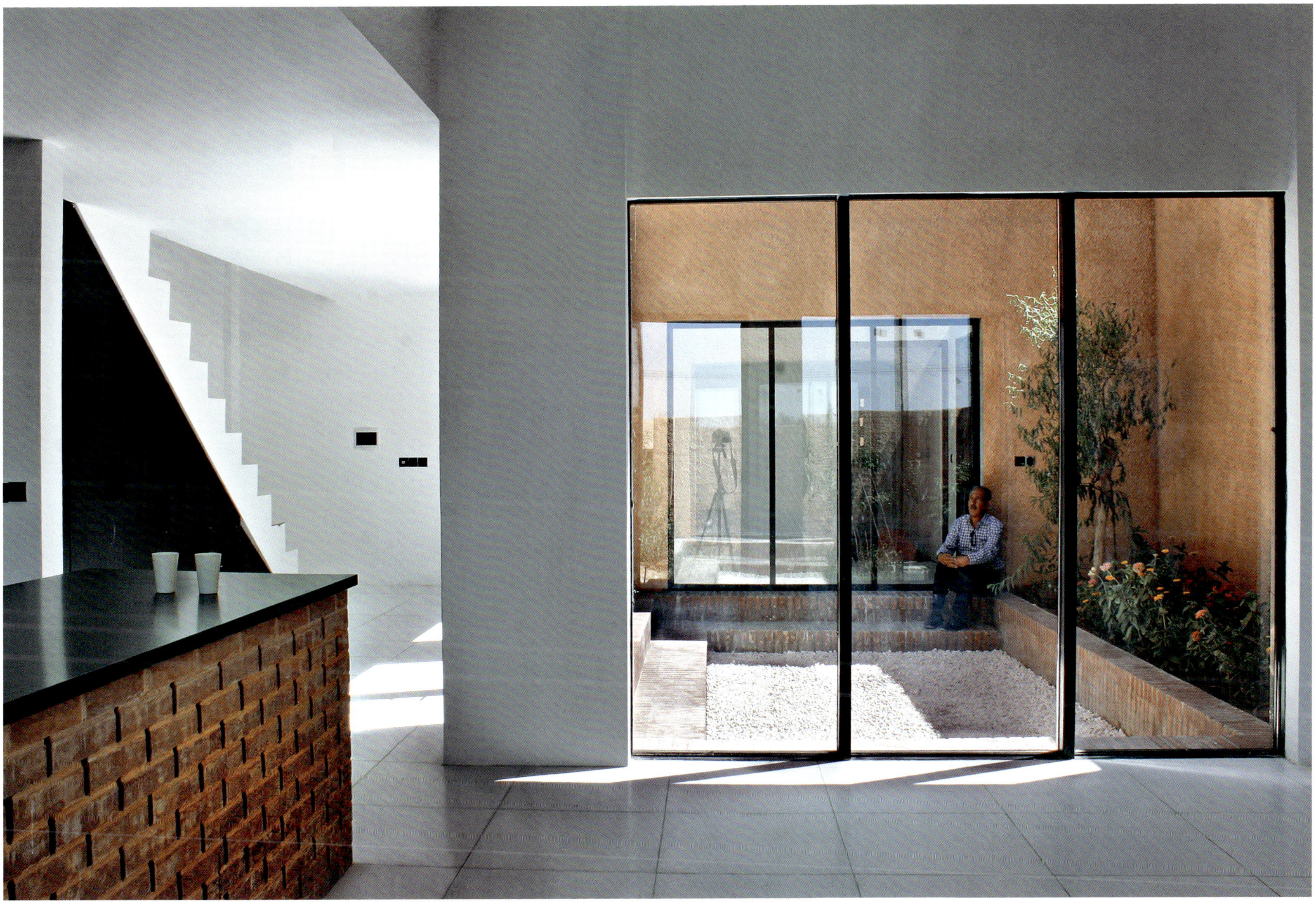

A-I-R, Inc. Darren Petrucci Architect
GHOST WASH HOUSE
2016 | Paradise Valley, AZ, USA

Located on a low hillside to the north of Camelback Mountain in Paradise Valley, Ghost Wash House uncannily imitates the surrounding Sonoran Desert in Arizona. Two brick-patterned volumes are flanked by natural washes—shallow dry riverbeds prone to flash flooding—with the space in between creating something akin to a third wash.

The east volume, housing the kitchen, informal dining room, office, and garage, is designed for protection from the low desert sun rising over the mountain in the morning. In the opposite structure, bedrooms and recreation spaces are shielded from bright beams of light later in the day. A third volume linking the two contains a living room and a more formal dining room, opening out onto a series of terraced courtyards, recreation spaces, and vegetation that lead to a pool house. A massive cantilevered roof that appears to float provides abundant shade outdoors, much like a nurse tree shields young cacti from extreme heat and sun. The roof also contains a rainwater collection system and photovoltaic panels, underscoring the house's connection to the desert-wash ecosystem it inhabits.

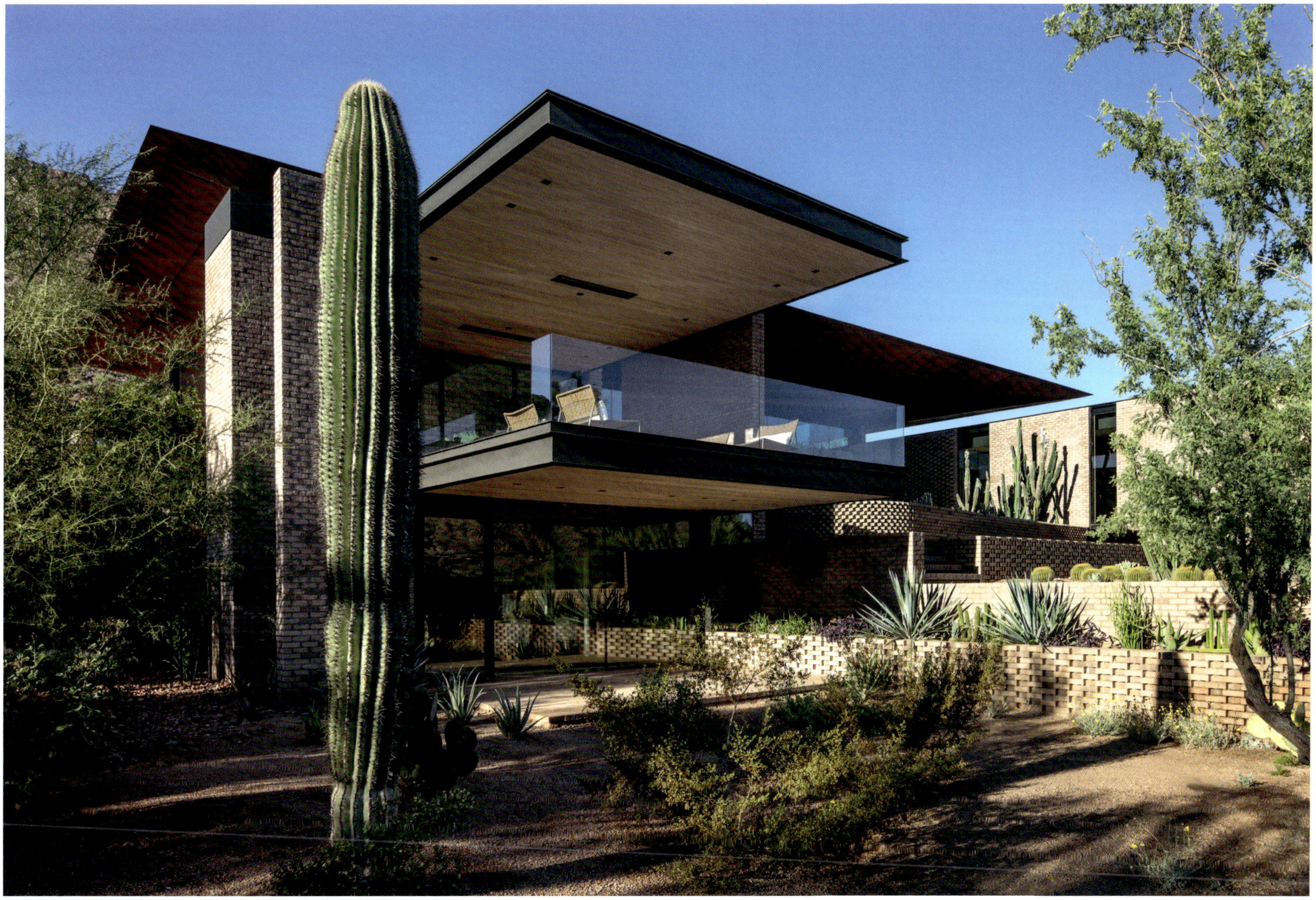

GHOST WASH HOUSE

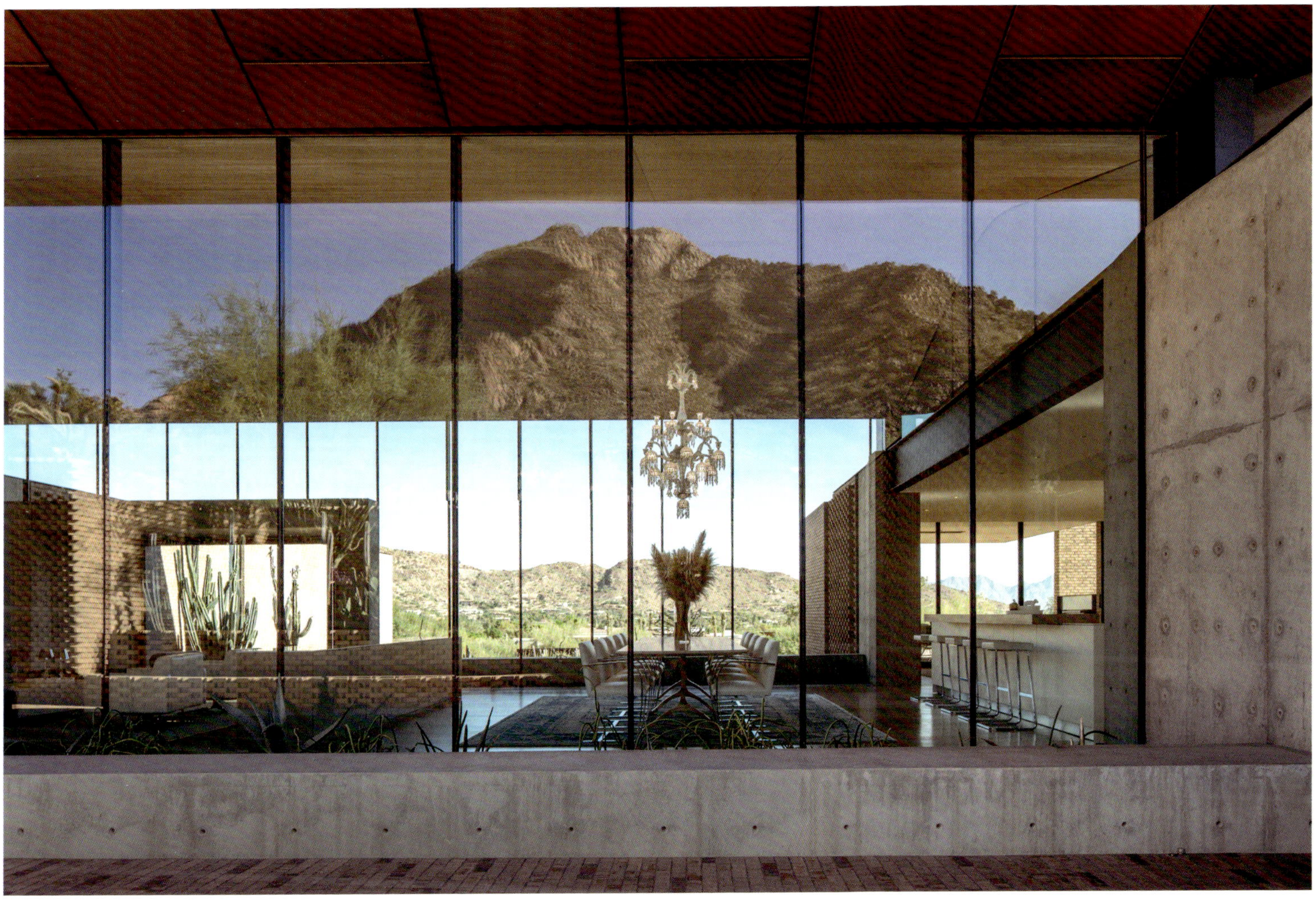

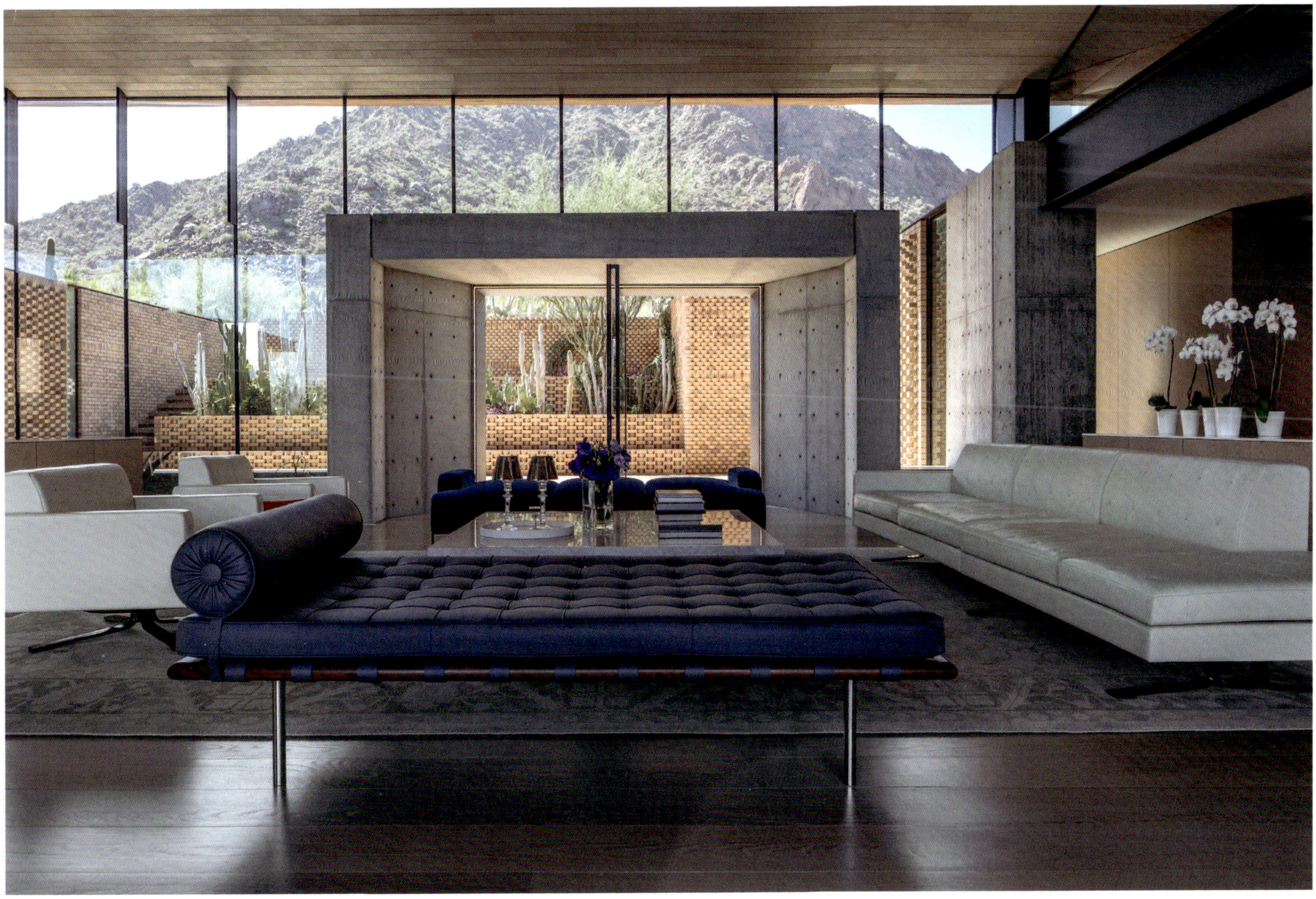

Carlos Arroyo Arquitectos
CASA ENCUENTRO
2007 | Almería, Spain

Only seemingly untouched, the desert of Tabernas in Almería has been traversed many times—and seen even more often by those who never actually set foot on its ground. It is called the Hollywood of Spain because many films are produced in the region due to its similarities to North American deserts. Functioning as an allegory of the area's history, Casa Encuentro is an old farmhouse that has been transformed and extended with the goal of emulating original details of the structure that address the intense heat and sunlight of the region: thick earth and stone walls, a flat roof, small windows, and a chalky white exterior. The additions are discreetly tucked away, camouflaged among terraces and hidden behind pine trees intersecting the property. A private area with an adjacent painting studio in the heart of an artificially created hill is reserved for the owners, while an additional bedroom provides space and equal privacy for visitors. A long narrow pool stretches along the upper terrace and allows for refreshment while the eye wanders over the land, studded with ancient olive trees that are harvested for olive oil production. The central courtyard is protected from the sun by another tree of importance, the fig tree. A retractable double lattice of galvanized steel, laser-cut to imitate the silhouette of the tree's distinct leaves, acts like a tree canopy when the sun is high overhead, with only dappled light penetrating the space.

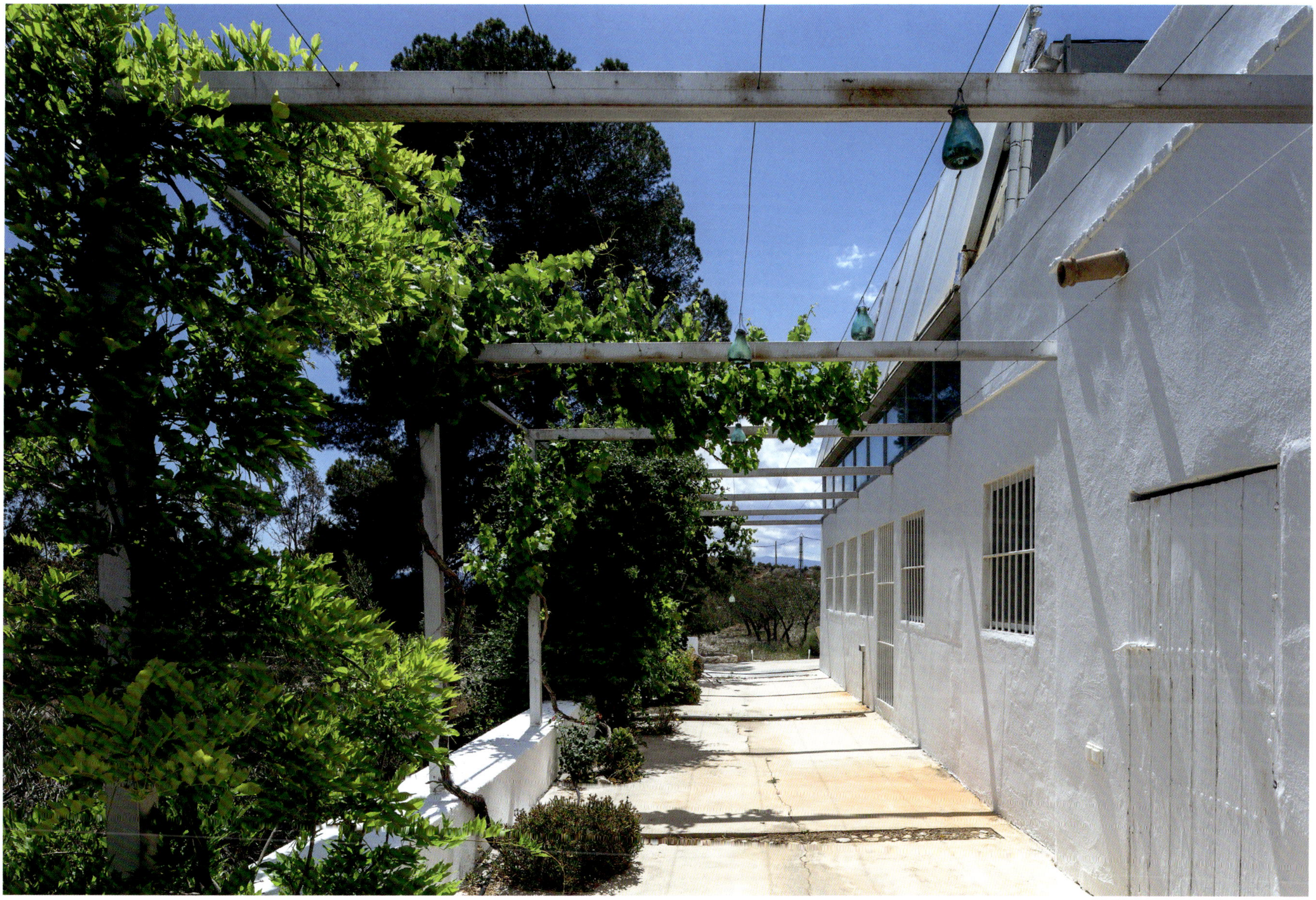

CASA ENCUENTRO

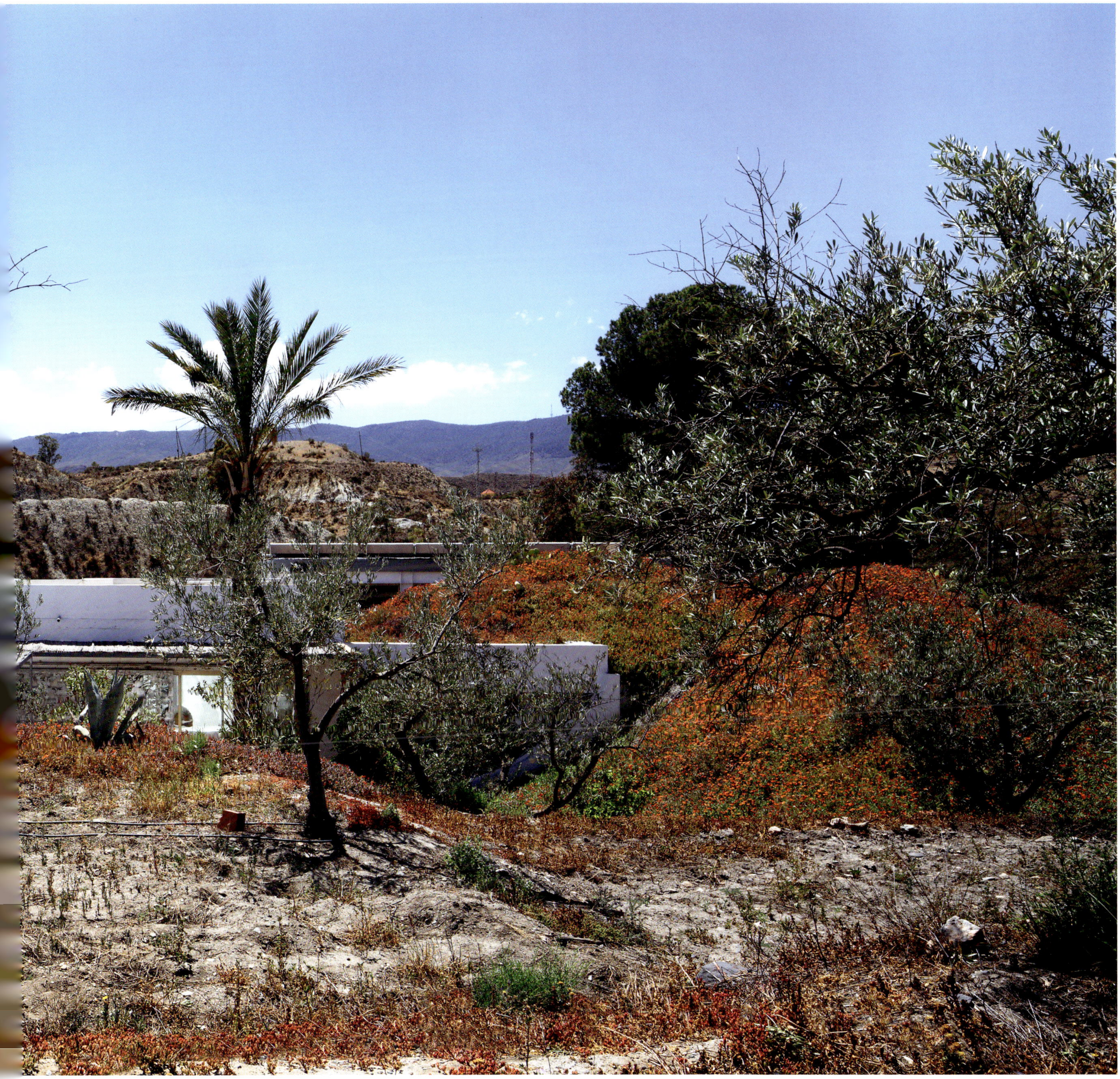

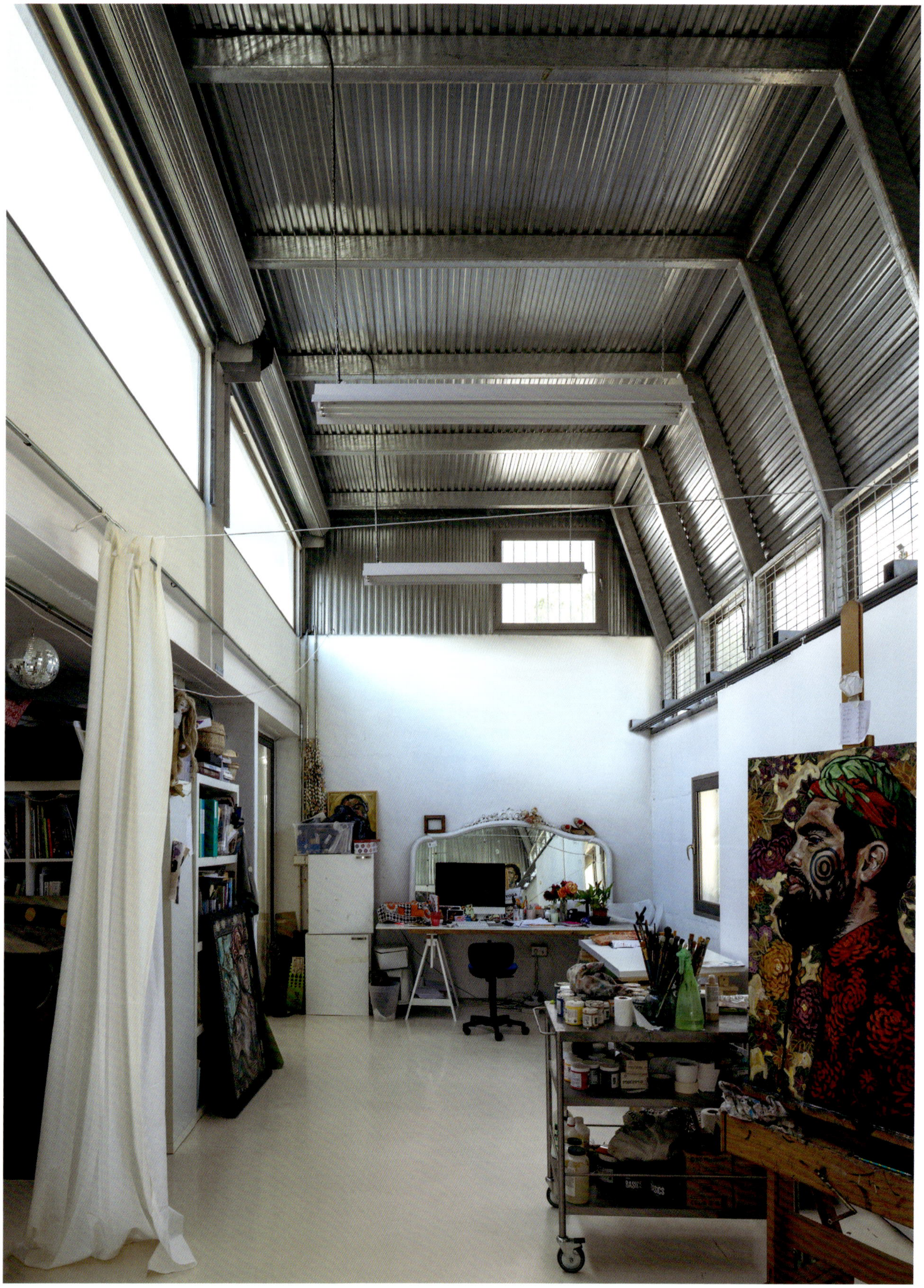

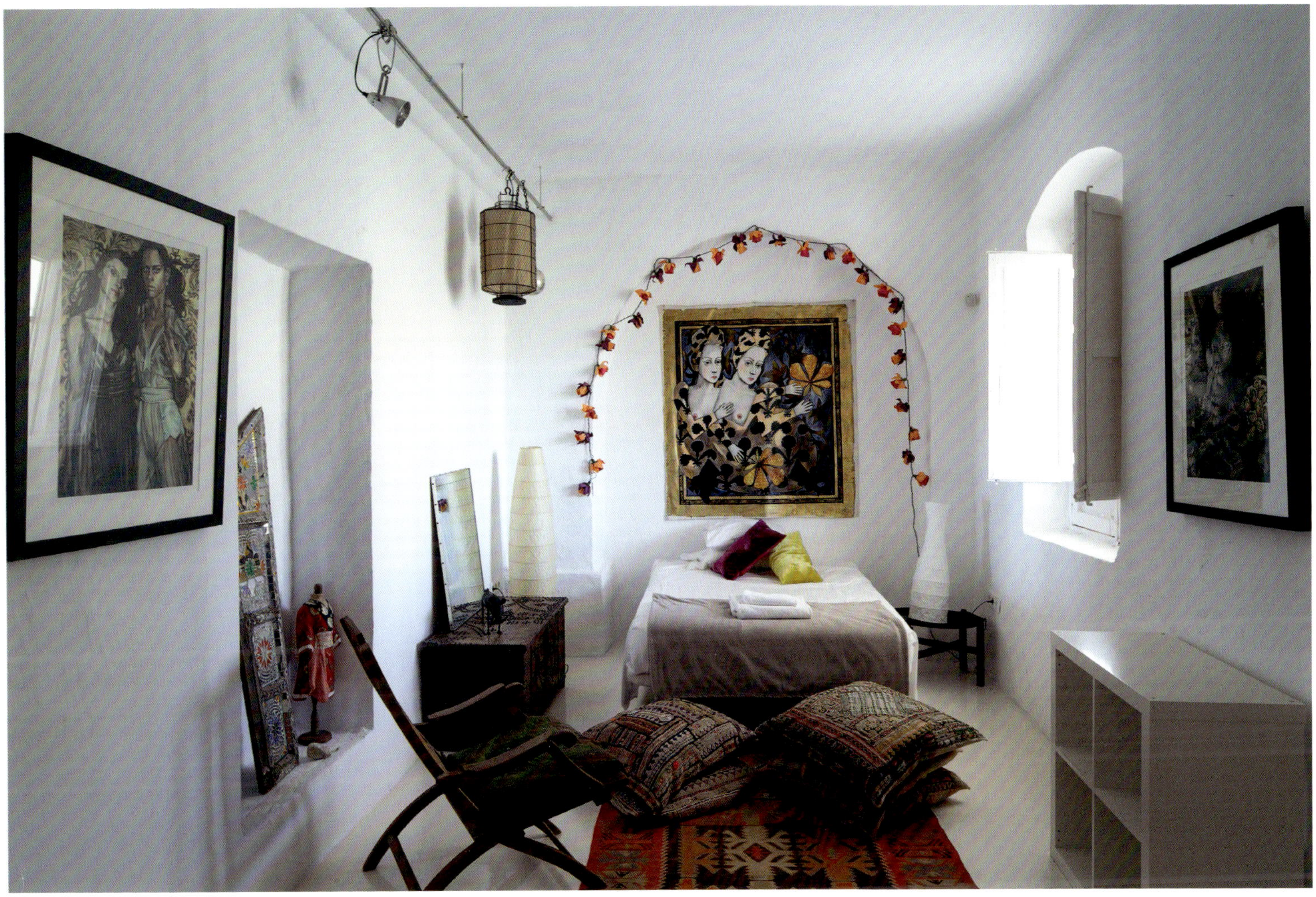

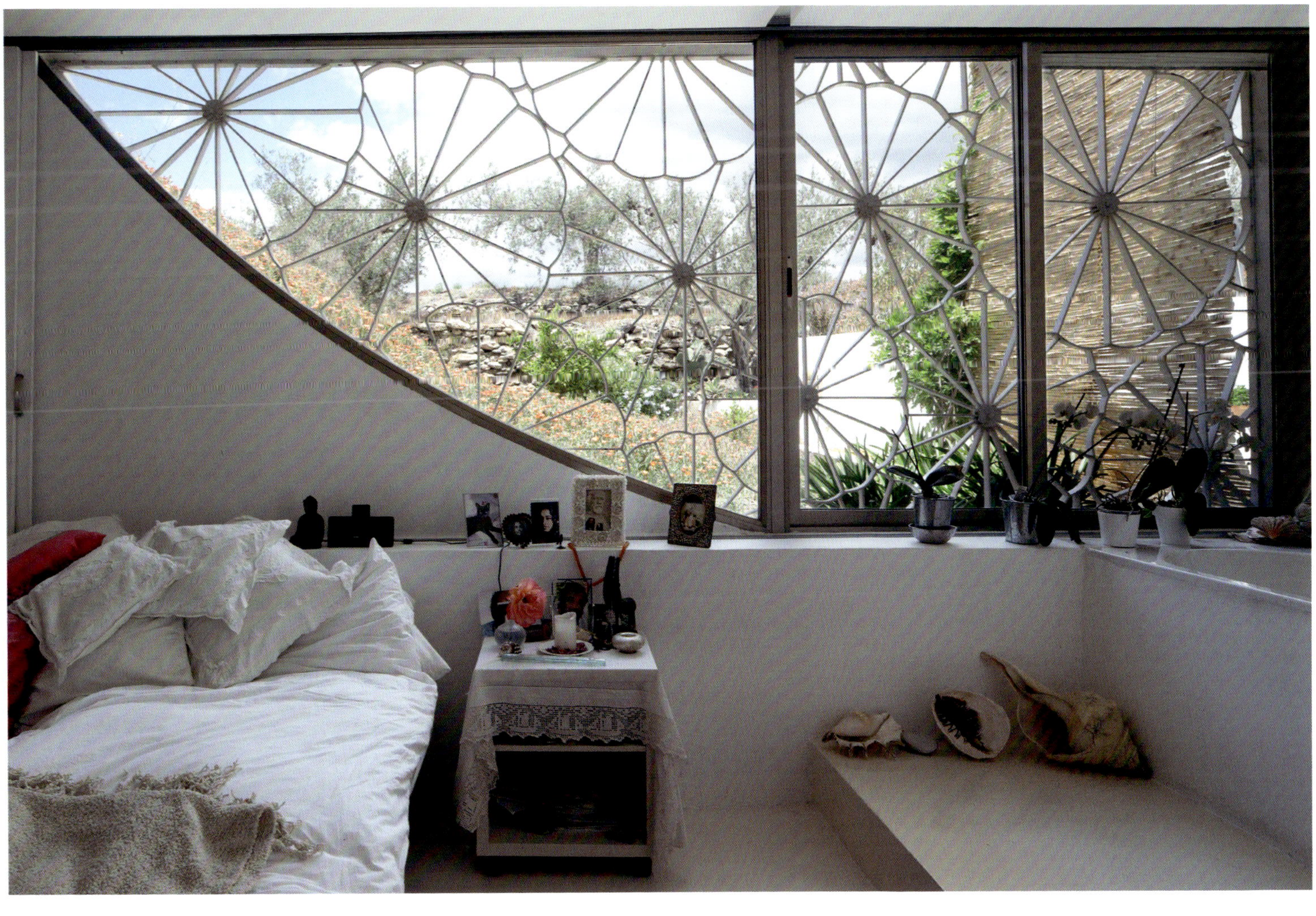

Marmol Radziner
SCOTTSDALE
2013 | Scottsdale, AZ, USA

Like the Sonoran Desert in which it is situated, Frank Lloyd Wright's winter residence, Taliesin West, in Scottsdale, is dominated by desert rock; Wright was convinced that Arizona's low lines and abstract shapes needed their own kind of architecture. Honoring but in no way attempting to re-create the iconic home, Marmol Radziner contributes its own modern typology to the region's architecture with Scottsdale, a house for which the horizontal lines of building and landscape are connected. Tall walls of cement studded with local stone are employed throughout the property, including the traverse leading to the threshold of the house through a native succulent garden. Stepped roofs, raised terraces, and fully glazed living spaces allow the house to extend into the landscape. Despite its relatively ambitious program, the residence doesn't overpower its setting, due to thoughtful choices of materials that blend naturally with the surroundings. The clever layout includes two offices stacked one atop the other and a roof garden on the upper level. Multiple exterior recreational spaces, framed by low concrete retaining walls, offer spectacular vistas for both group gatherings and private contemplation.

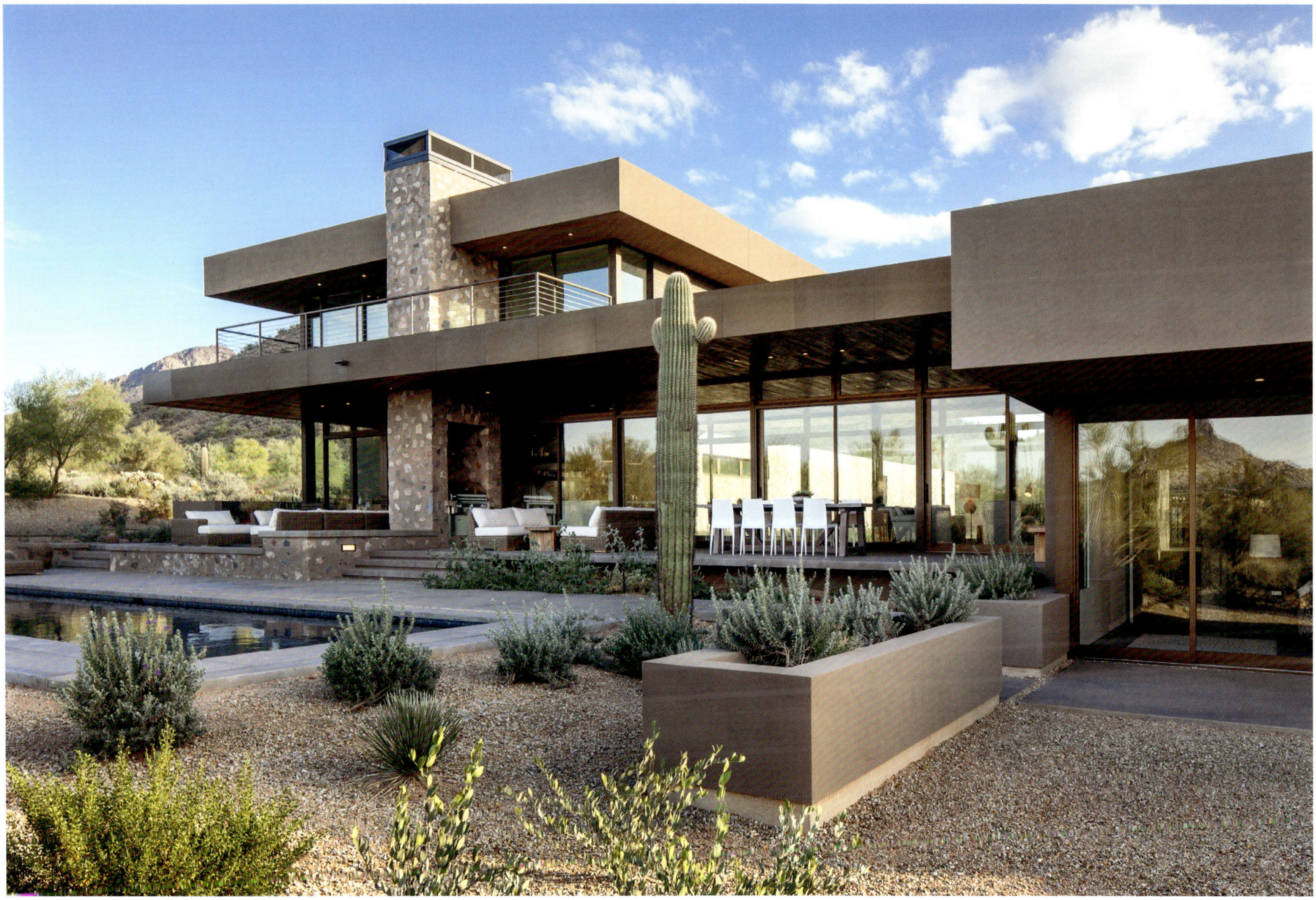

SCOTTSDALE

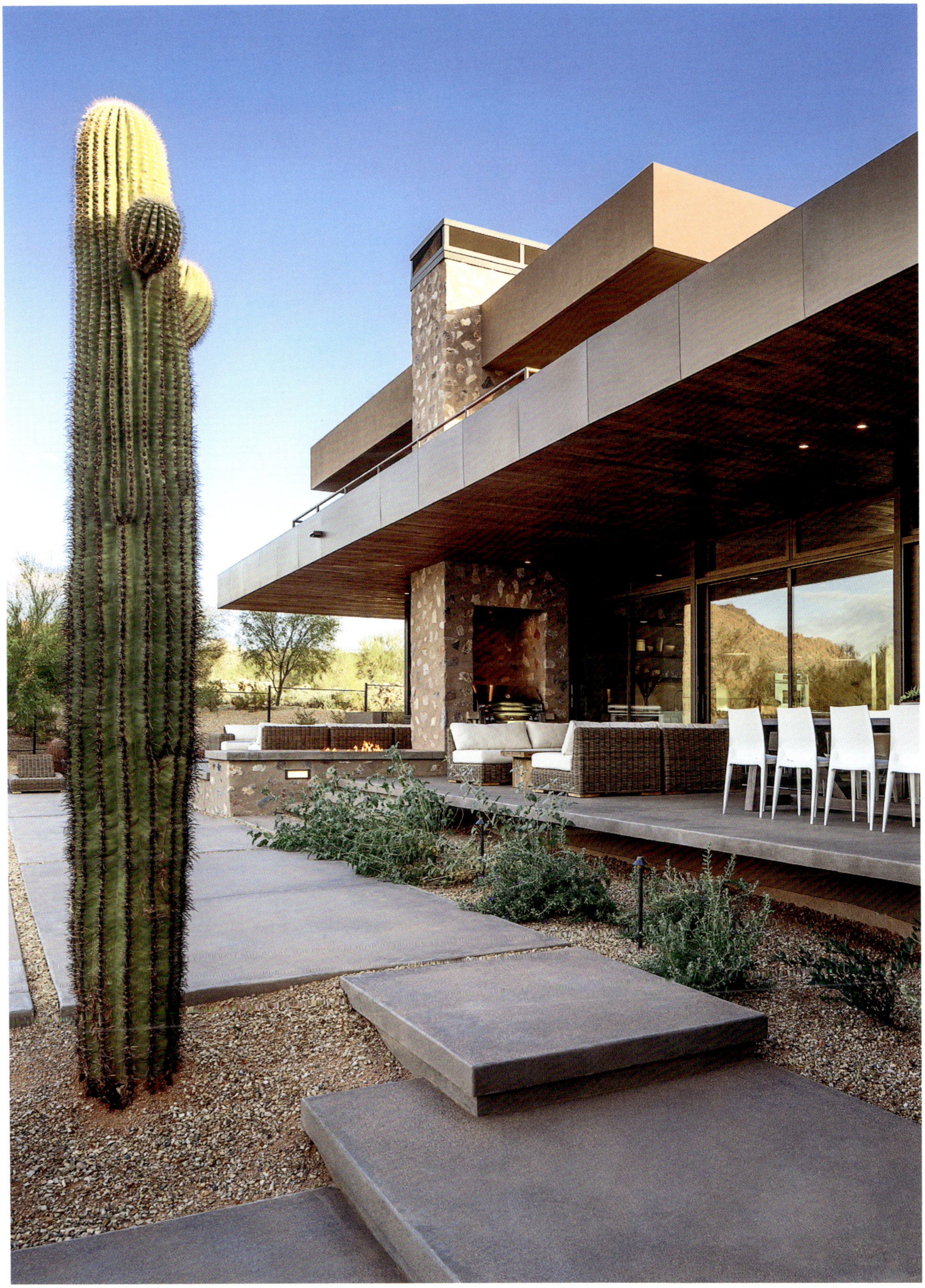

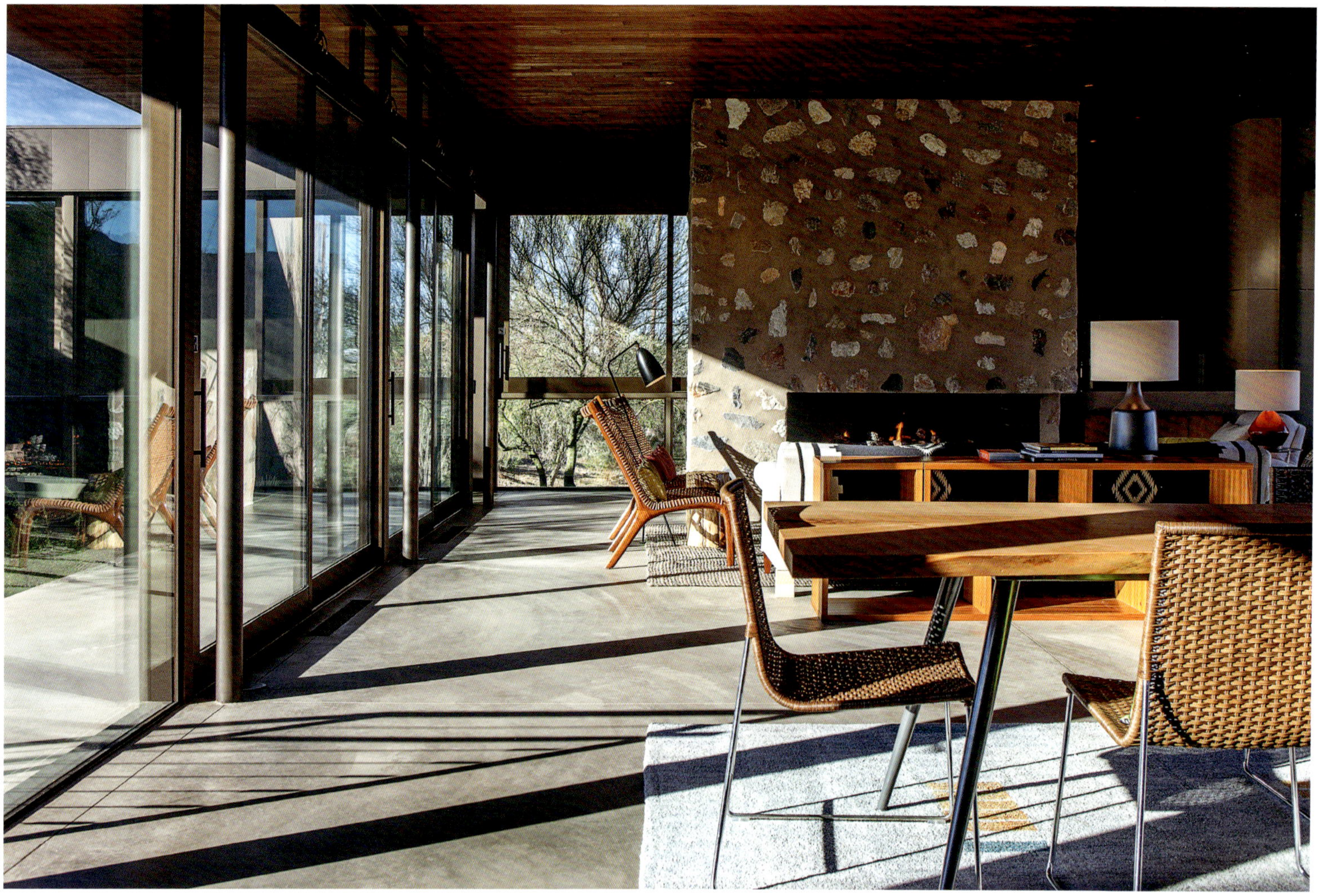

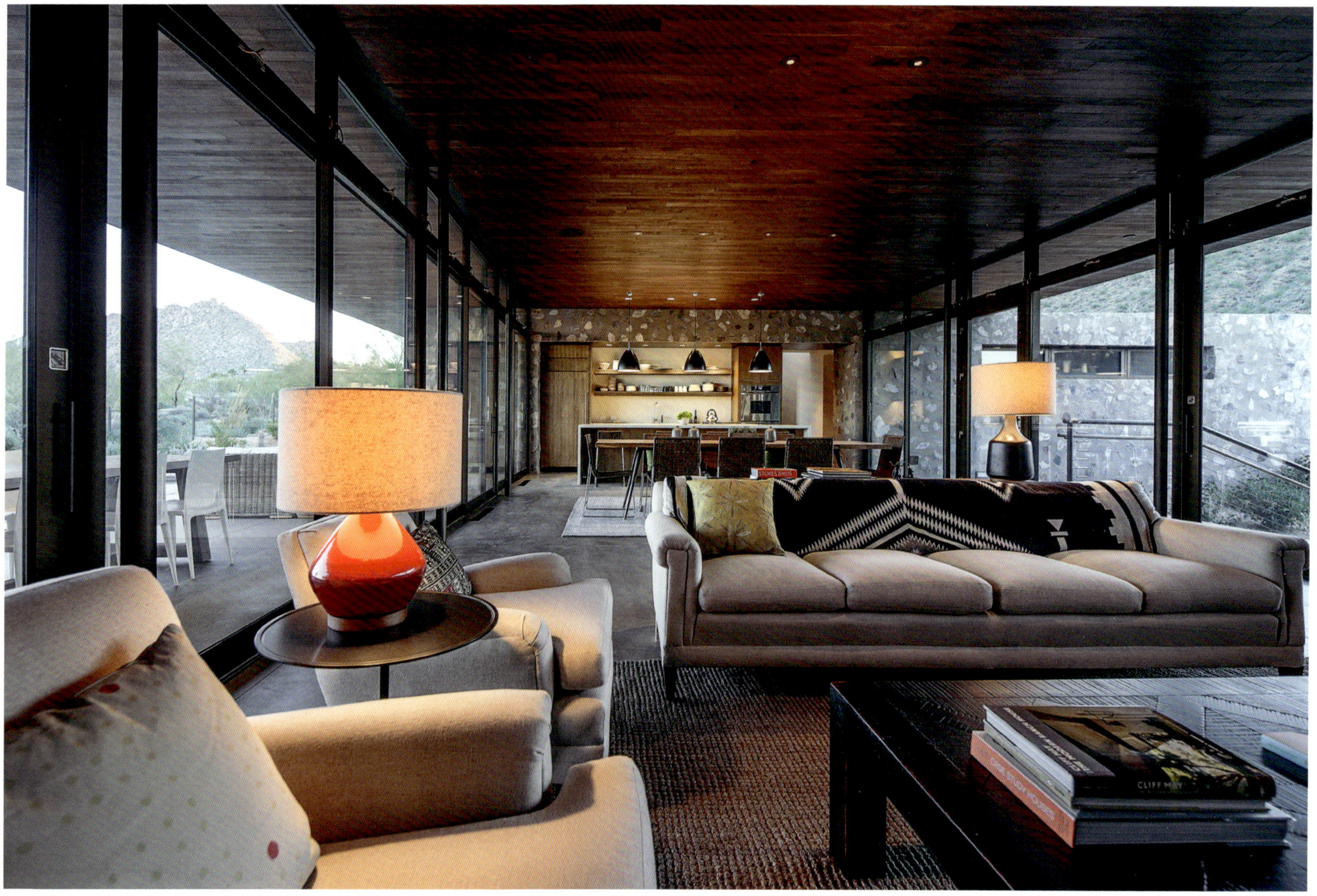

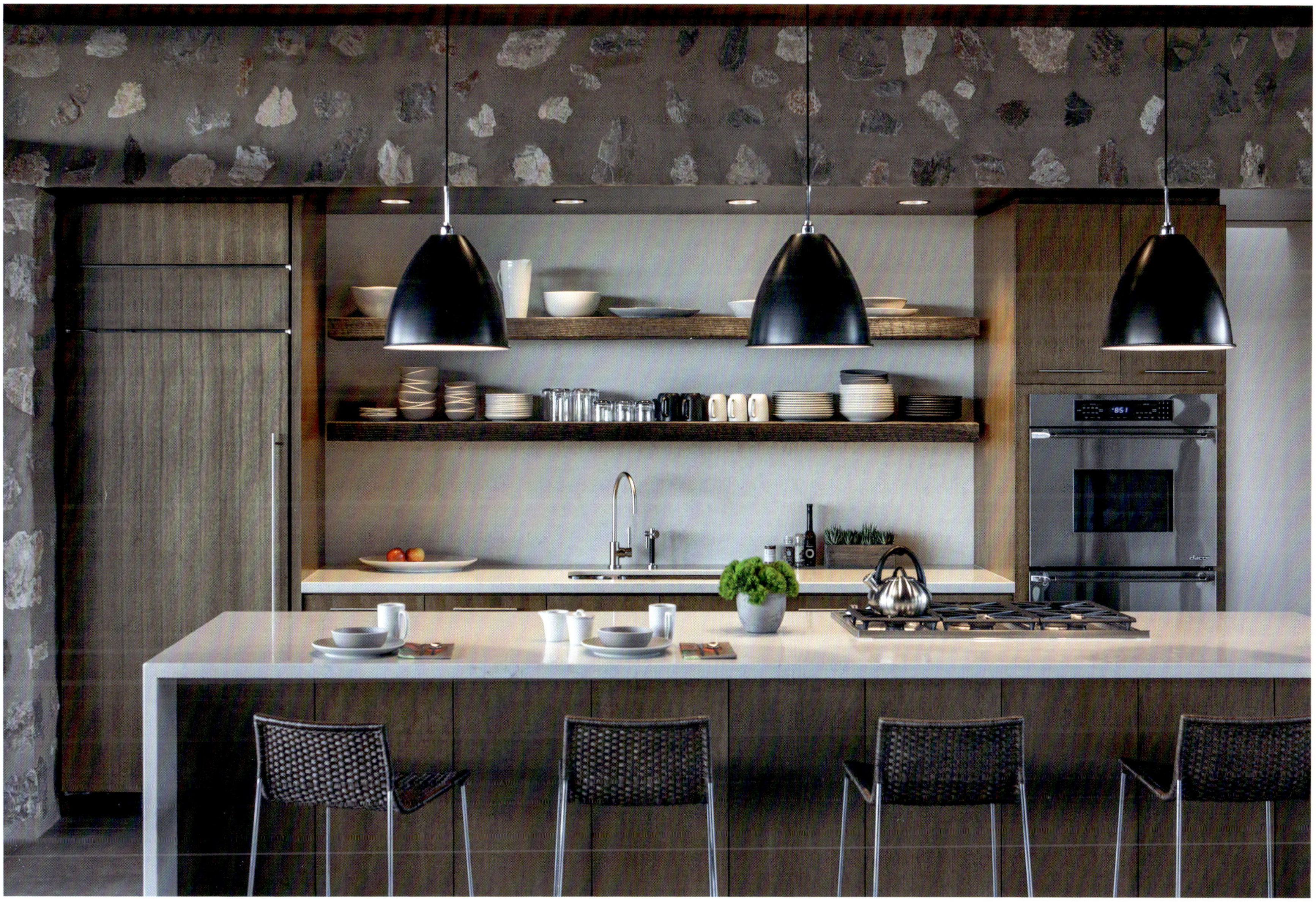

Olson Kundig
STUDHORSE
2012 | Winthrop, WA, USA

Studhorse is set in Washington's glacial Methow Valley in the northern Cascades, in Winthrop, about two hundred miles (322 kilometers) northeast of Seattle. Four separate structures are positioned to resemble a nomadic settlement or a circle of wagon trains. This resemblance is carried through to the design of each dwelling, giving expression to the clients' wish to be not only close to but also actively within nature. Three of the buildings, housing a living room, kitchen, and dining space, surround a central pavilion. It is a space where the family can come together outside as much as inside; all structures can be opened up to the open air and additionally, a TV and a bar are designed to be accessed from both the interior and the courtyard, enabling for entertainment to seamlessly traverse the threshold.

Boundaries are consistently blurred on purpose—even when gazing through the floor-to-ceiling windows, one has the feeling of being on the outside. The materials, too, fit perfectly into the landscape and over time will do so even more successfully; the salvaged woods and metals used on the exterior will weather and fade, taking on a closer resemblance to the surrounding rock formations. Similarly, the marine-grade plywood walls and ceilings of the interior will darken with age. A glacial erratic, an ancient migrant boulder that differs from the native rock, sits in the heart of the courtyard—serving as a fulcrum to unite the individual structures and a reminder of the history of the earth over several millennia.

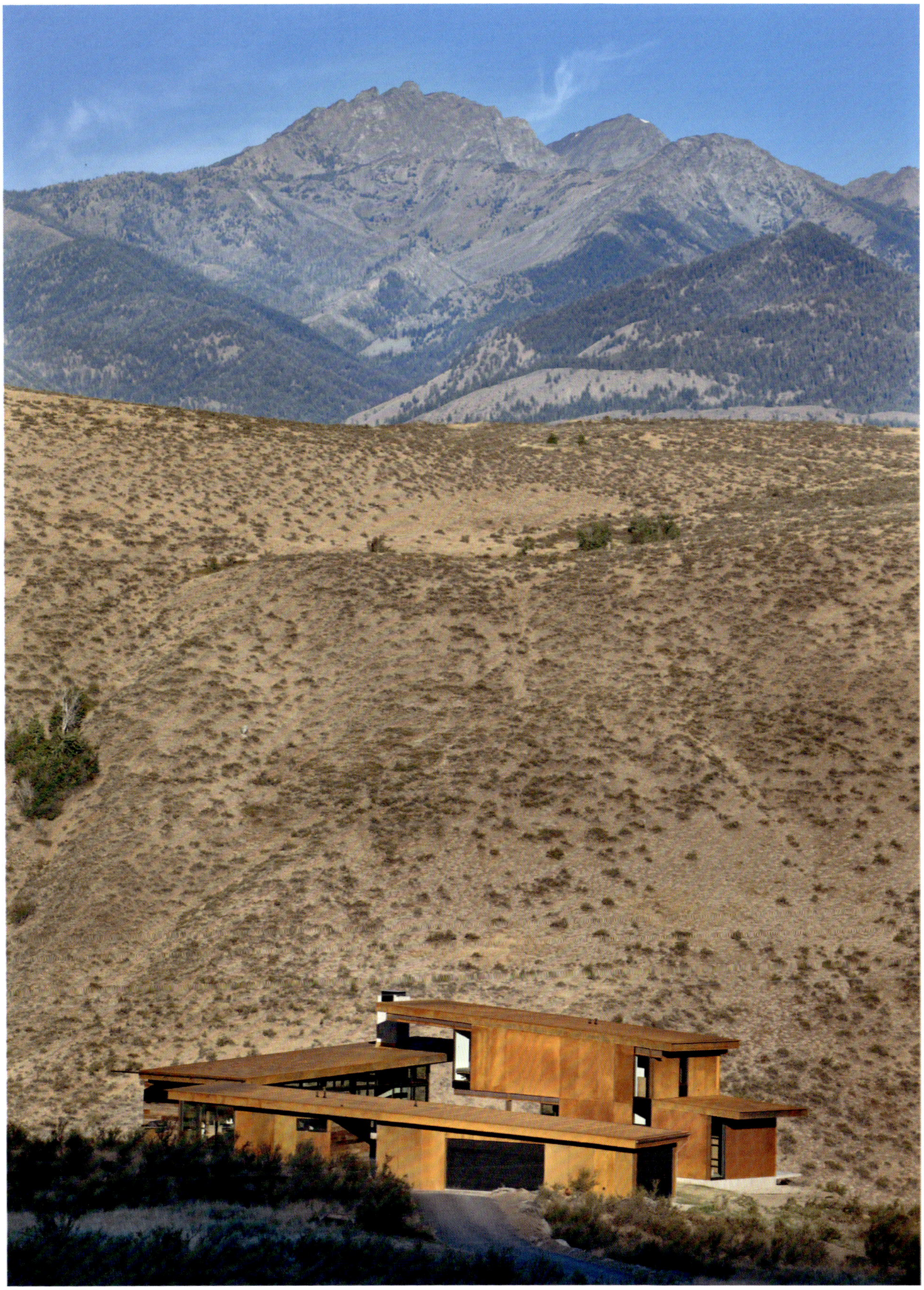

STUDHORSE

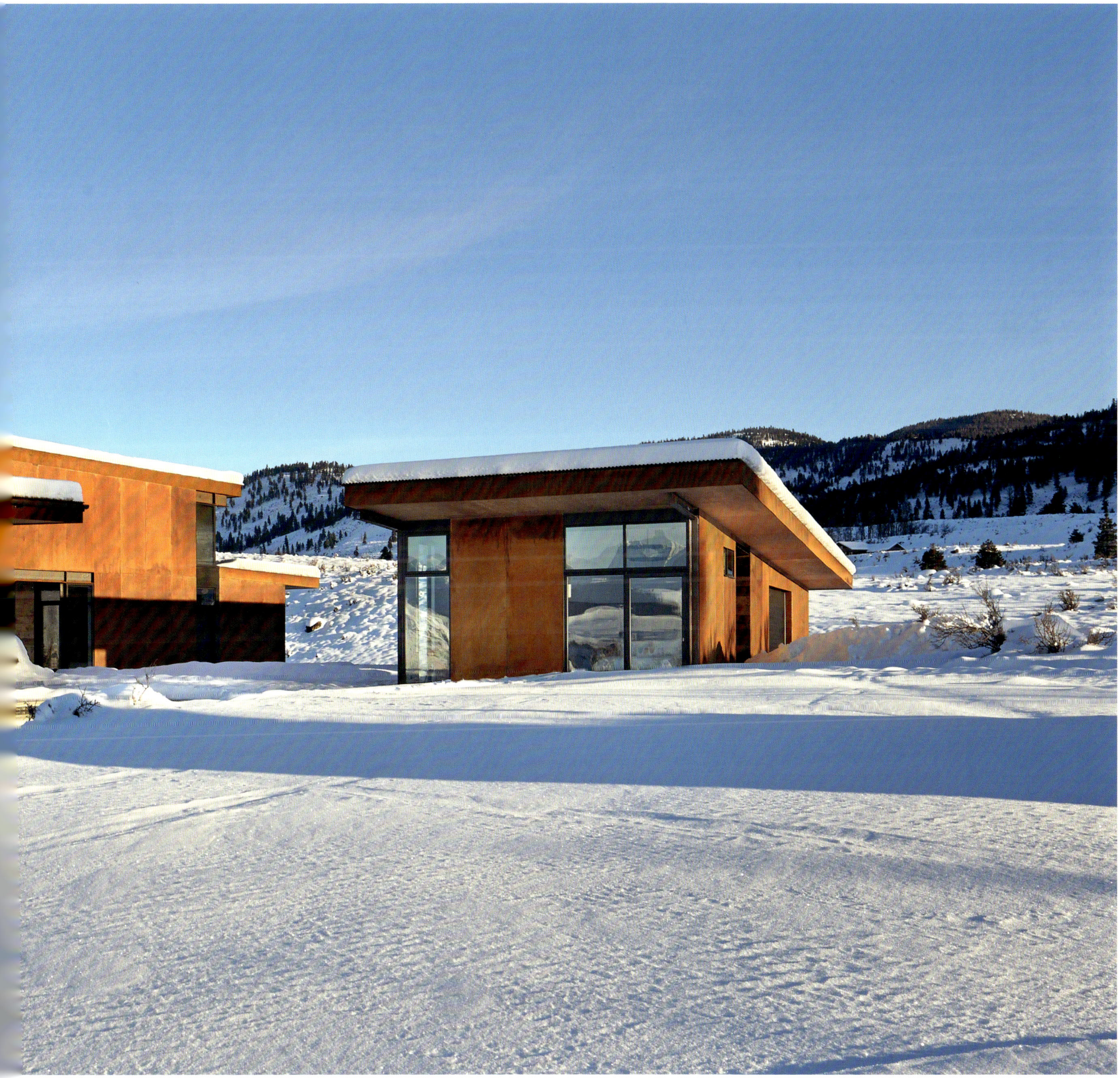

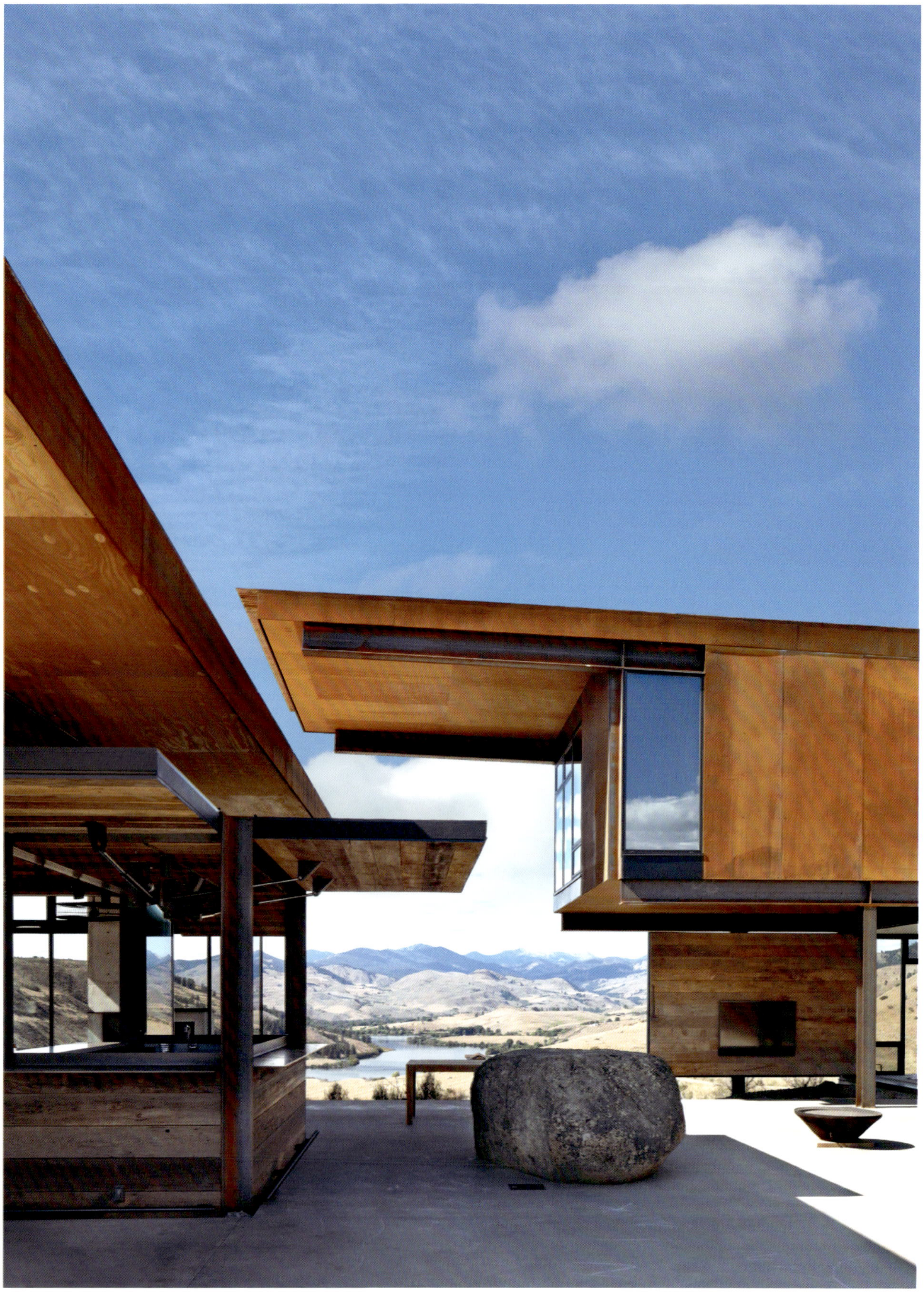

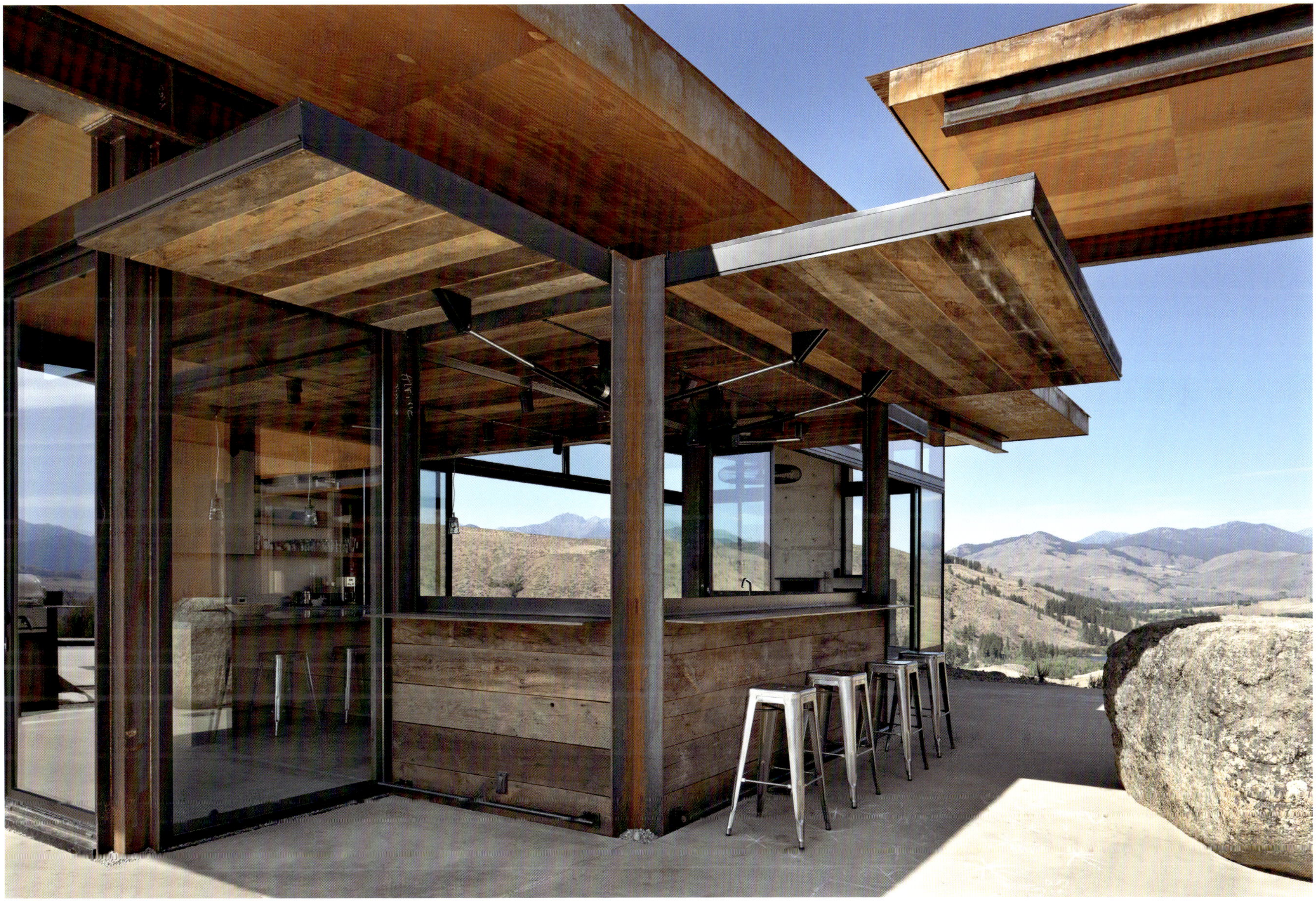

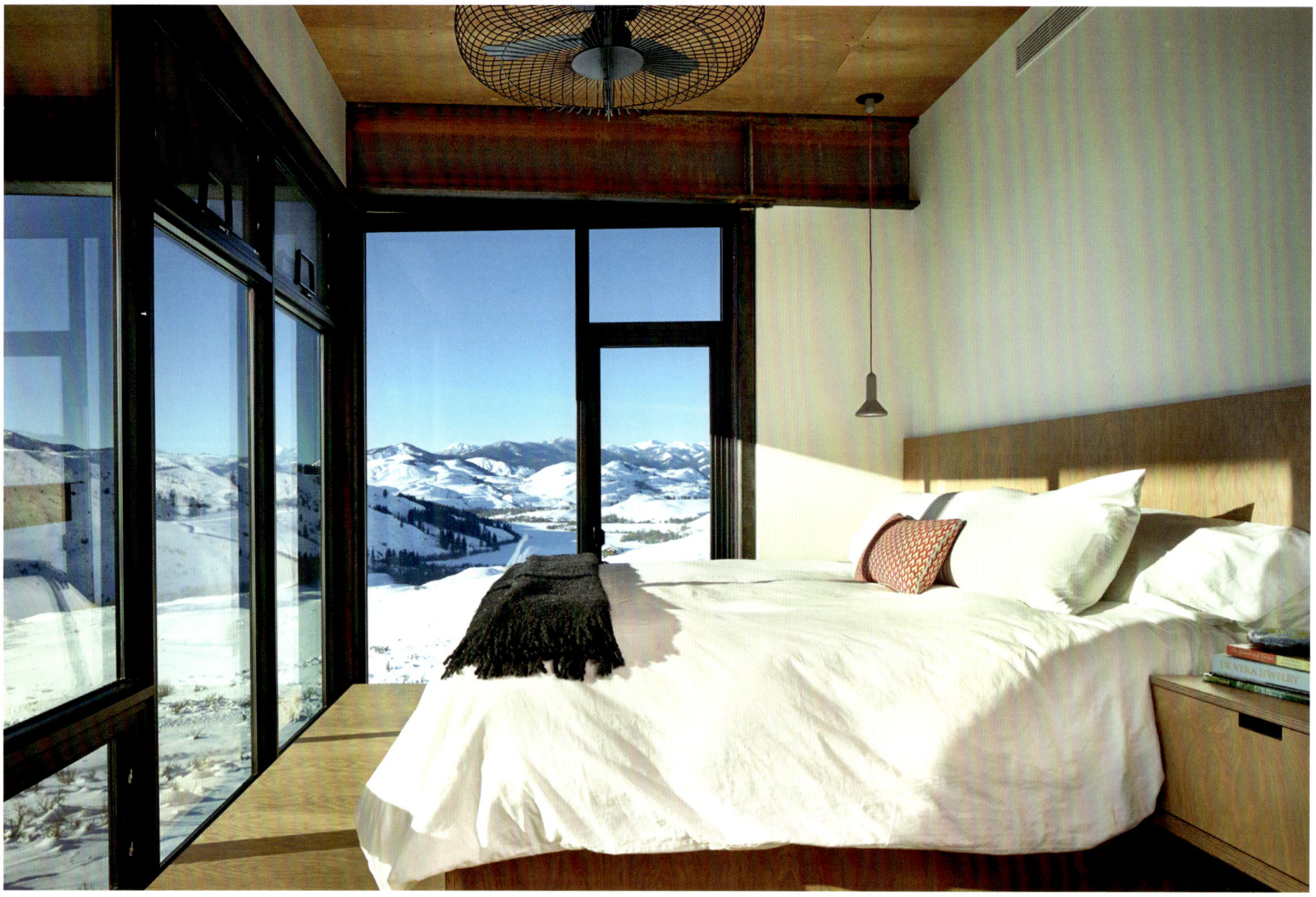

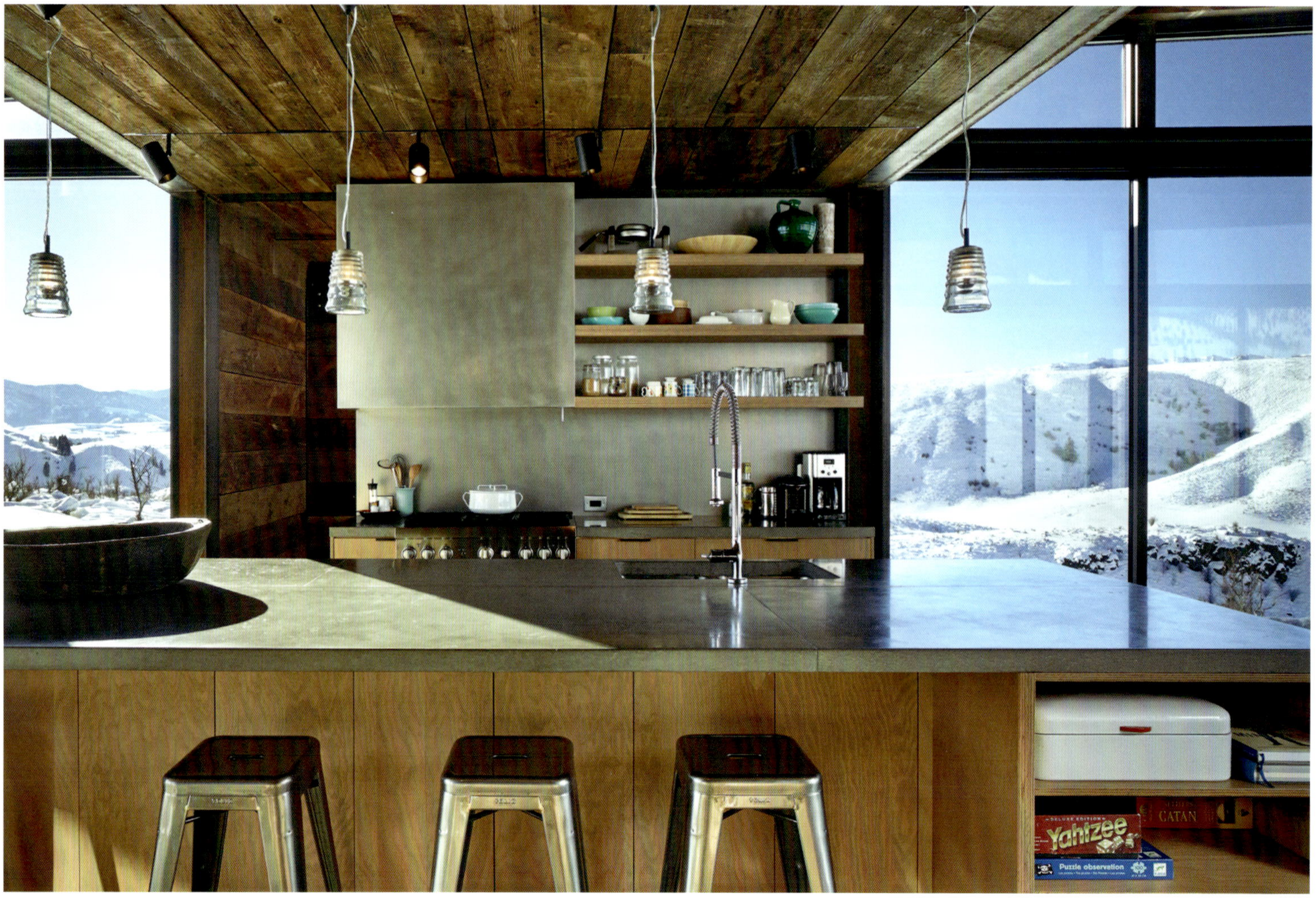

CATAN
Yahtzee
Puzzle observation

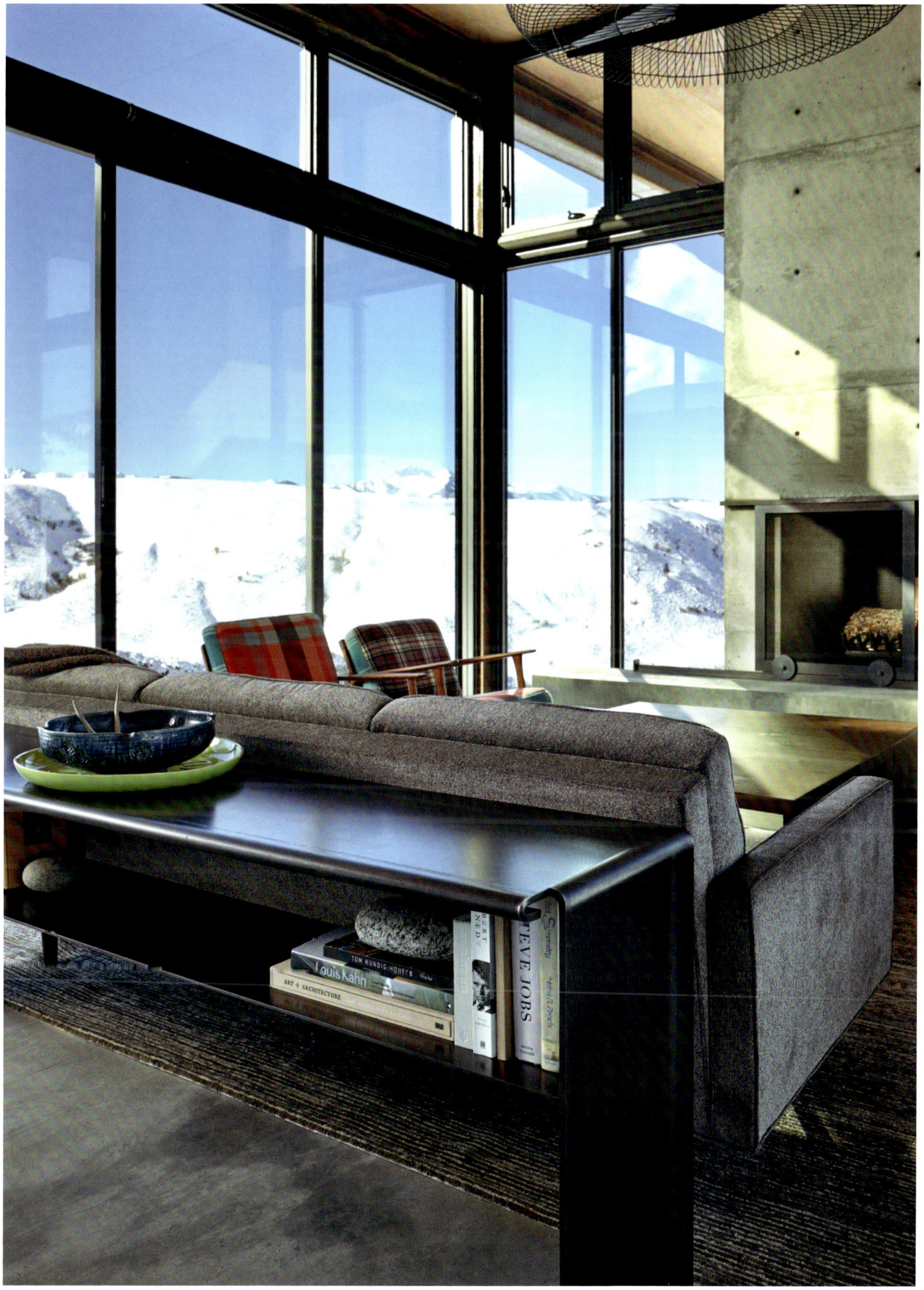
Louis Kahn

Studio Ko
VILLA D
2013 | Al Ouidane, Morocco

To draw inspiration from the existing landscape is not an uncommon design approach, though one decidedly more challenging if the plot in question consists mostly of dry, flat earth apart from the occasional shrub. Using sun-dried bricks made from local dirt, Karl Fournier and Olivier Marty of Studio Ko constructed Villa D in Al Ouidane as a house from the land rather than on the land. It is an homage to the mineral-rich earth of Morocco, where colors range from sandy beige tones to deeply saturated reds and dark browns, a scope that is reflected in the successively arranged rooms of the house.

Responding to the clients' wish, window sizes were kept to a minimum and create specific moments of light in the interleaved rooms, which are not fully revealed from any single viewpoint. Simplicity, fluidity, and traditional materials dominate the two-story complex. Ceilings soar dramatically to sixteen feet (five meters) in public rooms but drop lower in the private quarters, creating a sense of intimacy amid the oiled stone walls. Within the garden, rectangular water ponds cultivate life, contrasting both the arid landscape and building materials with precious water, sustainably provided through a rainwater collection system.

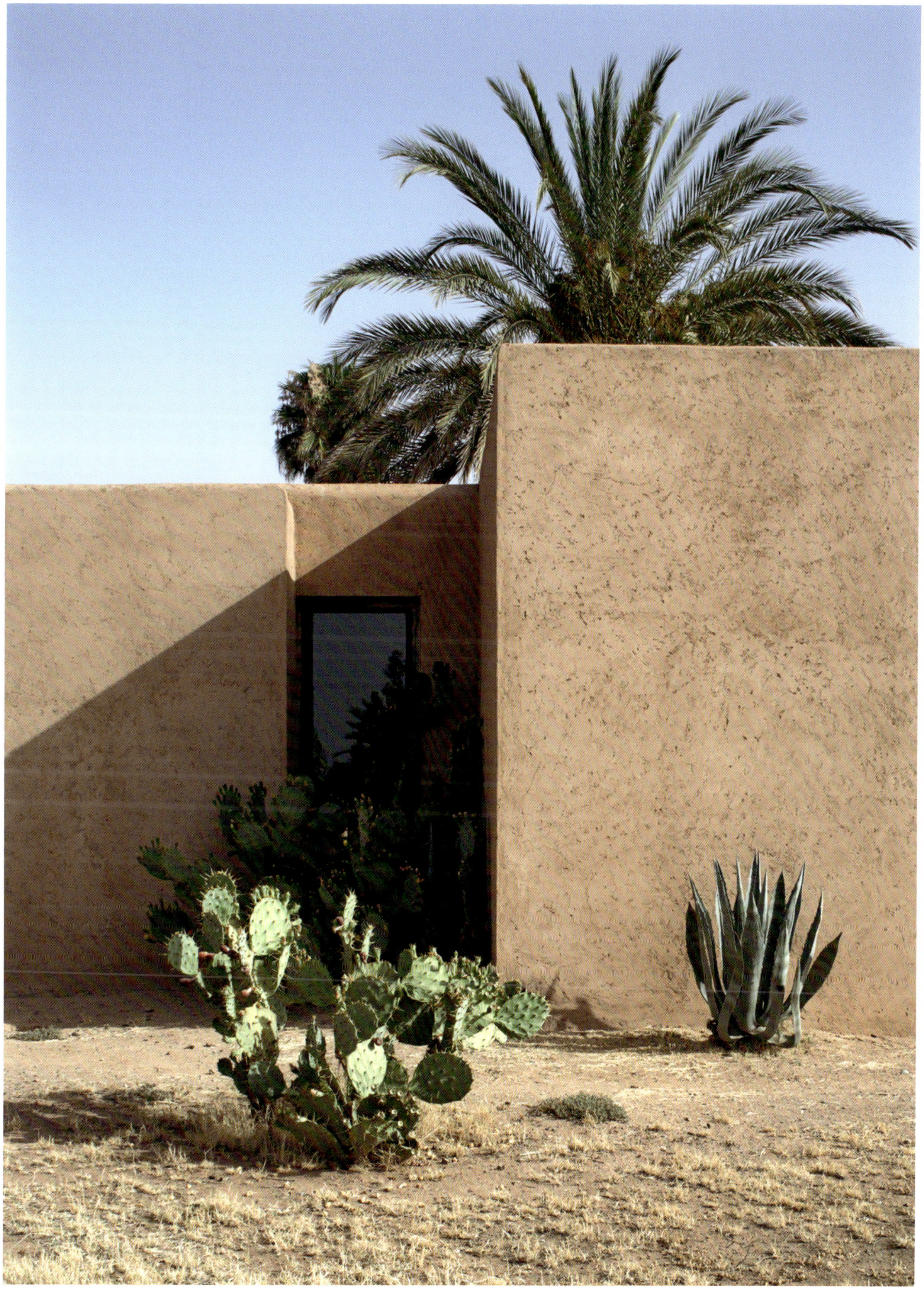

VILLA D

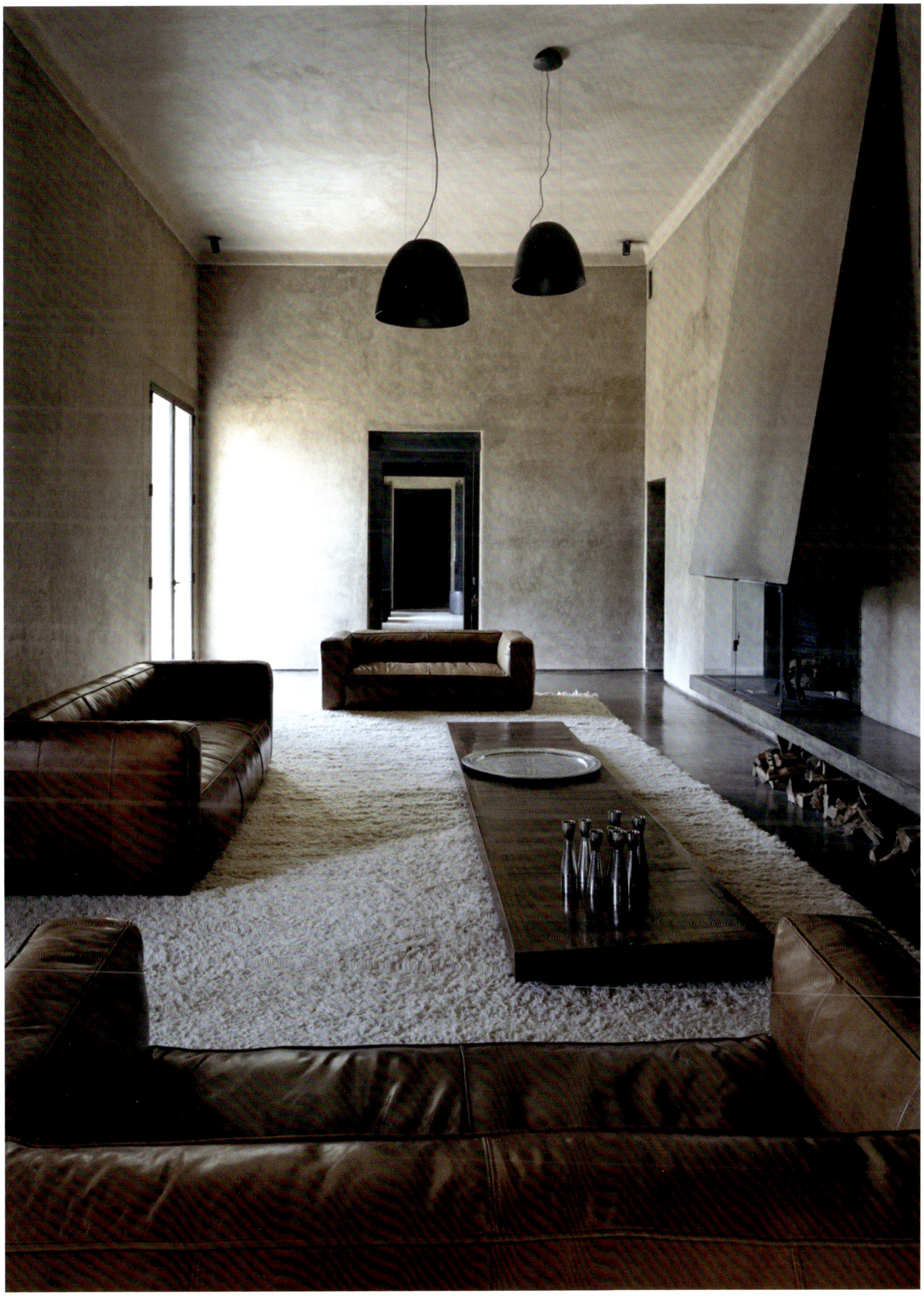

Gracia Studio
ENCUENTRO GUADALUPE
2013 | Valle de Guadalupe, Mexico

Valle de Guadalupe's inhabitants may number below five thousand and its location may be yet another arid spot on the Mexican side of the Sonoran Desert, but the local culinary delights of Baja Med, a new threefold-fusion cuisine, have brought the region an unexpected prominence. Encuentro Guadalupe is well situated within this area, also known as "Mexico's Wine Country." The development consists of a restaurant, a wine cellar, and a hotel of twenty-two individual cabins and villas scattered across the hillside. These diminutive pods, perched on low stilts with an adjoining platform deck are each framed in steel, faced in monochromatic timber, and appointed with glossy white interiors, industrial light fixtures, and plywood furniture with hairpin legs. The units read trendy—risking a chance that such determined stylization could be misunderstood as an effort-heavy endeavor in picture perfectness. Yet the careful adherence to uniformity and simplicity and a commitment to keep any contamination and destruction of the panorama as well as of the native soil to a minimum elevate the experience to something more contemplative and less decorative. The accommodations can be considered a more lavish version of camping. They elegantly provide the basic needs of overnight guests without distracting them from the breathtaking beauty of the surrounding nature. One can easily imagine sitting outside early in the morning, watching the fog dissipate across Baja California and the sagebrush in the valley below.

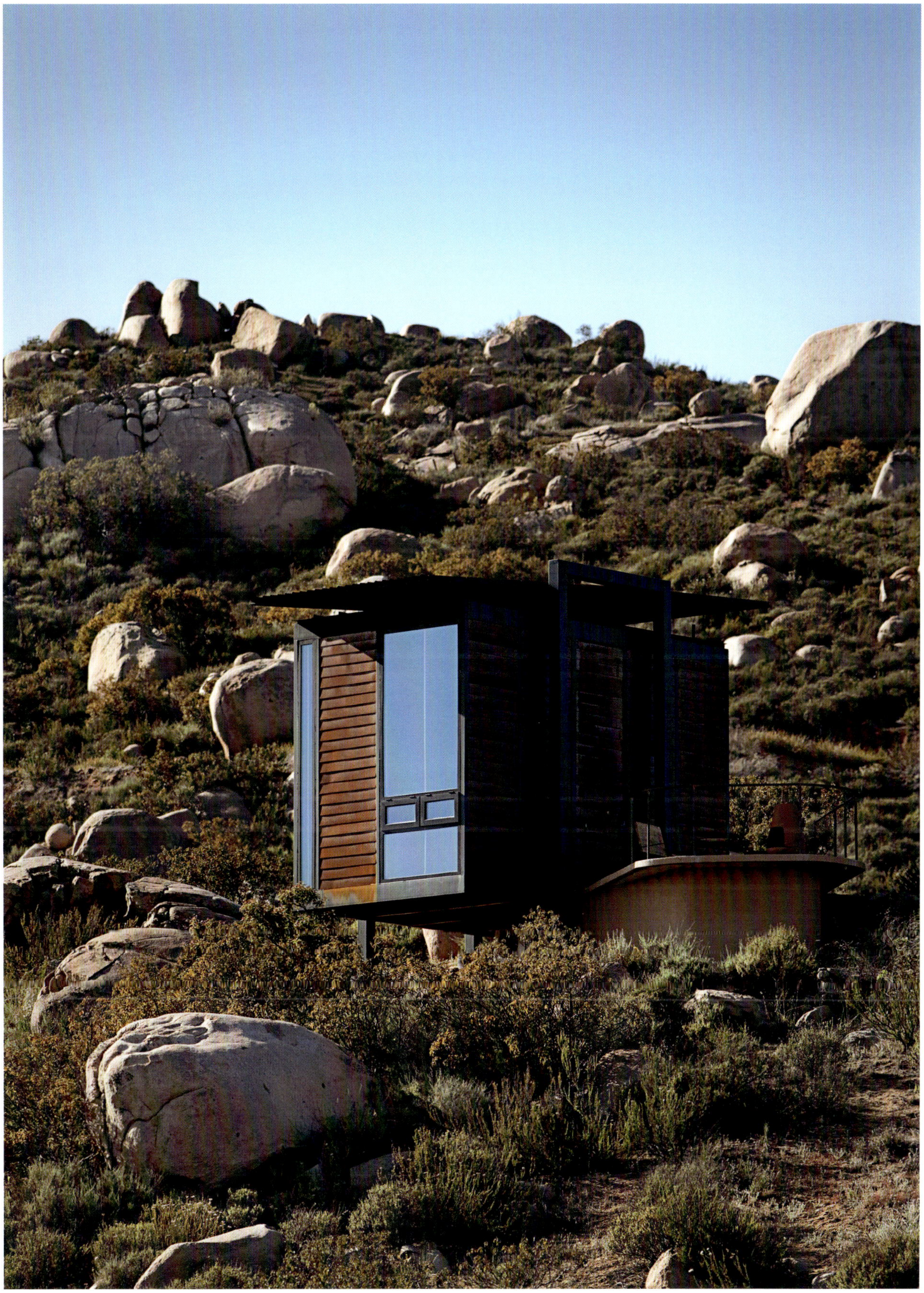

ENCUENTRO GUADALUPE

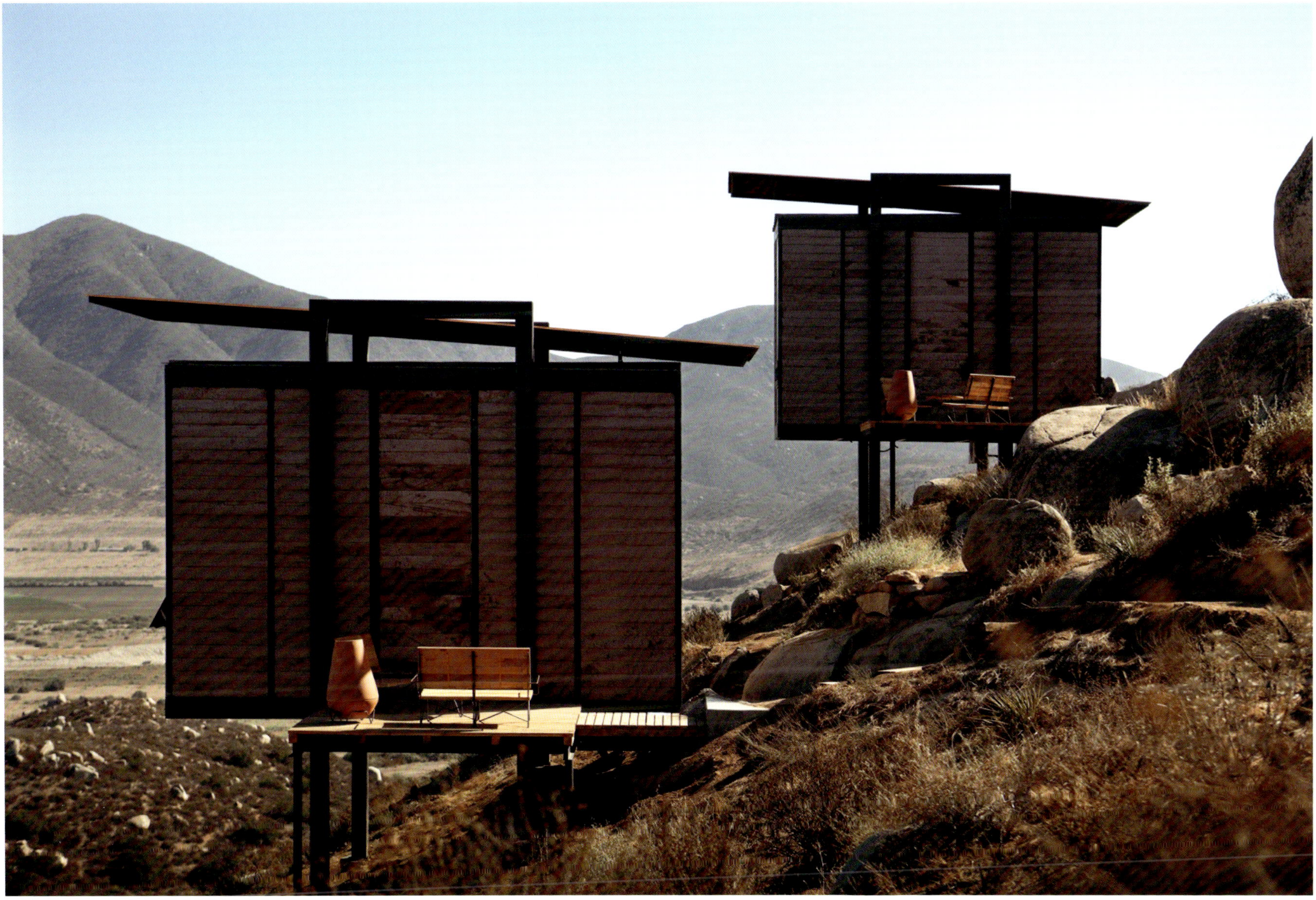

ENCUENTRO GUADALUPE

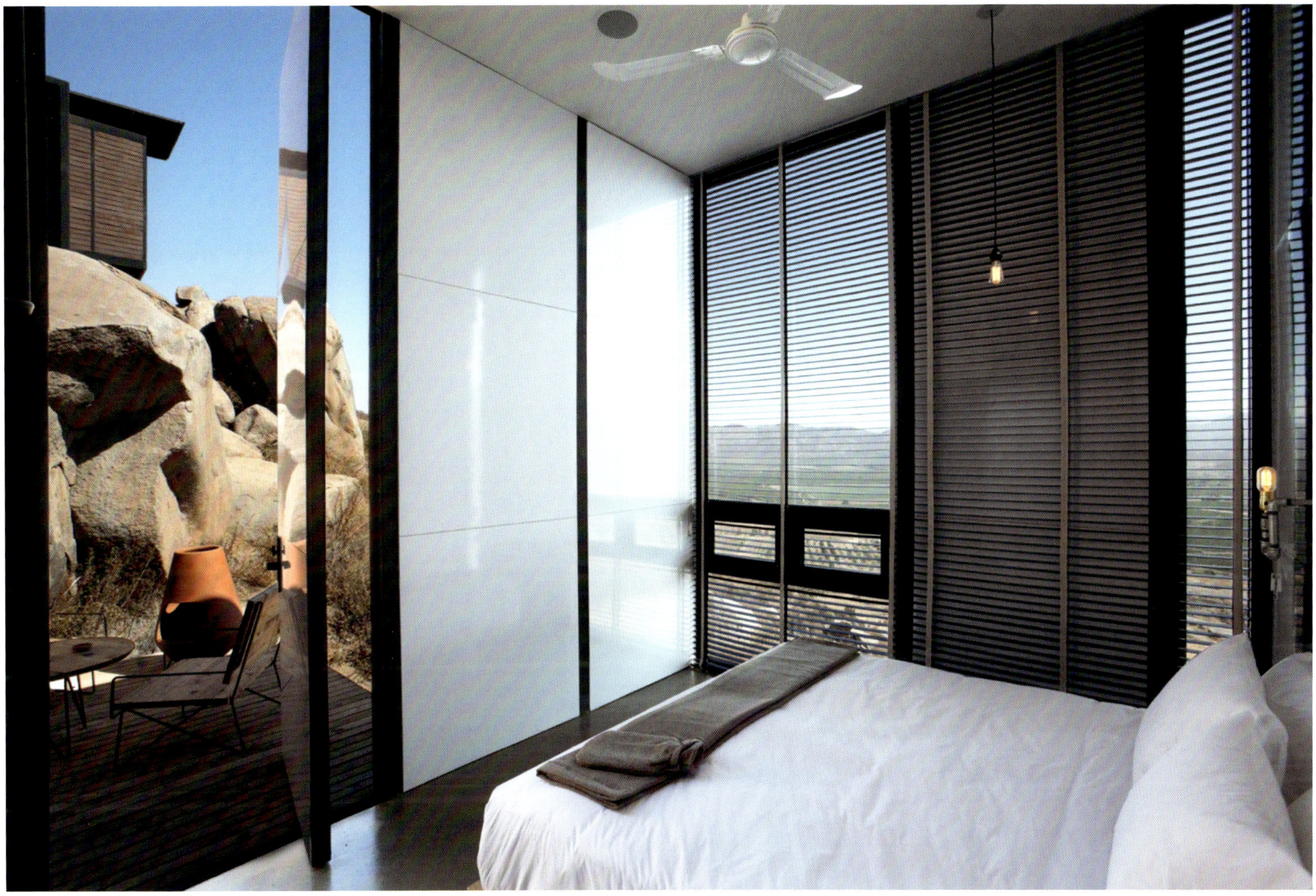
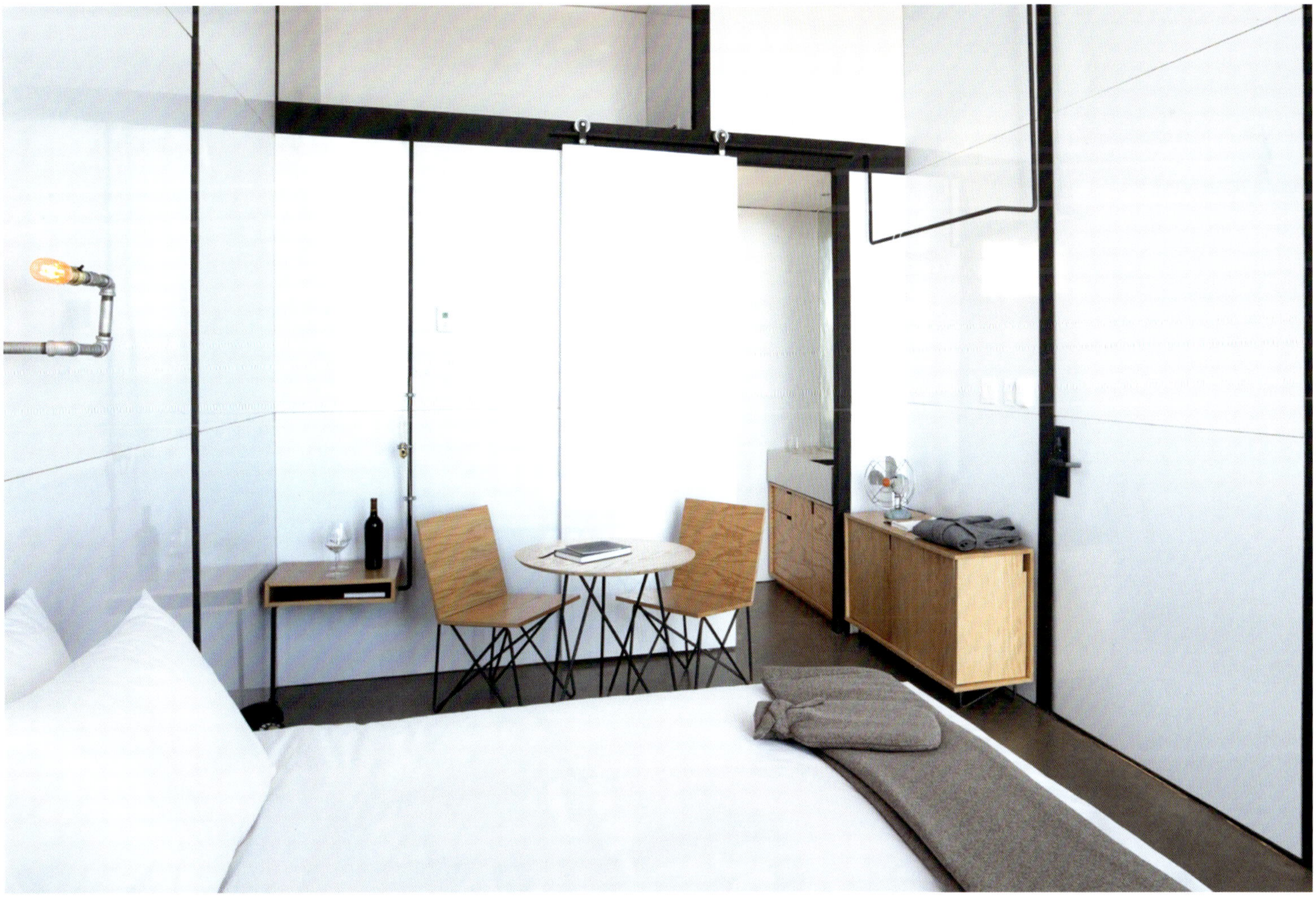

Johnston Marklee
MOUND HOUSE
2002 | Marfa, TX, USA

In spite of its small size, the town of Marfa carries a large legacy when it comes to design and architecture: it was once home to the minimalist artist Donald Judd, who came to rural Texas from New York in search of a slower-paced lifestyle and a sense of permanence. The conditions of the desert offer the perfect environment for showcasing his artworks and furniture, made up of geometric shapes of concrete, metal, plywood, and colored glass. Though Judd inspired—and continues to inspire—generations far beyond Marfa, this particular house by Los Angeles architecture firm Johnston Marklee is mostly based on Judd's design typology. Unpretentious straight lines and a space that appears to be mostly filled with a distinct aura characterize Mound House on the inside as well as the outside. To the north, the L-shaped house features a sizable glazed wall with a view to the courtyard, thereby bathing the living room and open-plan kitchen in light. Much attention has been paid to proportions and shapes, especially visible in the interior design and furniture choices. Every object relates to other objects spatially without the slightest sign of interference, and materials are kept to minimalist classics: concrete flooring, adobe bricks, maple plywood fittings and panels, and steel. As with Judd, a principal element of mystery remains: the mound on the other side of the house.

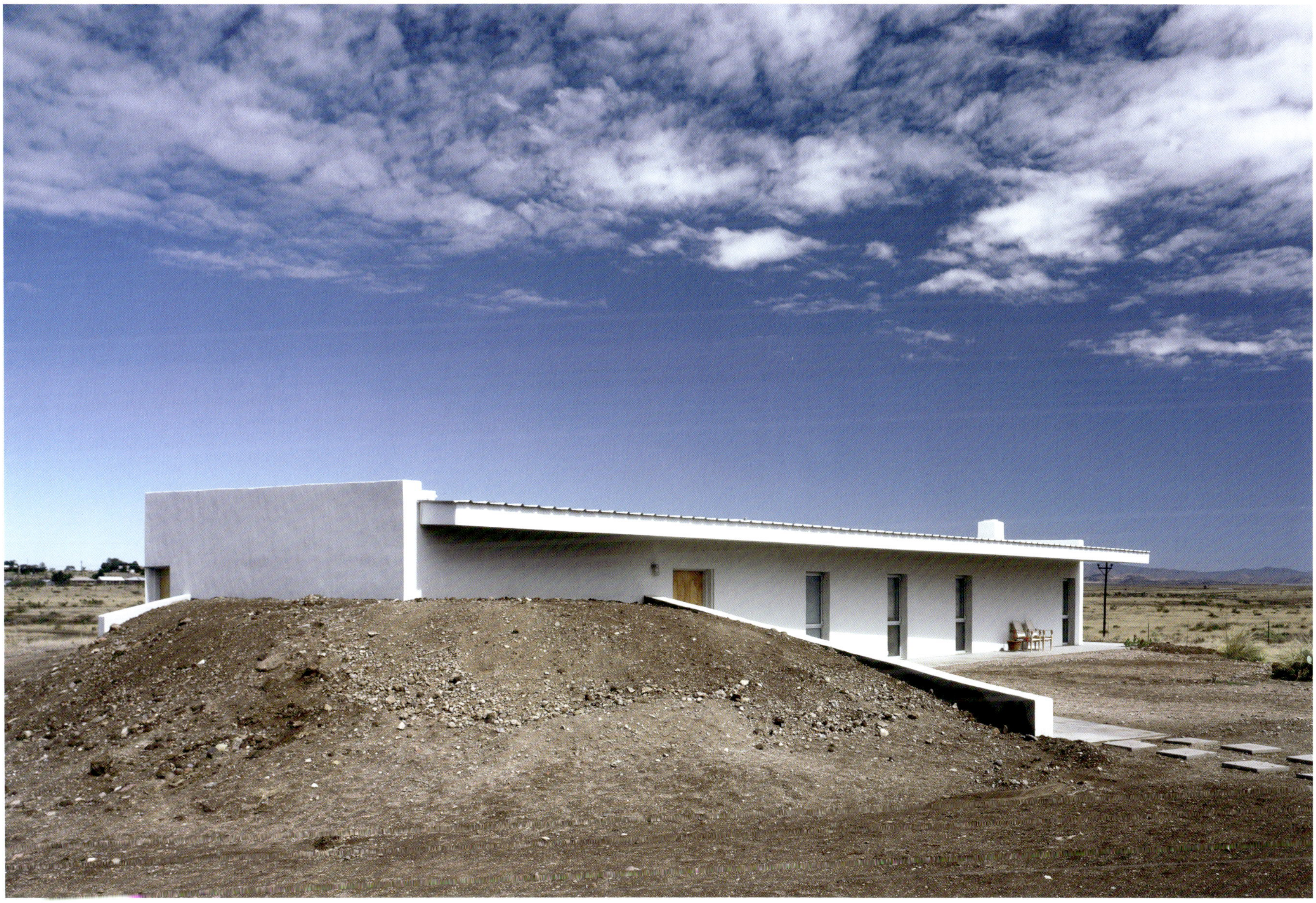

MOUND HOUSE

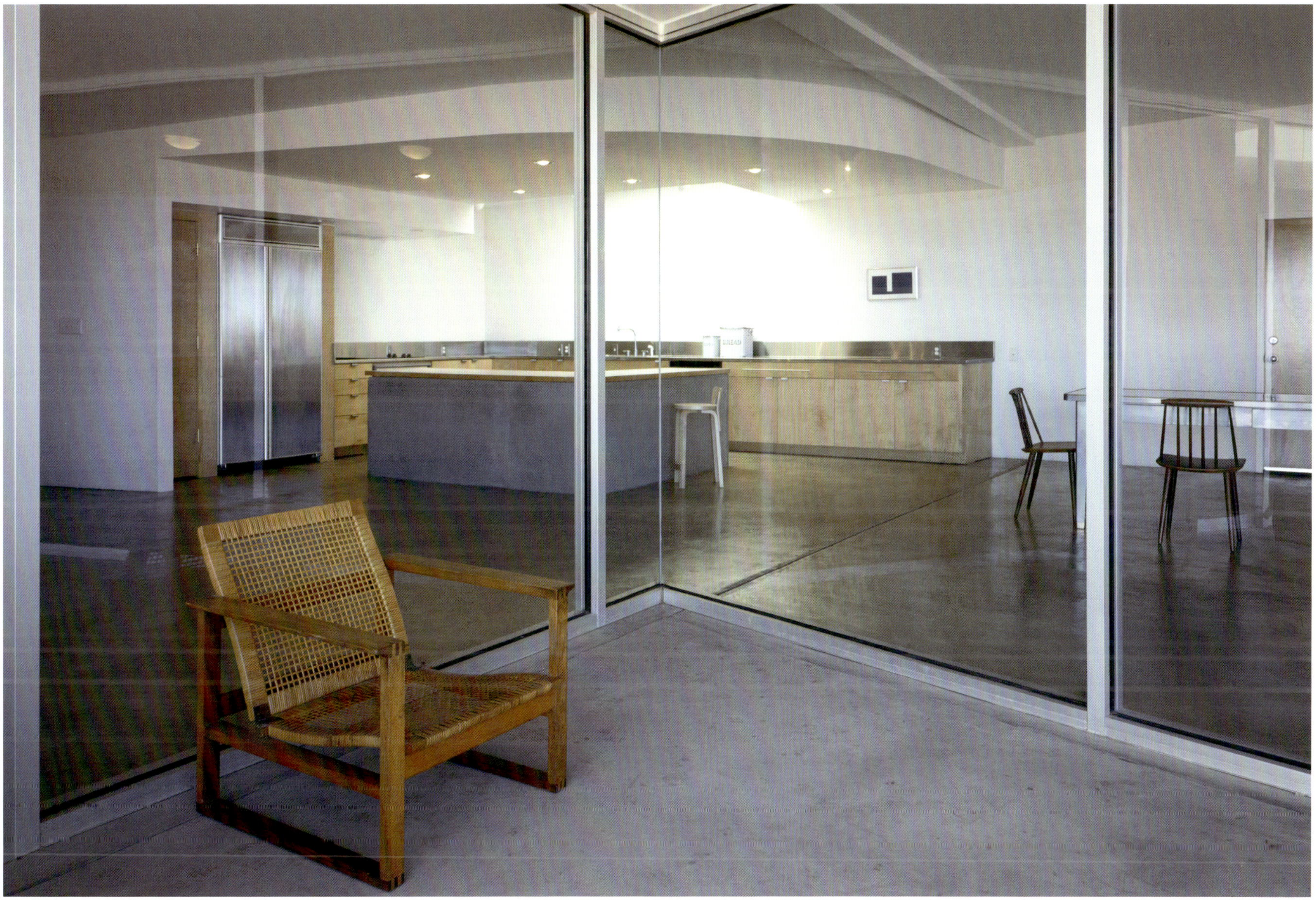

Scott Pask with Graydon Yearick
CASA PASK
2013 | Tucson, AZ, USA

There are two main characteristics forming the identity of Casa Pask, a home in Tucson, Arizona. Originally built in 1968 as an adobe-style building—adobe means "mud brick" in Spanish and can refer to any kind of earth construction—it was bought and redone by Broadway set designer Scott Pask in 2013. He put a strong emphasis on further bringing out the native structure of the pavilion by removing vestiges of the original interiors—dark bookcases, drywall, wall-to-wall carpeting, and forlorn bathroom tiles—thereby exposing features like Douglas fir ceilings, concrete floors, and indigenous adobe brick walls. Mexican Travertine, a type of limestone, was the choice for elements of the kitchen and bathrooms, the only addition aside from hand-plastered walls, neutral steel, and glass. The peach-colored exterior was repainted in a subtle gray selected by Pask to more accurately resemble Sonoran Desert tones.

Among the designer's goals was to invite the sun into the house and follow its ever-changing path through skylights that create shafts of light that shift throughout the day. As many desert visitors can testify, it is the strong white light hitting the earth at a straight angle that accounts for some of a barren landscape's dizzying beauty. As a house of its time, it had been conceived as a bright desert dwelling to start with. Pask further transformed it into a sanctuary flooded with light streaming through multiple windows and skylights, enabling a theatrical interplay with shadows during the day, not unlike a seemingly effortless but meticulously planned scenography on stage.

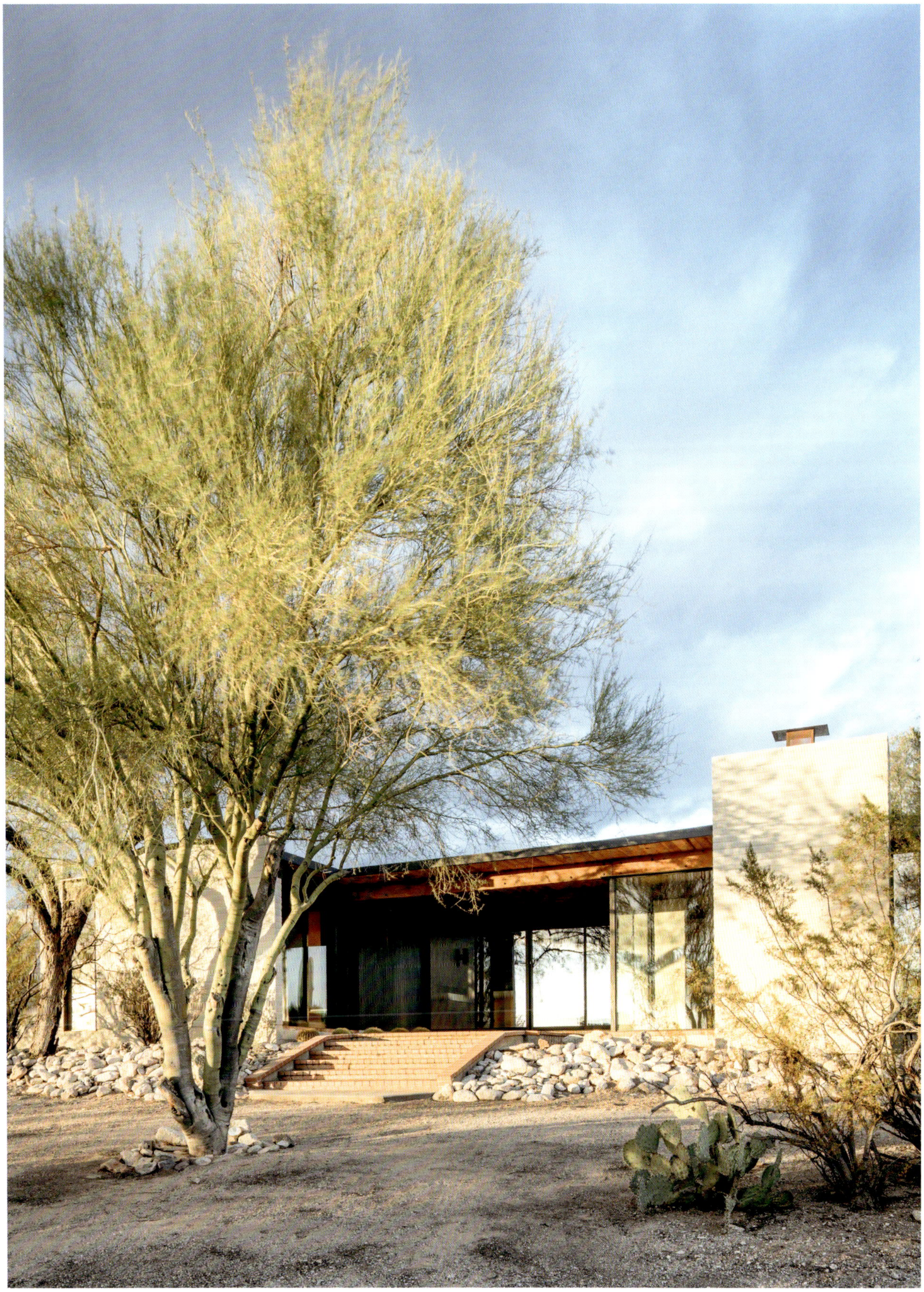

CASA PASK

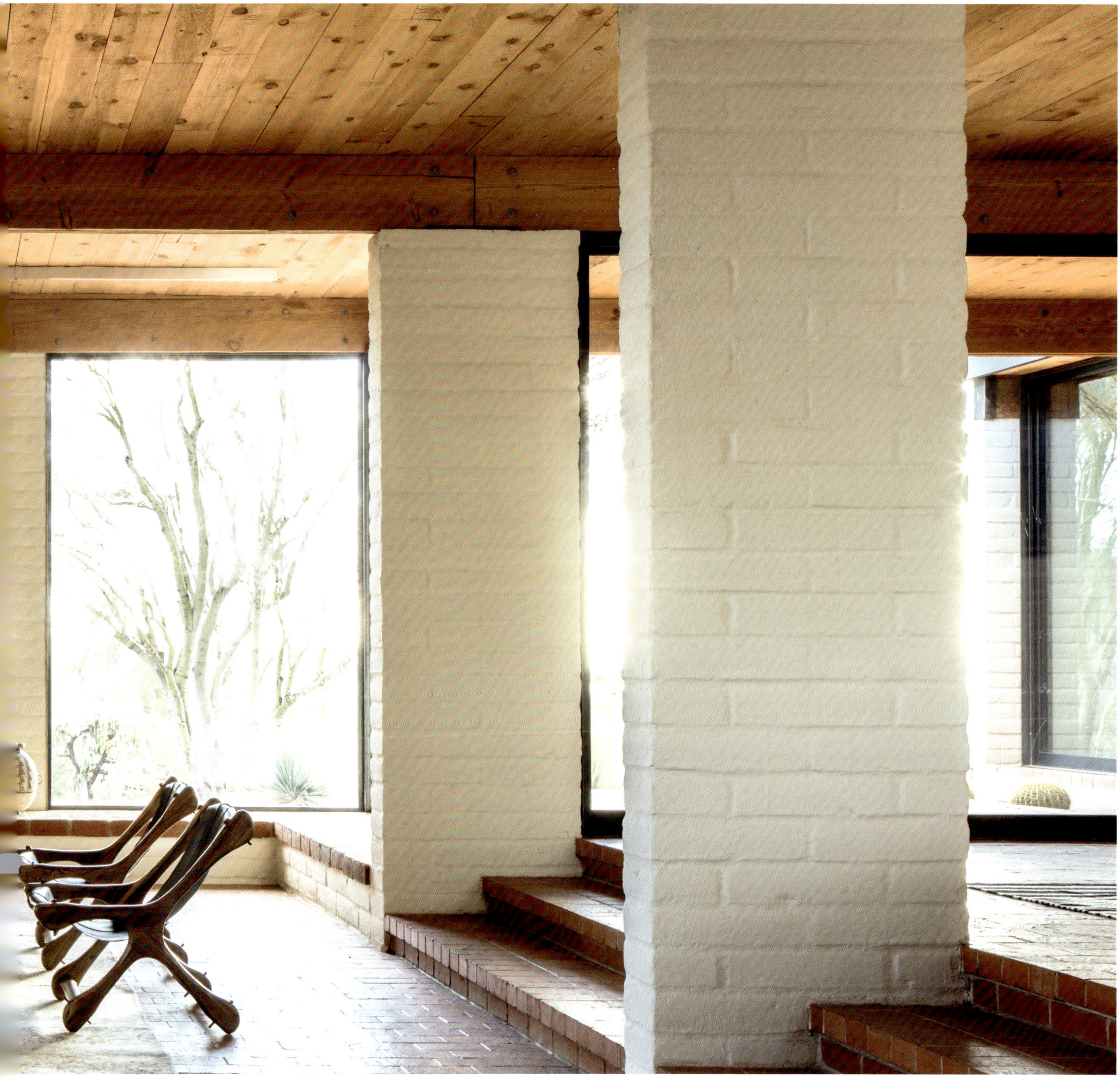

CASA PASK

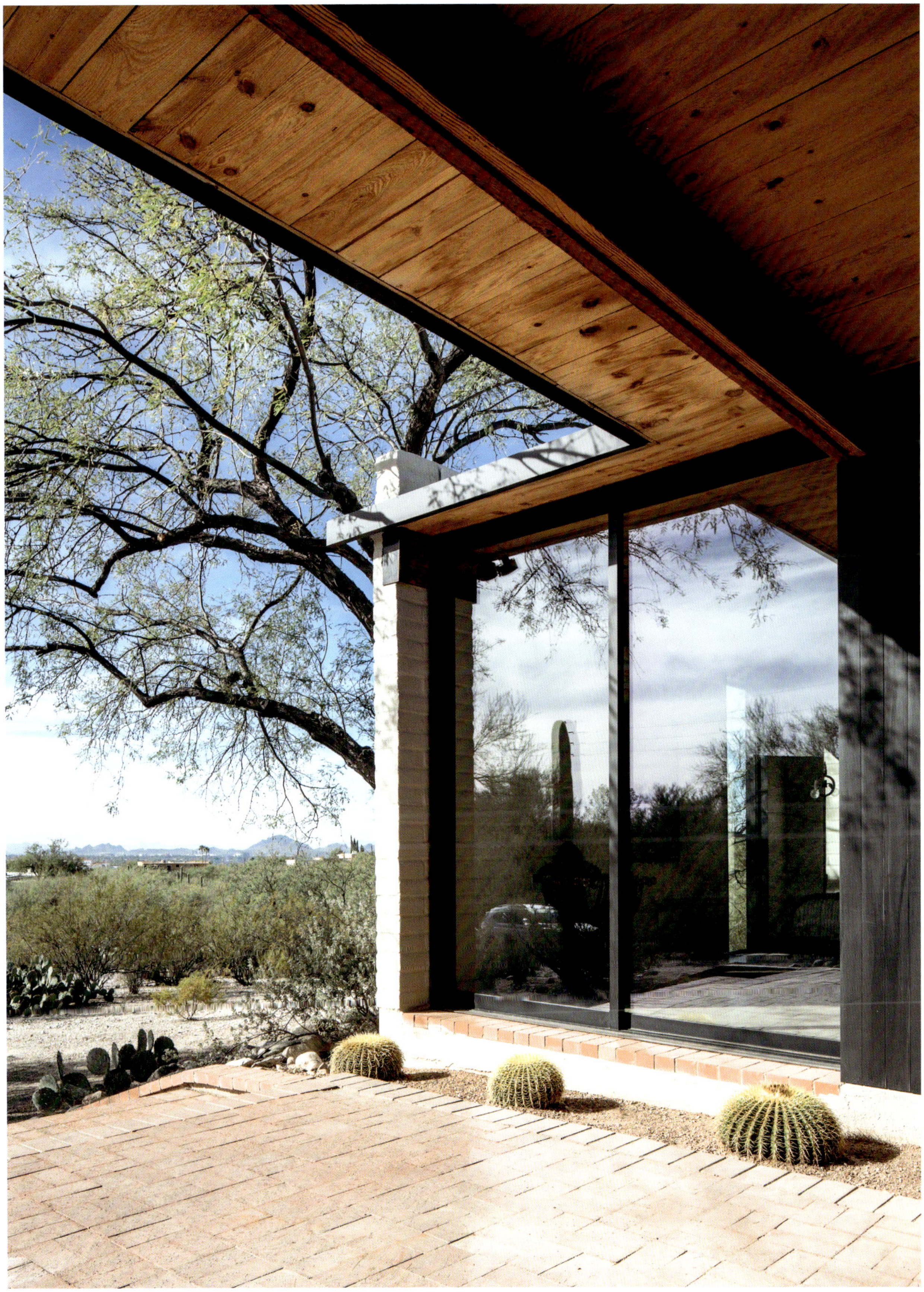

CASA PASK

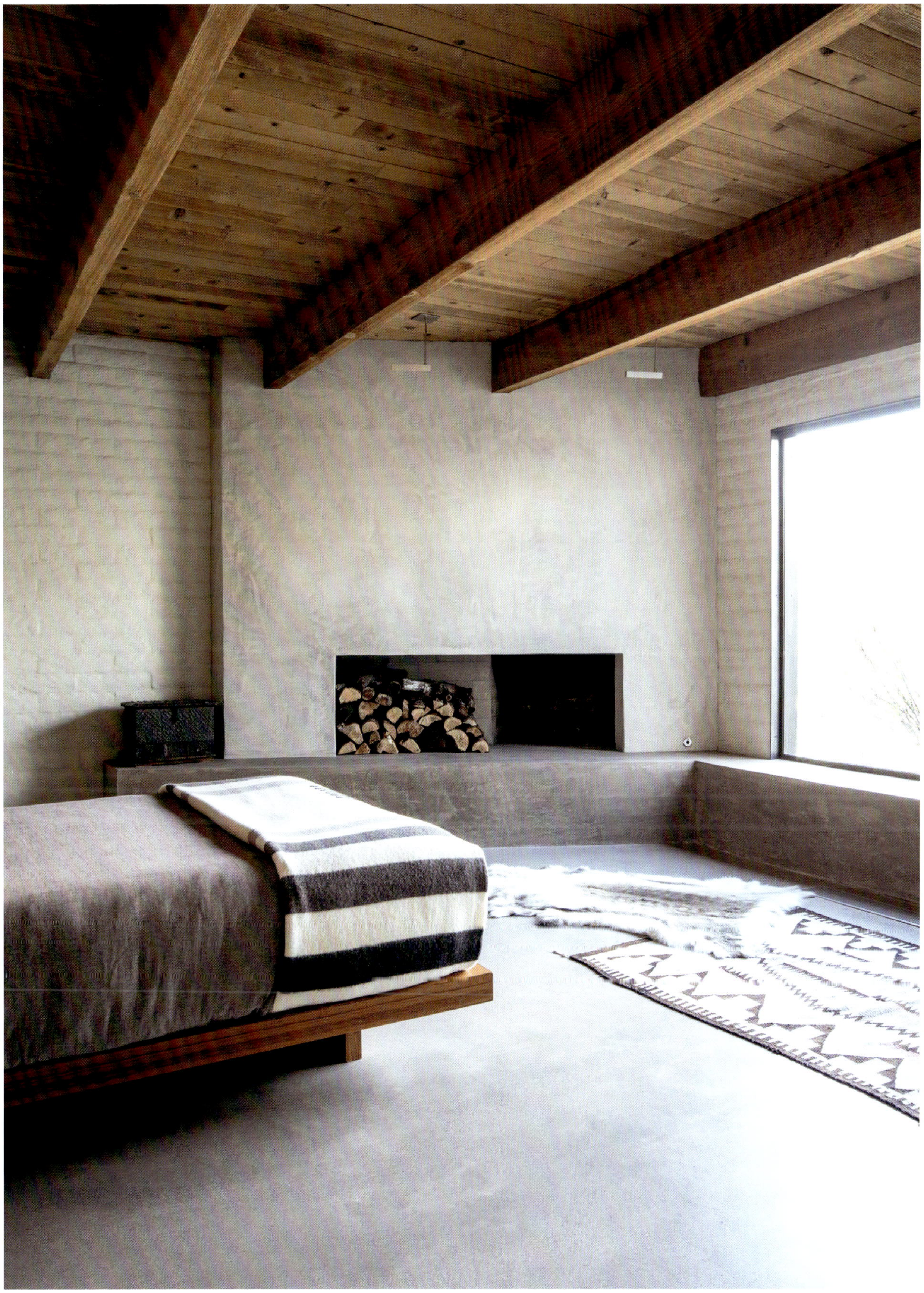

I-10 Studio
AMANGIRI RESORT
2009 | Canyon Point, UT, USA

True luxury lies in understatement, an old truth that rings true at Amangiri Resort's every corner. Located in Canyon Point, Utah, it is within the Grand Circle route that stretches over five states and contains America's largest concentration of monuments and national parks. The monolithic quality of the stunning geologic formations imbues the region with a serene tranquility. The same can be said of Amangiri: no ornamentation disturbs the wandering eye as it follows massively thick concrete and sandstone walls to various cuts and openings, narrow passages, and shaded seating corners. The sense of openness and the monumental scale are calming rather than overwhelming, because it is surrounded by the even greater scale of the immense canyon landscape. Beyond this play of volumes, it is the luminous colorways throughout that demand attention; the resort's palette of gentle whites, grays, and beiges is only occasionally interrupted by spots of yellow or a deep red. At night, the strong architectural geometry is highlighted with gentle lighting, which, if one pays close attention during the day, reveals itself to be the exact opposite of the rugged, organically shaped waves and sharp edges of the surrounding topography. Much of Amangiri's beauty lies in the fact that it does not try to overpower the breathtaking view but rather supports it, silently.

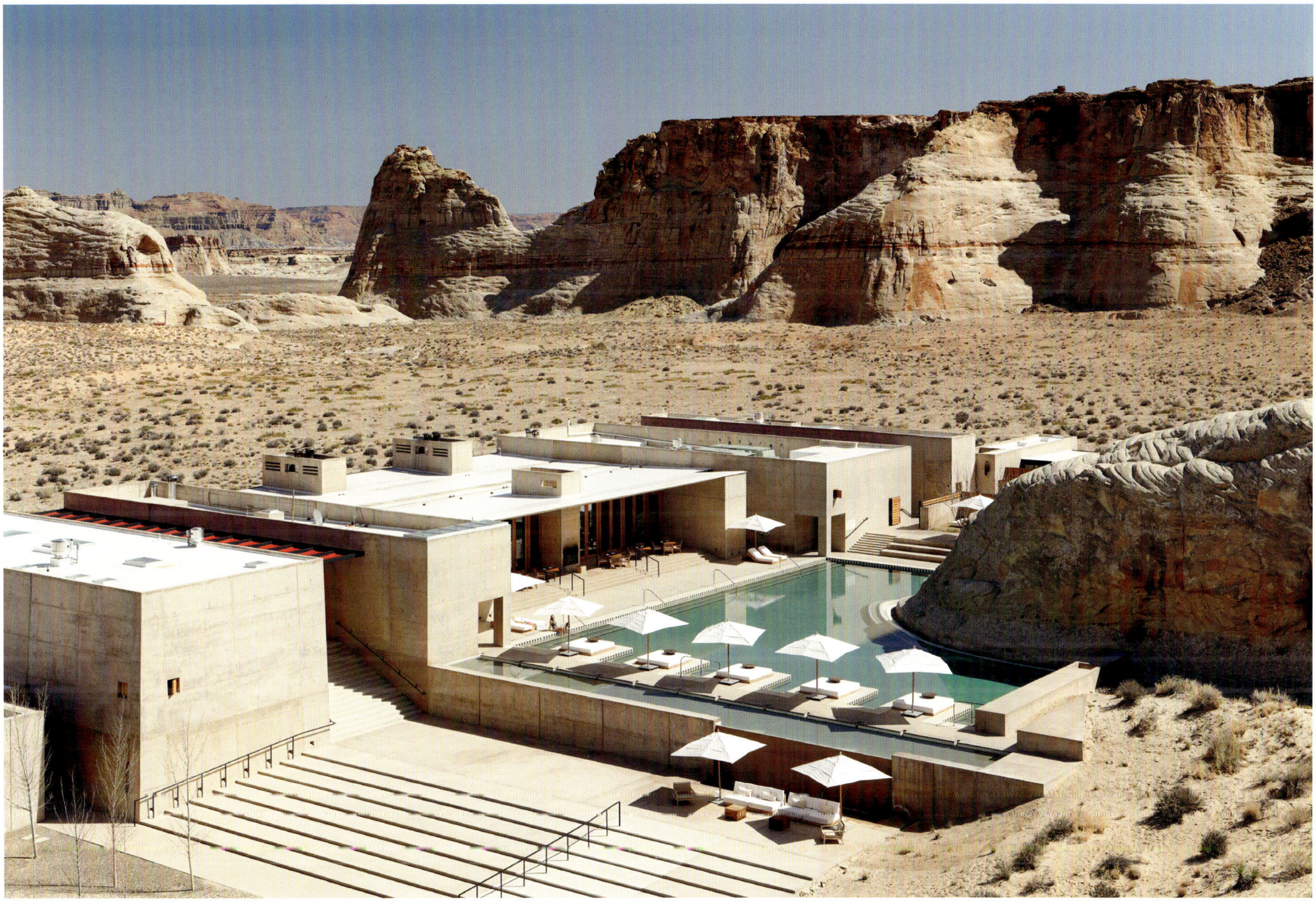

AMANGIRI RESORT

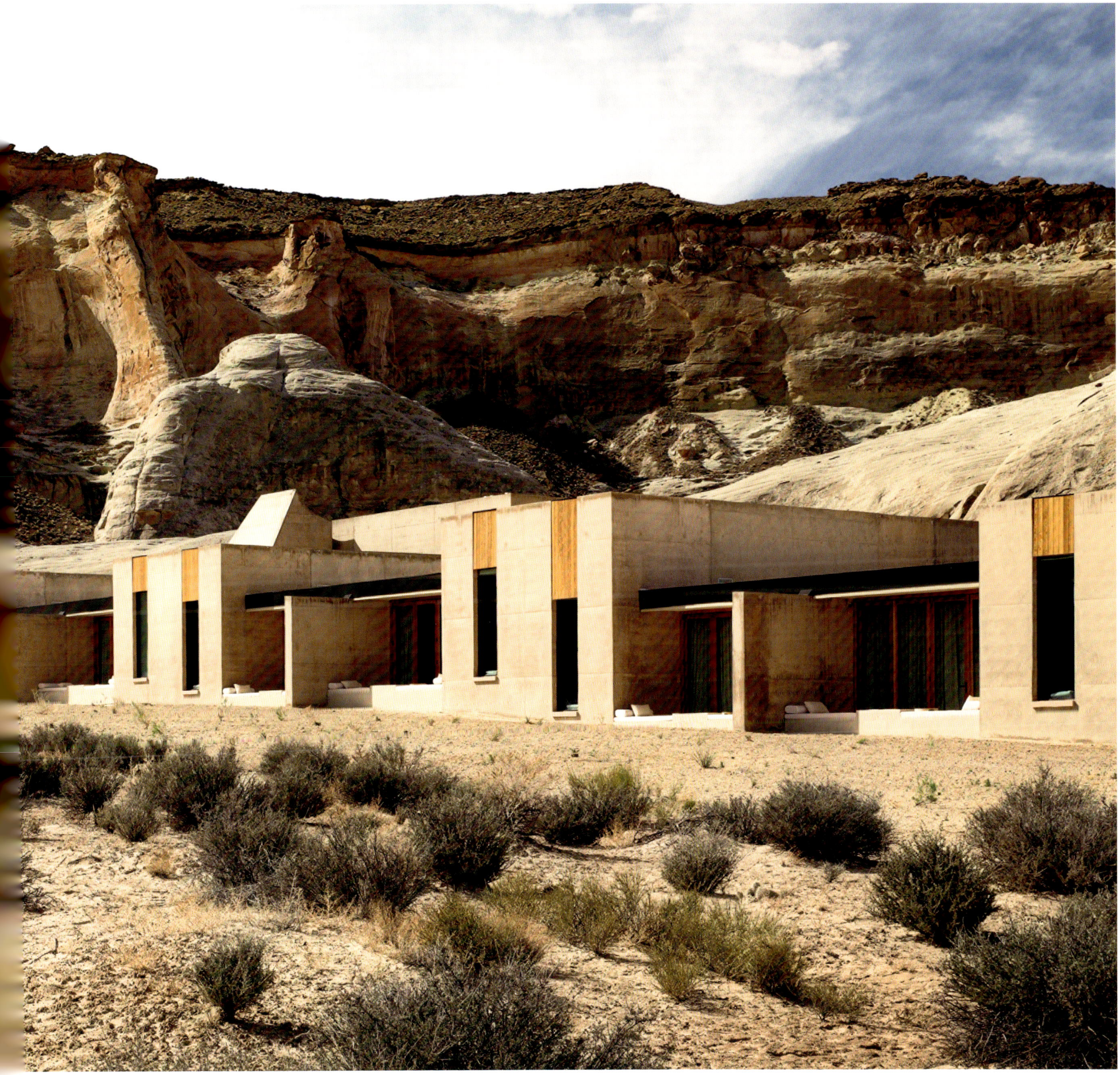

AMANGIRI RESORT

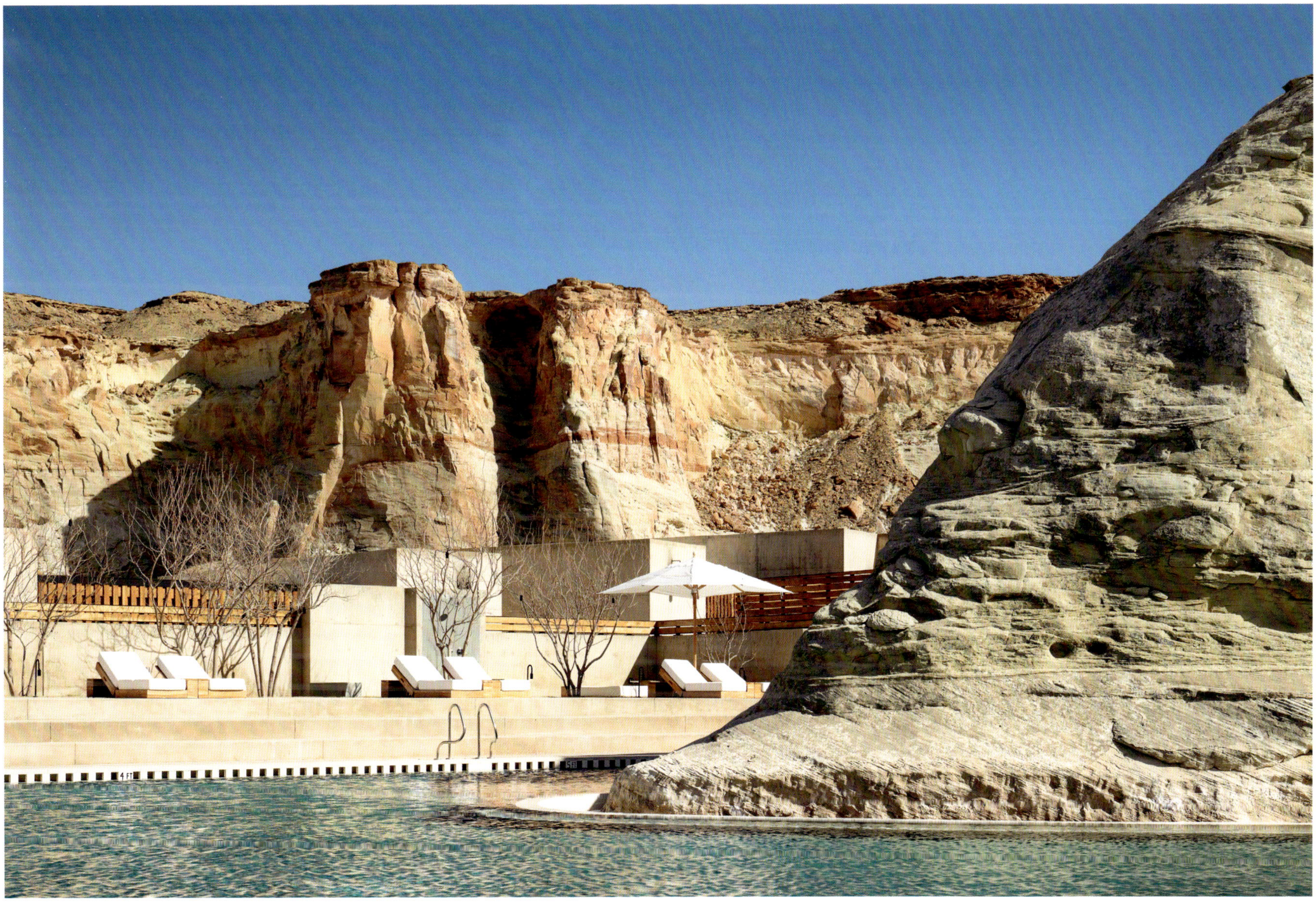

AMANGIRI RESORT

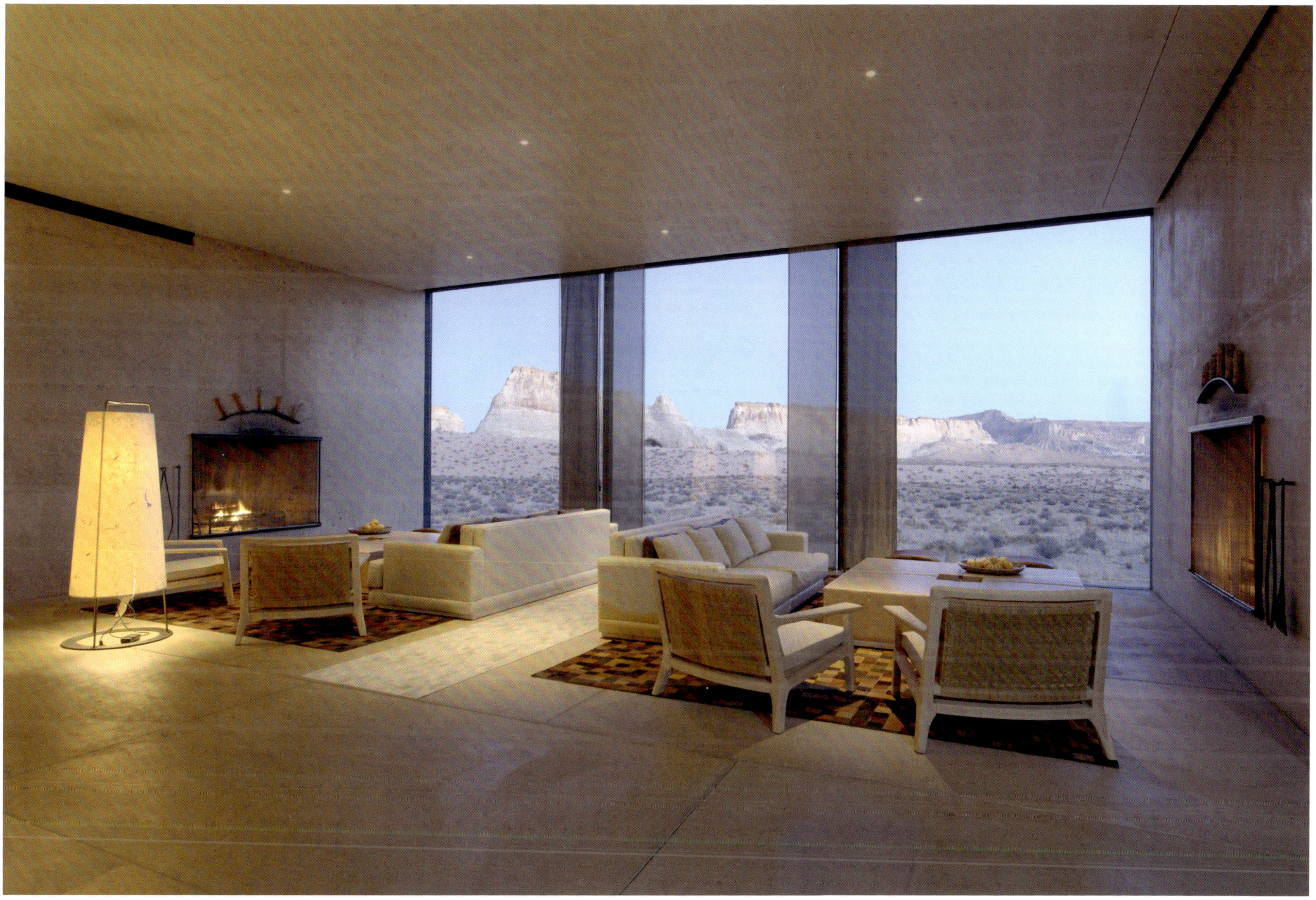

[3] BUILT TO RESIST THE DESERT

170 Dunn & Hillam Architects
DESERT HOUSE

176 Christian Félix et Laetitia Delubac Architectes
ECOLODGE I

180 Kendle Design Collaborative
DESERT WING HOUSE

186 Campos Leckie Studio
ZACATITOS 03

192 Marmol Radziner
MOAB

198 OFIS Arhitekti
THE GLASS PAVILION

204 Tate Studio Architects
SEFCOVIC RESIDENCE

208 Guilhem Eustache
FOBE HOUSE

214 Carlos Jiménez Studio
CROWLEY HOUSE

218 Marwan Al-Sayed, Inc.
STONE COURT VILLA

224 Kendle Design Collaborative
DANCING LIGHT

232 Marwan Al-Sayed, Inc.
DESERT CITY HOUSE

238 Olson Kundig
SAWMILL

246 Wendell Burnette Architects
DESERT COURTYARD HOUSE

Since ancient times, resilience has been an inherent feature of architecture. Buildings are designed to withstand the elements, and depending on the technological possibilities available, architects have introduced innovations to improve their structures' abilities to do so. Recent discourse has mainly focused disaster preparedness, architecture and science uniting to develop buildings that can withstand earthquakes, hurricanes, wildfires, or tsunamis. In the desert, such defiance is needed on a daily basis to respond to its inhospitable beauty. Sometimes this may mean using methods to overpower or outwit nature, with the benefit of ingenuity and funds—perhaps best illustrated by the prevalence of swimming pools and irrigated vegetation in arid zones—to build works of extremely high quality in an environment that challenges the basic skill of survival. It may also, however, mean the opposite: creating small, completely self-sufficient buildings that, unimpressed by outer circumstances, manage to quietly put into use the simplest tools necessary for their own perseverance. Neither of the two scenarios would be possible without a constant pushing forward and a creative ability to physically incorporate innovative practices. The desert has always been an extreme environment and, for a long time, even just attempting to cross it could pose a threat to health or survival. It is modern progress that allows us to spend extended periods of time—a lifetime, perhaps—in hostile environments and attempt to find a balance between radically taming one's surroundings and slowly, thoughtfully adjusting to them.

Celebrated on the next pages are examples by architects who challenge the status quo and push for architecture to discover and facilitate new possibilities of living.

Dunn & Hillam Architects
DESERT HOUSE
2013 | Alice Springs, Australia

Alice Springs is part of Australia's original outback and home to one of the largest Aboriginal populations in the country. The mostly dry Todd River cuts through the town and the MacDonnell Ranges to the west; the wider area is composed of multiple desert areas. According to the architects, for any living thing to survive in these harsh conditions requires patience, economy, strength, and responsiveness. In order to facilitate economy, Desert House was sited among layers of hard rock to take advantage of the earth's stable core temperature for cooling in the hot summer and warmth in winter. A slanted fly roof of corrugated steel cleverly generates shadow from the top, thereby shading a central courtyard that in turn sends cool air from the ground up for ventilation through floor-level windows. Warm air is released through roof vents to encourage the cycle. Its progressively sustainable program gives the modernist house a distinct deconstructivist aesthetic, ever so slight but nevertheless present. Photovoltaic arrays, solar evacuated tubes, and CoolMax coating rarely receive such overt placement; mechanical elements are often integrated or tucked away in an attempt to not lay bare the guts of a building. In the Desert House, the display of functional resilience is elevated to have its own appeal.

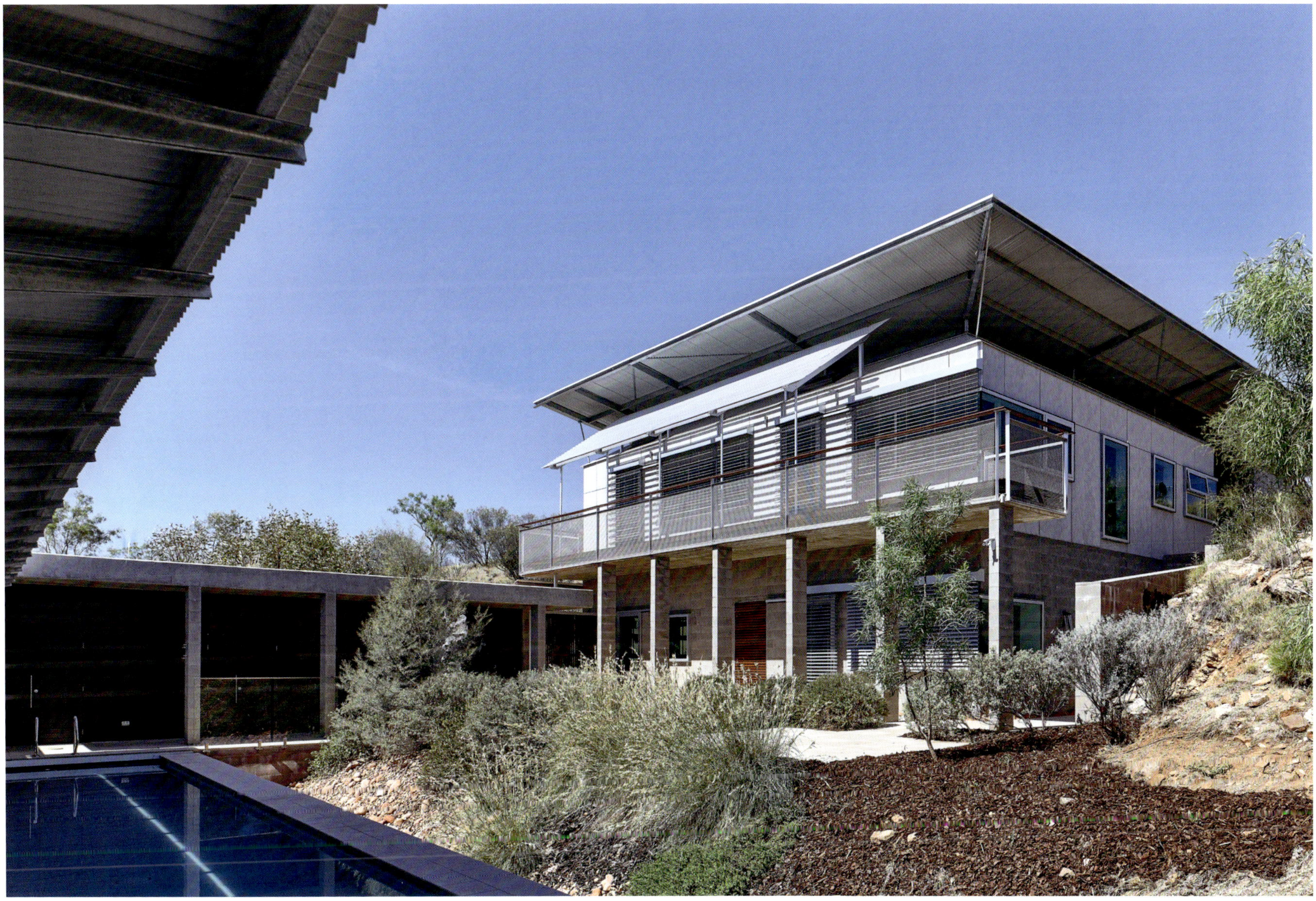

DESERT HOUSE

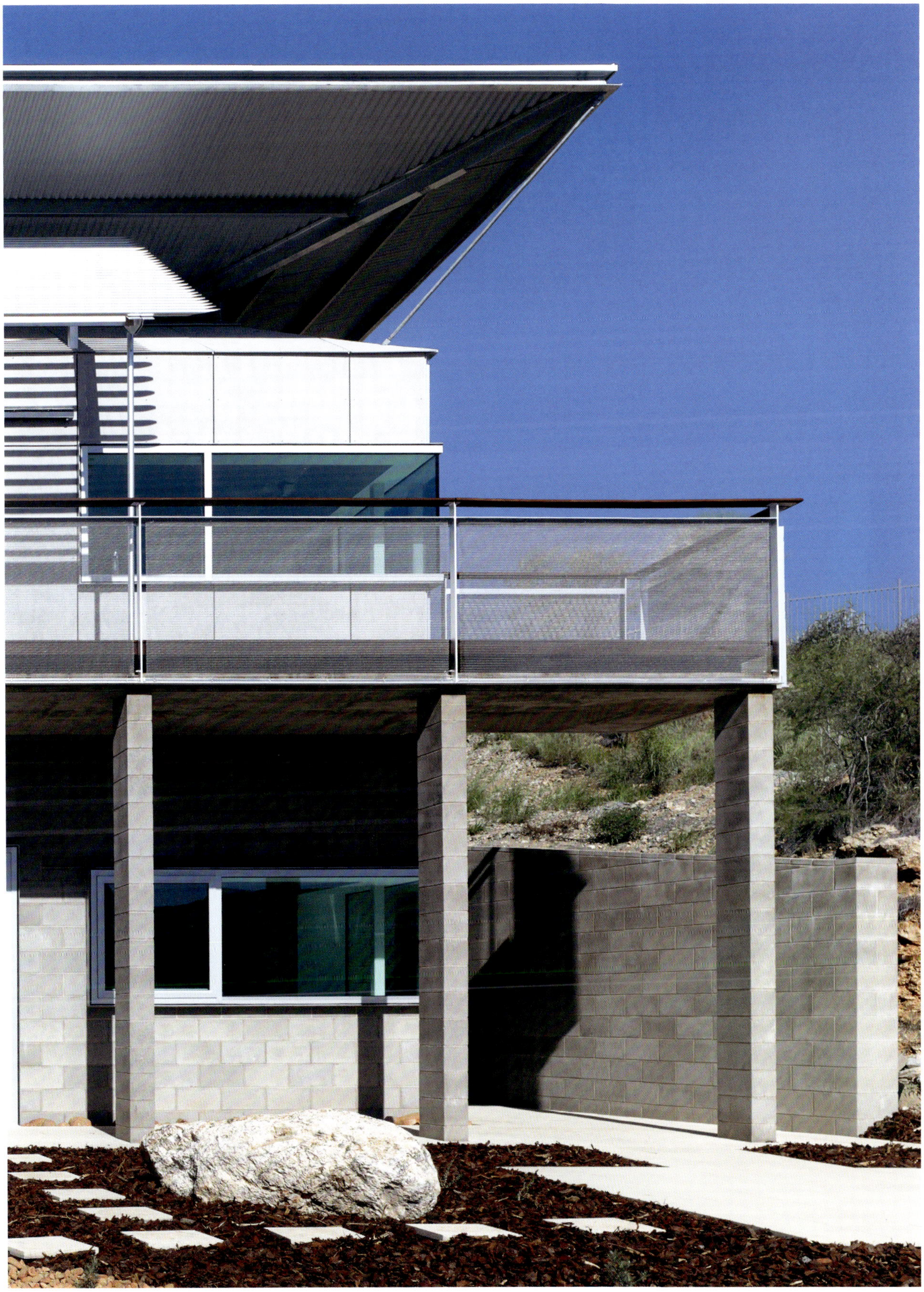

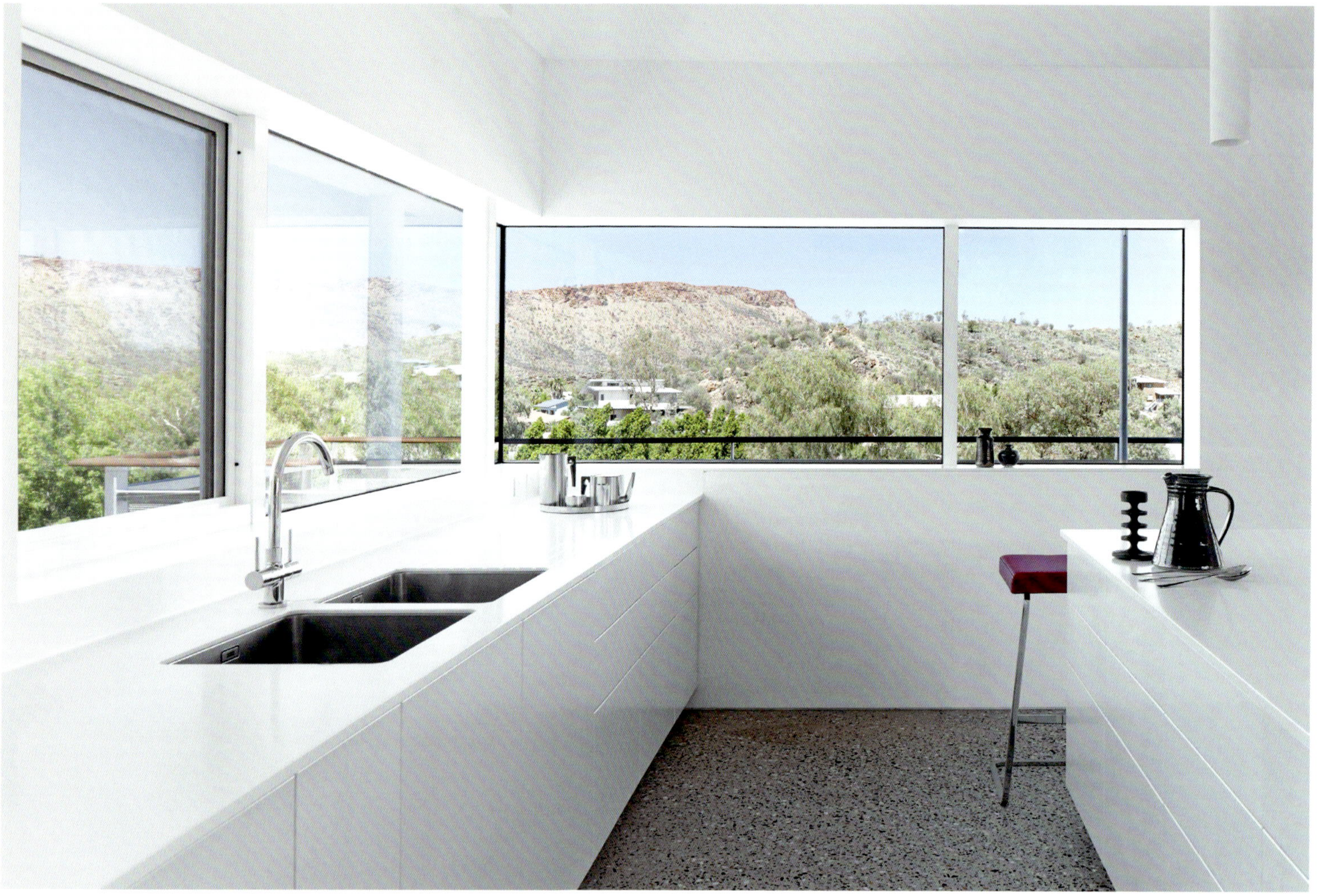

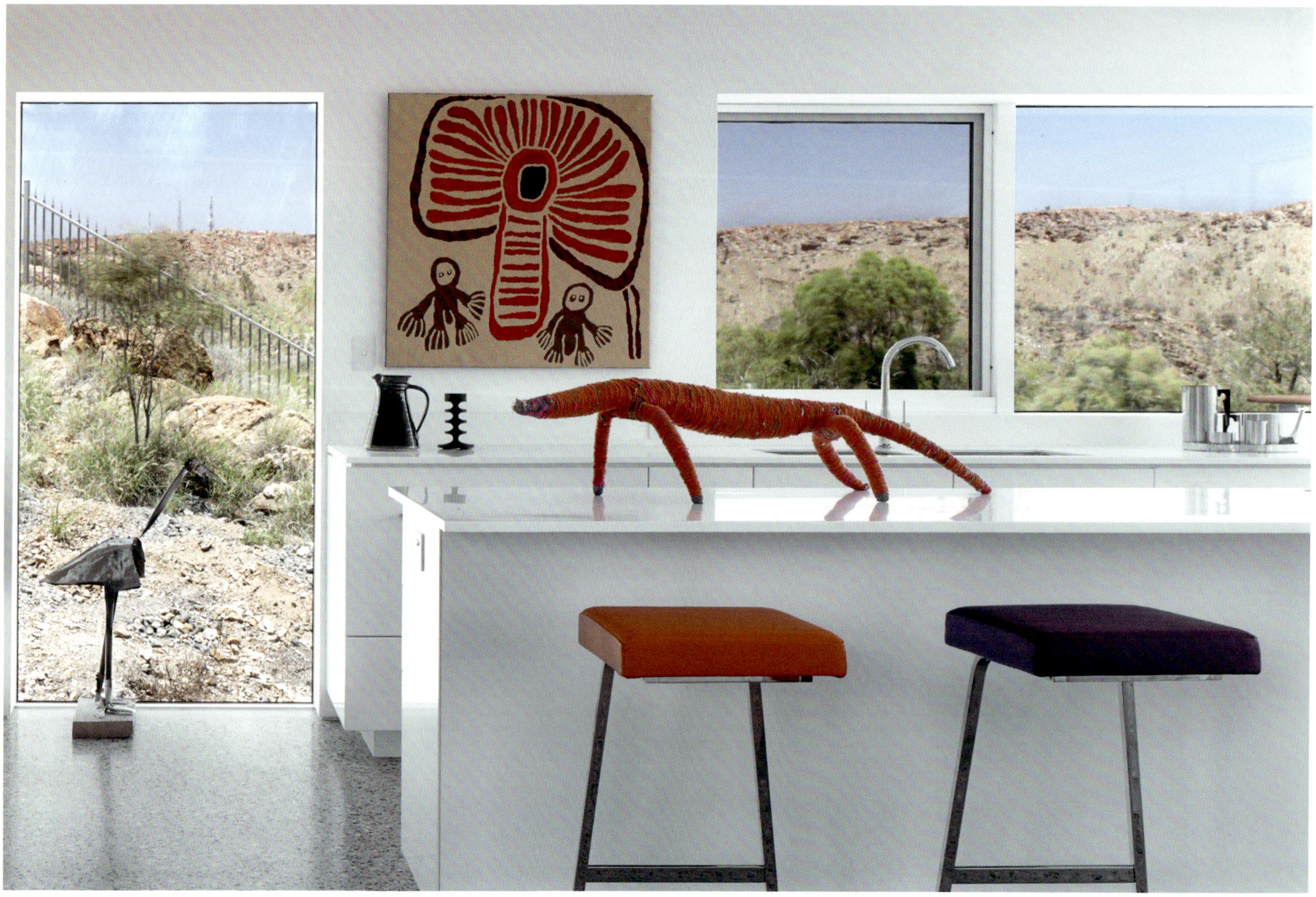

DESERT HOUSE

Christian Félix et Laetitia Delubac Architectes
ECOLODGE I
2011 | Siwa, Egypt

Located 350 miles (563 kilometers) west of Cairo and just thirty miles (forty-eight kilometers) east of the Libyan border, Egypt's Siwa Oasis is a very secluded settlement found at the bottom of Adrere Amellal, meaning "white mountain" in Tasiwit, the Berber dialect of this area. Mimicking the form of a quadrat that opens out on all four sides—with a pergola facing the adjacent salt lake— the floor plan of Ecolodge I clearly reflects the ideas of remoteness and serenity. Together with tradition, these are the concepts dominating most logistics and countenance, with the building materials of mud, sun-fired bricks, palm wood, reeds, red stone, and salt stone exclusively locally sourced. To build the walls, craftsmen harvested sun-dried salt from the lake and mixed it with mud and sand to make *kershef*, a traditional local building material and efficient insulator that helps keep indoor temperatures mild in every season. Candles placed in small niches in the thick walls light the way through the house. This feature is not just decorative but also performs a necessary function, as there is no electricity in the house—a gesture that can be understood as both strictly traditional and radically modern, as it succeeds in relieving visitors of the never-ending flow of technological chatter. And water? To really keep the impact on the land minimal, fresh water is sourced straight from a spring at the base of the mountain, later to be purified and recycled into nature again through a reed grove.

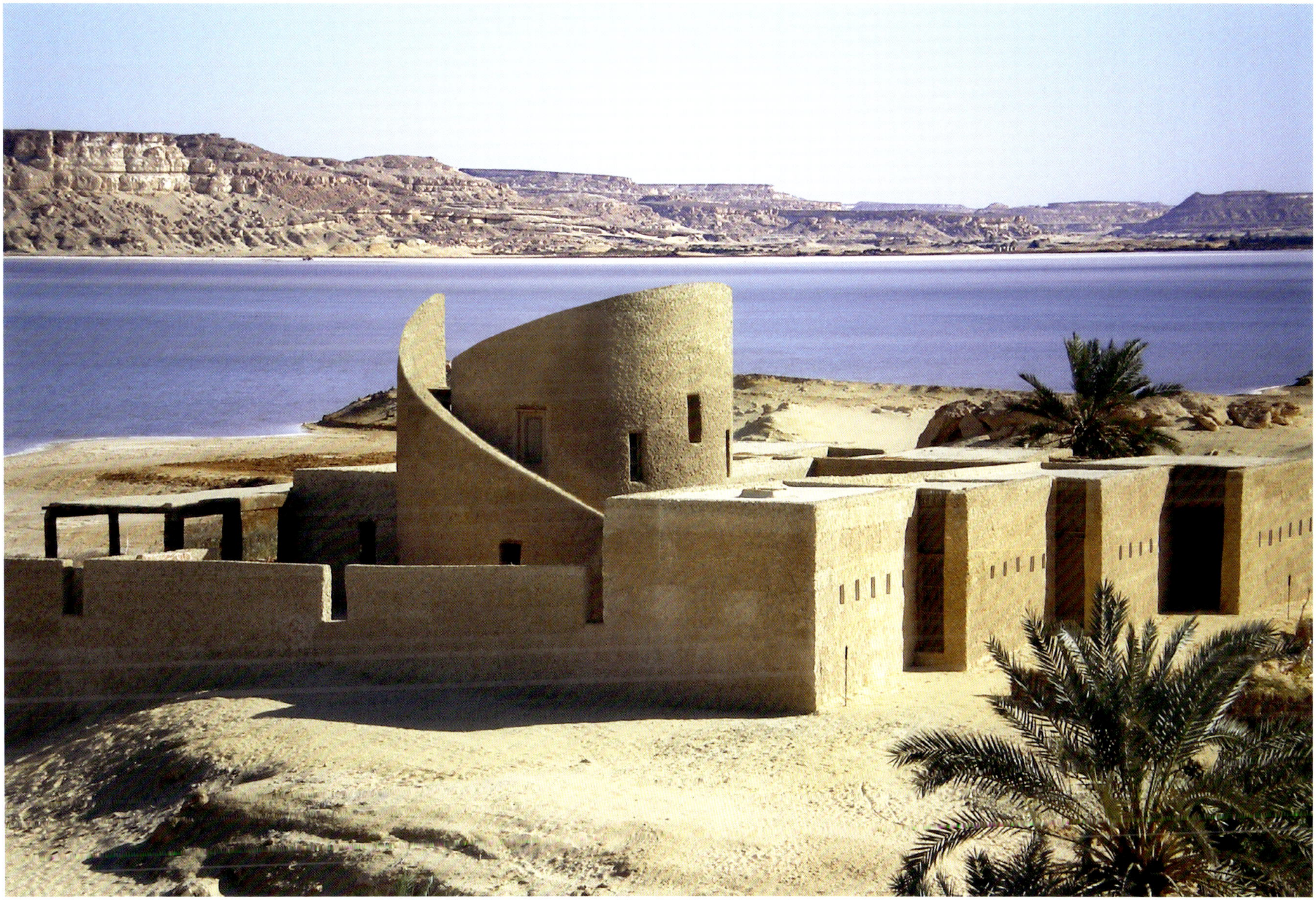

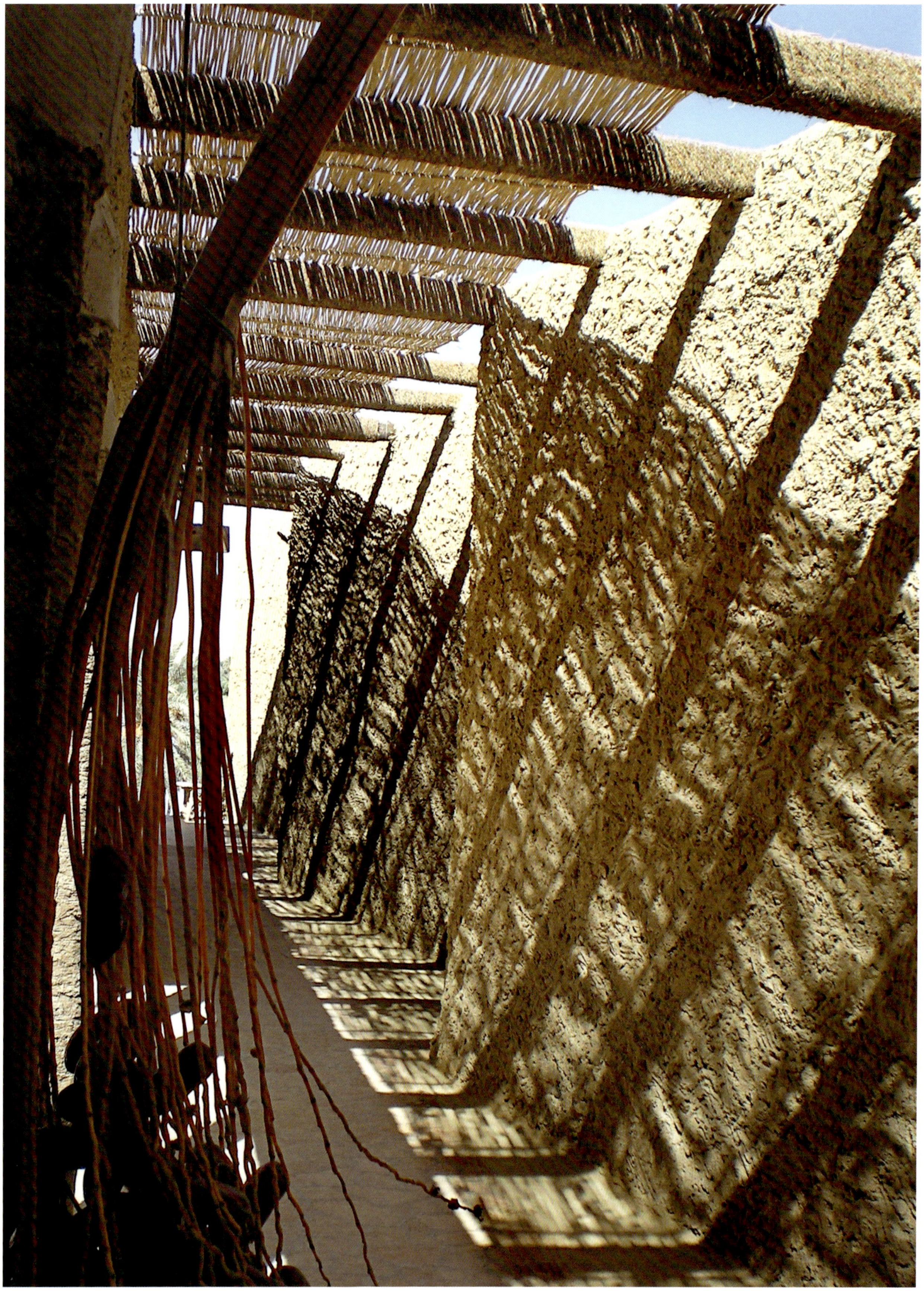

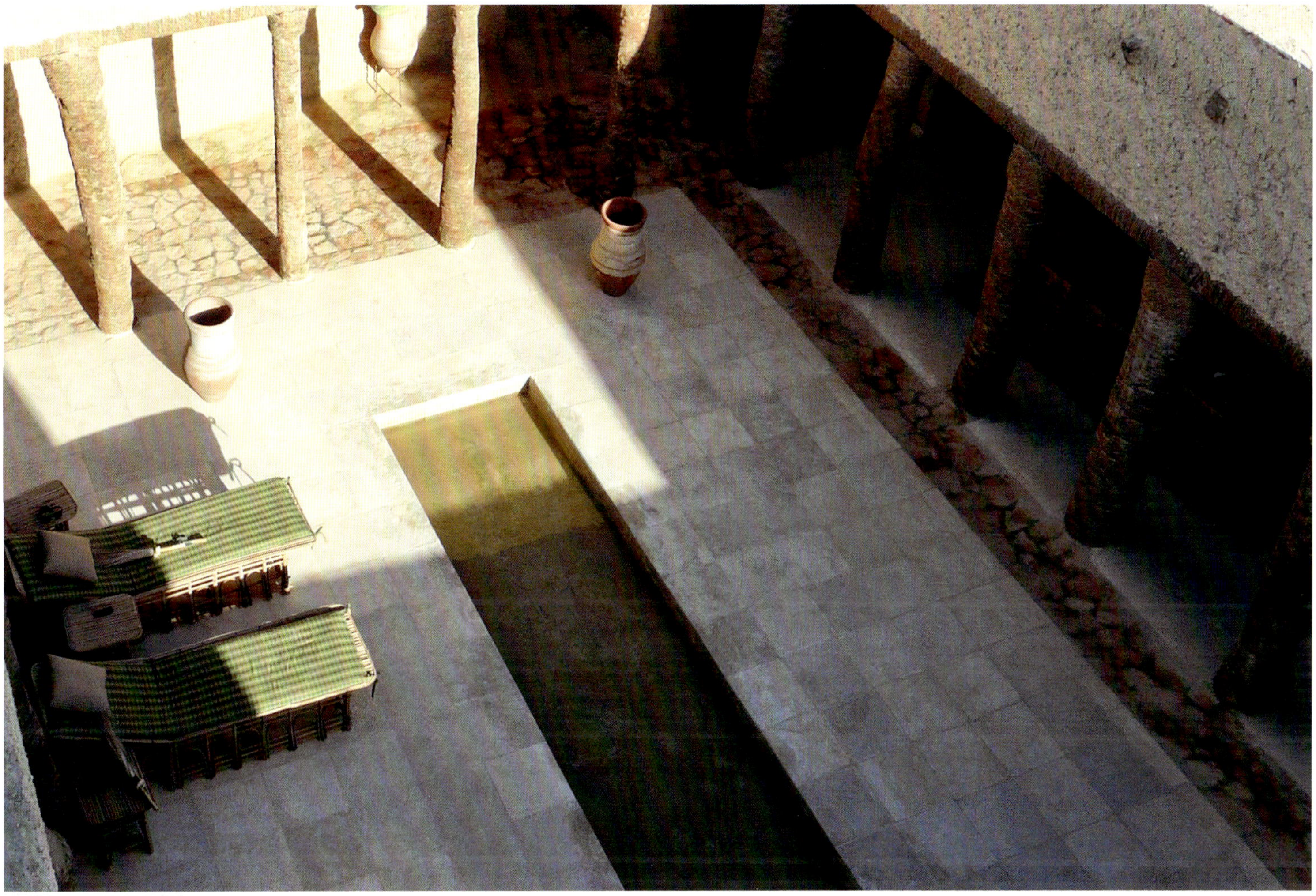

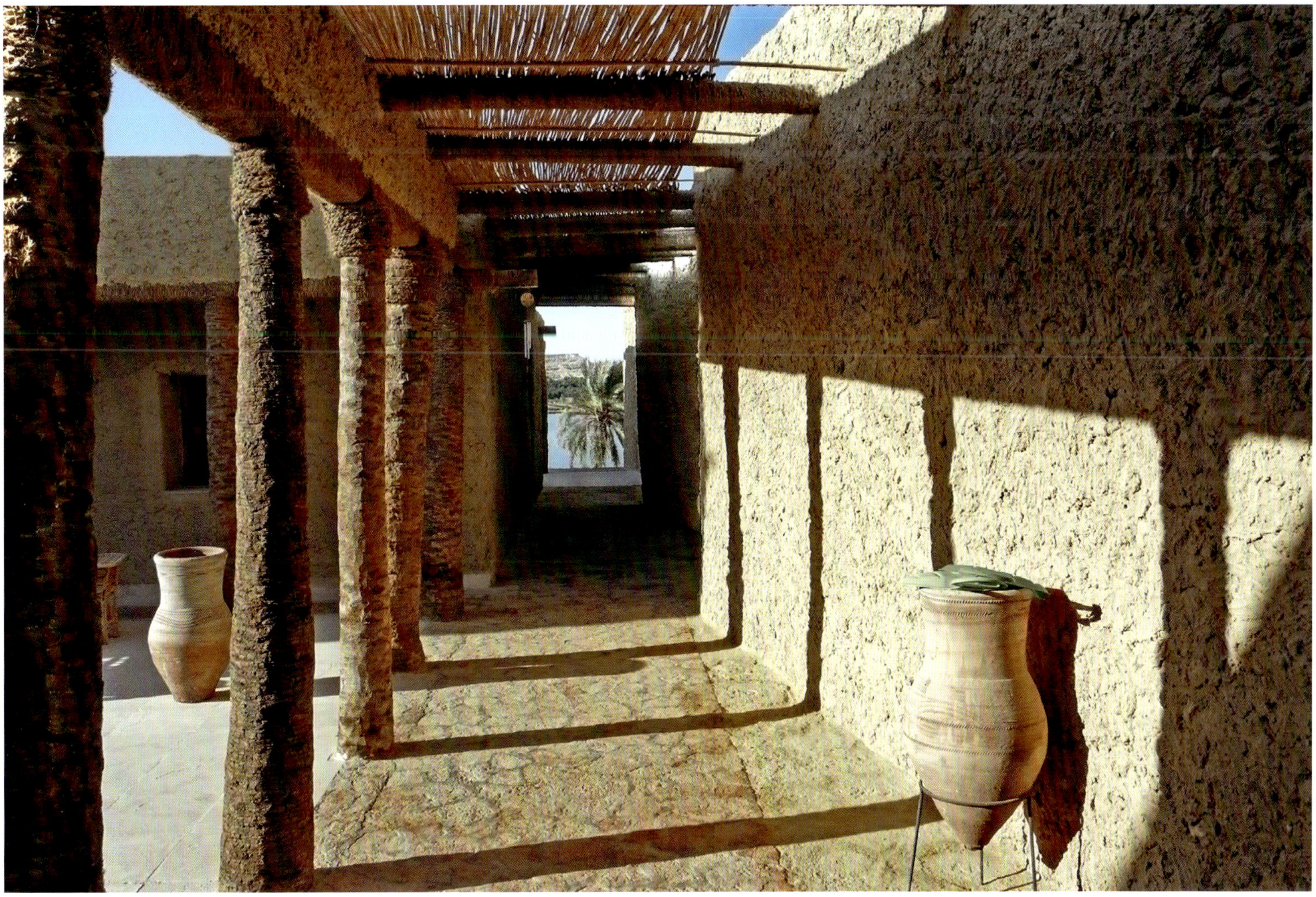

Kendle Design Collaborative
DESERT WING HOUSE
2013 | Scottsdale, AZ, USA

Rock solid, even when viewed from miles afar, is an accurate description of this Scottsdale, Arizona, residence. Desert Wing House's tremendously thick rammed-earth walls protrude from the Sonoran Desert; an equally immense overhanging roof of angled planes—designed to collect rainwater for circulation to the thirsty vegetation below—appears to float over the structure, like the wing of its name, and it very nearly does. The thick roofline, edged in locally mined copper cladding that radiates a warm orange glow when hit by the sun, lies above a thin strip of glass, creating the odd sense of lightness between the heavy forms.

Heat-balancing raw concrete walls are complemented by polished concrete floors and wooden ceilings. An overflowing pool, directly accessible from a large terrace off the open living space as well as a bedroom, is divided by a tall rammed-earth wall from which springs a fanciful fountain. It is not impossible to tame the desert.

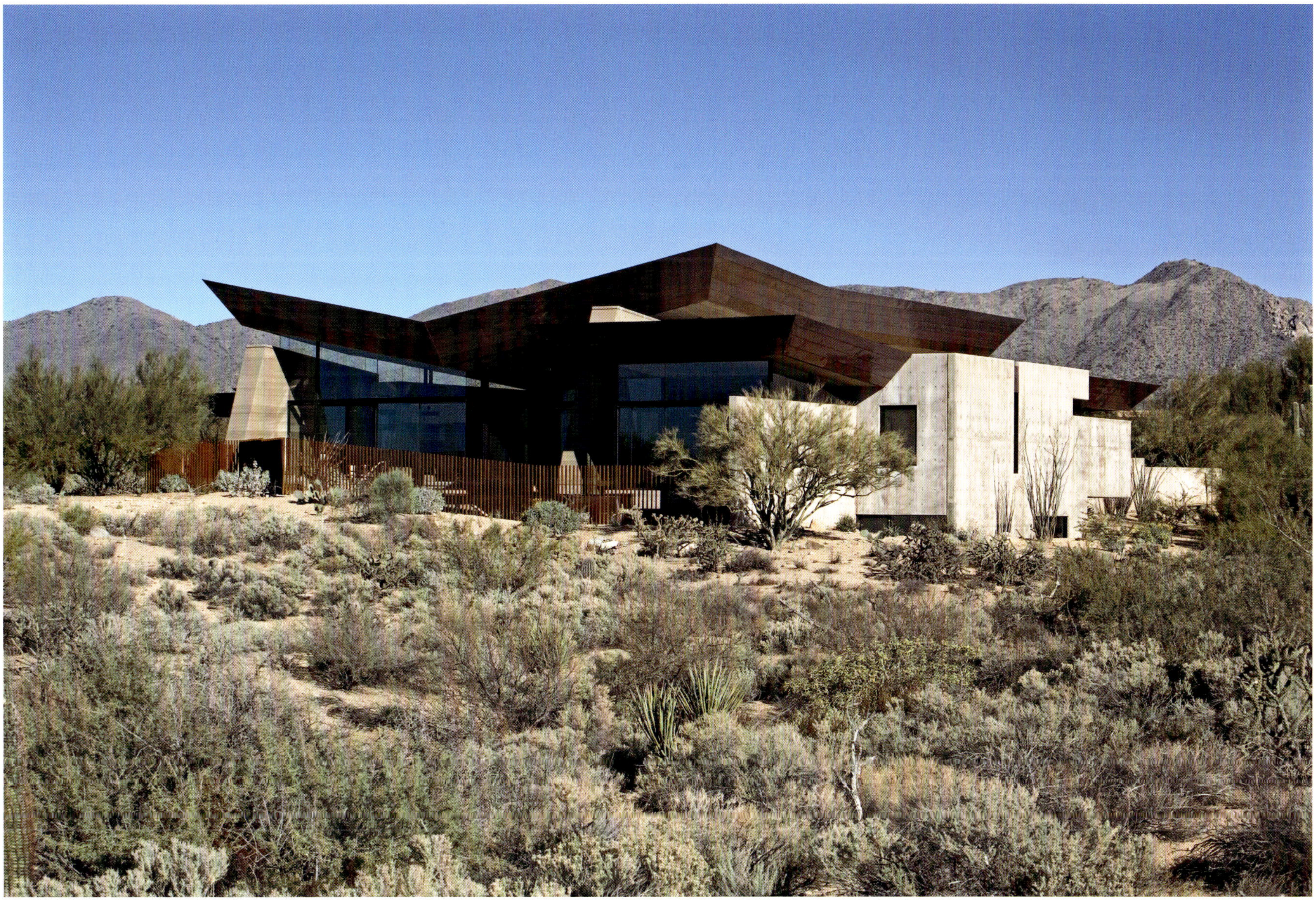

DESERT WING HOUSE

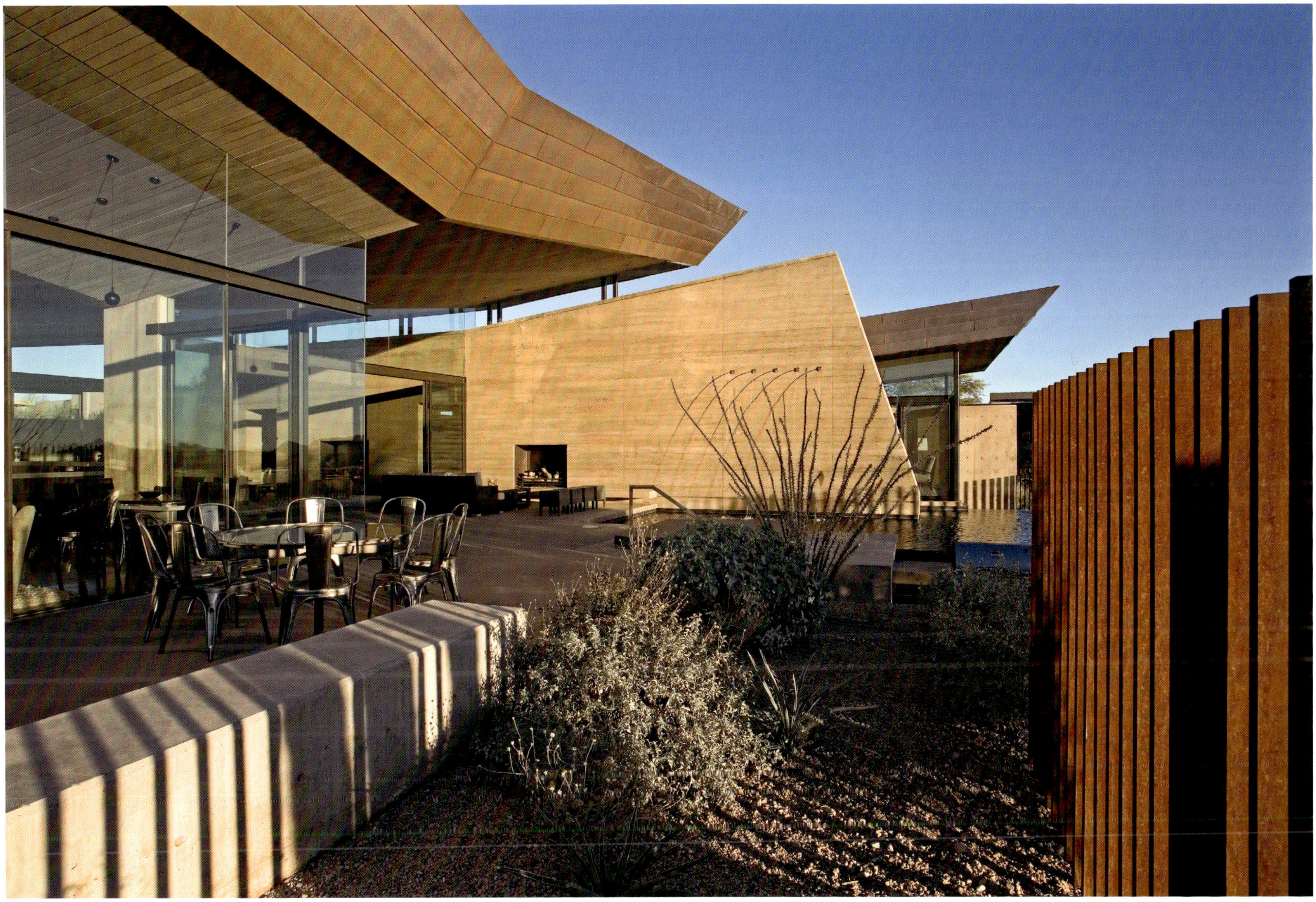

DESERT WING HOUSE

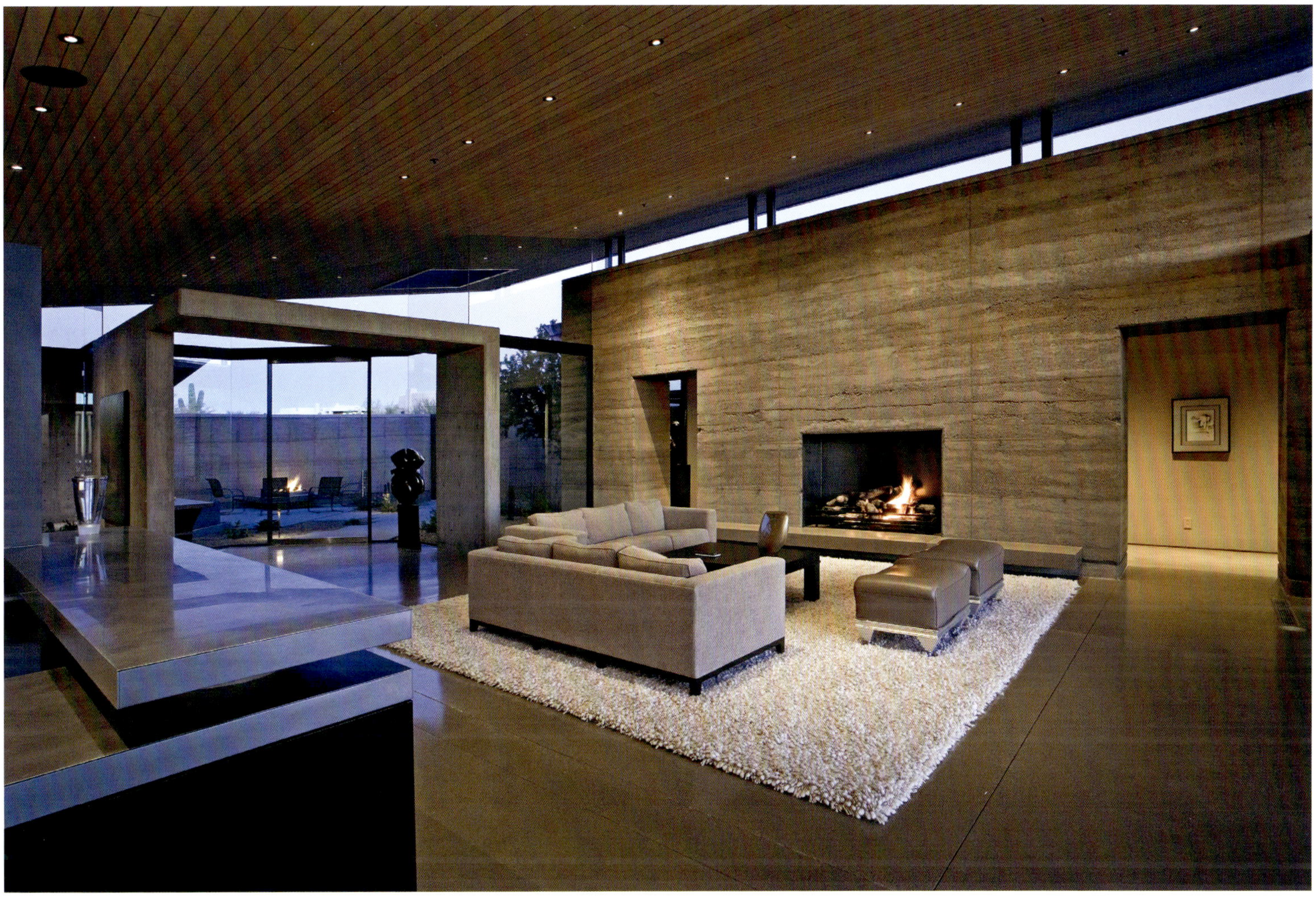

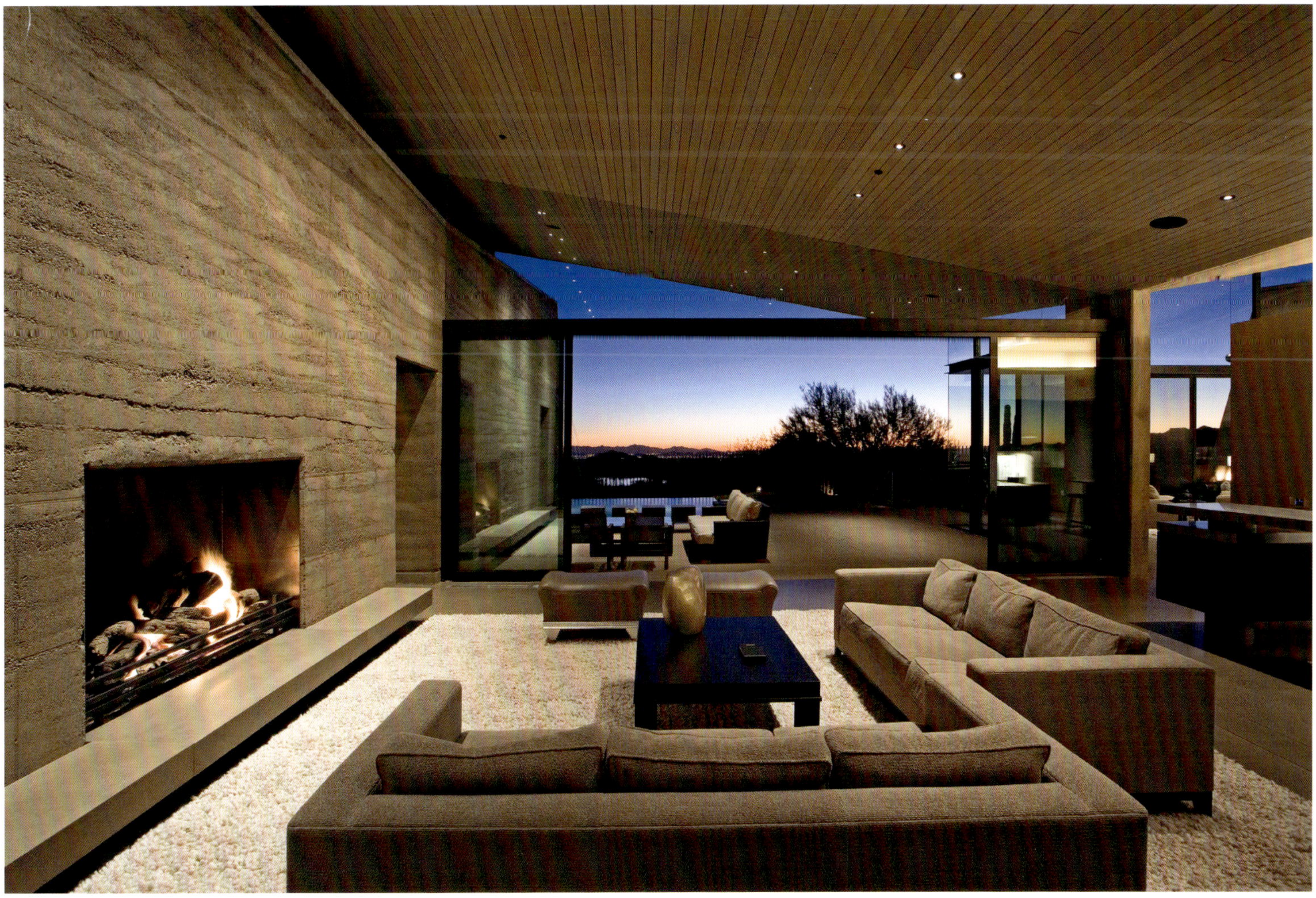

Campos Leckie Studio
ZACATITOS 03
2011 | Los Zacatitos, Mexico

On the Sea of Cortez north of Cabo San Lucas in Mexico's Baja California Sur lies Los Zacatitos, known mostly for its long beach of fine sand. On a stretch of land facing this beautiful vista, architects Michael Leckie and Javier Campos have constructed a series of prototype dwellings to explore the possibilities of sustainable off-grid construction in extreme climates. The third study—Zacatitos 03—consciously investigates the formal expressions of the local construction methodology based on the insulating properties of reinforced-concrete panels. Organized in a linear progression across the sloping side, the compact dwelling is lined on two sides with spaced panels forming breezeways that respond to the moving sun and the direction of prevailing breezes to minimize excessive heat and maximize ventilation. The simple palette of the materials—white and gray concrete, glass, steel, and aluminum—is a direct reflection of the monochromatic character of the desert. The allure of this project clearly lies in this kind of simplicity, partly facilitated through a commitment to a modest budget.

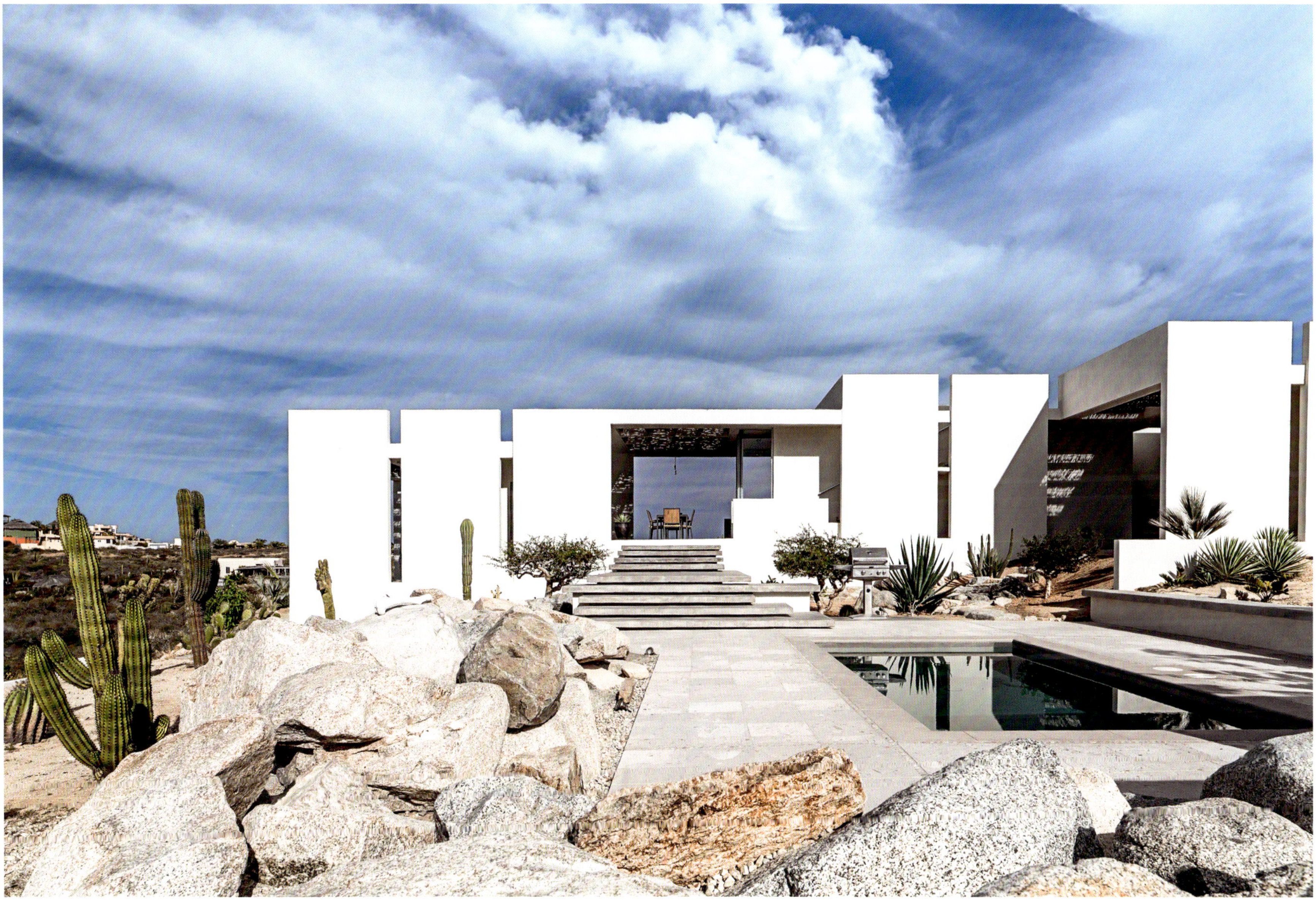

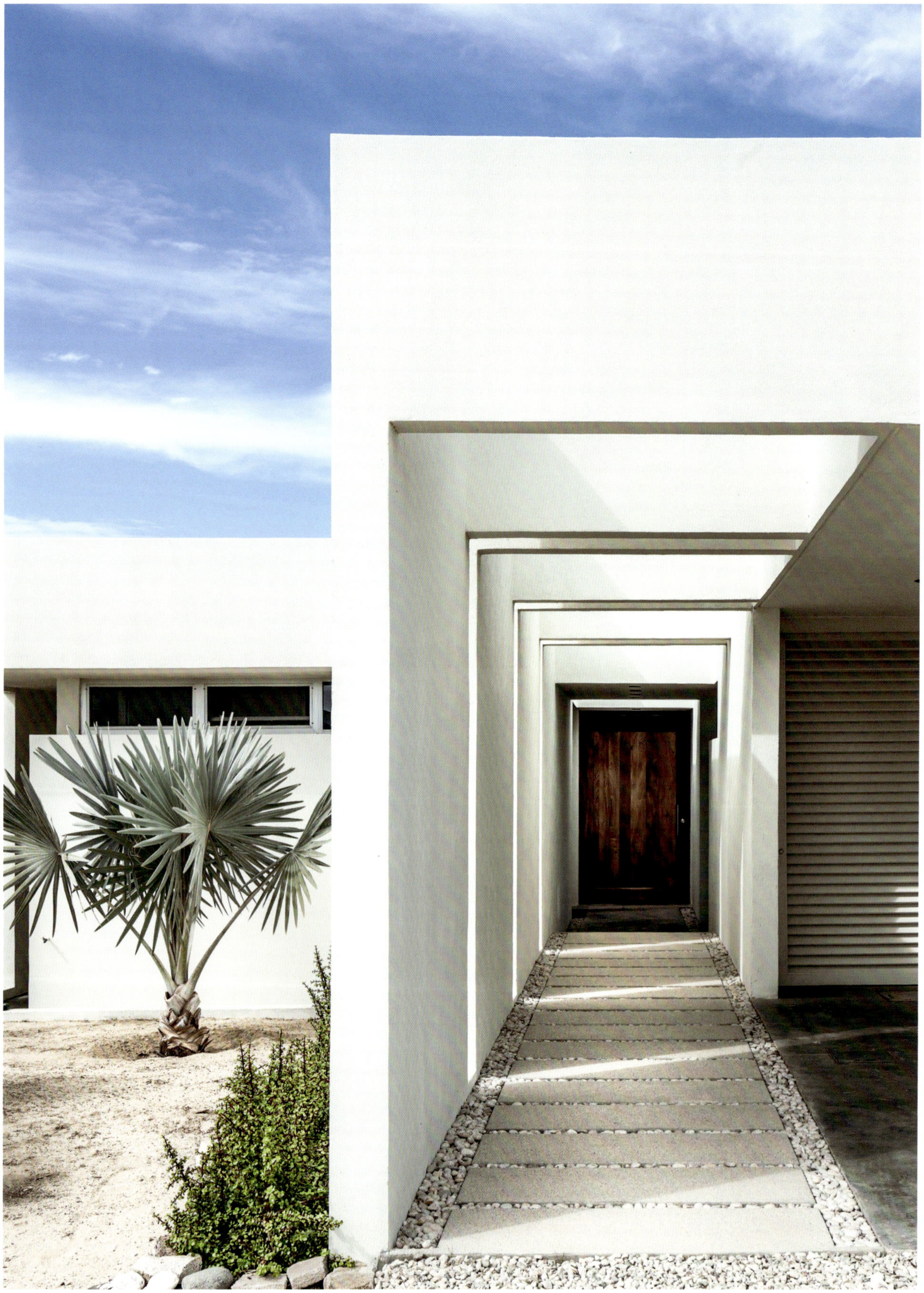

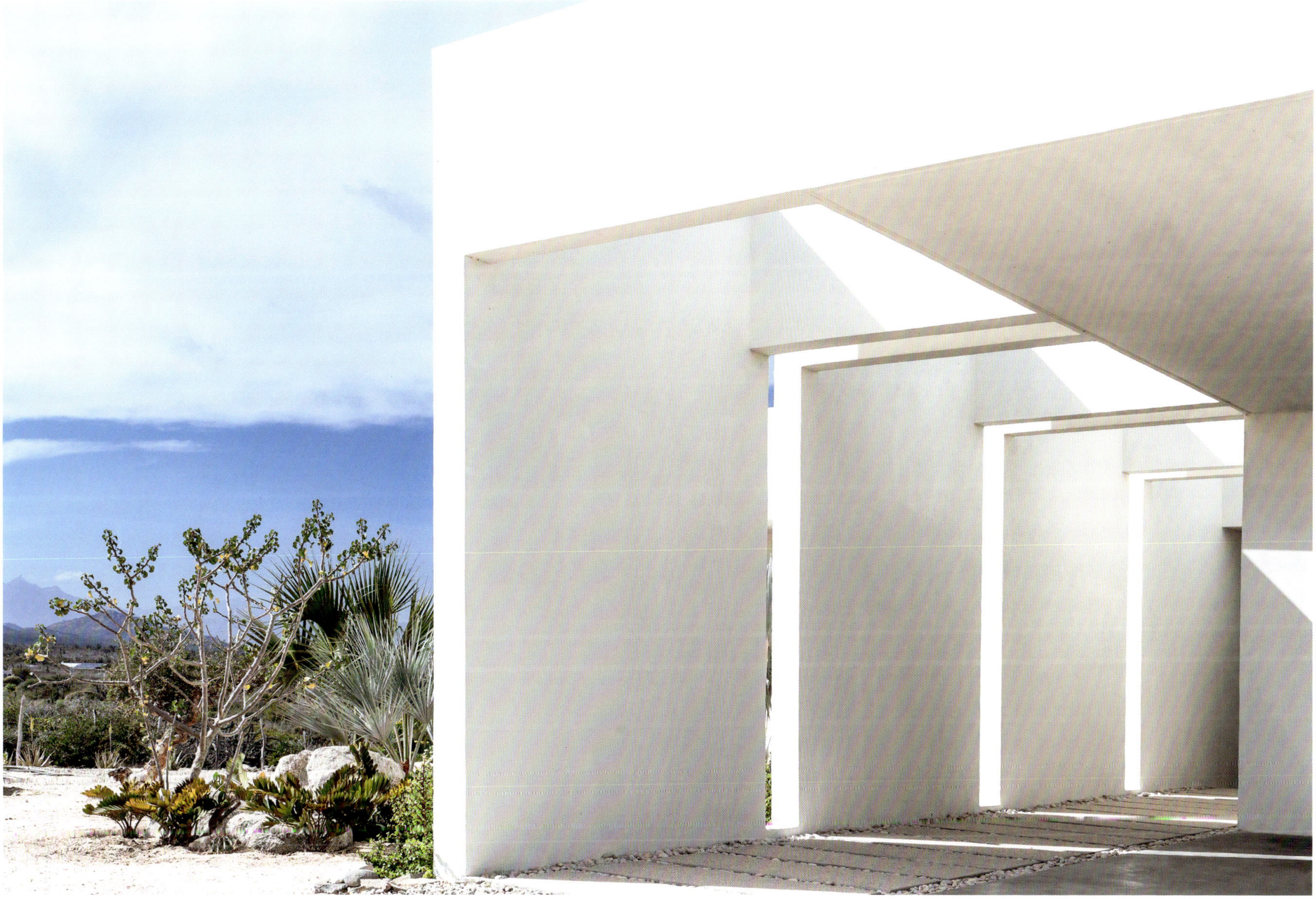

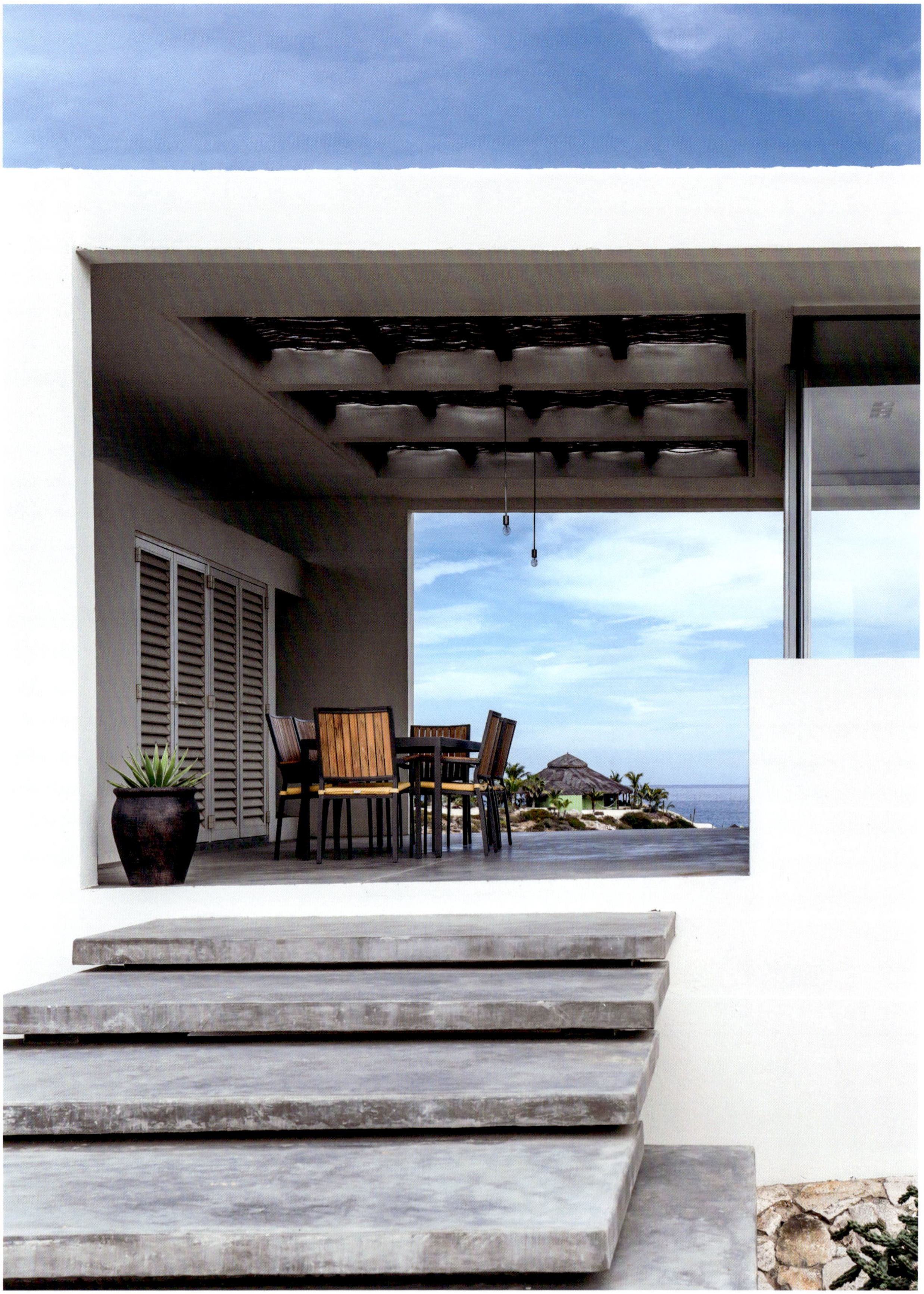

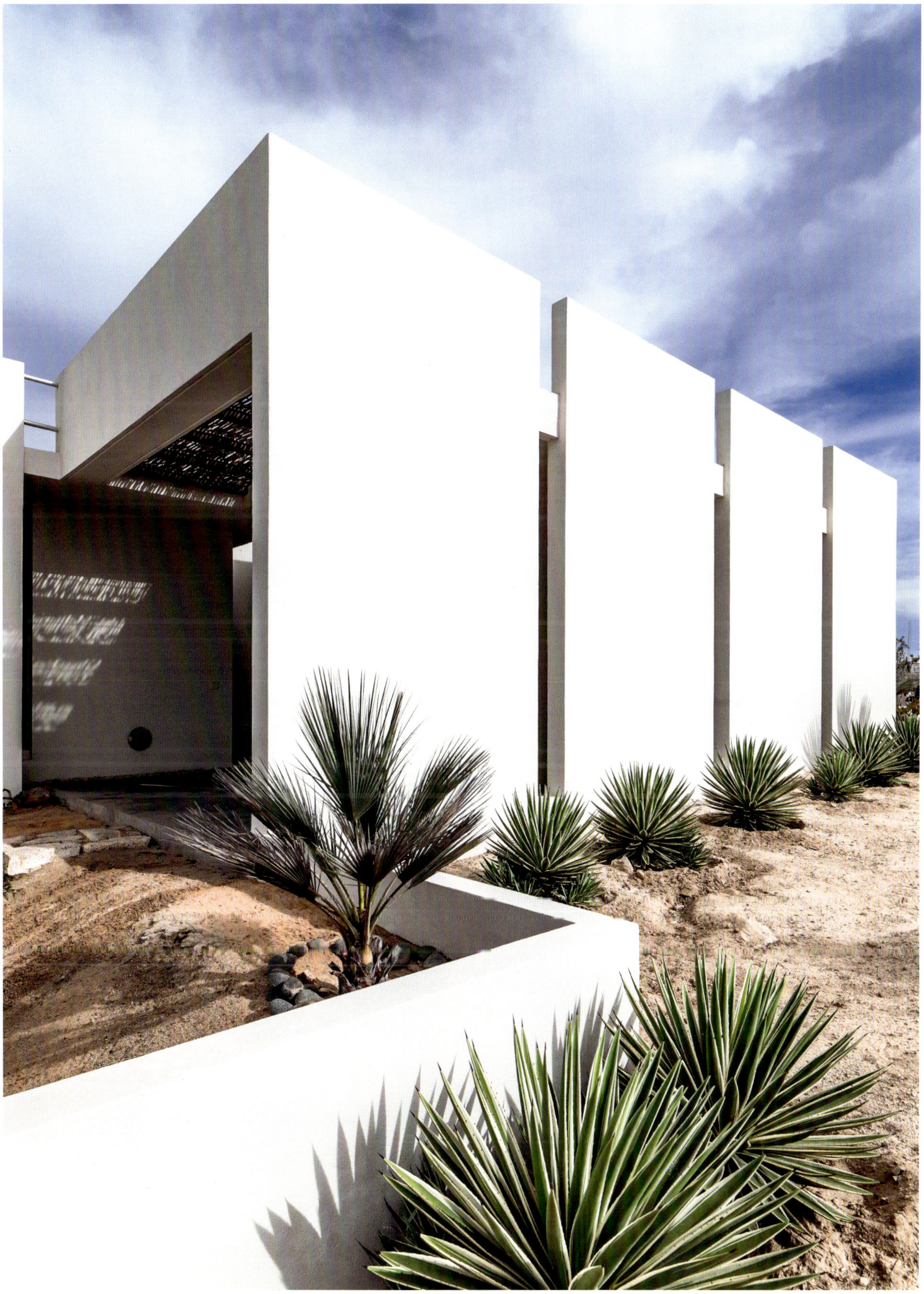

Marmol Radziner
MOAB
2007 | Hidden Valley, UT, USA

Found in eastern Utah's secluded desert outside Moab, this Hidden Valley home offers an uncommon solution to a primary challenge of construction in remote and inhospitable landscapes: the transportation and assembly of materials in a minimally invasive manner. Marmol Radziner resolved the issue using prefabricated steel units that were assembled on-site by crane. The resulting rectilinear building, with five interior and seven exterior modules, belies its industrial origins: it is a piece of avant-garde art sitting among rocks. In addition, it is designed to be eco-friendly and energy-efficient with solar and geothermal energy systems, creating as small a carbon footprint on the pristine, rugged terrain as possible. The primary axis follows an elevated rock ledge, giving way to extensive views over the valley, with dramatic red boulder formations and snow-capped mountains in the distance. The gift of a view is returned to the horizon: there is pleasure in seeing the modest and unassuming structure nestled quietly in the rocky topography studded with sagebrush. Its presence is calming because it comes without clutter—it did not bring anything to the desert that is not needed. The priorities are clear: the desert frames the house, not the other way around.

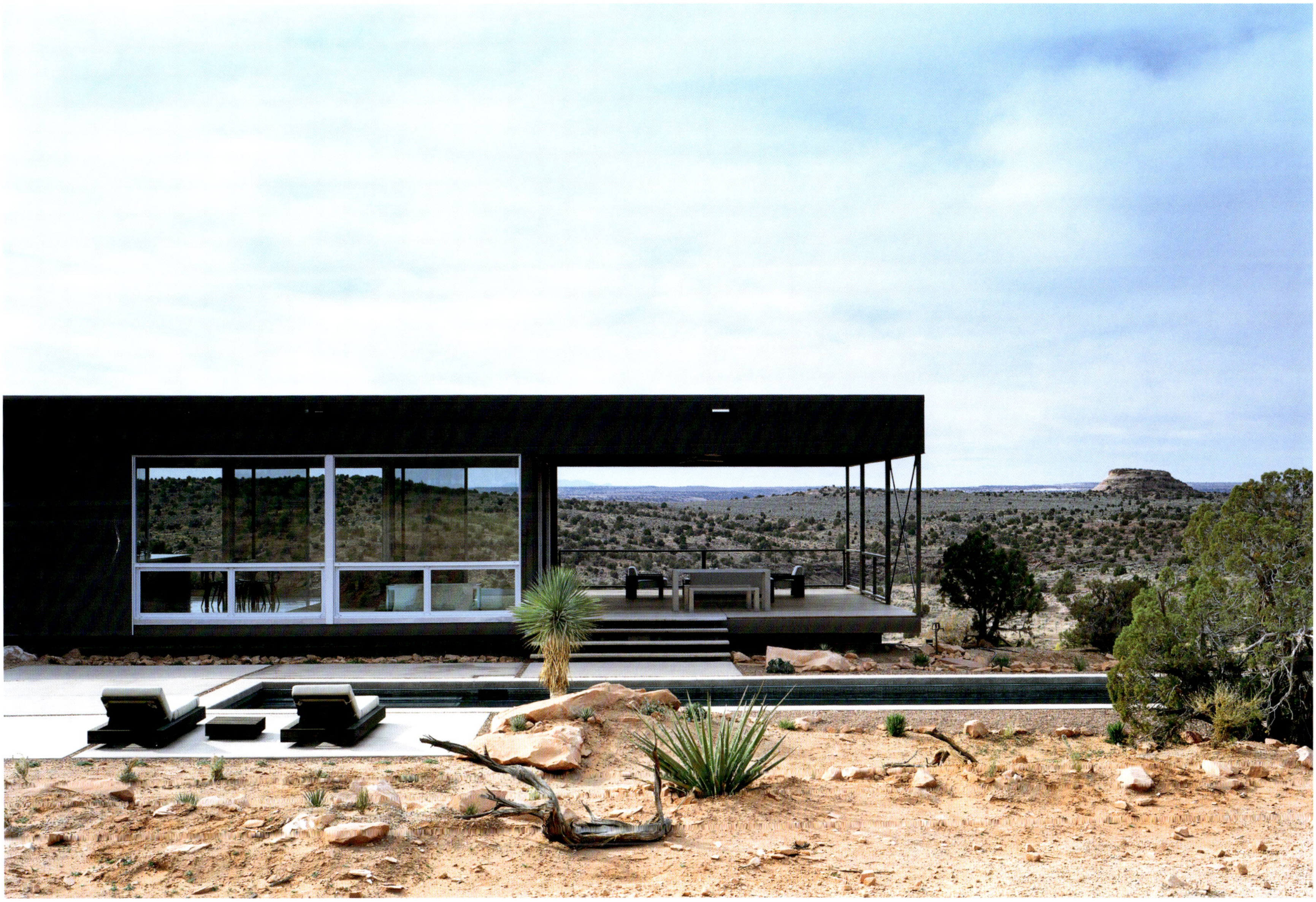

MOAB 194

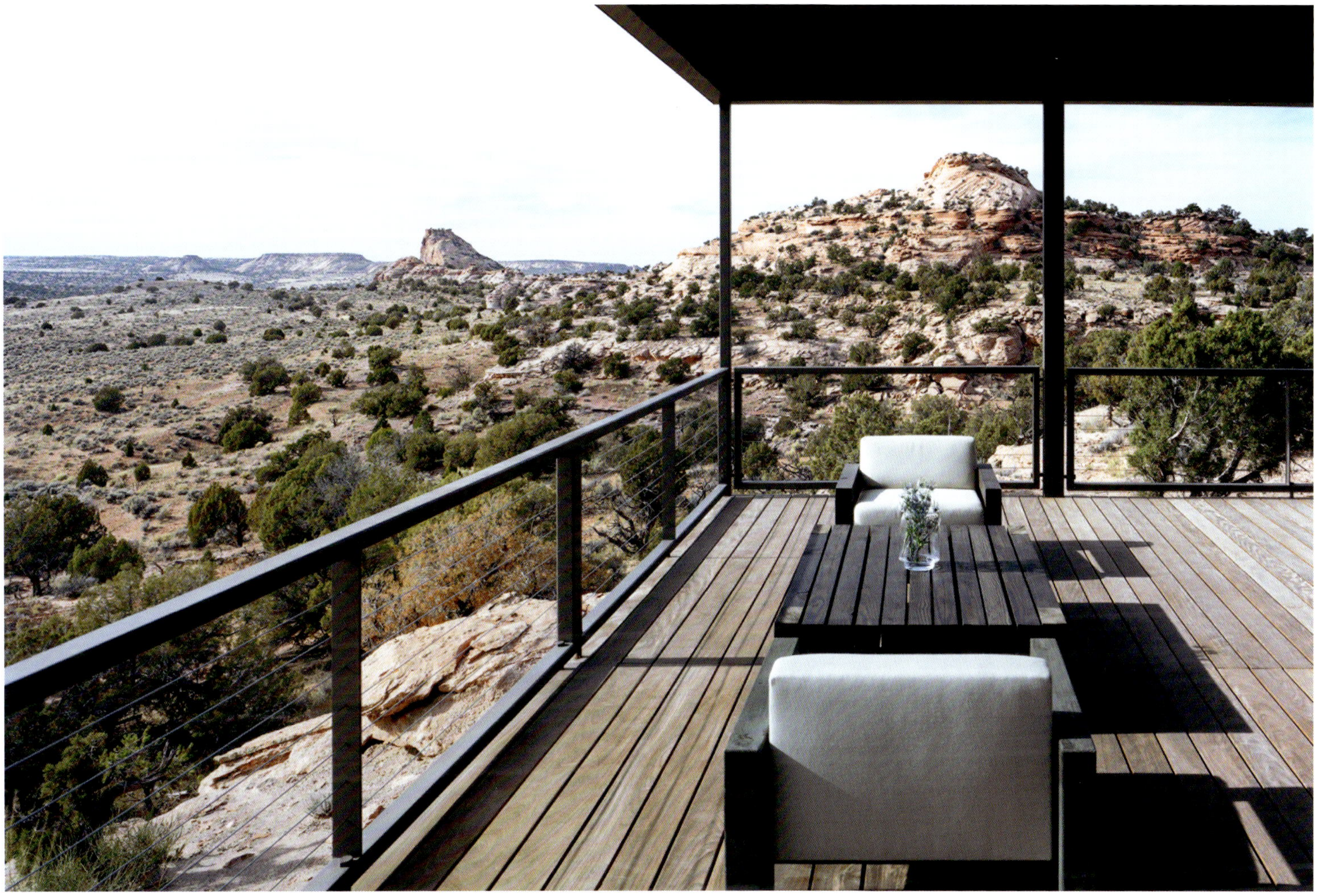
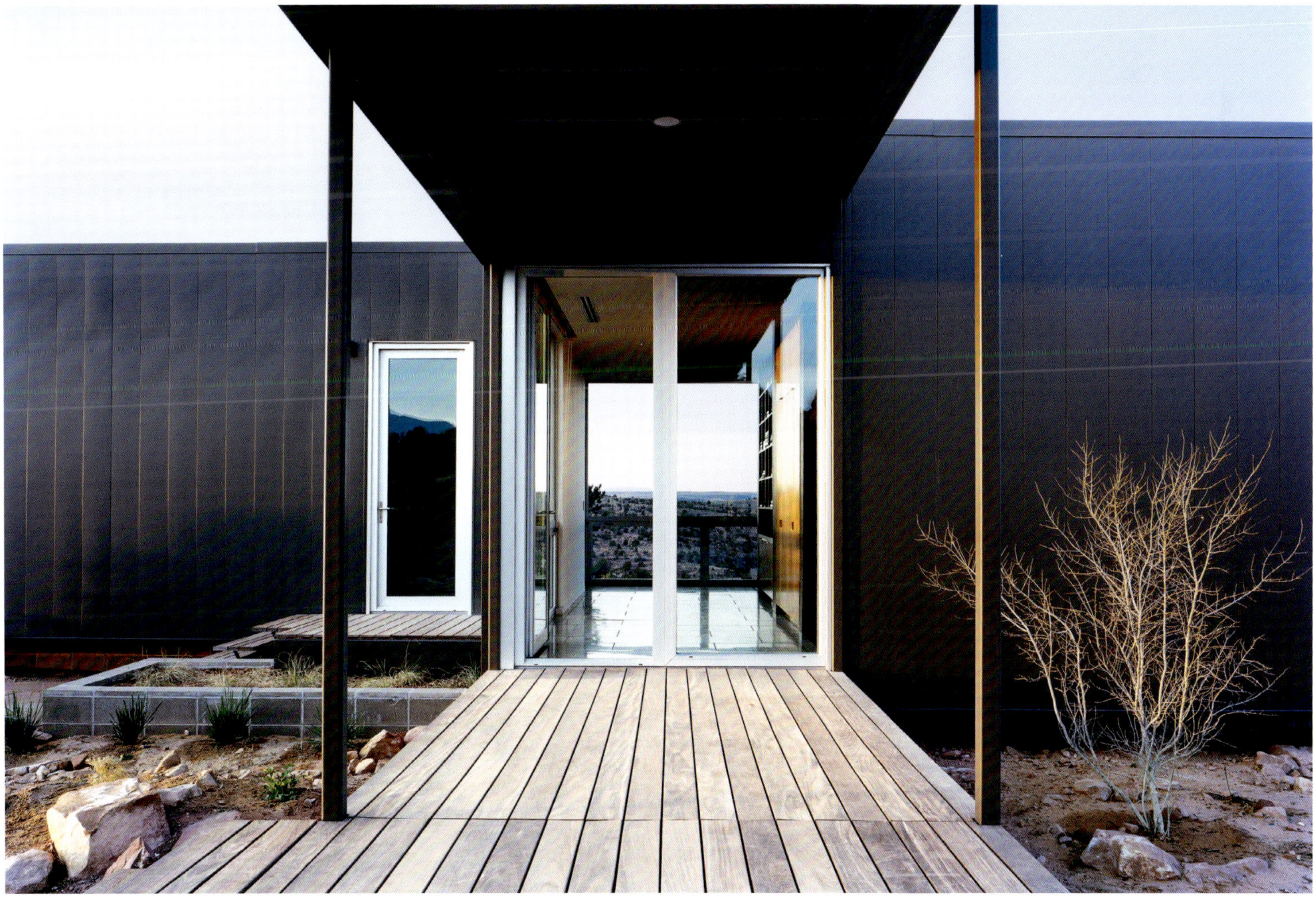

MOAB

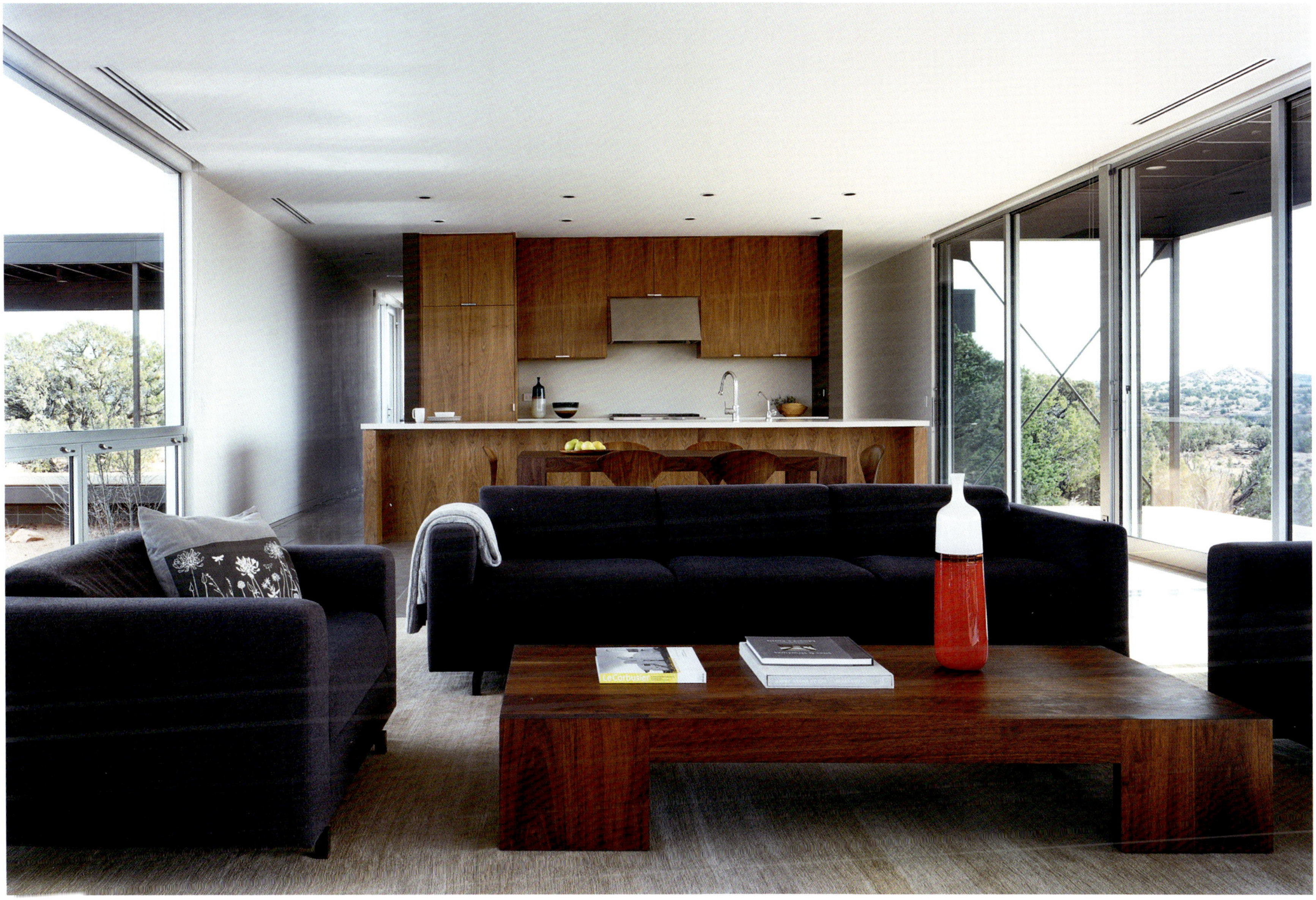

OFIS Arhitekti
THE GLASS PAVILION
2015 | Granada, Spain

In an area of Spain where local architecture responds to the harsh conditions with a traditional vernacular of troglodytic homes dug into the earth, Slovenian architecture firm OFIS Arhitekti shines by having constructed a building that does the exact opposite: it stands out. The Glass Pavilion is situated in one of Europe's harshest environments, Granada's Gorafe desert, which can reach temperatures up to 104 degrees Fahrenheit (forty degrees Celsius). It is a bold move to erect a glass pavilion beneath the soaring sun of a desert of such magnitude, but it is also a testament to the never-ending progress of modernity. Guardian Glass, a special glazing coated with an almost invisible film that is able to filter the sun's radiation almost completely, thus allowing the material to be used as structural walls, is used extensively on the Y-shaped floor plan. A wooden plinth underneath the volume provides a terrace that is shaded by the pavilion's overhanging roof, part of which is clad in mirrored panels that reflect the landscape.

The capsule dwelling's spare interior miraculously satisfies every elaborate need a traveler could have and more: it may be the sole fully panoramic desert structure to feature an indoor Jacuzzi. Complementing this comfort is the fact that the region's stars are not diminished by the slightest light pollution, granting the opportunity to experience the pleasures of nature from earth to sky.

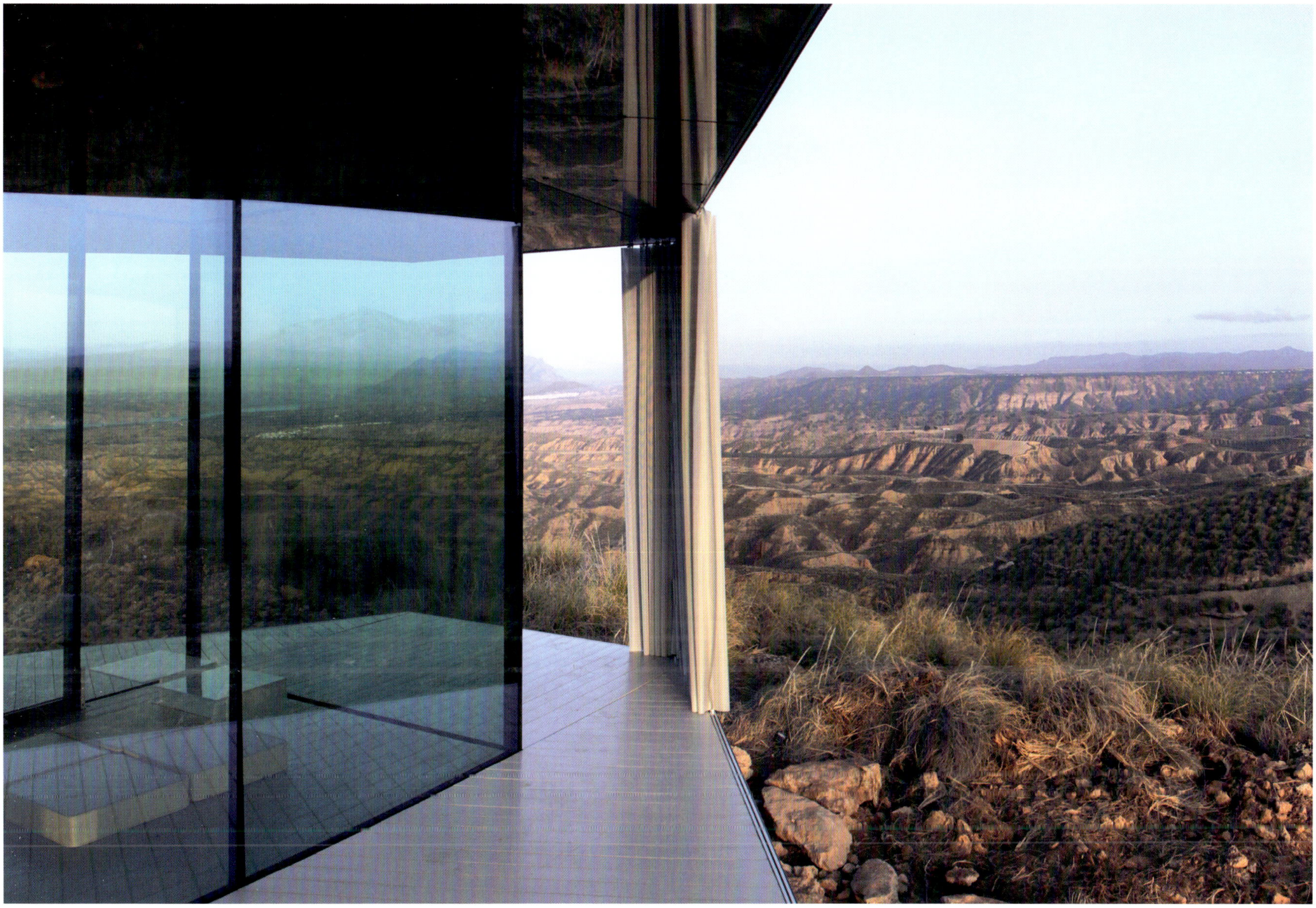

THE GLASS PAVILION

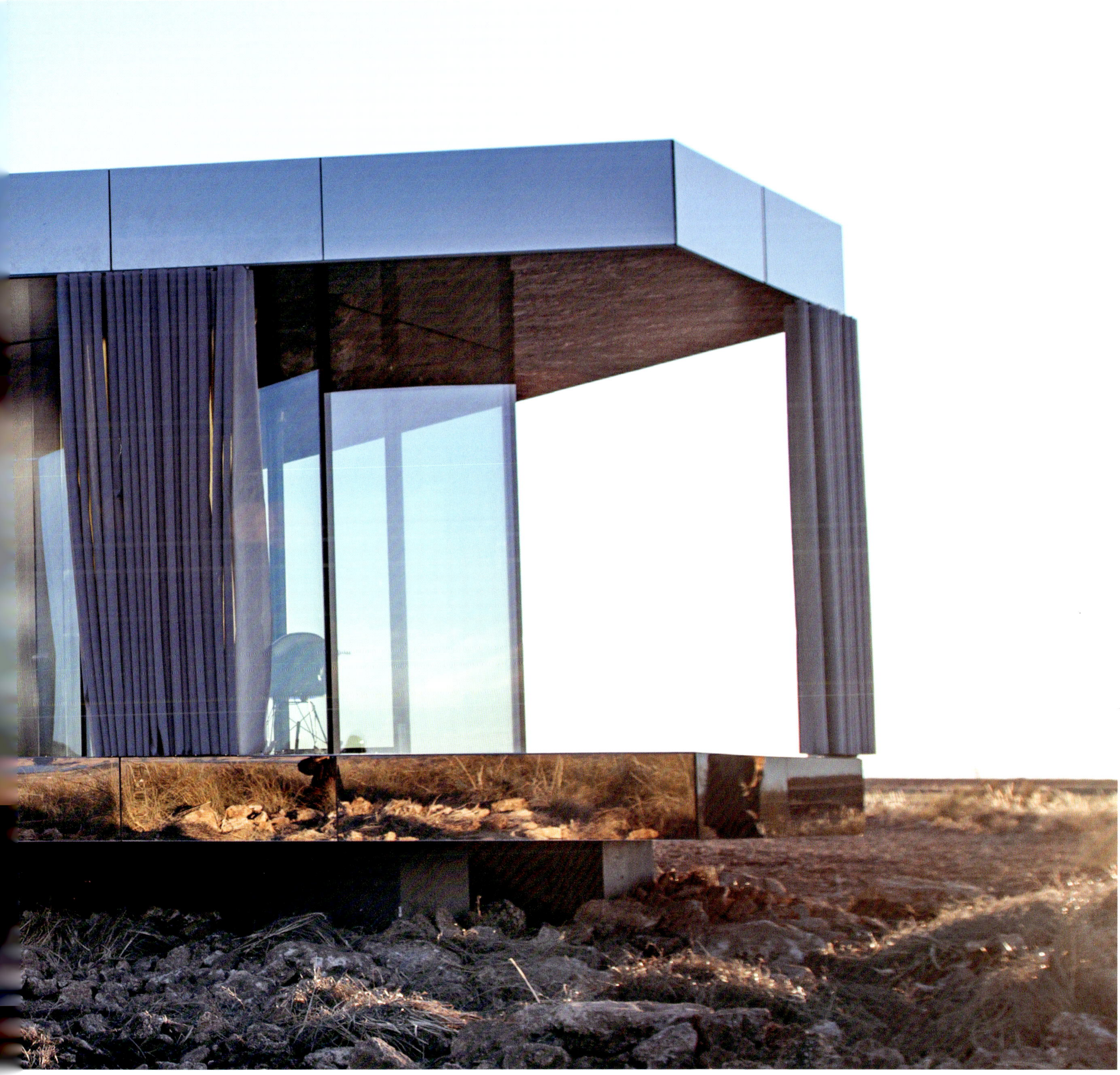

… THE GLASS PAVILION

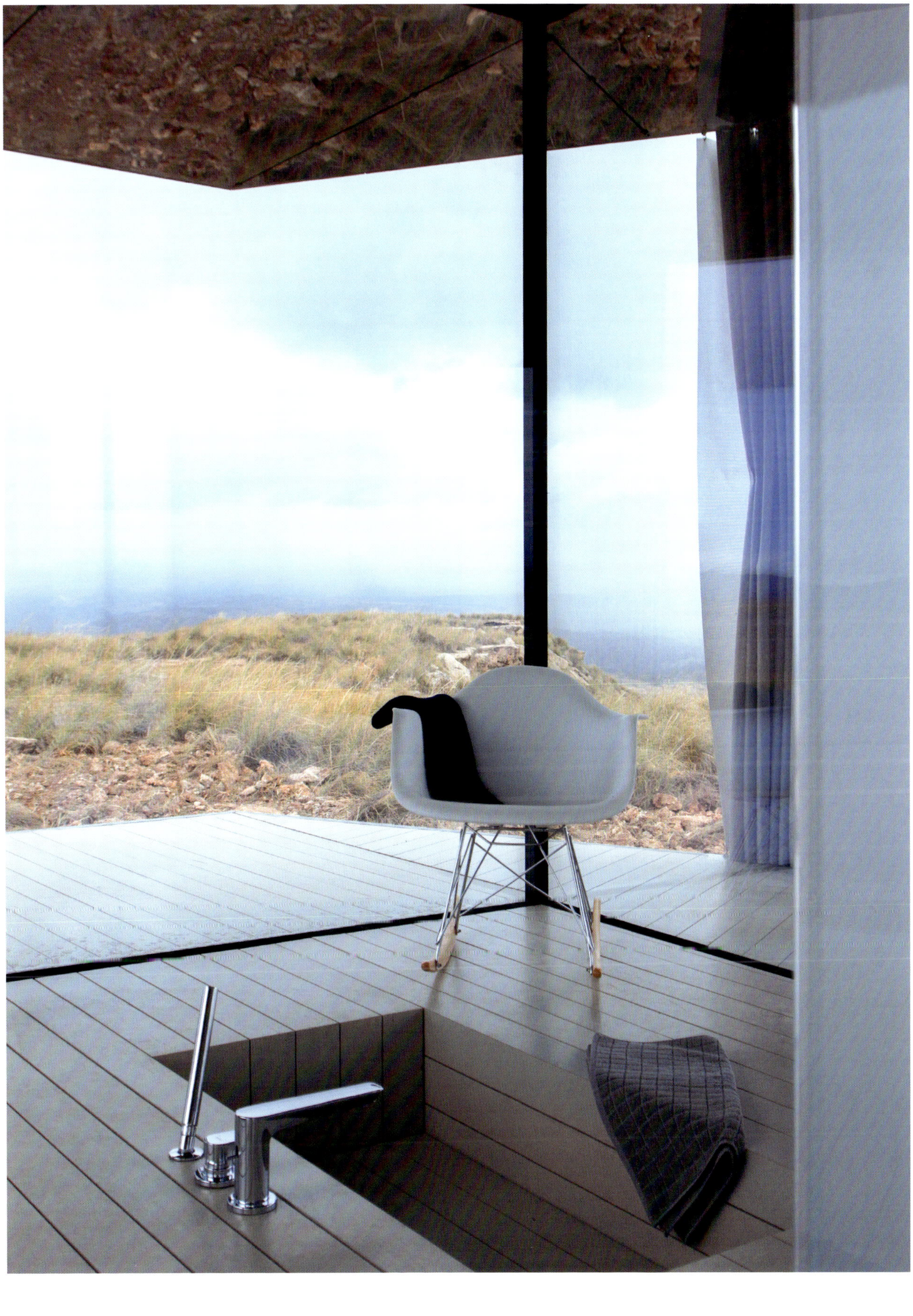

Tate Studio Architects
SEFCOVIC RESIDENCE
2011 | Scottsdale, AZ, USA

Rather than just living off the land, this man-made oasis takes from the no-man's-land what is most valuable—the views—to orientate itself on the arid site. Set within a hillside of Arizona's Desert Mountain in northern Scottsdale, the two-story Sefcovic Residence radially arcs along a central spine, following the natural ridge line and uncannily resembling the vertebrae of a desert reptile. Most of the exterior walls are constructed of glass, thus elevating the spectacular views in all directions as the main feature of the house. Cantilevered roofs edged in copper provide essential shade for the generously glazed surfaces during hot summer months, while an array of south-facing windows was put into place to capture sunlight during the colder months. Special emphasis has been placed on the consistent use of native materials, such as limestone and basalt, and a vernacular design while ensuring the availability of every possible comfort, ranging from expansive rooms to cultivated gardens with blooming cacti.

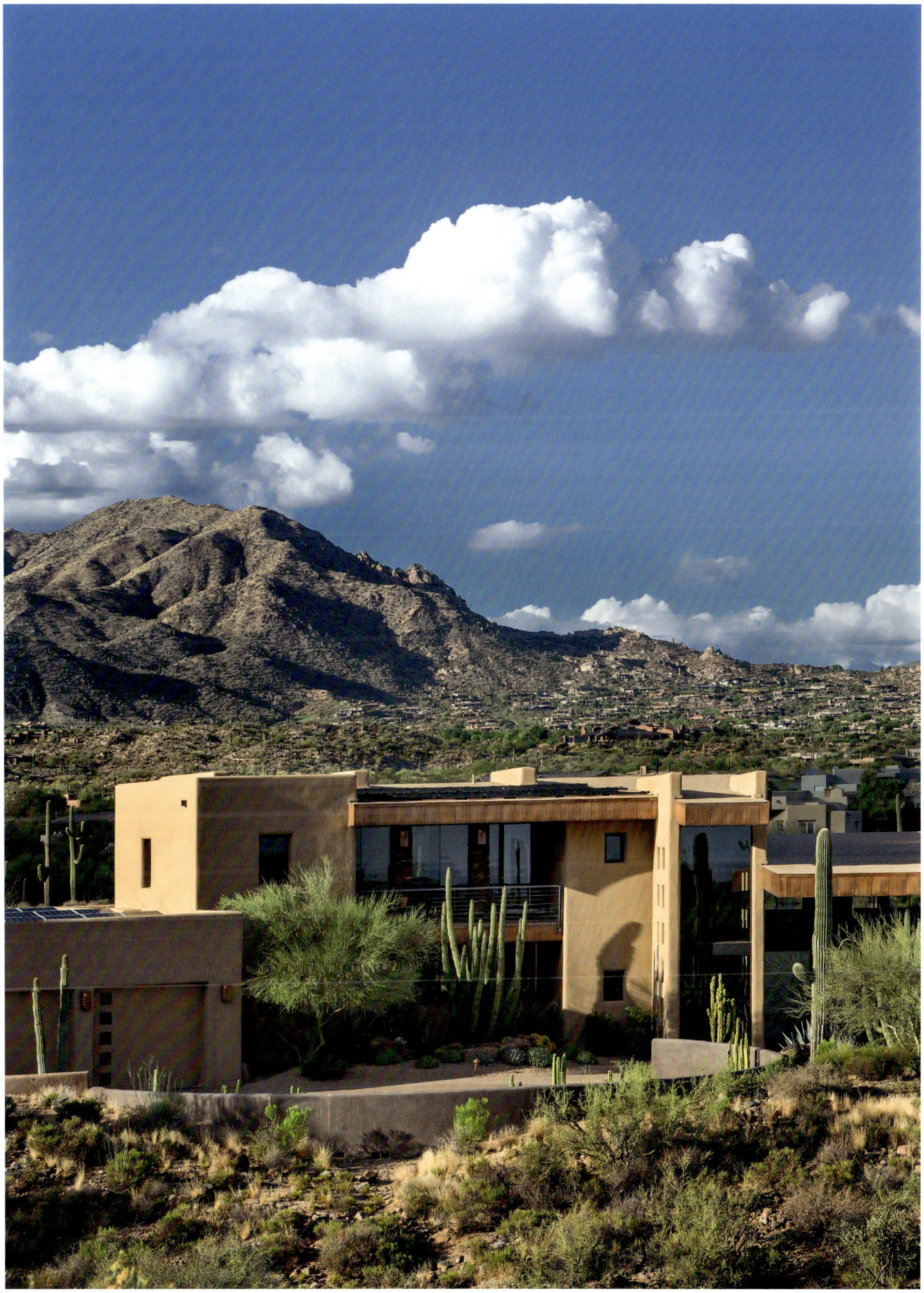

SEFCOVIC RESIDENCE

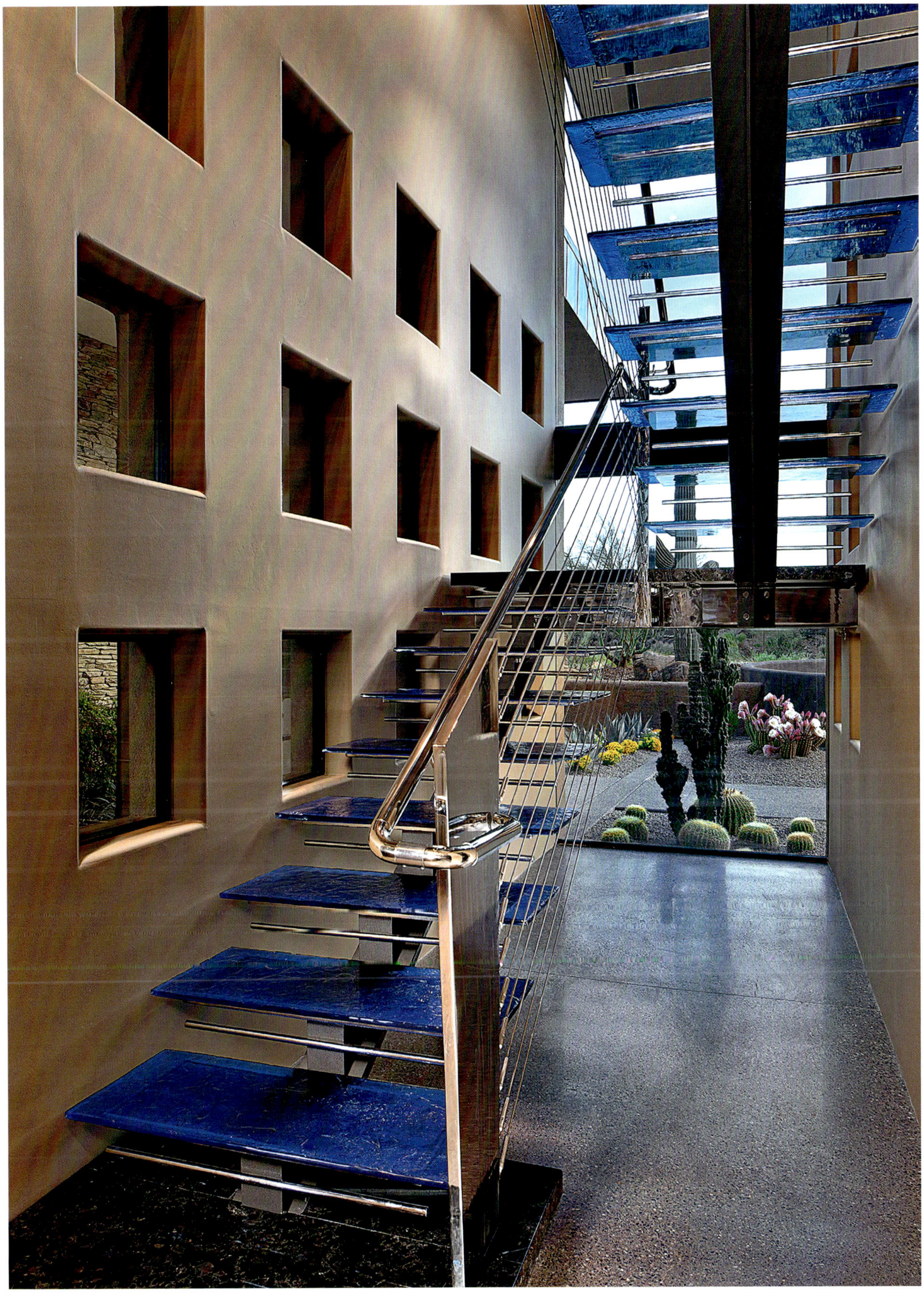

Guilhem Eustache
FOBE HOUSE
2014 | Marrakech, Morocco

It takes about two hours by car to reach the bottom of Morocco's Atlas Mountains from Marrakech, two hours in which the landscape changes—notably, but not completely. Spaces become wider and vegetation more sparse, apart from olive and argan groves, and hues change to darker green and brown. Located six miles (ten kilometers) south of Marrakech, Fobe House witnesses the beginning of this transformation. The site is left in a natural state on purpose, with artificial or superfluous efforts to sustain manicured greenery rejected in favor of what the land and the historic traditions of its cultivation—or benign neglect—have to offer. The conglomerate of boxy, stark white structures erected on the property, however, counter this approach by imposing a certain level of sophistication and rigidity. Despite being constructed with double-thick walls by artisan hands and with nothing but natural resources—proudly wearing the labels of sustainability and ecology—there is a visible tension in the interplay of the precision of the architecture against this setting. A Donald Judd–like geometry reveals itself as the eye takes in the individual forms, some slightly surreal, such as the outsized staircase to nowhere emerging from the edge of the swimming pool. Fobe House's dynamic appeal results from the decision to limit built-up areas, thereby preserving the typology—the negative space—of the land and giving way to the imagination. For the client, a cinematographer, this is certainly a paramount feature.

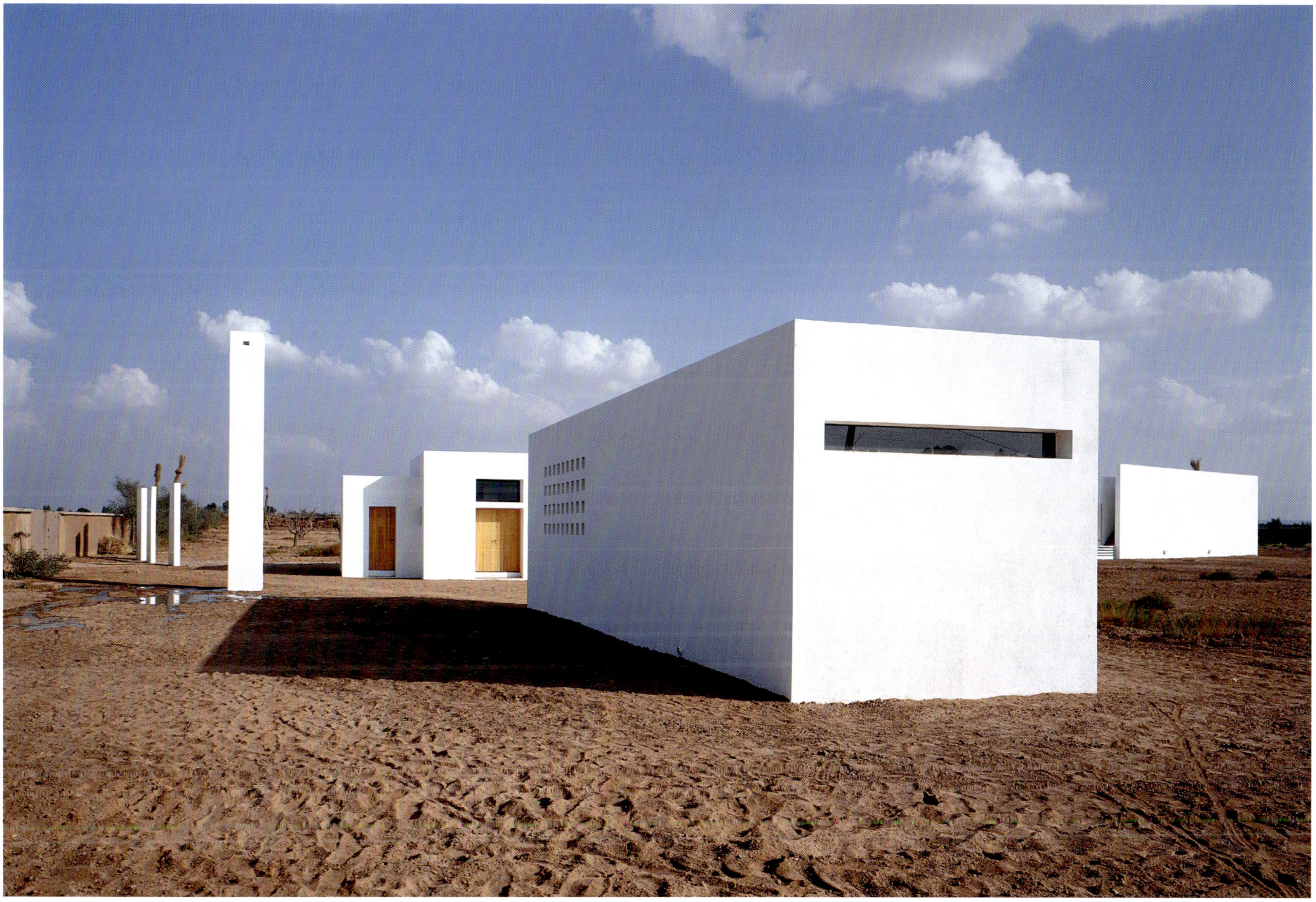

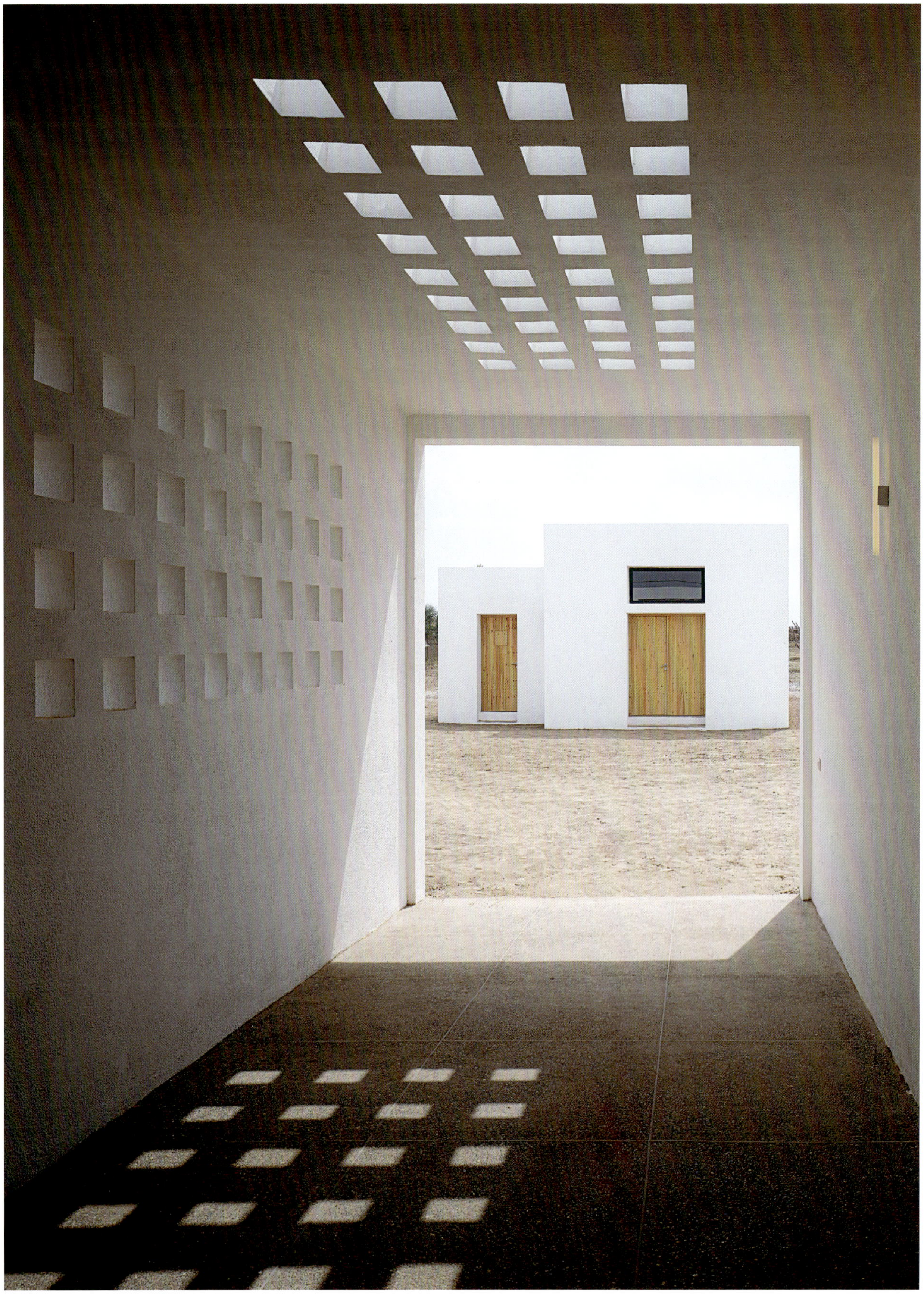

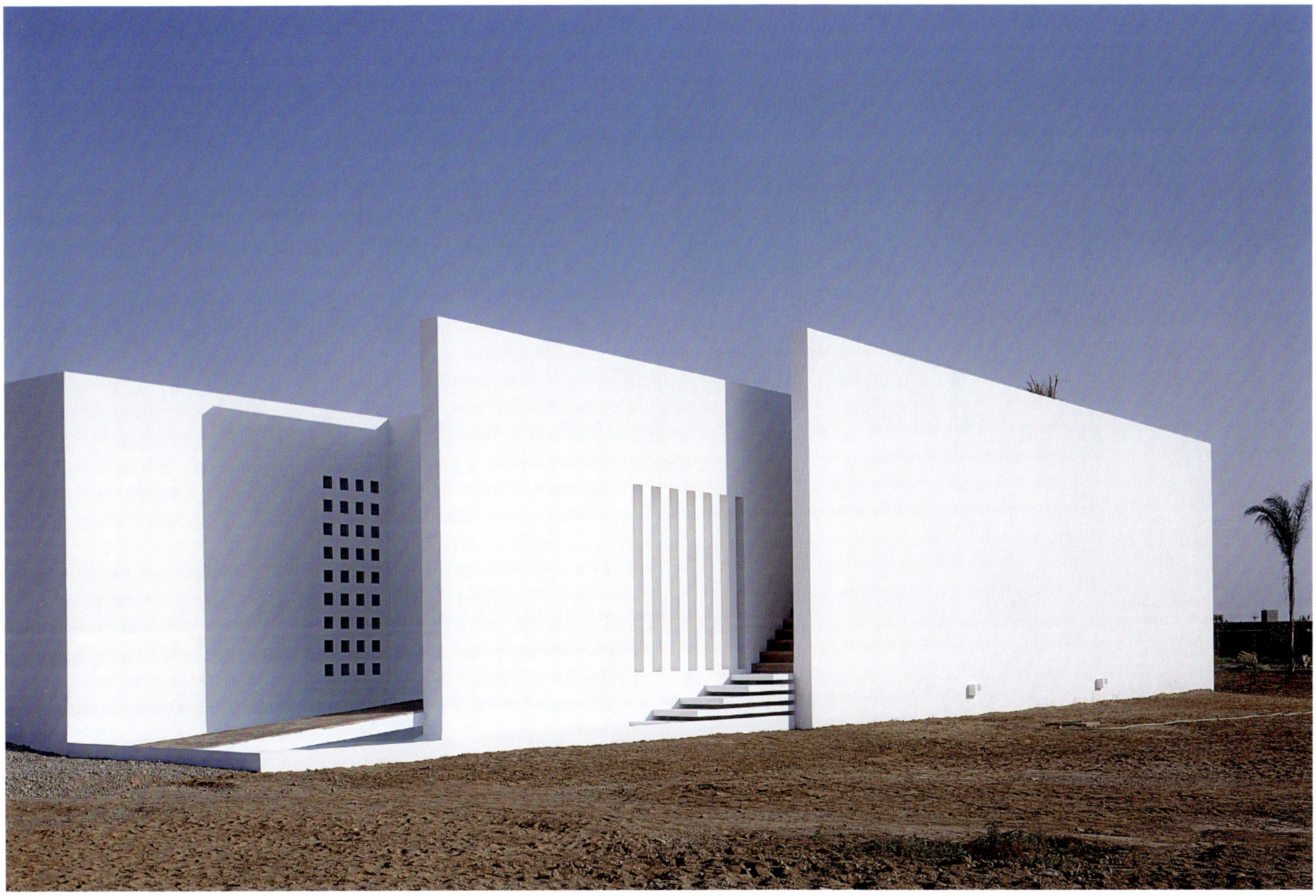

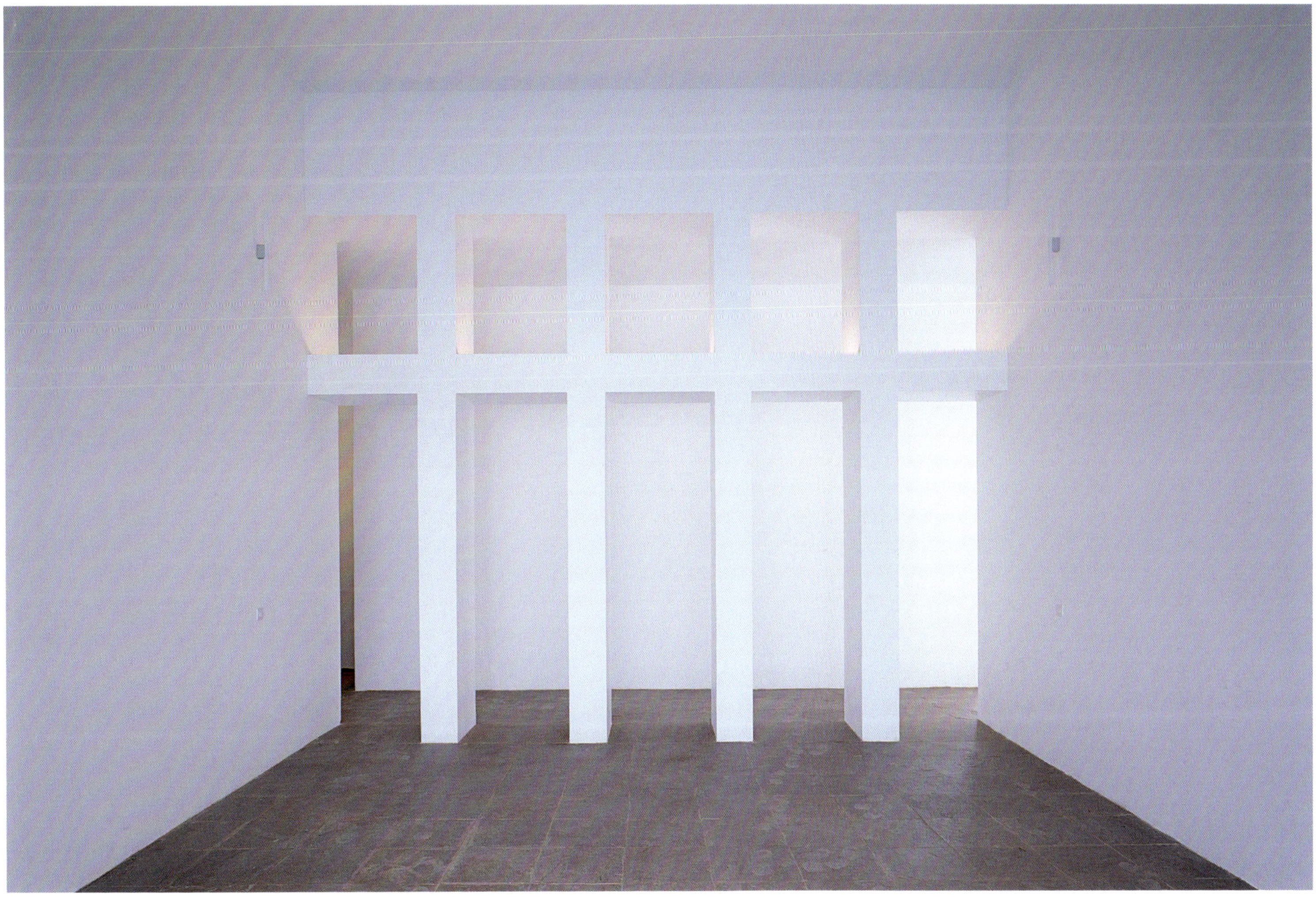

FOBE HOUSE

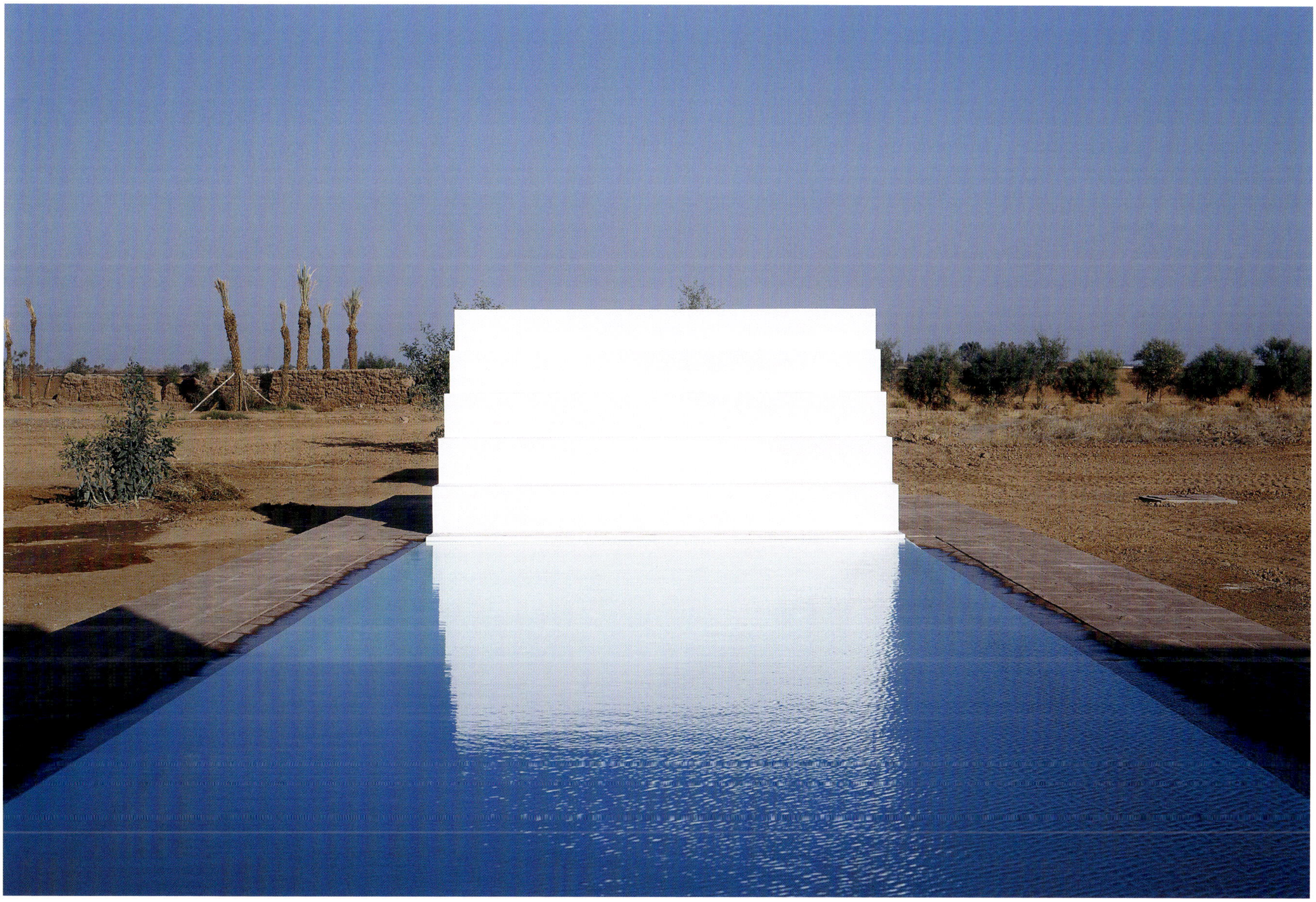

Carlos Jiménez Studio
CROWLEY HOUSE
2014 | Marfa, TX, USA

With minimal impact on the landscape, Crowley House rests on a flat hilltop in Marfa overlooking the rolling grass dunes of the Chihuahua Desert. As a Texas native, architect Carlos Jiménez knows the state's topography intimately. This single-story unit with uniform width unites within it the boundaries of interior and exterior space, its two separate courtyards protected by the house's structure. Marfa weather features intense afternoon sun and unforgivingly strong winds; materials like concrete, galvanized steel, and ipe wood were chosen to withstand the climate. Large aluminum-framed windows invite views of differing scales into the domestic space, showcasing the interplay between proximity and distance, the intimacy of native flora and the expansiveness of the chiseled mountain ranges on the borderless horizon. The muted color palette of earthy grays and warm browns allows the house to blend easily with nature's textures. Following the light's journey was a major consideration in order to create protection—important because of the owner's contemporary art collection—without inducing darkness.

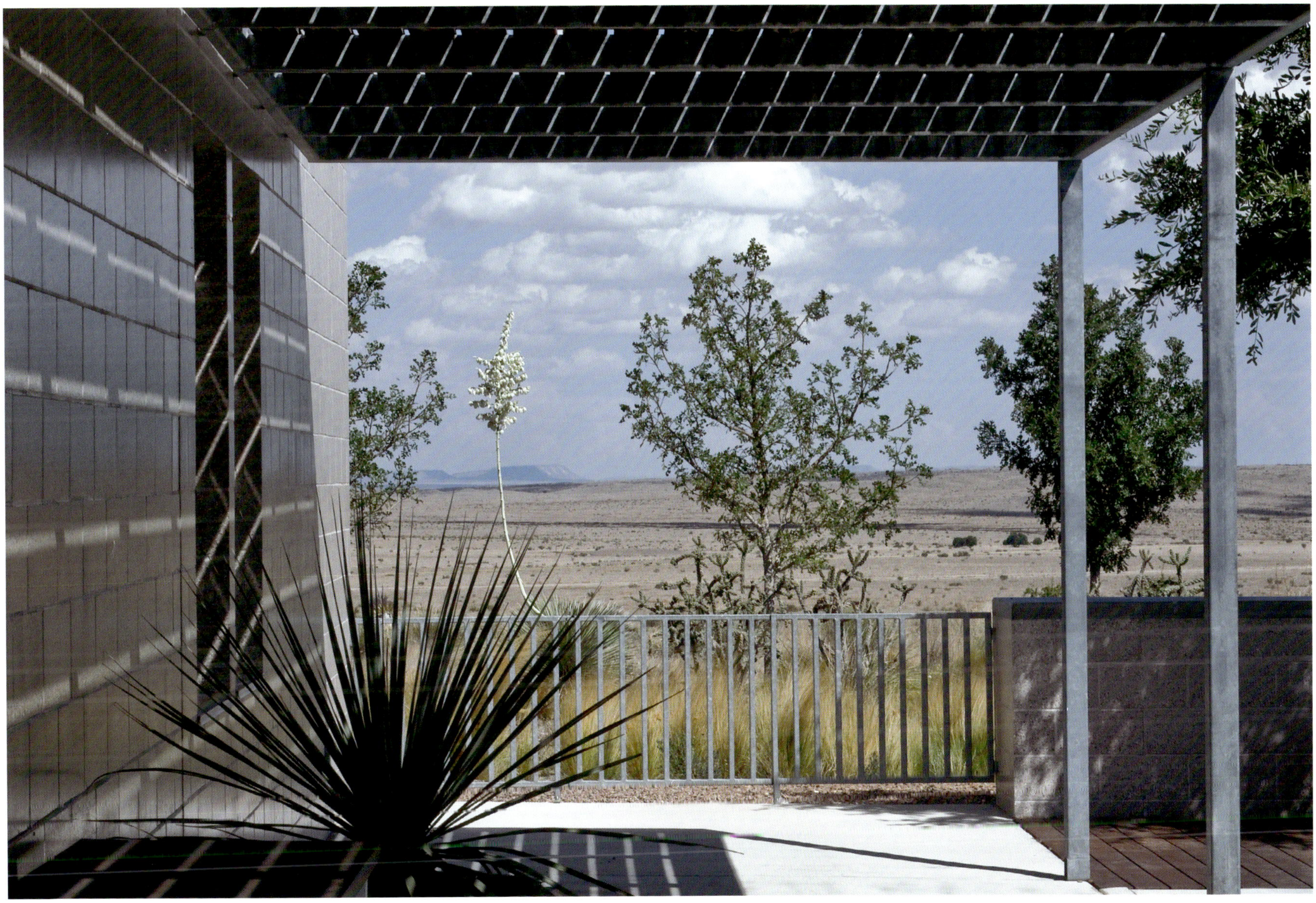

CROWLEY HOUSE

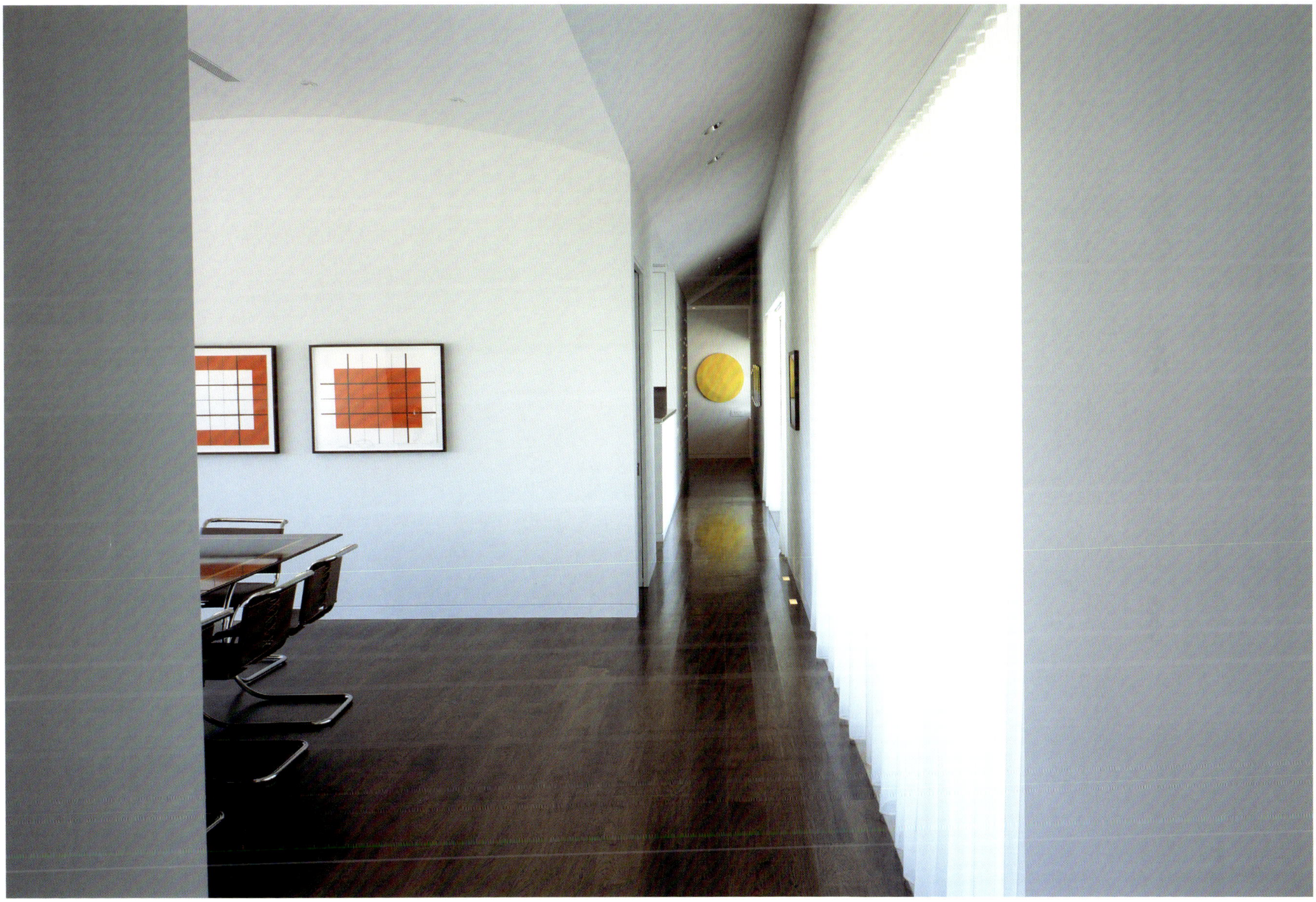

Marwan Al-Sayed, Inc.
STONE COURT VILLA
2014 | Paradise Valley, AZ, USA

In the rugged landscape of Arizona's Paradise Valley, Stone Court Villa rises as a four-bedroom residence of majestic scale. Its wide and boxy appearance immediately puts visitors under its spell, drawing in every pair of eyes with a subtle grandeur seen in modern Middle Eastern architecture. Hefty bricks of limestone—a sedimentary rock mainly composed of skeletal fragments of marine organisms—are the main building material.

It is the immense courtyard that forms the centerpiece of the structure. Like in a mosque, it manages to unite the outdoors with the indoors, aided in this pursuit by full-frame wooden doors that rotate completely open and create continuing vistas if desired. Large floor-to-ceiling windows also afford views over the entire property, giving an additional feeling of openness. Privacy is not of concern, as the villa provides secluded space for its owners and separate facilities for guests that include a kitchenette and a yoga room. A seemingly still, endlessly reflecting pool with a negative edge separates private from public functions and also hides a second, deeper pool for swimming that extends onto a lower pool terrace. The cooling system will fill engineering enthusiasts with joy: a series of tubes runs cold water through the thick ceilings, providing more efficient and subtle coolness than air-forced mechanisms.

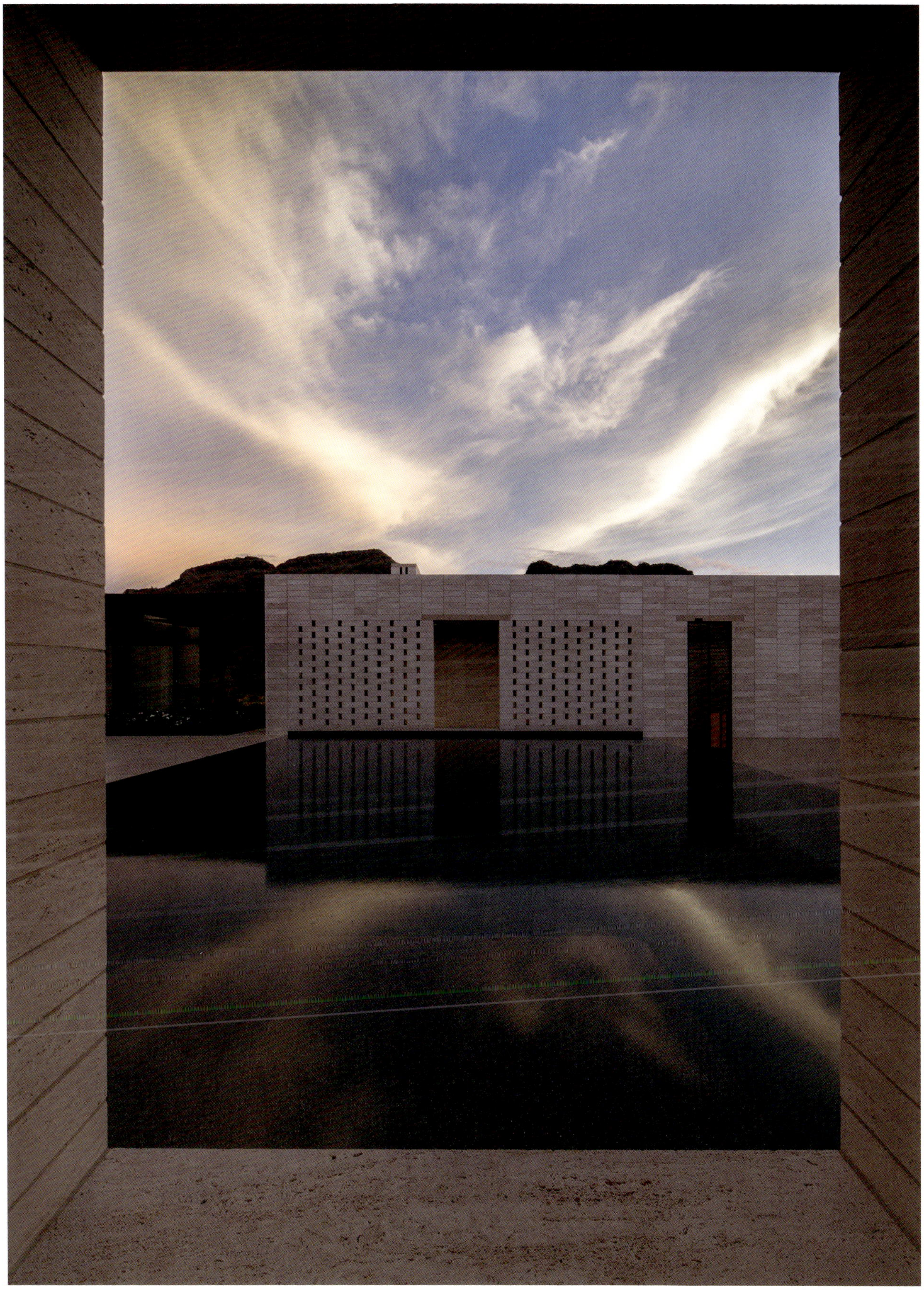

STONE COURT VILLA 220

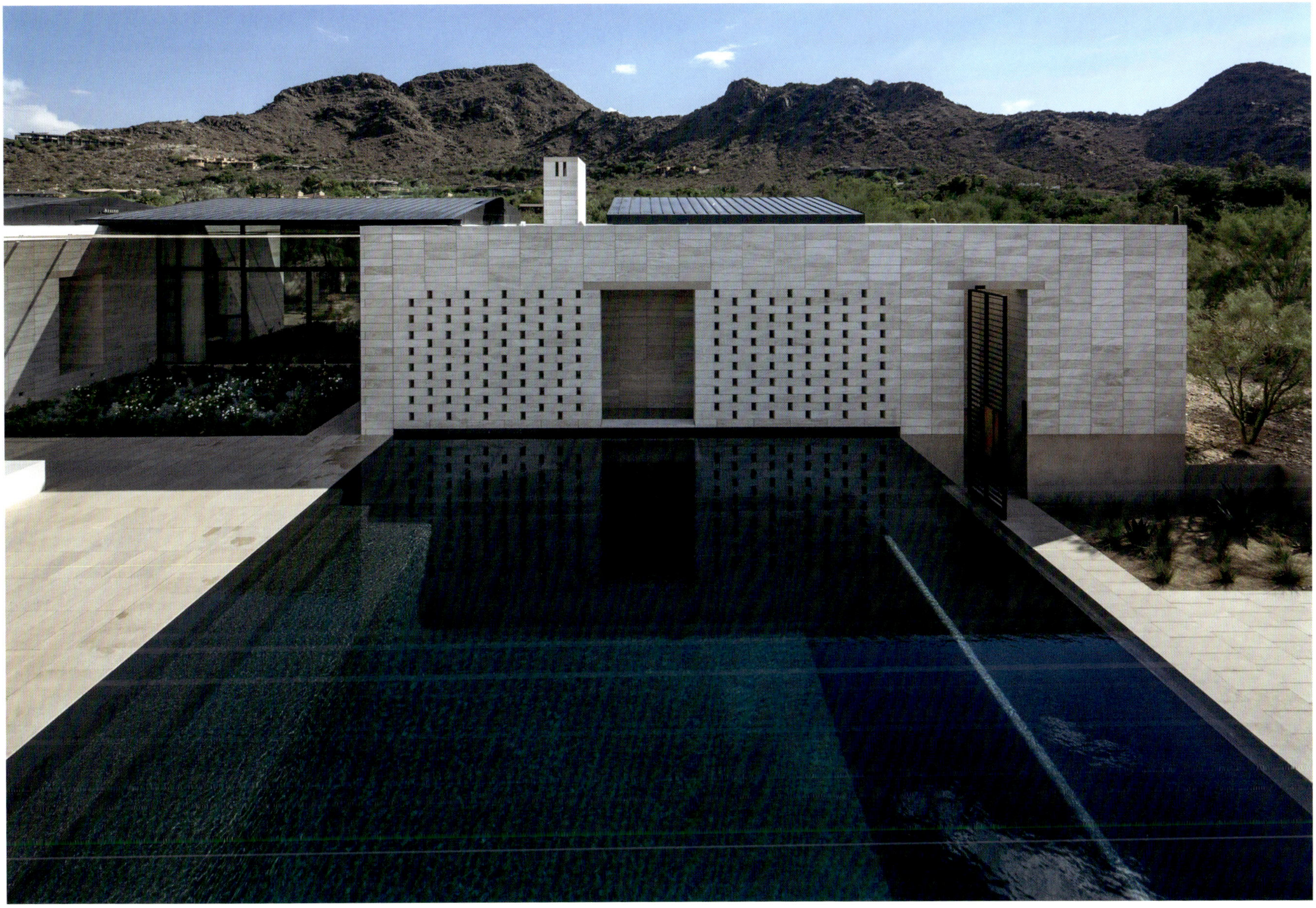

STONE COURT VILLA

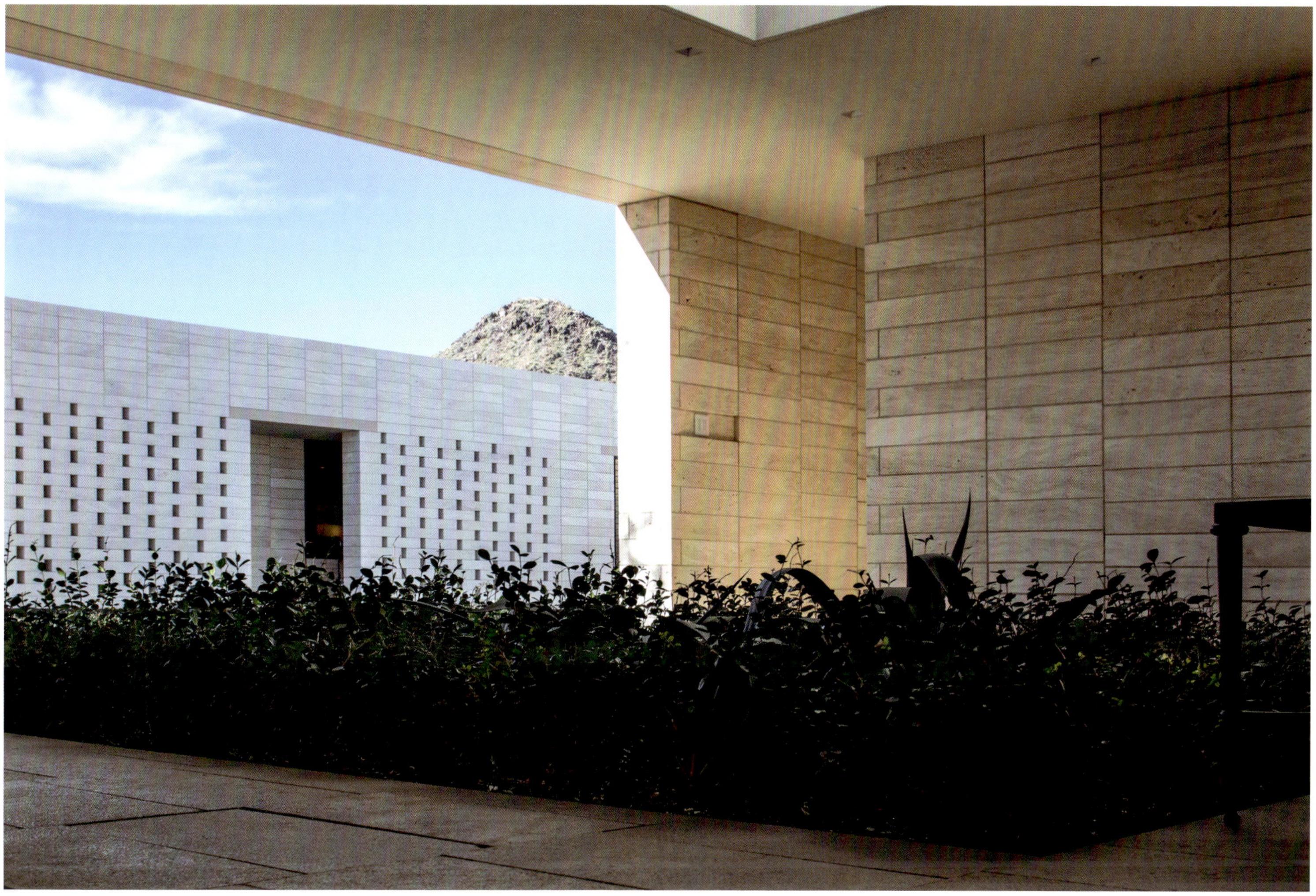

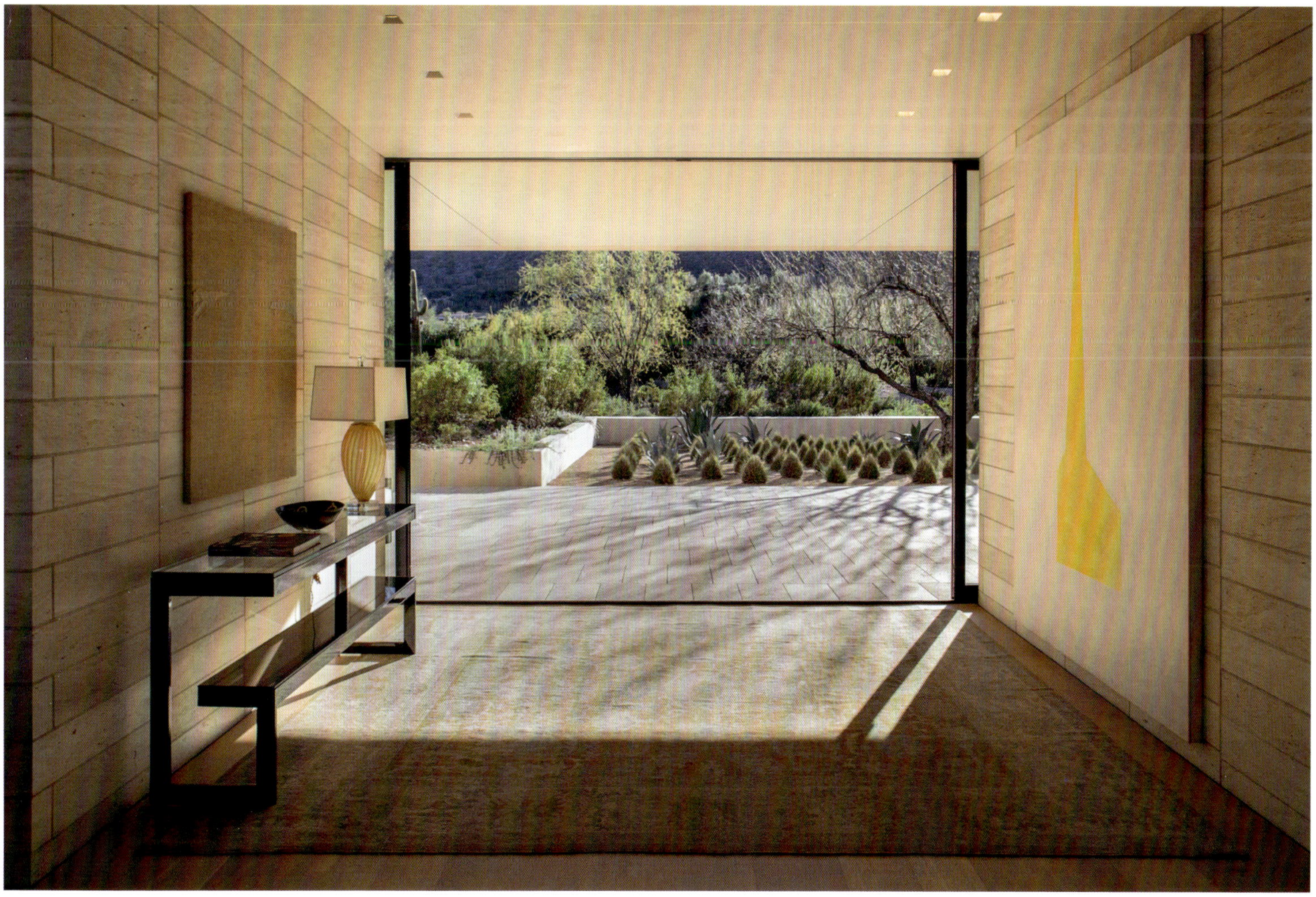

Kendle Design Collaborative
DANCING LIGHT
2016 | Paradise Valley, AZ, USA

Situated on a parcel of land with direct views of Camelback Mountain, this residence in Paradise Valley gives priority to the spectacle of nature in one way or another. The first and most visible is a canopy of overlapping and sharply angled wood planes that soar high above an outdoor living room, providing shelter from the Arizona sun. Its form appears to be directly drawn from the mountain and immediately sets the tone of the experience for the first-time visitor. Further sustaining a dialogue with the geology of the region are the indigenous materials used: concrete, rammed earth, and natural woods. While these materials from the soil lend a presence, they don't take center stage; the extensive use of glass and metal makes the house decidedly modern and provides a conduit for the play of luminous desert light. The public spaces are arranged around the wide terrace with a wall of glass that fully retracts, enabling air and light to circulate freely and fill the home with life and movement during the day. The multitude of glazed surfaces and unusual angles provides an interesting spectrum of patterns of light and shadow throughout the house, appropriately named Dancing Light.

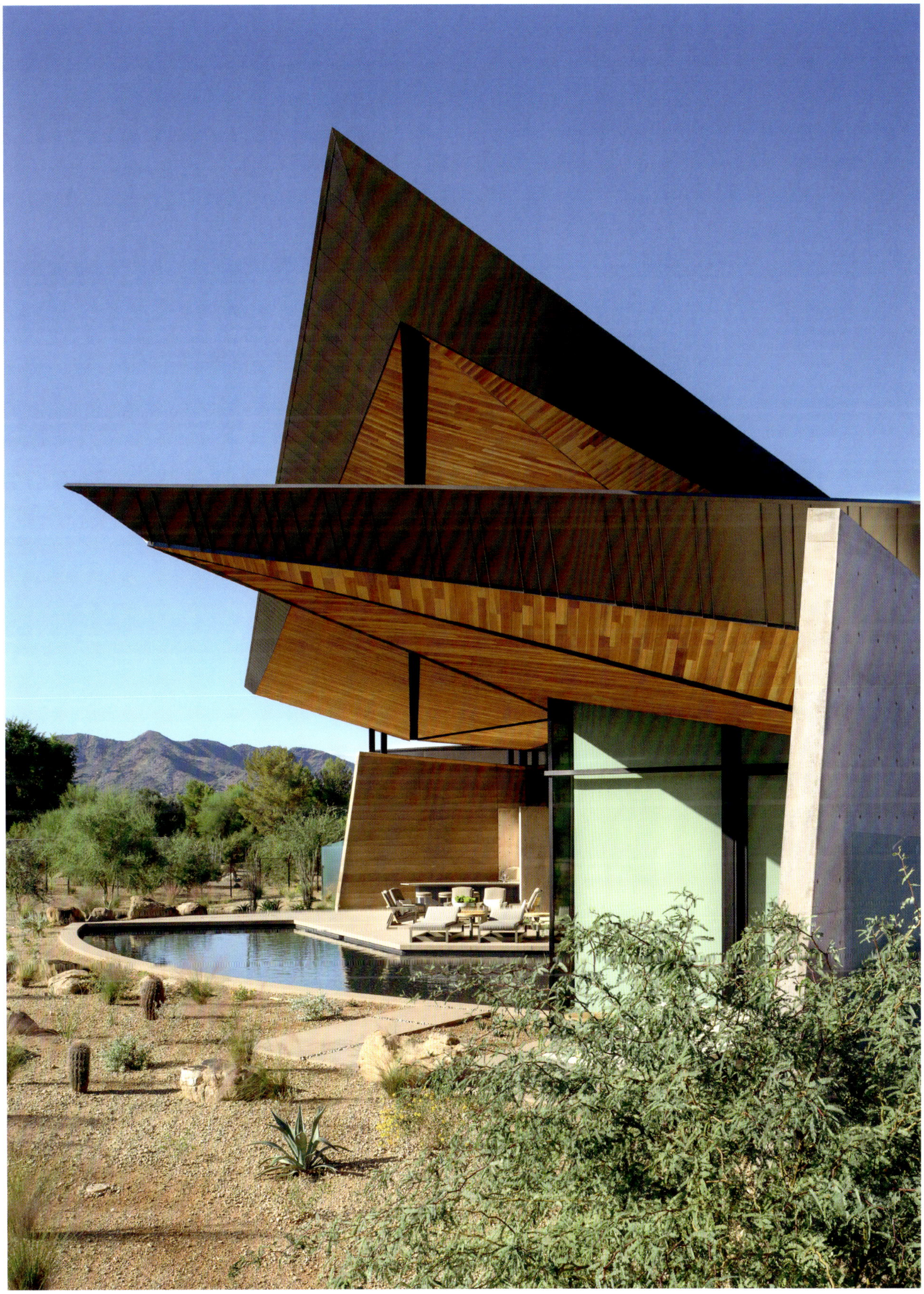

DANCING LIGHT

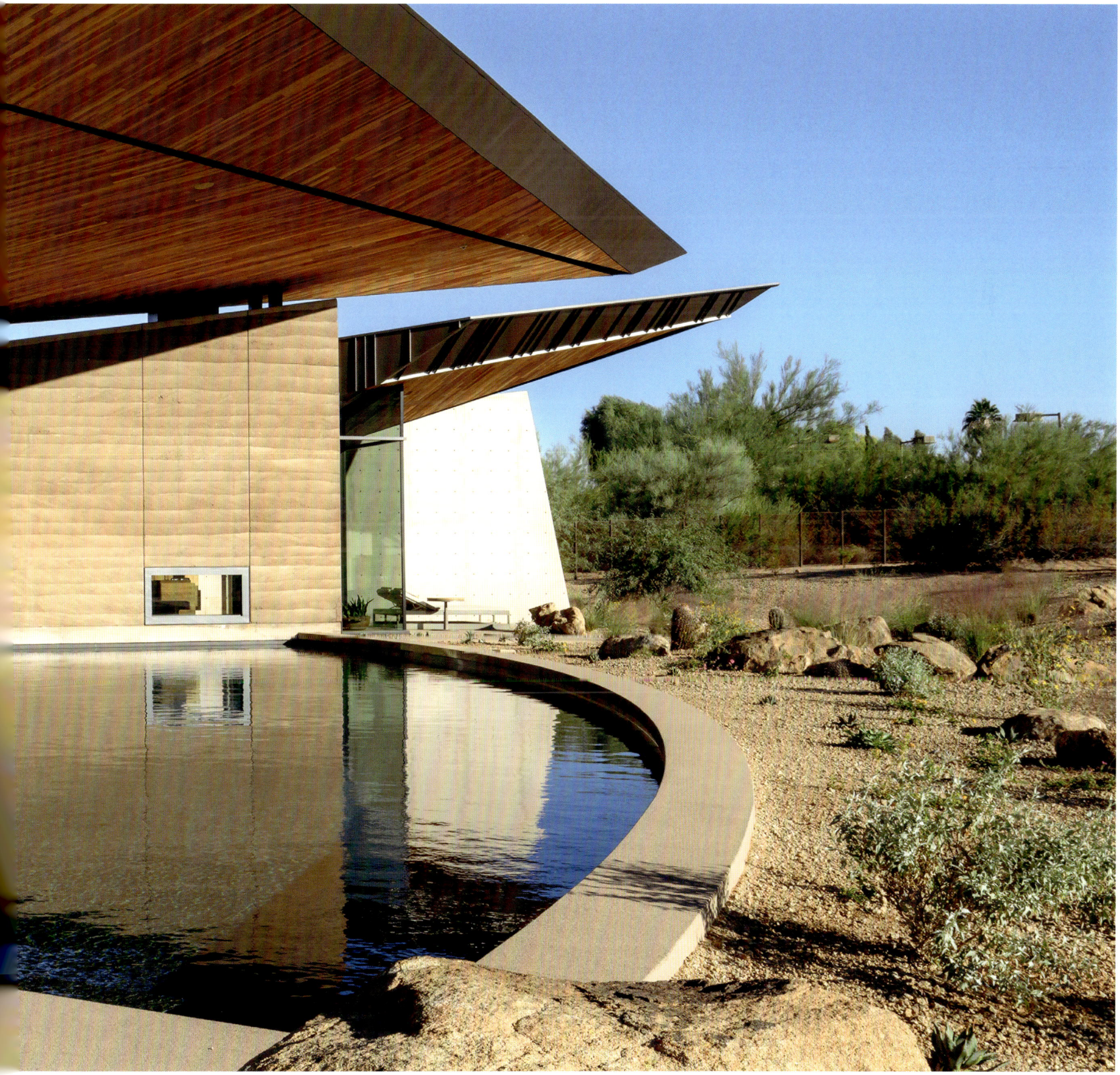

DANCING LIGHT

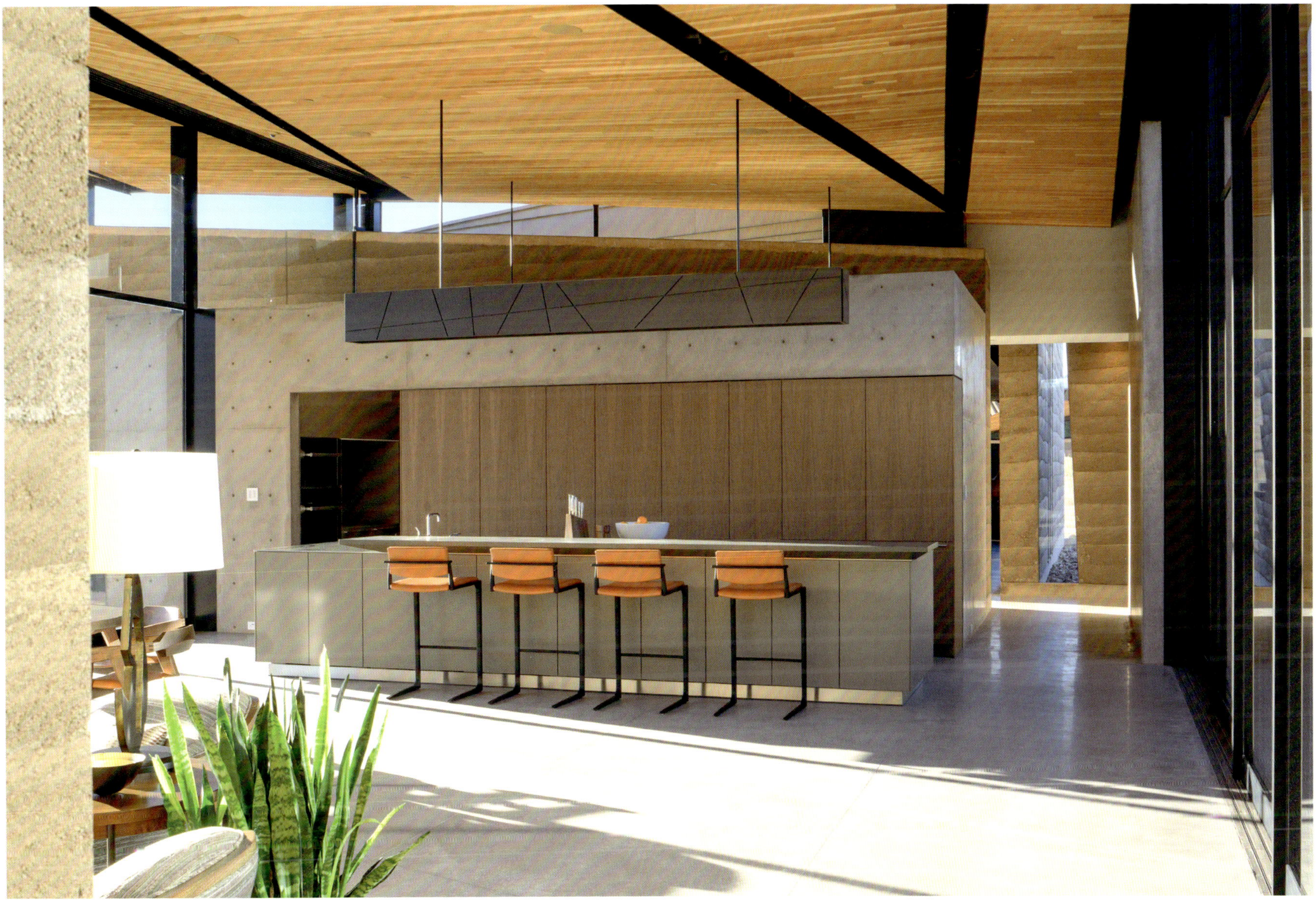

DANCING LIGHT

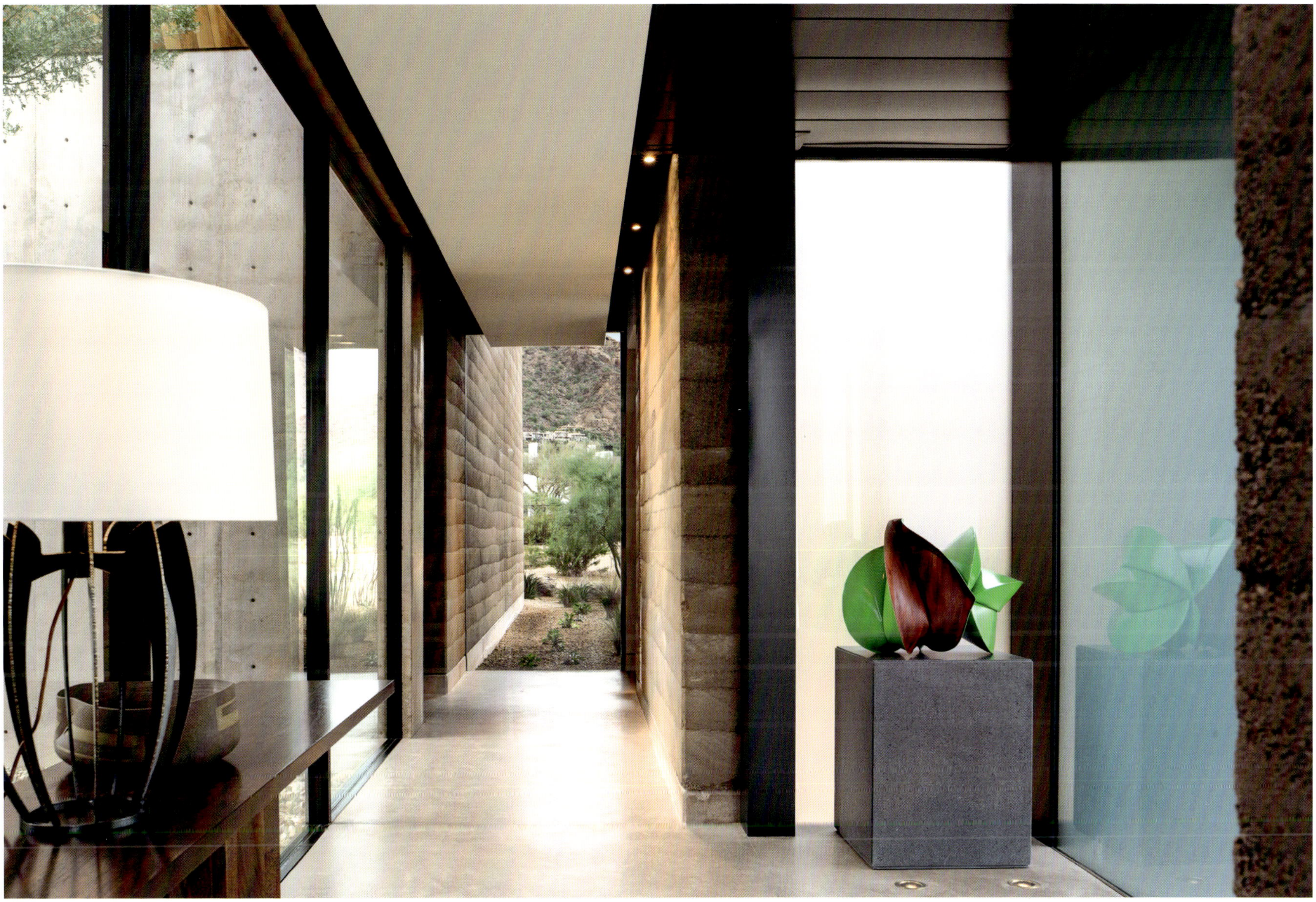

Marwan Al-Sayed, Inc.
DESERT CITY HOUSE
2012 | Paradise Valley, AZ, USA

Located in Paradise Valley, in the suburban sprawl of Phoenix, the Desert City House was originally conceived to be a zero net energy dwelling. Though most certainly the desire of many environmentally conscious house builders, in reality it can be a difficult goal to achieve, as local expertise can be sparse and the costs for innovative systems high. But sometimes alternatives are better than the initial plan. Since utilizing cast-earth walls was not possible, the decision was made to use single-cast concrete—a common building material in hot climates and now the main characteristic of this Arizona house. The walls feature a thermal lag effect that completely shields the structure from eastern and western exposure, while white plaster reflects sunshine off other exposed surfaces. Both materials are appealing beyond their aesthetic and thermic qualities for their longevity and low need for maintenance. Two one-story volumes flank the entry courtyard and anchor a two-story volume that houses the main living, dining, and kitchen spaces as well as outdoor dining decks. This "reverse" living plan keeps bedrooms and bathrooms on the lower level cool in the desert heat, while the more public level above grants generous views of the topography. Through its twenty-inch-thick (fifty-one centimeters) walls and its sheer scale, this modern monolith carries connotations of Mediterranean classicism; its proportions strengthen impressions of grandeur. Two towerlike slender volumes, faced primarily in glass, rise an additional story and are designed to absorb the abundant sunlight during the day and simultaneously act as a fresh air draw to cool the house and keep the low-impact mission alive. At night, the monitors mystically glow like beacons in the dark.

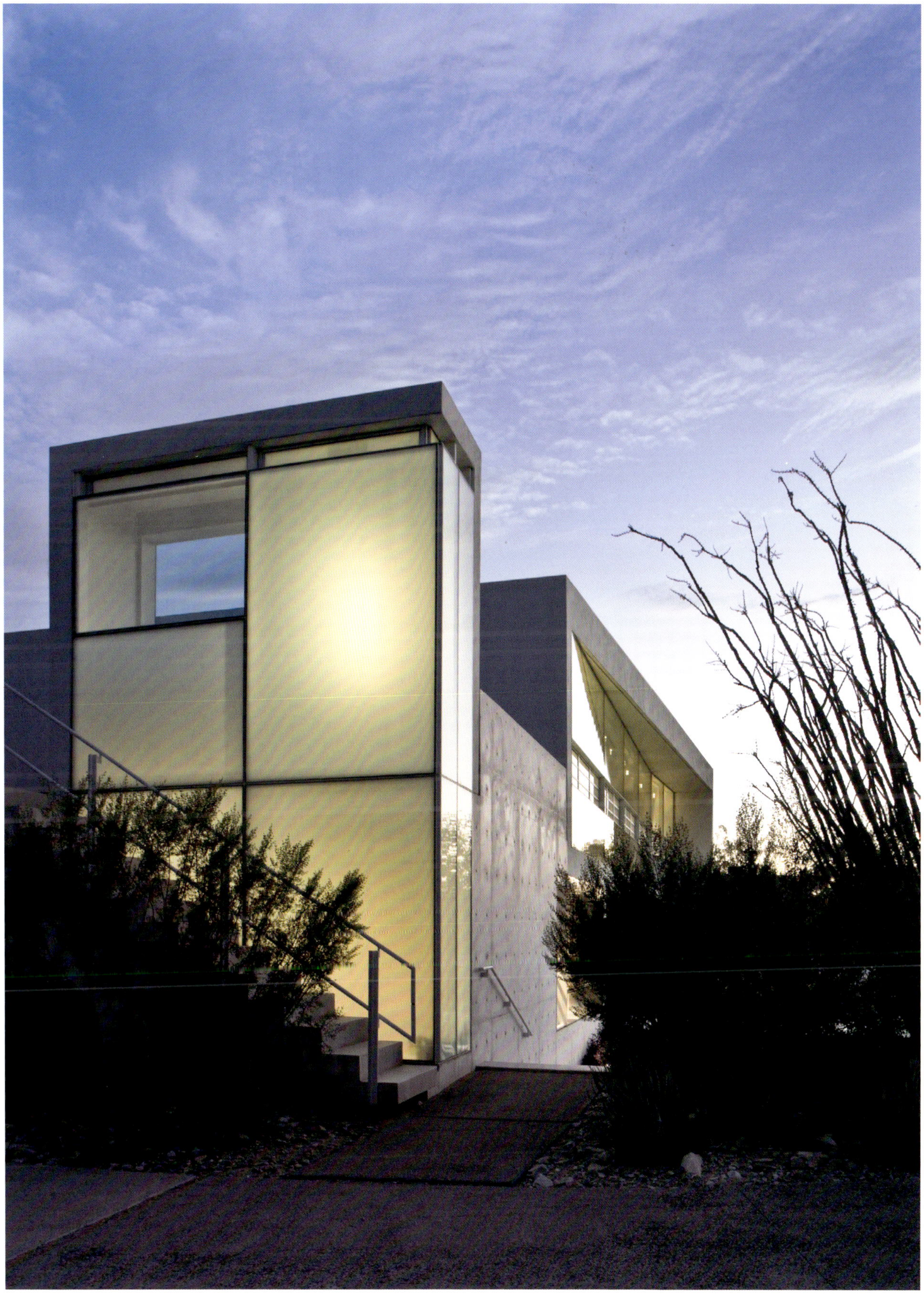

DESERT CITY HOUSE

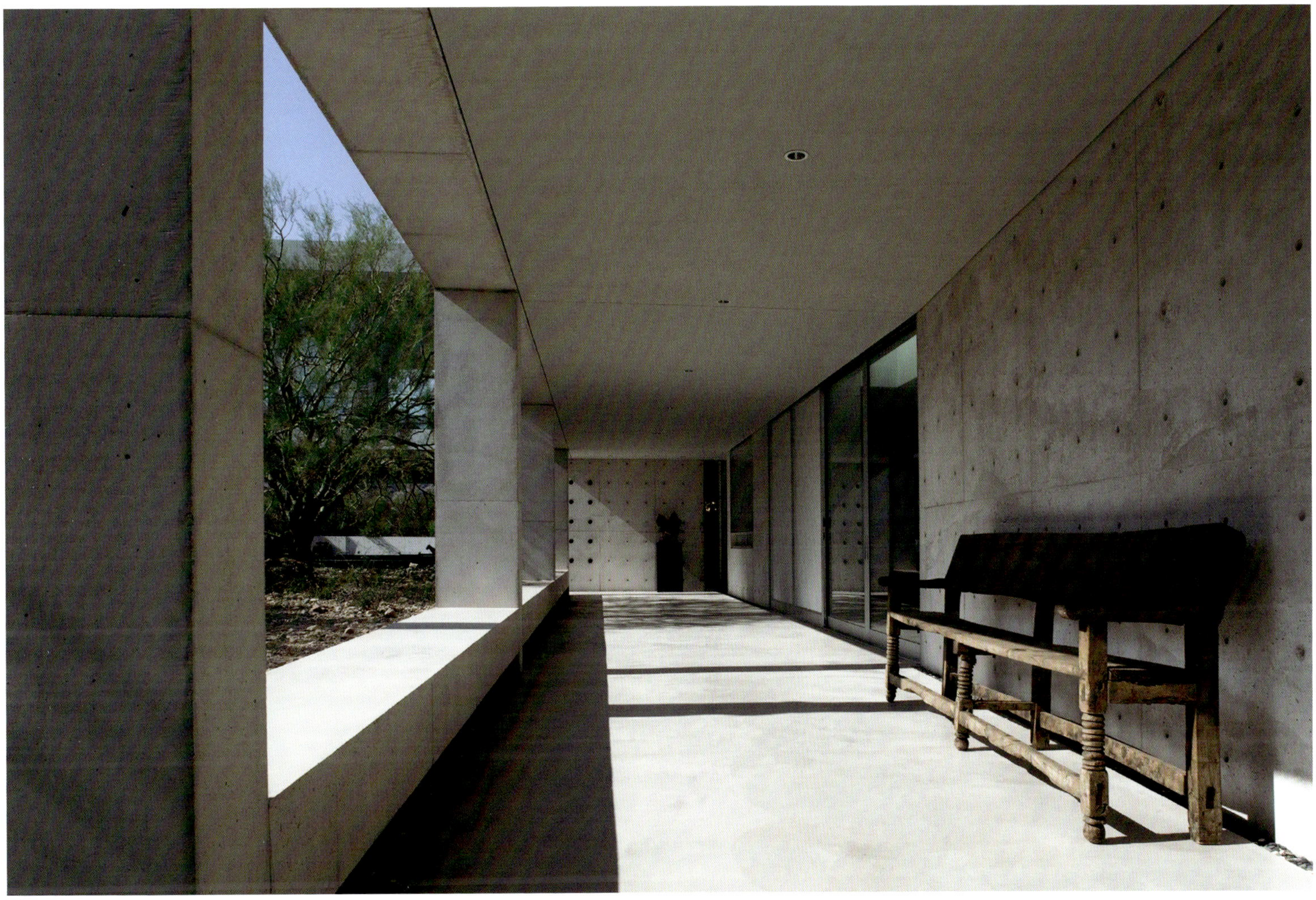

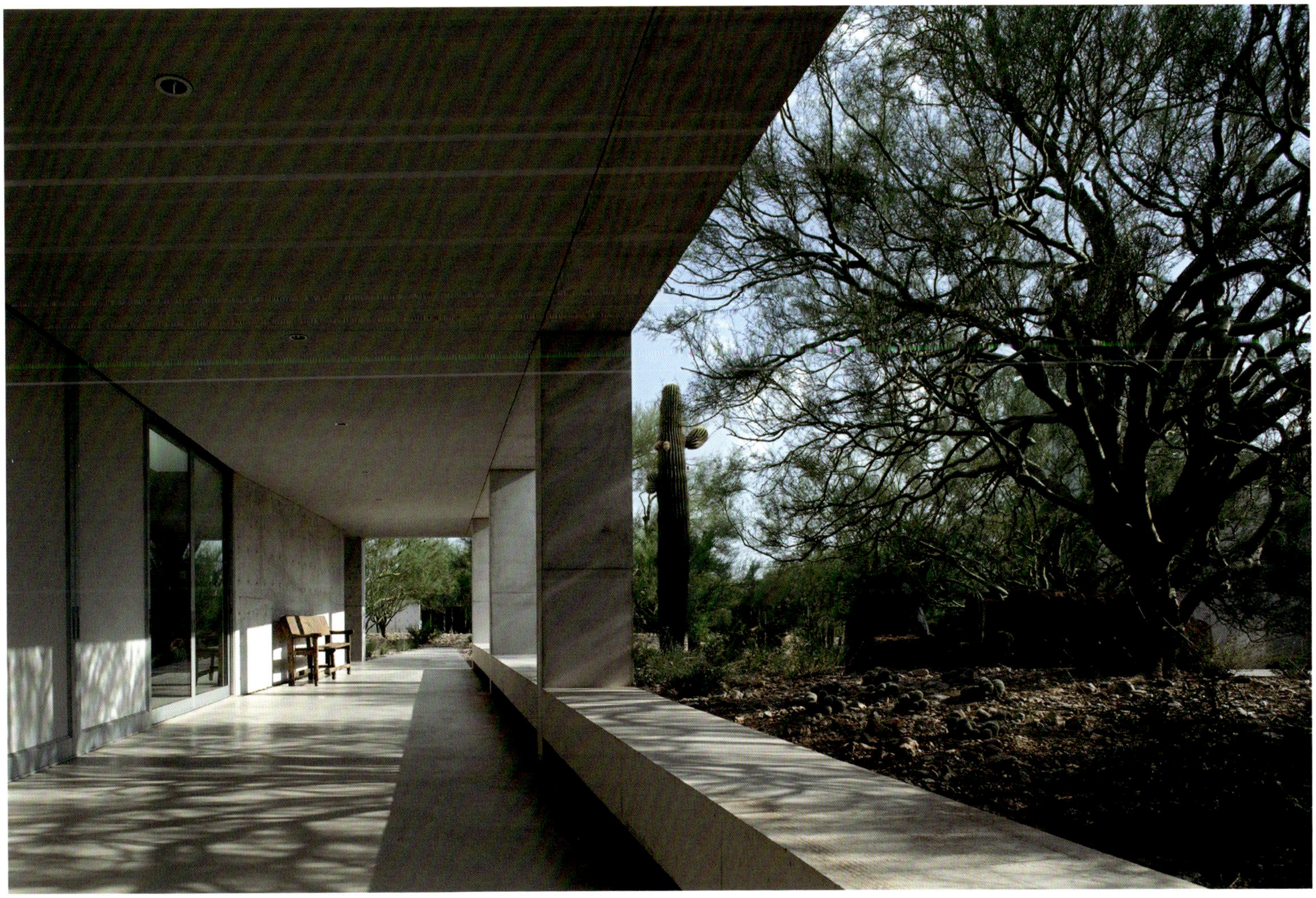

DESERT CITY HOUSE

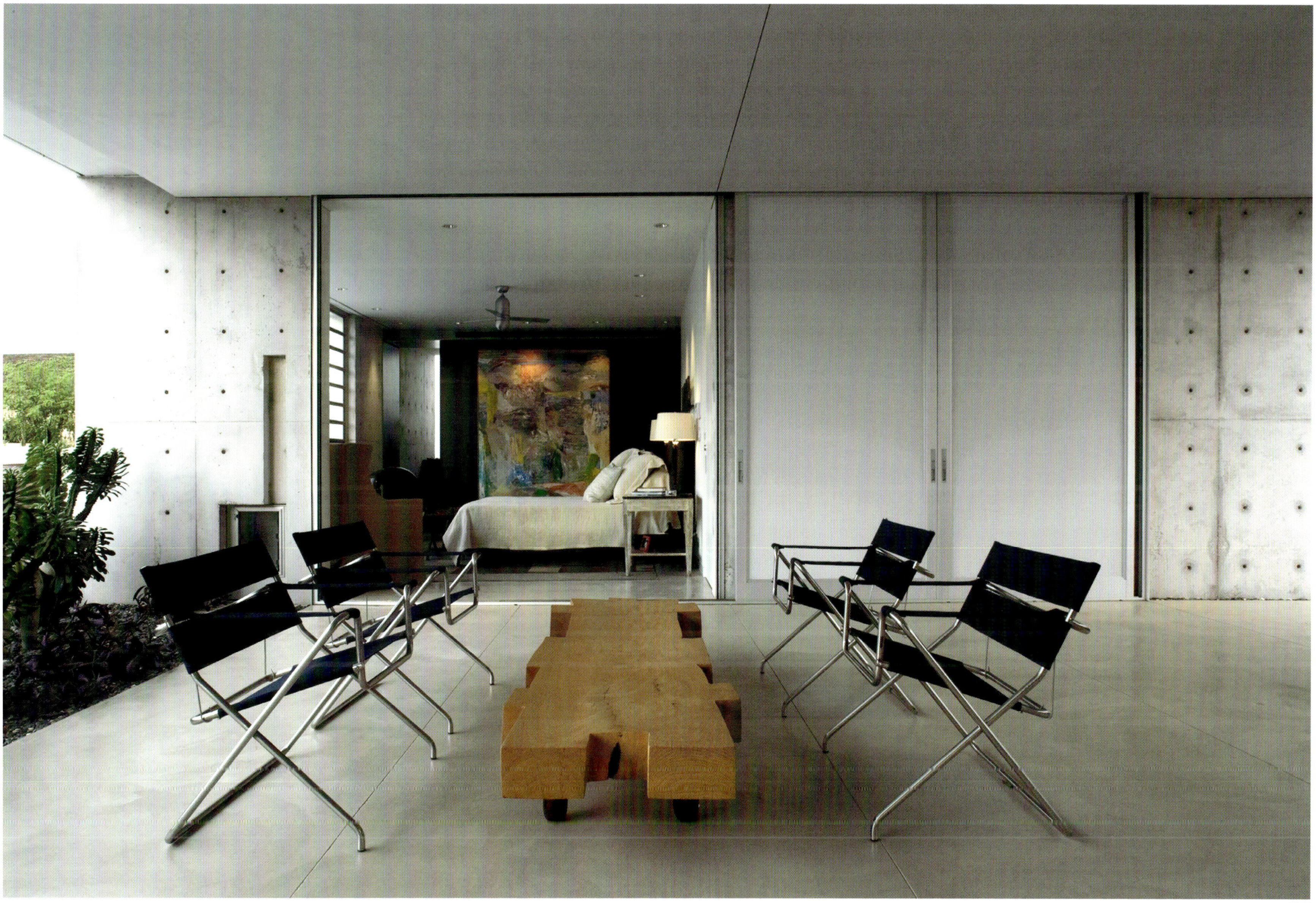

Olson Kundig
SAWMILL
2014 | Tehachapi, CA, USA

Without question, the remoteness of a desert landscape attracts visionaries; in the case of Sawmill, a house in the Tehachapi Mountains in central California, it turns these visionaries into collaborators. Five miles (eight kilometers) off the paved road and at an altitude of five thousand feet (1,524 kilometers), the plot of land was purchased by a couple whose intentions were to build a modest vacation home to reunite a family of four. Architect Tom Kundig, a California native, proposed a structure with three private wings radiating from a gathering space centered around a large hearth—a place to be together and to be alone. The materials were carefully chosen to withstand the sun but to also take into account the possibility of wildfires common to the area: cement brick, steel beams, and salvaged corrugated metal sheets form the exterior. Built mostly on weekends over the course of several years, often with the help of three generations of family members, the cabin features thoughtful details and ideas honed over time, such as the gearbox of an old irrigation pump that is used as a wheel to open a glazed wall. At this high altitude, even the desert of California can receive snow in winter; radiant-heat floors are powered by electricity provided through solar panels if the necessity arises, and a well supplies water. It is rare that consideration and respect are articulated with such consistency and eloquence.

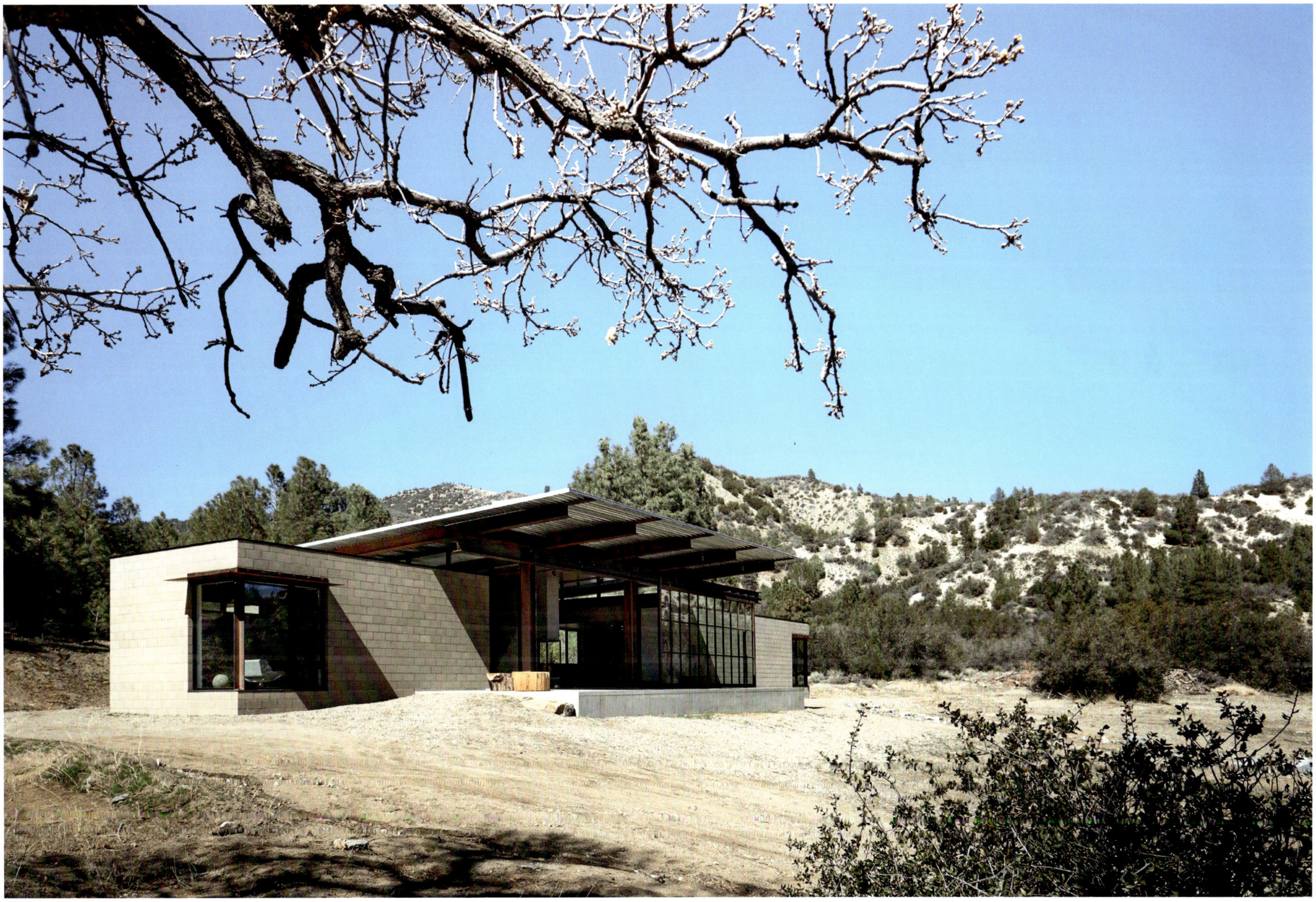

SAWMILL

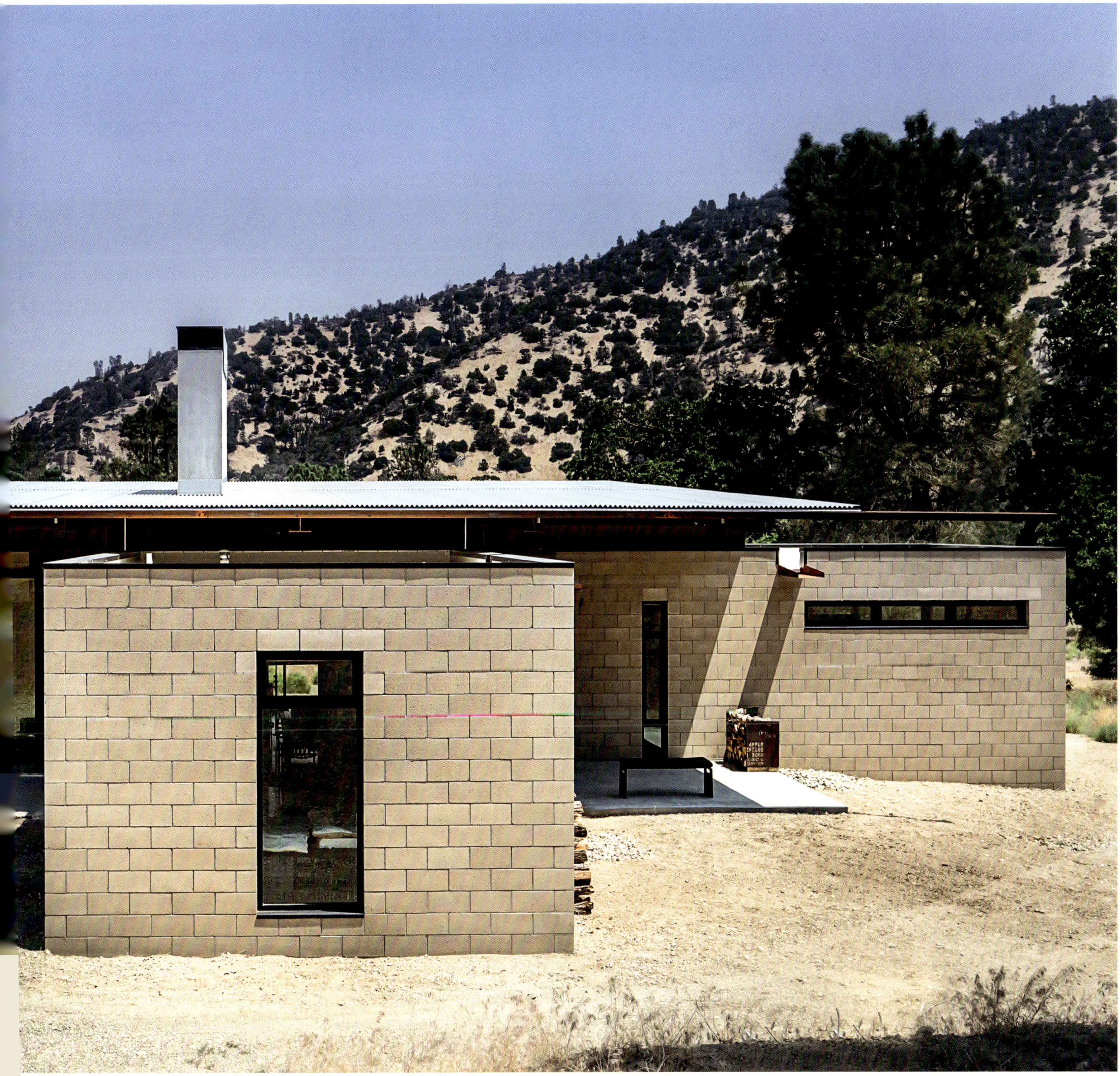

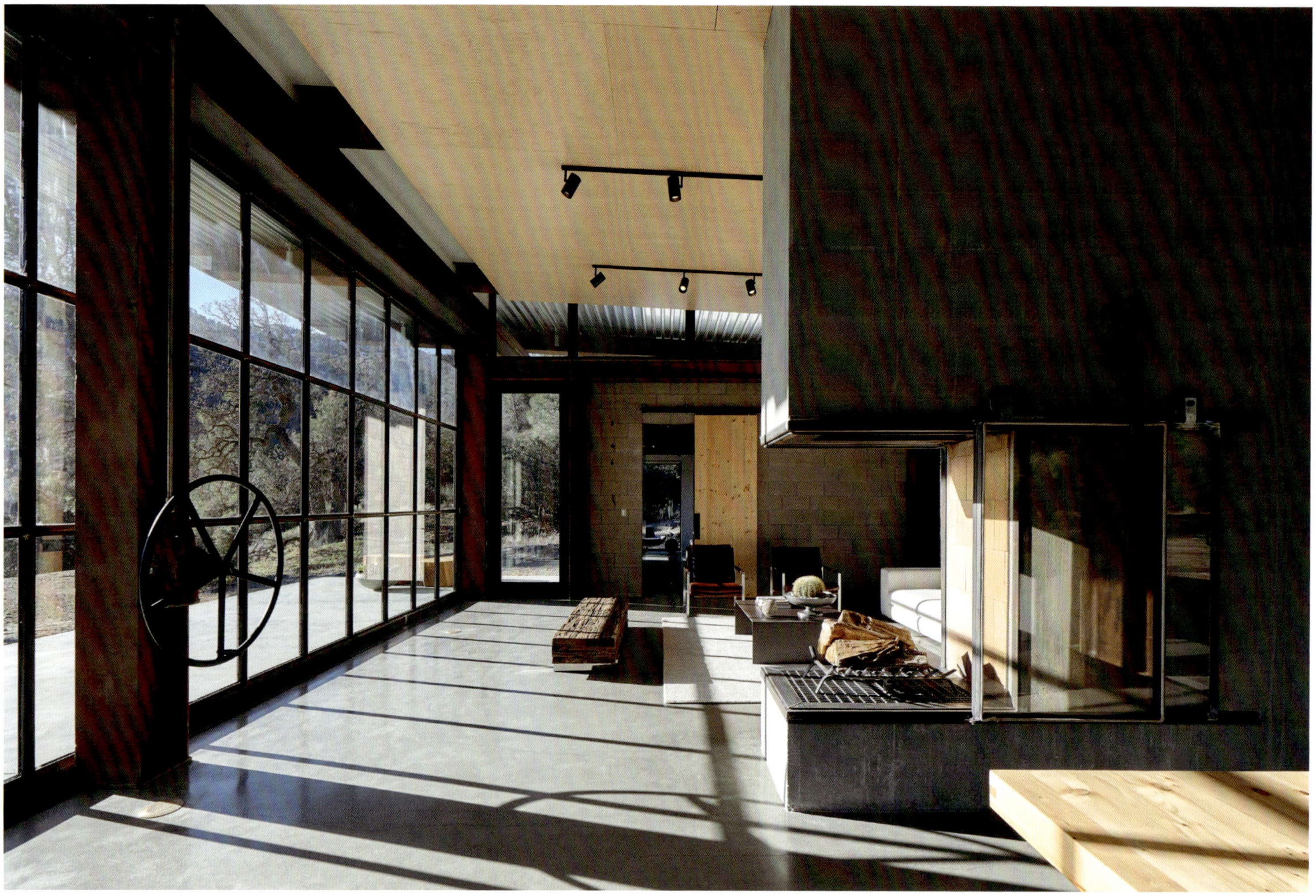
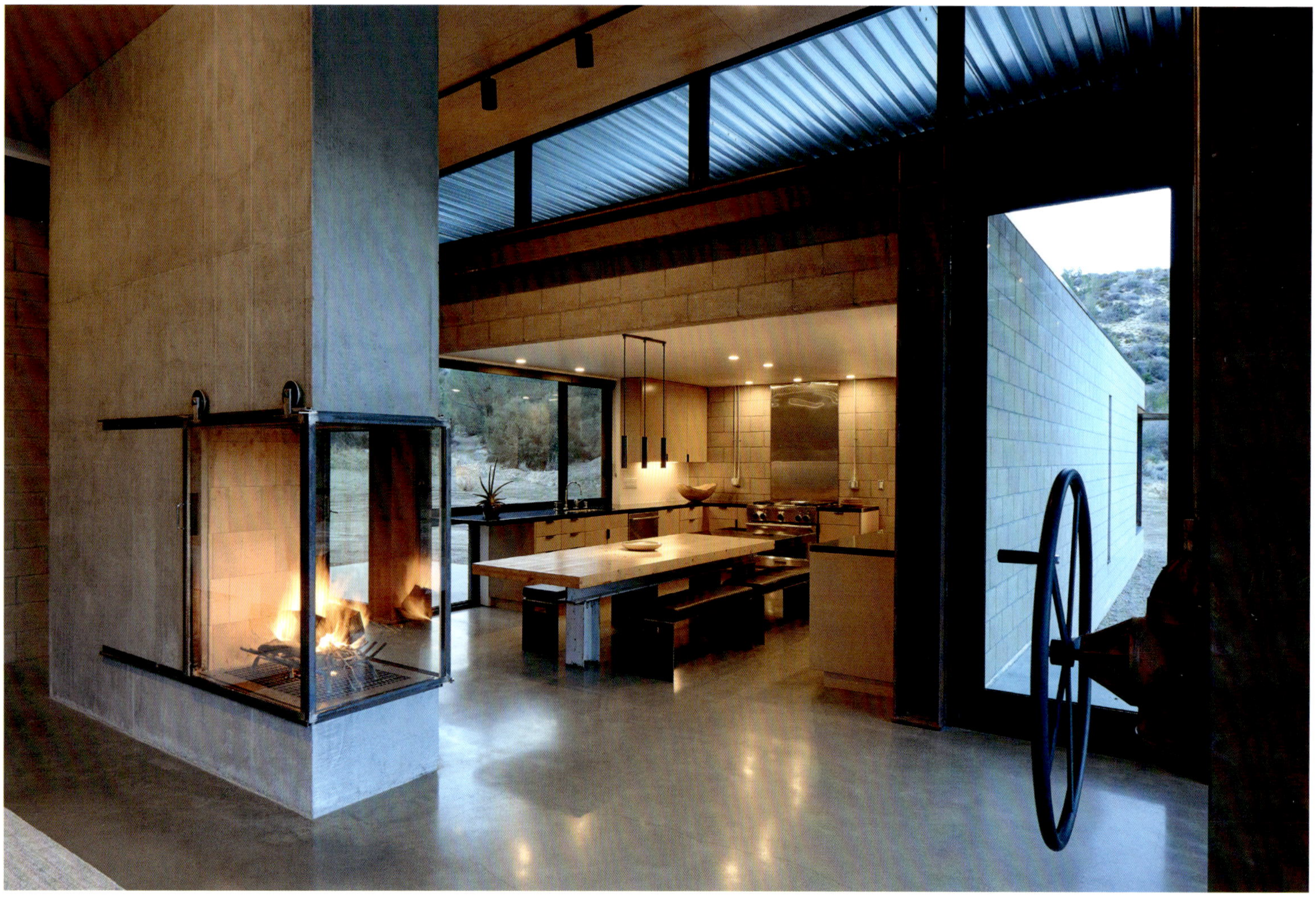

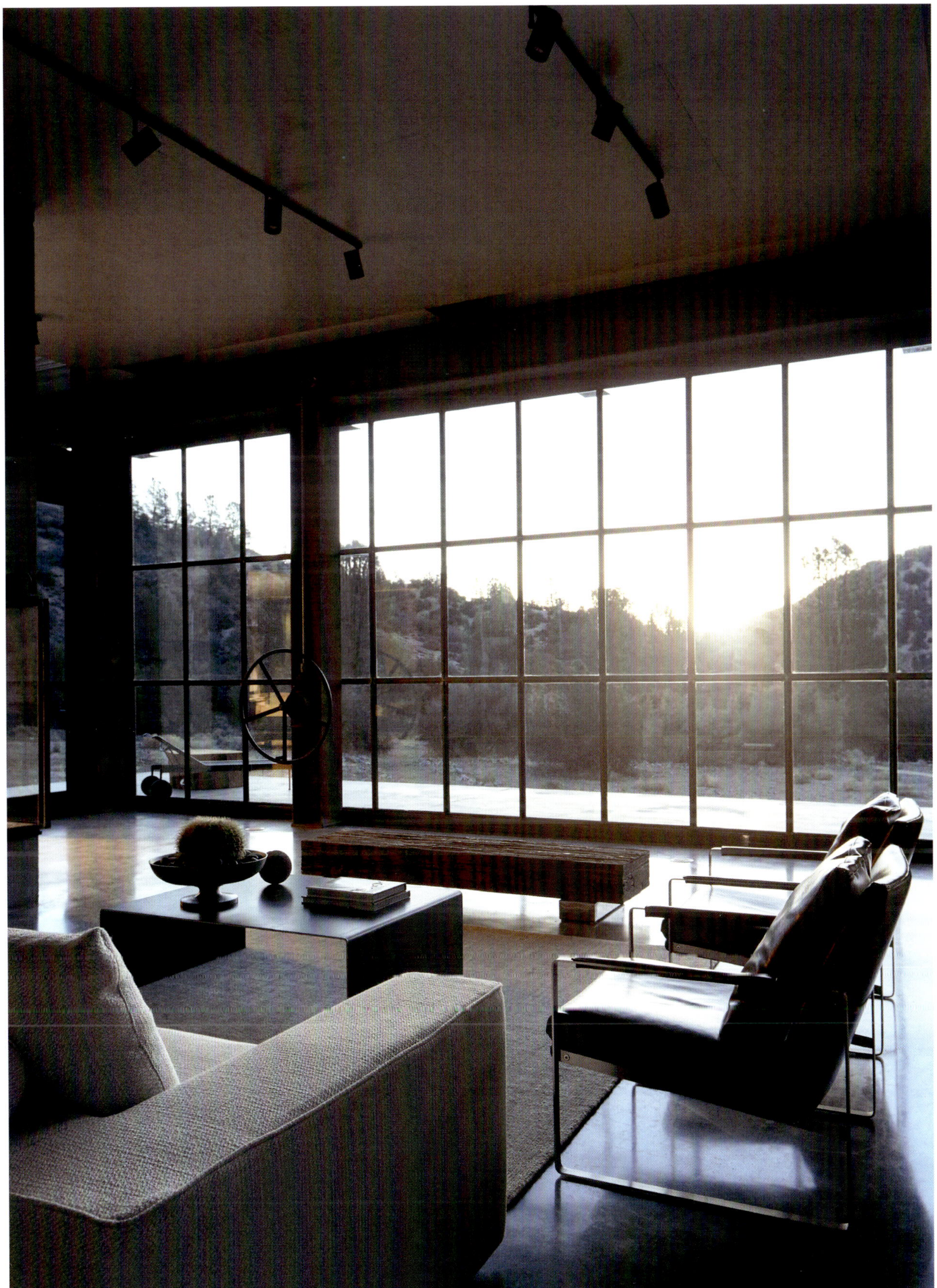

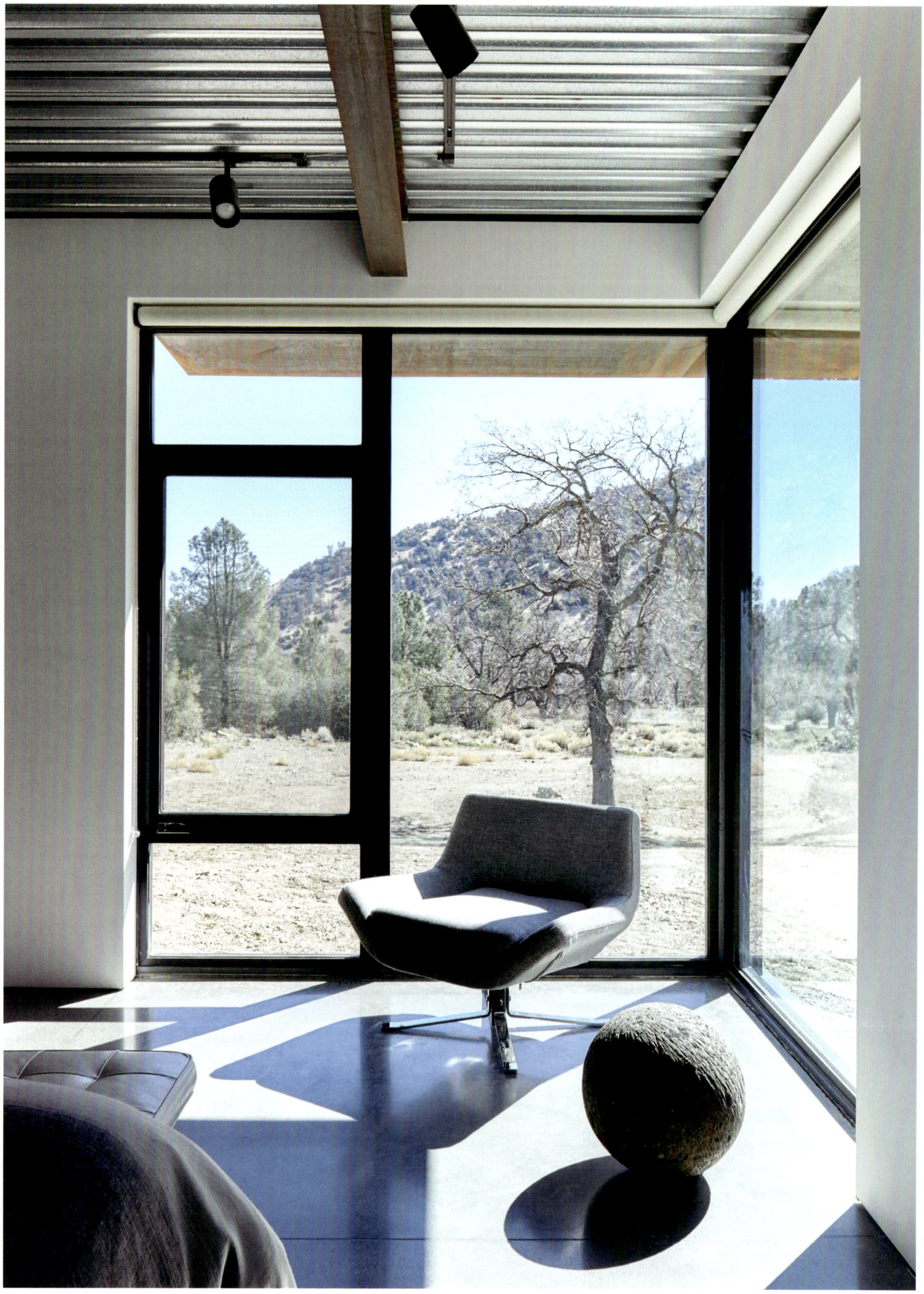

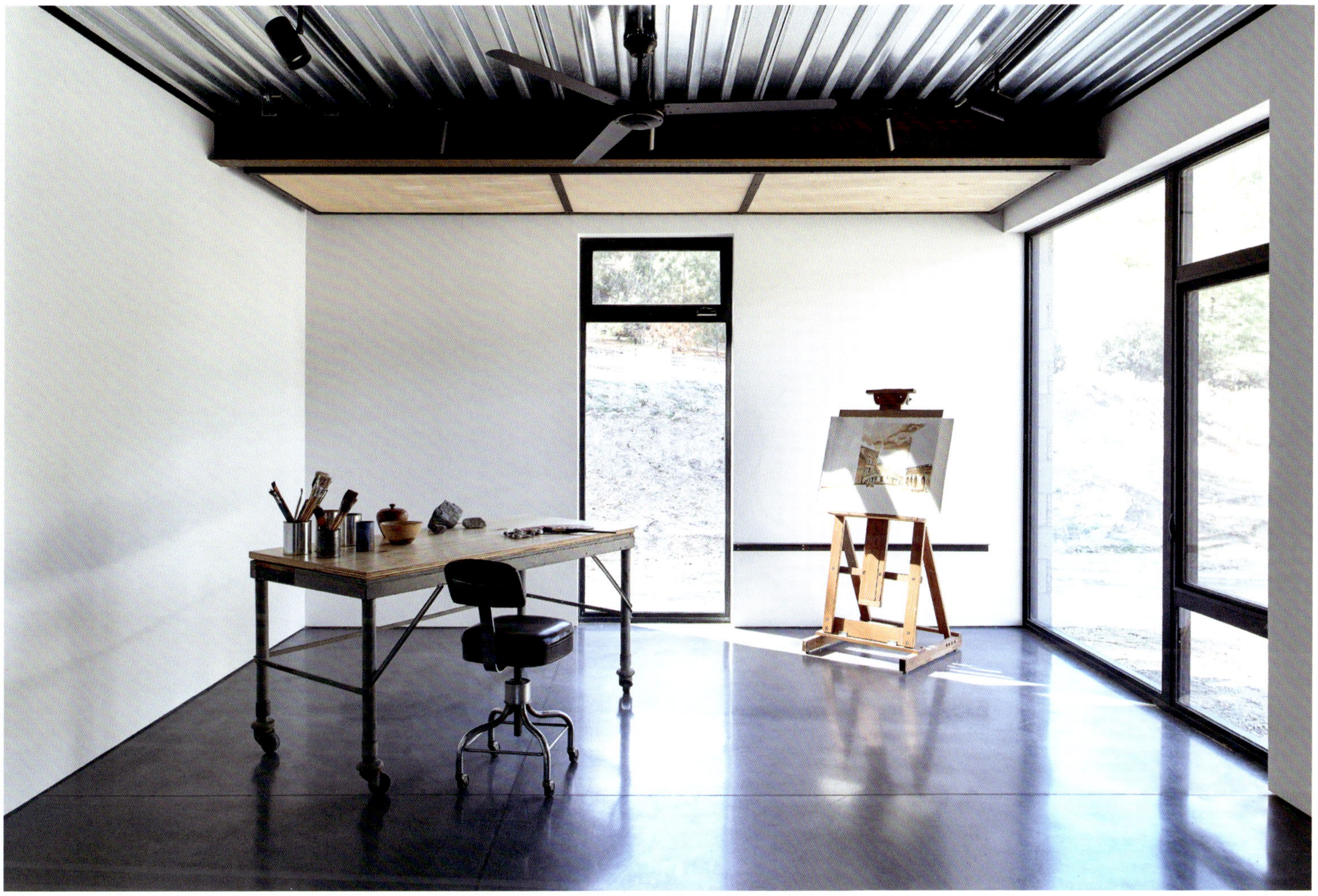

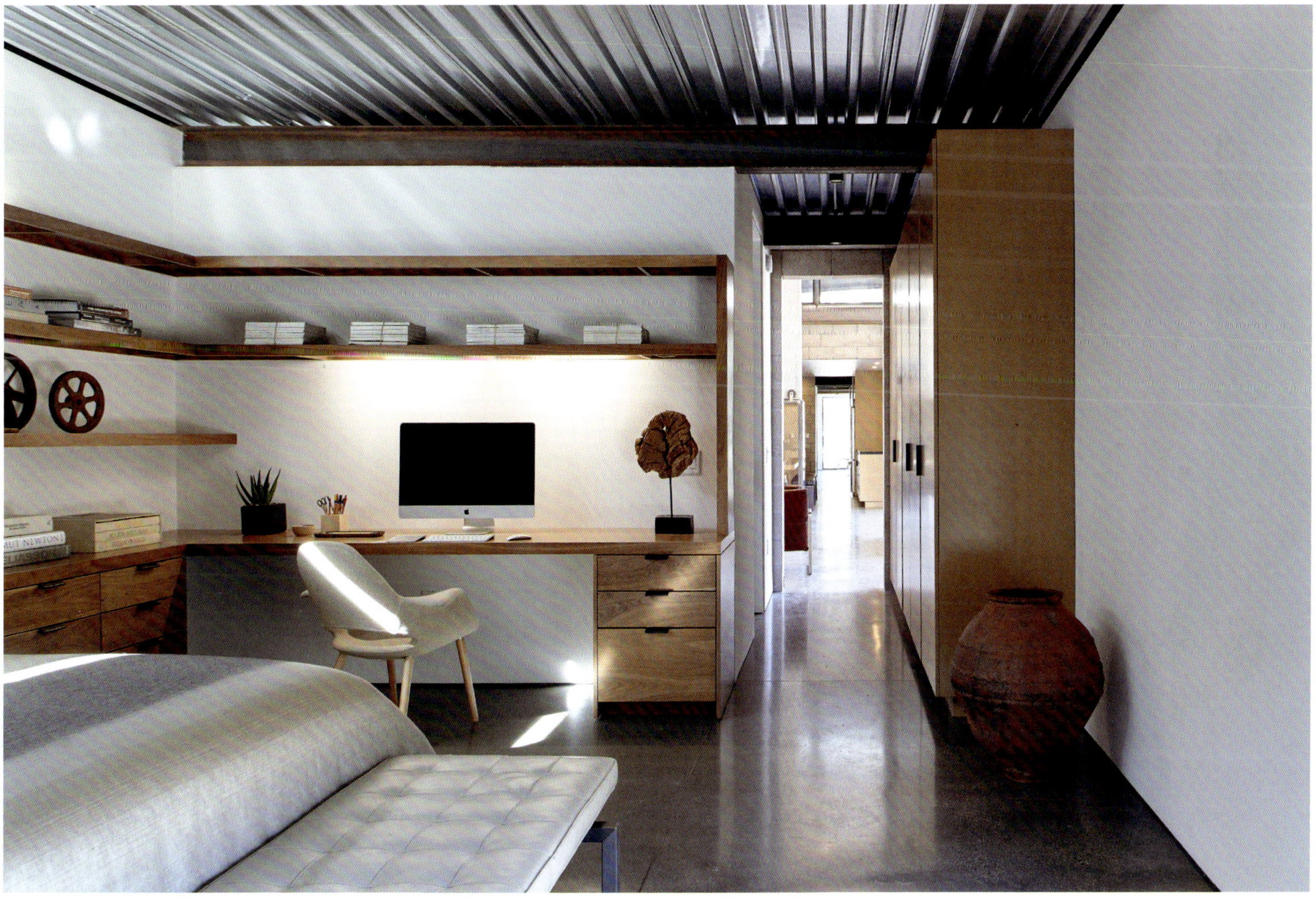

Wendell Burnette Architects
DESERT COURTYARD HOUSE
2013 | Scottsdale, AZ, USA

This unusual Arizona structure emerges from Scottsdale's desert terrain in the form of a fortress wrapped in a patinated-steel envelope. As the low-lying site hinders privacy from neighbors' views, the house was designed to recede into the landscape, with apertures centered primarily on an expansive central courtyard. The interior is more cheerful than the exterior but no less impressive. Thick rammed-earth walls are made from the local soil, which is uniquely suited for this process. A concrete plinth cast with cement harvested from the nearby Salt River merges exterior with interior, and a glass-floored corridor reveals the desert topography below. It is well-considered details such as these that render the project special and reveal the architects' respect for the land, a sentiment that is at the heart of the decision to arrange the main living spaces around the courtyard and thus invite the desert features to the center of the house. Because of the owners' appreciation of the darkness of desert nights, the ceilings are made from mill-finished steel; as the deep-hued, glowing material recedes into dimness at the close of day and the fully glazed walls become invisible, interior and exterior appear to unite into a single space. Regardless of its effort to shield itself from the outside world, Desert Courtyard House permits intimate connections to the land—the entire bathroom wall, for example, can be opened mechanically if one desires to shower in the company of the desert.

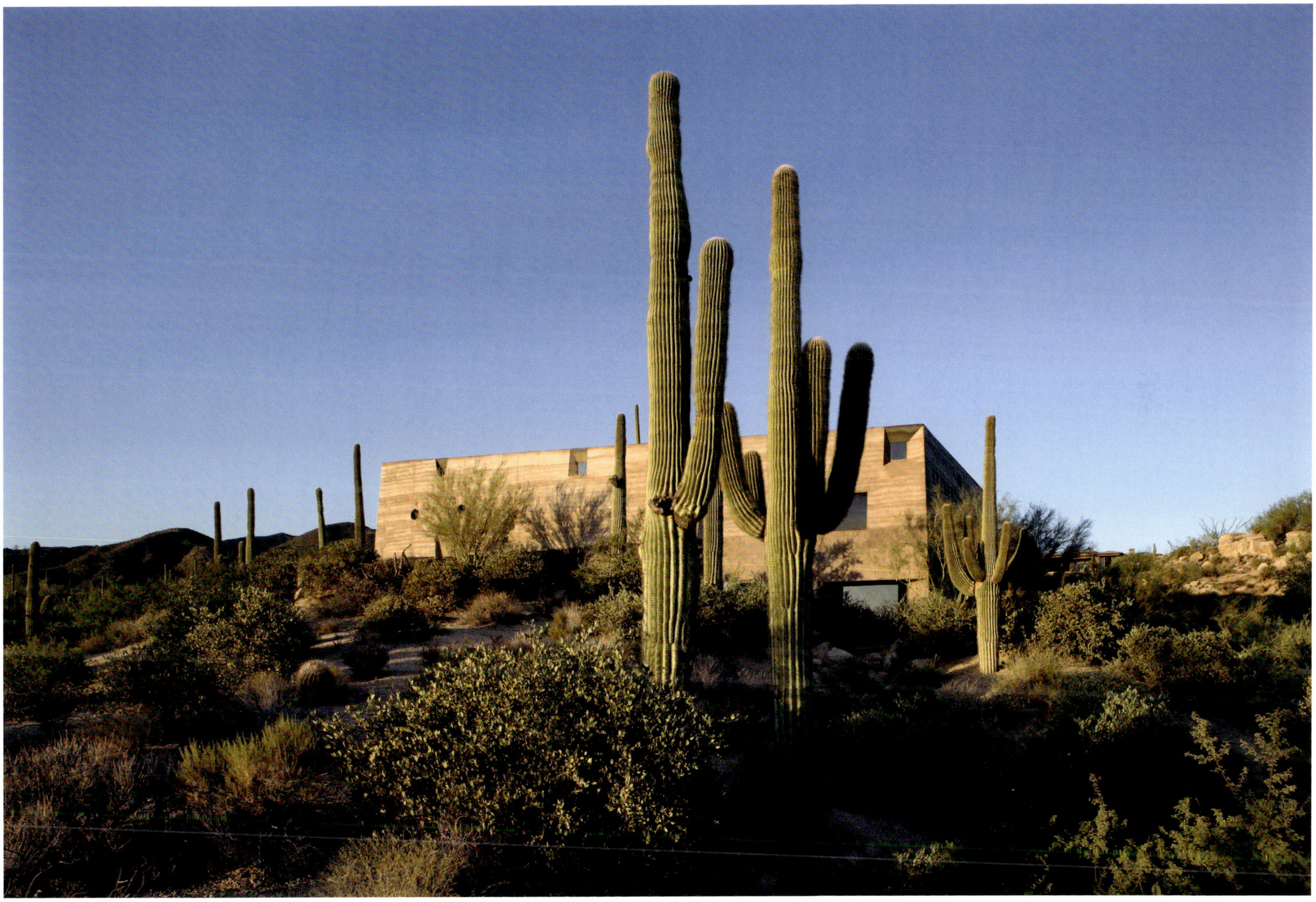

DESERT COURTYARD HOUSE

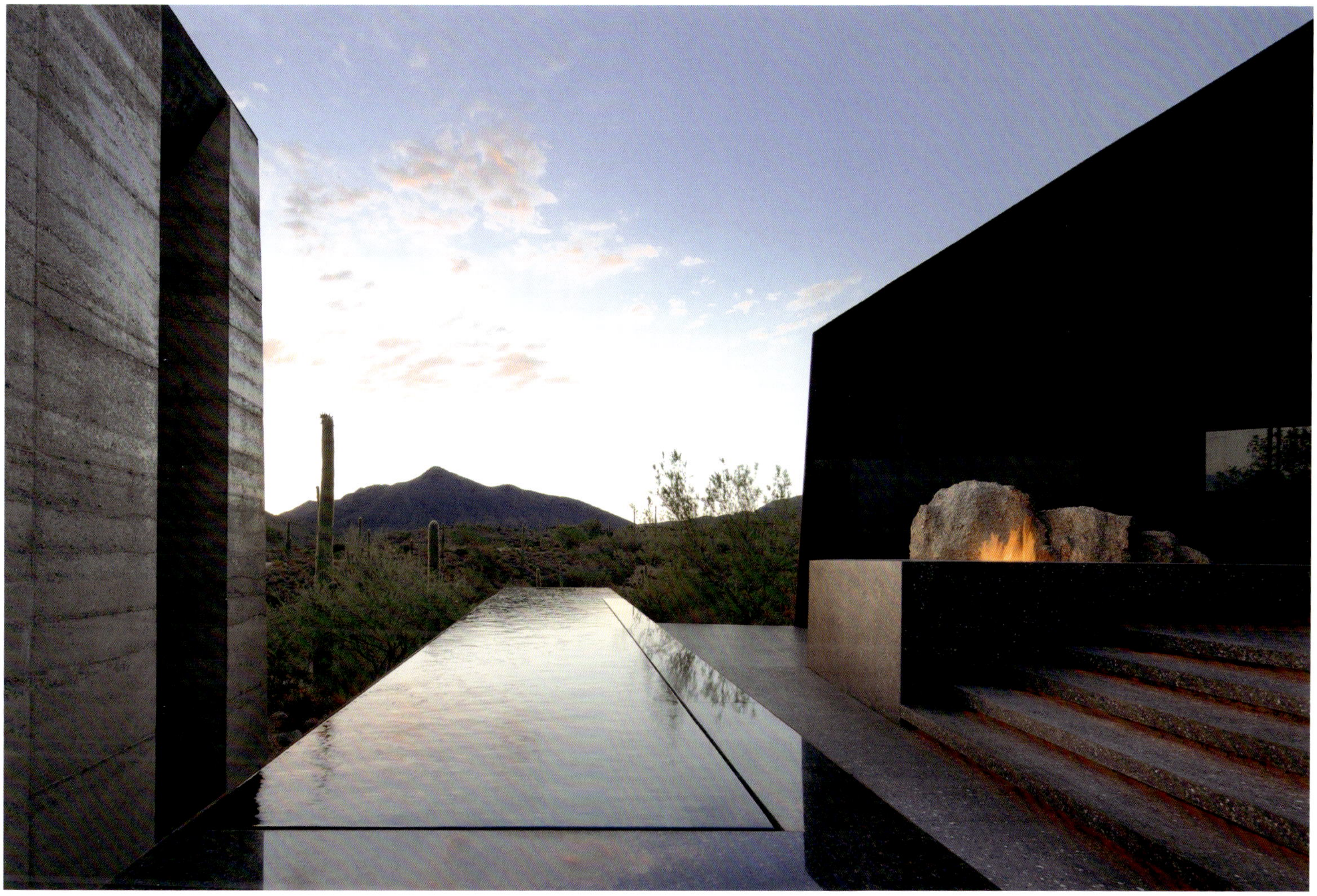

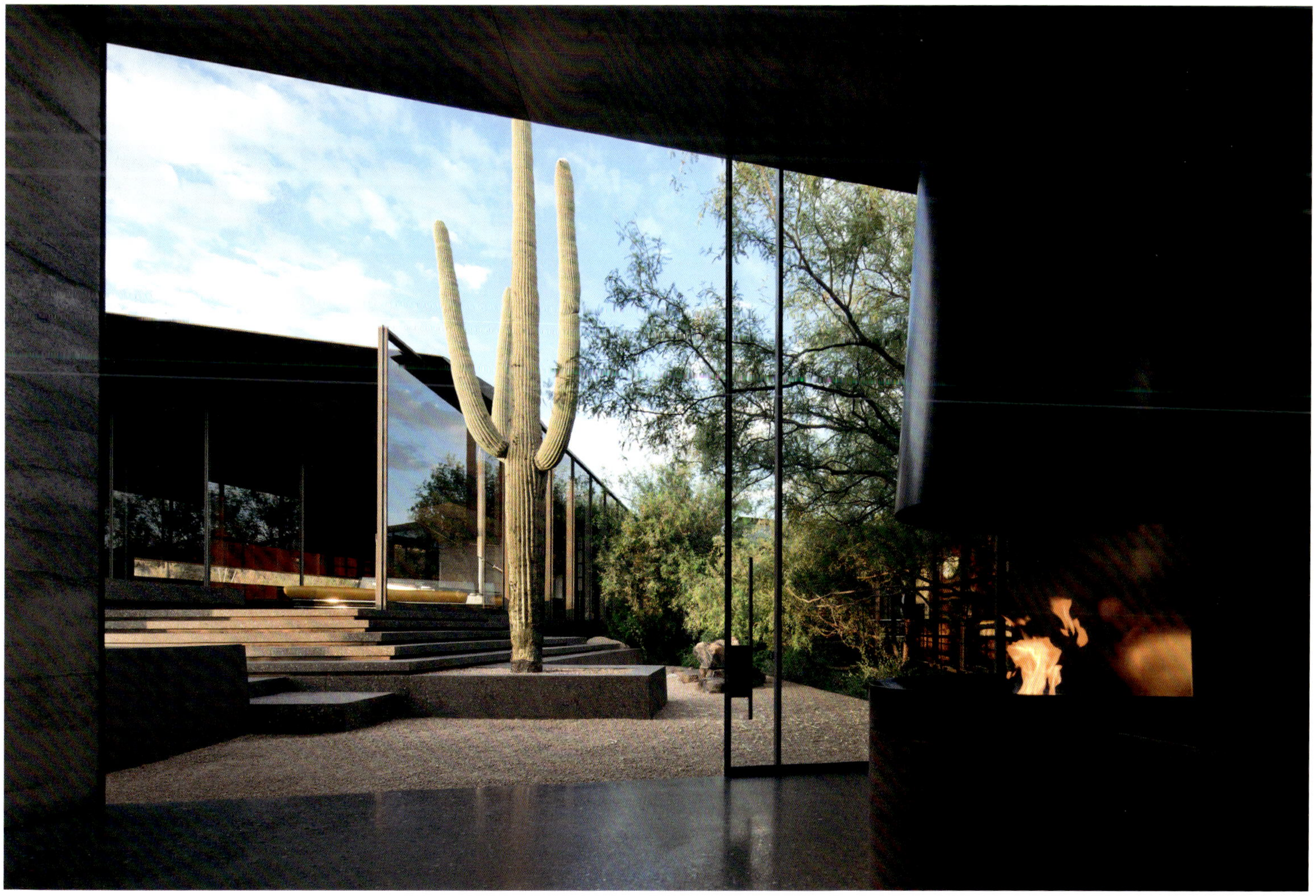

DESERT COURTYARD HOUSE

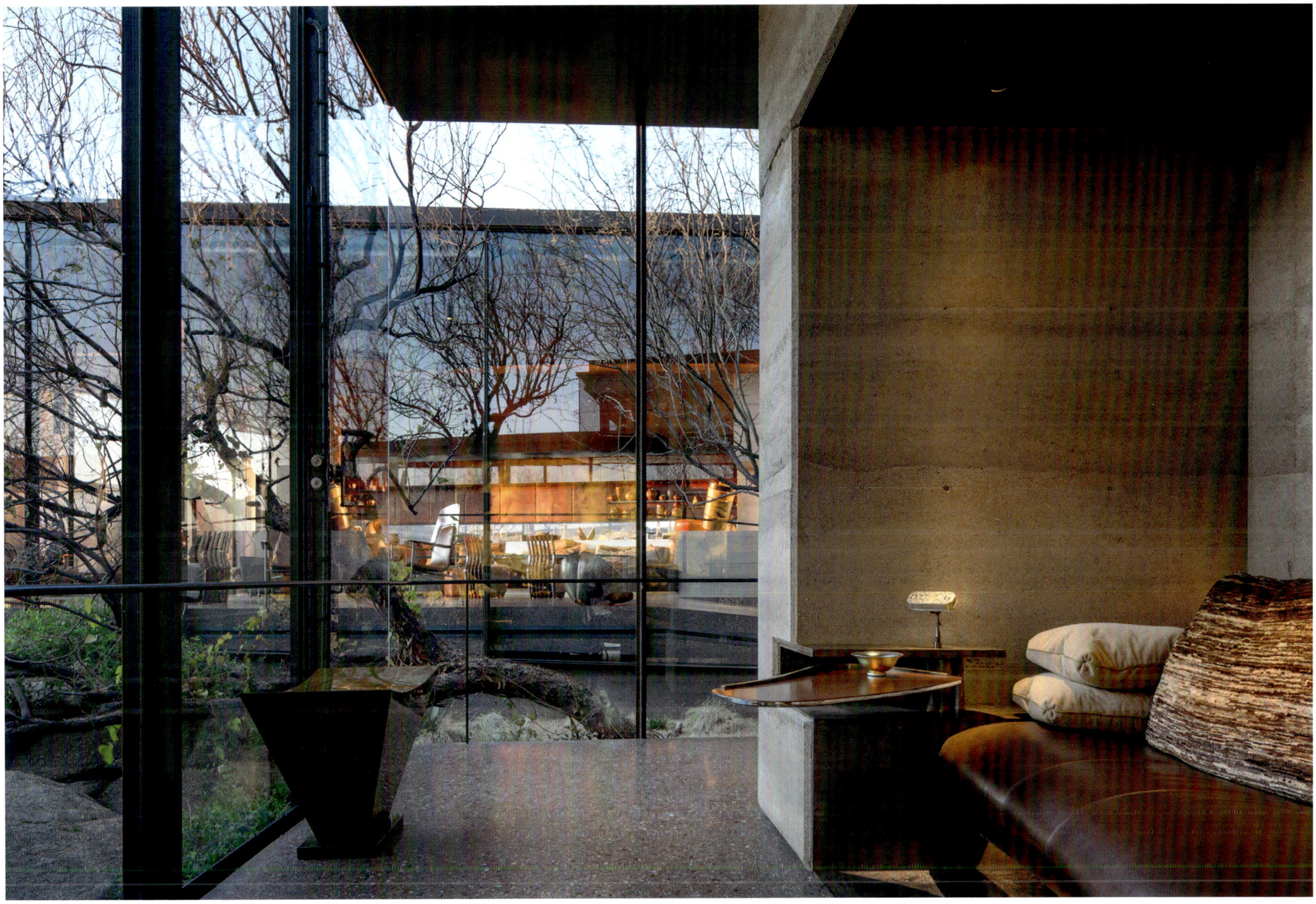

INDEX
Page references for illustrations appear in **boldface**.

A-I-R, Inc. Darren Petrucci Architect
   Ghost Wash House 112, **113–15**
Aitken, Doug
   Mirage 68, **69–71**
Aladab, Niger 44, **45–47**
Alentejo, Portugal 88, **89–91**
Alice Springs, Australia 170, **171–75**
Almería, Spain 116, **117–21**
Al Ouidane, Morocco 136, **137–39**
Amangiri Resort (I-10 Studio) 158, **159–65**
Ancón District, Lima Province, Peru 16, **17–21**
AutonomeForme Architettura
   Deserti Tascabili DJ Complex #2 102, **103–5**

BAM Architects Office
   Through Gardens House 106, **107–11**
Barclay & Crousse Architecture
   C3 House 16, **17–21**
Black Desert House (Oller & Pejic Architecture) 54, **55–61**
Blank Studio
   Xeros Residence 48, **49–53**

C3 House (Barclay & Crousse Architecture) 16, **17–21**
Campos Leckie Studio
   Zacatitos 03 186, **187–91**
Canopea
   Casa Nahas 28, **29–31**
Canyon Point, UT, USA 92, **93–97**, 158, **159–65**
Capitol Reef National Park, UT, USA 98, **99–101**
Carlos Arroyo Arquitectos
   Casa Encuentro 116, **117–21**
Carlos Jiménez Studio
   Crowley House 214, **215–17**
Casa Encuentro (Carlos Arroyo Arquitectos) 116, **117–21**
Casa Nahas (Canopea) 28, **29–31**
Casa Pask (Pask, Yearick) 150, **151–57**
Chicureo, Chile 78, **79–83**
Christian Félix et Laetitia Delubac Architectes

Ecolodge I 176, **177–79**
Coachella Valley, CA, USA 72, **73–77**
Crowley House (Carlos Jiménez Studio) 214, **215–17**

Dancing Light (Kendle Design Collaborative) 224, **225–31**
Desert City House (Marwan Al-Sayed, Inc.) 232, **233–37**
Desert Courtyard House (Wendell Burnette Architects) 246, **247–51**
Desert House (Dunn & Hillam Architects) 170, **171–75**
Deserti Tascabili DJ Complex #2 (AutonomeForme Architettura) 102, **103–5**
Desert Nomad House (Rick Joy Architects) 62, **63–67**
Desert Wing House (Kendle Design Collaborative) 180, **181–85**
Djerba, Tunisia 102, **103–5**
Dungeness, Kent, UK 22, **23–27**
Dunn & Hillam Architects
   Desert House 170, **171–75**

Ecolodge I (Christian Félix et Laetitia Delubac Architectes) 176, **177–79**
Edward Ogosta Architecture
   Four Eyes House 72, **73–77**
Encuentro Guadalupe (Gracia Studio) 140, **141–45**
Eustache, Guilhem
   Fobe House 208, **209–13**

Fobe House (Eustache) 208, **209–13**
Four Eyes House (Edward Ogosta Architecture) 72, **73–77**

Ghost Wash House (A-I-R, Inc. Darren Petrucci Architect) 112, **113–15**
Glass Pavilion, The (OFIS Arhitekti) 198, **199–203**
Gracia Studio
   Encuentro Guadalupe 140, **141–45**
Graeme Williamson Architects
   Shingle House 22, **23–27**

Granada, Spain 198, **199–203**
GZ House (Studio Cáceres Lazo) 78, **79–83**
Hidden Valley, UT, USA 192, **193–97**
High Desert Dwelling (Imbue Design) 98, **99–101**
House to Watch the Sunset (Vital) 44, **45–47**

I-10 Studio
   Amangiri Resort 158, **159–65**
Ibarra Rosano Design Architects
   Levin Residence 38, **39–43**
Imbue Design
   High Desert Dwelling 98, **99–101**

Johnston Marklee
   Mound House 146, **147–49**
Joshua Tree National Park, CA, USA 10, **11–15**

Karoo Desert, South Africa 32, **33–37**
Kendle Design Collaborative
   Dancing Light 224, **225–31**
   Desert Wing House 180, **181–85**

La Ventana, Mexico 28, **29–31**
Levin Residence (Ibarra Rosano Design Architects) 38, **39–43**
Los Zacatitos, Mexico 186, **187–91**

Marana, AZ, USA 38, **39–43**
Marfa, TX, USA 146, **147–49**, 214, **215–17**
Marmol Radziner
   Moab 192, **193–97**
   Scottsdale 122, **123–27**
Marrakech, Morocco 208, **209–13**
Marwan Al-Sayed, Inc.
   Desert City House 232, **233–37**
   Stone Court Villa 218, **219–23**
Mesa at Amangiri (Selldorf Architects) 92, **93–97**
Mirage (Aitken) 68, **69–71**
Moab (Marmol Radziner) 192, **193–97**
Mound House (Johnston Marklee) 146, **147–49**

INDEX

OFIS Arhitekti
   Glass Pavilion, The
     198, **199–203**
Olgiati, Valerio
   Villa Além 88, **89–91**
Oller & Pejic Architecture
   Black Desert House 54, **55–61**
Olson Kundig
   Sawmill 238, **239–45**
   Studhorse 128, **129–35**
Openstudio Architects
   Swartberg House 32, **33–37**

Palm Springs, CA, USA 68, **69–71**
Paradise Valley, AZ, USA 112, **113–15**, 218, **219–23**, 224, **225–31**, 232, **233–37**
Parvaneh Village, Borkhar County, Isfahan Province, Iran 106, **107–11**
Pask, Scott
   Casa Pask 150, **151–57**
Phoenix, AZ, USA 48, **49–53**

Rick Joy Architects
   Desert Nomad House 62, **63–67**

Sawmill (Olson Kundig) 238, **239–45**
Scottsdale (Marmol Radziner) 122, **123–27**
Scottsdale, AZ, USA 122, **123–27**, 180, **181–85**, 204, **205–7**, 246, **247–51**
Sefcovic Residence (Tate Studio Architects) 204, **205–7**
Selldorf Architects
   Mesa at Amangiri 92, **93–97**
Shingle House (Graeme Williamson Architects) 22, **23–27**
Siwa, Egypt 176, **177–79**
Stone Court Villa (Marwan Al-Sayed, Inc.) 218, **219–23**
Studhorse (Olson Kundig) 128, **129–35**
Studio Cáceres Lazo
   GZ House 78, **79–83**
Studio Ko
   Villa D 136, **137–39**
Swartberg House (Openstudio Architects) 32, **33–37**

Tate Studio Architects
   Sefcovic Residence 204, **205–7**
Tehachapi, CA, USA 238, **239–45**
Through Gardens House (BAM Architects Office) 106, **107–11**
Tucson, AZ, USA 62, **63–67**, 150, **151–57**

Valle de Guadalupe, Mexico 140, **141–45**
Villa Além (Olgiati) 88, **89–91**
Villa D (Studio Ko) 136, **137–39**
Vital, Not
   House to Watch the Sunset 44, **45–47**

Wagon Station Encampment (Zittel) 10, **11–15**
Wendell Burnette Architects
   Desert Courtyard House 246, **247–51**
Winthrop, WA, USA 128, **129–35**

Xeros Residence (Blank Studio) 48, **49–53**

Yearick, Graydon
   Casa Pask 150, **151–57**
Yucca Valley, CA, USA 54, **55–61**

Zacatitos 03 (Campos Leckie Studio) 186, **187–91**
Zittel, Andrea
   Wagon Station Encampment 10, **11–15**

[1] BUILT TO EMBRACE THE DESERT

Marc Angeles: 54, 55, 56, 57, 58, 59, 60, 61; Louis Botha: 35; Studio Cáceres Lazo: 78, 79; Pablo Casals-Aguirre: 80, 81, 82, 83; Richard Davies: 32, 33, 34, 36, 37; Alan Gastelum: 69; Lance Gerber: 70; ESTO/Jeff Goldberg: 62, 63, 64, 65, 66, 67; Charles Hosea: 22, 23, 24, 25, 26, 27; Ryan Houchin: 68; © Raimund Koch/VIEW: 48, 49, 50, 51, 52, 53; Conner MacPhee: 71; Chloe Nahas: 28, 29, 30, 31; Not Vital: 44, 45, 46, 47; Edward Ogosta Architecture: 72, 73, 74, 75, 76, 77; Cristóbal Palma: 16, 17, 18, 19, 20, 21; Bill Timmerman: 38, 39, 40, 41, 42, 43; © Andrea Zittel, courtesy the artist and Sadie Coles HQ, London: 10, 11, 12, 13; © Andrea Zittel, courtesy the artist and Sadie Coles HQ, London. Photo by Lance Brewer: 14, 15.

[2] BUILT WITHIN THE DESERT

© Archivio AutonomeForme: 102, 103, 104, 105; Tahsin Baladi: 106, 107, 108, 109, 110, 111; Benjamin Benschneider: 128, 129, 130, 131, 132, 133, 134, 135; Joe Fletcher: 159, 160, 161, 162, 163, 164; Photographs by Luis Garcia: 140, 141, 142, 143, 144, 145; Dan Glasser: 136, 137, 138, 139; Ken Hayden, Courtesy of Selldorf Architects: 92, 93, 94, 95, 96, 97; Photography: imagensubliminal.com: 116, 117, 118, 119, 120, 121; Imbue Design: 98, 99, 100, 101; © Archive Olgiati: 88, 89, 90, 91; Stefan Ruiz: 150, 151, 152, 153, 154, 155, 156, 157; Richard Se: 158, 165; Eric Staudenmaier Photography: 146, 147, 148, 149; Bill Timmerman: 112, 113, 114, 115, 122, 123, 124, 125, 126, 127.

[3] BUILT TO RESIST THE DESERT

Gabe Border: 240, 241; © Courtesy of Guardian Glass_photo-Gonzalo Botet: 198; rickbrazil.com: 180, 181, 182, 183, 184, 185; Photographs: Laetitia Delubac: 176, 177, 178, 179; Joe Fletcher/OTTO: 192, 193, 194, 195, 196, 197; Paul Hester, Hester + Hardaway Photogypsies: 214, 215, 216, 217; Jean-Marie Monthiers: 208, 209, 210, 211, 212, 213; © José Navarrete Jiménez: 199, 200, 201, 202, 203; © Kilian O'Sullivan/VIEW: 170, 171, 172, 173, 174, 175; Kevin Scott, Olson Kundig: 238, 239, 242, 243, 244, 245; John Sinal: 186, 187, 188, 189, 190, 191; Steve Thompson: 204, 205, 206, 207; Bill Timmerman: 246, 247, 248, 249, 250, 251; © Alexander Vertikoff | Vertikoff Archive: 224, 225, 226, 227, 228, 229, 230, 231; Photos: Matt Winquist: 218, 219, 220, 221, 222, 223, 232, 233, 234, 235, 236, 237.

Phaidon Press Limited
Regent's Wharf
All Saints Street
London N1 9PA

Phaidon Press Inc.
65 Bleecker Street
New York, NY 10012

phaidon.com

First published 2018
© 2018 Phaidon Press Limited

ISBN 978 0 7148 7689 4

A CIP catalogue record for this book is available from the British Library and the Library of Congress.

All rights reserved. No part of this publication may be reproduced, stored in a retrieval system or transmitted, in any form or by any means, electronic, mechanical, photocopying, recording or otherwise, without the written permission of Phaidon Press Limited.

Commissioning editor: Emilia Terragni
Project editor: François-Luc Giraldeau
Production controller: Sarah Kramer
Design: Studio Joost Grootens/Joost Grootens,
    Dimitri Jeannottat, Julie da Silva
Text: Izabela Anna Moren

Printed in China

The publisher would like to thank Tanya Heinrich, Lisa Delgado, Susan Clements, and Laura Loesch-Quintin for their contributions to the book.